Literature and Sacrament

Medieval & Renaissance Literary Studies

Literature & Sacrament

The Sacred
and the Secular
in John Donne

Theresa M. DiPasquale

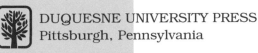
DUQUESNE UNIVERSITY PRESS
Pittsburgh, Pennsylvania

Published in the United States of America by

DUQUESNE UNIVERSITY PRESS
600 Forbes Avenue
Pittsburgh, Pennsylvania 15282

Library of Congress Cataloging-in-Publication Data
DiPasquale, Theresa M., 1962–
    Literature and sacrament: the sacred and the secular in John
Donne / Theresa M. DiPasquale.
    p. cm. — (Medieval and Renaissance literary studies)
  Includes bibliographical references (p.) and index.
  ISBN 0-8207-0309-5 (alk. paper)
    1. Donne, John, 1572–1631—Criticism and interpretation. 2.
Christianity and literature—England—History—17th century. 3.
Christian poetry, English—History and criticism. 4. Lord's
Supper—History of doctrines—17th century. 5. Baptism—History of
doctrines—17th century. 6. Donne, John, 1572–1631—Religion. 7.
Sacraments in literature. 8. Holy, The, in literature. 9. Theology
in literature. I. Title. II. Series.
    PR2248 .D5 1999
    821'.3—dc21
                              99-6301
                               CIP

Contents

Part I: Devotional Poetry

ONE   Sacramental Crossing

TWO   "Deigne at My Hands"

To my mother, Charlotte Rose Fasnacht DiPasquale
and
my father, Pasquale DiPasquale, Jr.

Acknowledgments

A portion of part 1, chapter 3 appeared as "Cunning Elements: Water, Fire, and Sacramental Poetics in Donne's 'I am a little world'" (*Philological Quarterly* 73.4 [1994]: 403–15), and is reprinted with the permission of *Philological Quarterly*. An earlier version of chapter 4 appeared as "Donne's Catholic Petrarchans: The Babylonian Captivity of Desire" in *Renaissance Discourses of Desire*, edited by Claude J. Summers and Ted-Larry Pebworth (1993); the material is reprinted by permission of the University of Missouri Press. Chapter 5 was previously published as "Receiving a Sexual Sacrament: 'The Flea' as Profane Eucharist" in *John Donne's Religious Imagination: Essays in Honor of John T. Shawcross*, edited by Raymond-Jean Frontain and Frances M. Malpezzi (UCA Press, 1995) and is reprinted by permission of the editors.

A writer completing a book many years in the making has many people to thank. The weaknesses that remain in this study must, of course, be laid solely to my charge. But whatever merit (to use a theologically loaded term) this study possesses, is due in significant part to the generous contributions of my teachers, colleagues, friends, and family.

I owe a debt of gratitude to faculty and fellow alumni of the

University of Virginia, particularly to my dissertation director, James C. Nohrnberg, and to Gordon Braden, William Kerrigan, Hoyt Duggan, Daniel Kinney, Monica Potkay, and Mary Stone. I am also indebted to my dear friends and colleagues at Florida International University, especially Mary Free and Meri-Jane Rochelson, who read portions of the manuscript and offered helpful criticism, and to Lynne Barrett, Peter Craumer, Chuck and Mary Jane Elkins, Bruce Harvey, Jeffrey Knapp, Marta Lee, Barbara Murphy, Ken Rogerson, Dick Sugg, Donald Watson, and Butler Waugh, all of whom provided friendship, collegial support and helpful advice. The students in my seventeenth century literature courses at Sweet Briar College, Carleton College, and F.I.U. have been a constant source of new inspiration and insight into Donne's poetry.

I also wish to thank the many other friends and colleagues—from Sweet Briar, Carleton and St. Olaf, and the John Donne Society—who have influenced and assisted me through their published work and through their constructive responses to and comments on my research and writing: Helen Brooks, Gale Carrithers, Ross Dabney, Steve Davis, John and Sharon Day, Daniel Doerksen, Susan Dykstra-Poel, Robert Fallon, Dennis Flynn, Raymond-Jean Frontain, Kate Frost, Chanita Goodblatt, Achsah Guibbory, Paul Harland, Joan Hartwig, Dayton Haskin, Judith Scherer Herz, M. Thomas Hester, Anne Hurley, Elena Levy-Navarro, Louis Martz, Noralyn Masselink, Frank Morral, Paul Parrish, Ted-Larry Pebworth, Anne Lake Prescott, Michael Price, Stella Revard, John R. Roberts, Graham Roebuck, Emma Roth-Schwartz, Maureen Sabine, Maria Salenius, Michael Schoenfeldt, Joshua Scodel, Jeanne Shami, John Shawcross, D. Audell Shelburne, Terry G. Sherwood, Robert "Sparks" Sorlien, George and Caroline Soule, P. G. Stanwood, Gary Stringer, Ernest W. Sullivan II, Claude Summers, Richard Todd, Julia M. Walker, Hugh Wilson, Richard Wollman, Cathy Yandell, Julie Yen, R. V. Young, and particularly the editor of this series, Albert C.

Labriola. Duquesne University Press Editor in Chief Susan Wadsworth-Booth has been both helpful and patient during the preparation of the manuscript. As will be clear from the extent of my allusions to their arguments, I am also indebted to the scholarly and critical work of Eleanor McNees, Helen Gardner, A. J. Smith, A. B. Chambers, John Carey, Barbara Lewalski, Arthur Marotti, Ernest Gilman, and Richard Baumlin.

I am grateful to Whitman College, which graciously funded the indexing of this volume.

I am most particularly grateful to my family: my parents, Pasquale DiPasquale, Jr., and Charlotte R. DiPasquale, who taught me to read and write, as well as how to pray and how to love; my sisters, Cathy DiPasquale Conroy and Maria DiPasquale Phifer; and my husband, Lee Keene, the best librarian and the most loving man on earth.

Editorial Note

I quote the poetry of John Donne (with parenthetical citations by abbreviated poem-title and line number) from *The
Complete Poetry of John Donne*, edited by Shawcross. The
abbreviations are those established in the currently available
volumes (6 and 8) of the *Variorum Edition of the Poetry of
John Donne* (ed. Stringer et al.); see the list following this note.
The dedicatory epistles to *Metempsychosis* and "A Hymn to
the Saints . . ." are also quoted from Shawcross's edition and
cited parenthetically by line number. Quotations from the
annotations and apparatus of Shawcross's edition are cited
as *Complete Poetry* by page number; other editions are cited
parenthetically by editor's name and page number; these editions are included in the bibliography under the editors' names.

I quote Donne's sermons (cited parenthetically as *Sermons*
by volume and page number) from *The Sermons of John Donne*,
ed. Potter and Simpson. Except where otherwise noted, I quote
Donne's letters (cited parenthetically as *Letters* by page number) from the facsimile reprint of *Letters to Severall Persons
of Honour* (1651), introduction by M. Thomas Hester. Donne's
Devotions Upon Emergent Occasions are quoted from Anthony Raspa's edition and cited parenthetically as *Devotions*

by page number and by the number of the Meditation, Expostulation, or Prayer.

Scriptural texts are quoted from *The Holy Bible . . . Set Forth in 1611 and Commonly Known as the King James Version* and cited parenthetically by book, chapter, and verse. Though some of the works I discuss were written before the Authorized Version was published, I quote it throughout for the sake of consistency. Wherever relevant, I note differences in translation and marginal glosses as they appear in *The Geneva Bible: A Facsimile of the 1560 Edition* and *The Geneva Bible: A facsimile of the 1599 edition with undated Sternhold & Hopkins Psalms*. When quoting Roman Catholic documents that include quotations from scripture, I retain the wording chosen by the translators of the ecclesiastical documents but alter chapter and verse numbers to correspond to those used in the King James Bible, which sometimes differ from those of the Vulgate and the Douay-Rheims translation.

Several key theological and liturgical texts are quoted repeatedly throughout. The Series Latina and Series Graeca of Migne's *Patrologiae Cursus Completus* are cited as *PL* and *PG* by volume and column number. Quotations from the *Canons and Decrees of the Council of Trent*, trans. J. J. Schroeder, are cited as pronouncements of the Council by session number, title of decree, and chapter number and/or canon number. The *Catechism of the Council of Trent for Parish Priests*, trans. John A. McHugh and Charles J. Callan, is cited as *Catechism* by page number. The Latin text of the Tridentine liturgy is quoted from William Maskell, *The Ancient Liturgy of the Church of England According to the Uses of Sarum, York, Hereford, and Bangor and the Roman Liturgy Arranged in Parallel Columns*, 3rd ed. and cited parenthetically as the *Roman Liturgy* by page number. English translations of the Tridentine Mass are quoted from a facing-page Latin/English edition by Sylvester P. Juergens, *The New Marian Missal for Daily Mass* and cited parenthetically as *Missal* by page number.

The liturgy of the Church of England is quoted from *The Book of Common Prayer 1559. The Elizabethan Prayer Book*, edited by John E. Booty, and cited parenthetically as *BCP* by page number. The official book of Elizabethan homilies is quoted from *Certaine Sermons or Homilies Appointed to be Read in Churches In the Time of Queen Elizabeth I (1547–1571). A Facsimile Reproduction of the Edition of 1623*, introduction by Mary Ellen Rickey and Thomas B. Stroup, and cited parenthetically as *Homilies* by page number. The Thirty-nine Articles of the Church of England are quoted from *Articles whereupon it was agreed by the Archbishoppes and Bishoppes . . . 1562* and cited parenthetically by article number. Calvin's *Institutes* is quoted from John Calvin, *The Institution of the Christian Religion*, translator Thomas Norton, and cited parenthetically as *Inst.* by book, section, and subsection. Hooker's *Of the Lawes of Ecclesiasticall Politie* is quoted from *The Works of that Learned and Judicious Divine Mr. Richard Hooker*, ed. John Keble, 7th ed., rev. R. W. Church and F. Paget and cited parenthetically as *Laws* by book, chapter, and section number.

Memorial elegies on Donne printed in the 1633 edition of his poems, as well as the front matter of that edition, are quoted from the facsimile of that edition and cited parenthetically as *Poems* by page number or folding. Quotations from the works of other major Renaissance authors are taken from the editions listed in the Works Cited. Poems are cited by author, title of the individual poem, and line numbers; lyric sequences are cited by title, poem number, and line numbers; prose works are cited by author, title of the individual work, and page number; plays are cited by author, title of the individual work, act, scene, and line numbers.

LIST OF ABBREVIATIONS

Short Forms of Reference for Donne's Works as specified in the *Variorum Fdition of the Poetry of John Donne*

(List of Short Forms Used in this Study)

Air	"Aire and Angels"
Anniv	"The Anniversary" ["All kings and all their favorites"]
Annun	"Upon the Annunciation and the Passion"
BedfDead	"To the Countess of Bedford: Begun in France"
BedfReas	"To the Countess of Bedford" ["Reason is our soul's left hand"]
BedfRef	"To the Countess of Bedford" ["You have refined me"]
Carey	"A Letter to the Lady Carey and Mrs. Essex Rich"
Corona	*La Corona*
Cor1	"Deign at my Hands"
Cor2	"Annunciation"
Cor3	"Nativitie"

Cor4	"Temple"
Cor5	"Crucifying"
Cor6	"Resurrection"
Cor7	"Ascension"
Cross	"The Crosse"
Eclog	"Eclogue at the Marriage of the Earl of Somerset"
ElFatal	"On His Mistress" ["By our first strange and fatal interview"]
ElProg	"Love's Progress" ["Whoever loves, if he do not propose"]
ElVar	"Variety" ["The heavens rejoice in motion"]
EpEliz	"An Epithalamion . . . on the Lady Elizabeth"
Fun	"The Funerall"
Goodf	"Goodfriday, 1613. Riding Westward"
GoodM	"The Good Morrow"

Holy Sonnets:

HSDue	"As due by many titles"
HSScene	"This is my play's last scene"
HSSighs	"O might those sighs"
HuntUn	"To the Countess of Huntingdon" ["That unripe side of earth"]
HWKiss	"To Sir Henry Wotton" ["Sir, more then kisses"]
Ind	"The Indifferent"
Sgo	"Song" ["Go, and catch a falling star"]
Sickness	"Hymn to God my God, in My Sickness"
Triple	"The Triple Foole"

INTRODUCTION

John Donne's conception of poetry was influenced by his engagement in the theological debate over the sacraments. Many of his poems—sacred and profane—may be better understood in light of sixteenth and seventeenth century sacramental theology, which helped to shape Donne's understanding of the written word as a visible sign, of the poet as the quasi-divine maker or priestly minister of that sign, and of the reader as its receiver.

Critics have often underscored the importance of Donne's religious milieu in defining the form and content of his poetry, and several studies have made invaluable contributions to Donne scholarship by focusing on specific theological and devotional sources and analogues: Louis Martz's *The Poetry of Meditation* demonstrated the influence of Catholic devotional models on Donne's sacred verse; Barbara Lewalski's *Protestant Poetics and the Seventeenth-Century Religious Lyric* stressed the impact of Protestant theology on Donne's devotional lyrics; and Terry Sherwood's *Fulfilling the Circle: A Study of John Donne's Thought* outlined the influence of Augustinian epistemology and psychology on Donne's religious and secular poetry.

1

None of these studies, however, accounts adequately for Donne's fluid maneuvering amid the current of theological and ecclesiological debate, or for the definitive impact of his religious experience as a Catholic who became a Protestant. John Carey's critical biography *John Donne: Life, Mind, and Art* focuses directly on that experience; indeed, Carey portrays Donne's "apostasy"—and the "ambition" he assumes to have motivated it—as the driving force behind all of Donne's writings, religious and secular. But Carey's project is a critical biography; he is thus more interested in evaluating Donne's psychology as it is expressed through the poetry than in executing detailed close readings of individual poems or defining the principles of Donne's poetics.

Carey's portrait of a man fascinated by power and motivated by raw ambition presupposes, moreover, the validity of Donne's twentieth century reputation as a royalist Arminian priest, aligned theologically with Andrewes and Laud and politically with the absolutist policies of the Stuart monarchy.[1] This conception of Donne has, however, been strongly challenged by recent scholarship. As Jeanne Shami observes, "It cannot be said too often that Donne's views on any subject are complex and elusive" ("Donne's Sermons," 383). Attempts to tag Donne with one or another partisan label underestimate the complexity of his responses to the politics of his time and ignore the findings of "recent historical research [which] has made it clear that the simple categories of power and submission, authority and resistance, Royalist and Parliamentarian just don't hold" (Shami, "Donne's Sermons," 392).[2] Similarly, attempts to classify Donne simply as an "Anglican" or a "Puritan" distort the complexities of the late sixteenth and early seventeenth century English Church and oversimplify Donne's constantly evolving sense of his place within it.[3] As Shami points out, it is only through a process of selective, decontextualized quotation of the *Sermons* that "Horton Davies can group Donne exclusively among the metaphysical Arminians . . ., or that Lewalski . . . and Sellin can find in Donne a consistently Calvinist theology" (Shami, "Donne's Sermons," 383).[4] A more comprehensive reading reveals that Donne can, for example, defend conservative ceremonial—including the sign of the cross in Baptism, kneeling at Holy Communion, and the use of the wedding ring—while departing broadly from Hooker and his successors on the role of sermons—insisting, as did "Puritans" like Cartwright and Perkins, that preaching is no less essential than the sacraments.[5]

Also oversimplified is the view of post-Reformation English Catholicism underlying Carey's critical biography. His sweeping account of Donne the Apostate has been revised in recent essays by M. Thomas Hester, R. V. Young, and Dennis Flynn, and in Flynn's *John Donne and the Ancient Catholic Nobility*.[6] A biographical portrait of the youthful Donne as a member of the English recusant subculture, Flynn's book clarifies the nature of recusant experience, revising and correcting many ingrained misconceptions about late sixteenth and early seventeenth century English Catholicism.[7] Flynn explores the political, theological, psychological and pastoral complexities that affected recusants' experience and their sense of their own identity; in so doing, he provides the critic with a fresh perspective on the religious and theological contexts of Donne's poetry, as well as a wealth of new information bearing upon the poet's sense of his audience. Taking Flynn's fruitful insistence on the complexity of Donne's religious identity as my point of departure for reading Donne's lyrics in their post-Reformation context, I focus on sacramental theology and on conflicting conceptions of the Eucharist as particularly significant parts of that context; that focus, in turn, leads me to emphasize Donne's concern with the function of literary works and with his own ability to direct and manipulate the reading experience.

My argument is in part a response to two recent books on

Donne that challenge an author- or text-centered hermeneutics: Thomas Docherty's *John Donne, Undone* and James
S. Baumlin's *John Donne and the Rhetorics of Renaissance
Discourse*. Docherty's book censures the emphasis on authorial "real presence" in twentieth century criticism; in place of
the "post-Eliotic Donne," whose "poetry passes itself off as a
pure medium or enactment or materialization of the poet's
thought" (3), Docherty presents a postmodern Donne, whose
writing is characterized by its "obscurity or secrecy, . . . its
transgressive stance" (5). In reconstructing the cultural context of that poetry, Docherty emphasizes three "problem-
atical areas which bear on Donne's writings: the scientific
discourse, which troubles secular historicity itself; the socio-
cultural, in which woman raises certain defenses in this male
poet; and the aesthetic, in which mimetic writing itself becomes fraught with difficulty" (1). These three areas are all
contrasted with what Docherty represents as the phallo-
centric certainty of religion and theological discourse. This
approach provides a needed corrective to criticism that takes
the idea of authorial "presence" for granted, but it does not
fully account either for the diversity and conflict within theological discourse itself, or for Donne's exploration of what
Baumlin calls a "rhetoric of incarnationism," a discourse that
"seeks to move beyond persuasion, literally to embody [the]
truth that it will . . . celebrate, sustain, and defend through
language" (9).

In *John Donne and the Rhetorics of Renaissance Discourse*,
Baumlin finds the poet experimenting with a variety of different rhetorics, from the radically skeptical to the incarnational;
and he argues that, while Donne thinks of spoken language as
capable of incarnational power, the poet sees written language
as troubled by a more "problematic relation to the poet's living voice and presence" (19). Baumlin argues persuasively that,
for Donne, the question of "whether the poem or *written
word*" can evoke presence depends upon the possibility that

"the act of reading" may be "a sacramental event" (19).
Baumlin's readings of these events tend, however, to rely
upon an essentially binary model of reformation controversy
as a matter of debate between two clearly defined semiotic
systems.

In pitting a "Catholic" concept of Real Presence against a
"Protestant" insistence on memory and absence, Baumlin
assumes the validity of such categorical distinctions, distinctions that Donne himself—in negotiating his own spiritual
crisis—defied. Baumlin makes considerable use of seventeenth
century theological texts in reading Donne's valedictory lyrics as unresolved confrontations with the "crisis of presence
and absence . . . that lies at the center of Western metaphysics"
(191). But his conclusion that these poems are informed by
a poststructuralist "Poetics of Absence" (159) is distortive.
For despite certain similarities linking Calvinism to post-
structuralism, Donne—as this study will demonstrate—did
not define Protestant sacramental theology as a theology of
absence. Thus, though Calvinist thought did influence both
Donne's theology and his poetics, Baumlin oversimplifies
when he dubs the product of that influence a "Poetics of
Absence."

In approaching Donne's sacramental poetics with less faith
in the binary model of "Protestant" versus "Catholic" or even
"Anglican" versus "Puritan" beliefs, I attempt to reconstruct
Donne's own, more nuanced theology of sacrament as a guide
to his poetics and, in particular, to his conception of the exchange between author and reader. In this effort, I am strongly
influenced by the theoretical stance of John Shawcross in his
Intentionality and the New Traditionalism. Though he distinguishes between "the reader's text," which is defined by
the reader's experience, and "the author's text," which "emphasizes . . . the craft" of the writer and "defines continuing
authorial presence" (4), Shawcross underscores the interde-
pendence of the two:

> [W]hat the reader elicits from a literary work is a major fac-
> tor in determining what the author does or does not do. The
> author's input and the reader's output are both, therefore, sig-
> nificant in evaluation. The text is an experience that the reader
> undergoes; it is an experience whose lineaments, however, have
> been laid out by the author. (1)

John Donne and his contemporaries would not, of course,
have used the terms "input" or "output" to describe the exchange between author and audience; but they would have
found an argument analogous to Shawcross's (and expressed
with comparable patience and urbanity), in Hooker's account
of the Eucharist:

> The real presence of Christ's most blessed body and blood is
> not . . . to be sought for in the sacrament, but in the worthie
> receiver of the sacrament. (*Laws* 5.67.6)

And yet,

> our participation of Christ in this sacrament dependeth on
> the co-operation of his omnipotent power which maketh it his
> body and blood to us . . . (*Laws* 5.67.6)

According to Hooker, the "real presence" of Christ that is
the substance and significance of the sacramental sign is
the receiver's "participation" in that presence; it is, like the
reader's text in Shawcross, not an essence but "an experience
that the [receiver] undergoes" (1). But Hooker, like Shawcross,
asserts that this experience, this participation, depends upon
an Author's work, a "power which maketh" (*Laws* 5.67.6).
Shawcross is making a point designed to encourage the analysis of authors' methods, while Hooker's aim is to discourage
what he sees as impertinent arguments about "the manner
how" God works in the Eucharist; but the analogy between
art and sacrament is Hooker's own:

> When I behold with mine eyes some small and scarce discern-
> ible grain or seed whereof nature maketh promise that a tree

shall come, and when afterwardes of that tree any skilful arti-
ficer undertaketh to frame some exquisite and curious work,
I look for the event, I move no question about performance
either of the one or of the other. Shall I simply credit nature
in things natural, shall I in things artificial rely myself on art,
never offering to make doubt, and in that which is above both
art and nature refuse to believe the author of both, except he
acquaint me with his way, and lay the secret of his skill before
me? (*Laws* 5.67.12)

Ironically enough, Hooker's anti-analytical analogy provides
an appropriate framework for the study of John Donne's
poetry. For Donne takes the "ways" of the divine artist as his
inspiration and models many of his poems on those most mysterious yet most accessible divine works, the sacraments.
Though Hooker maintains that the "the secret of [God's] skill"
as the author of the sacraments is "above both art and nature," Donne aspires to a poetic achievement that—as Sidney
puts it in his *Defense of Poesy*—"surpass[es]" nature's "do-
ings" and dares even to "imitate the unconceivable excellen-
cies of God" (217). And as Donne himself exclaims in his
Devotions, God is a poet—"a *figurative*, a *metaphoricall*
God"—not only in his words (the Scriptures) but in his
works, such as the ceremonies and sacraments of the Old
and New Testaments (99, 100; Expostulation 19).

In aspiring to emulate this particular mode of divine creativity, Donne is situating his art in a war zone; for one major
focus of the theological controversy that raged throughout the
Reformation was the question of how to interpret the sacramental works of God, how to read them reverently and with
due regard for authorial intention. Donne was deeply familiar
with the complexities of that theological debate; in the preface to *Pseudo-Martyr*, he insists that "I used no inordinate
hast, nor precipitation in binding my conscience to any locall
Religion," and did not make "any violent and sudden deter-
mination, till I had, to the measure of my poore wit and

iudgement, survayed and digested the whole body of Divinity, controverted betweene ours and the Romane Church" (fol. B2v–B3r).

In this passage, Donne not only bears witness to a wide-ranging knowledge of religious controversy, but alludes punningly to one of the most important topics of debate: the Eucharist. As M. Thomas Hester reads it, Donne's description of his course of study evokes the debate over the presence of Christ's Body and Blood in the sacrament, "collaps[ing] the Protestant figure of the primacy of reading or *survaying* and the Catholic figure of eating or *digesting* 'the whole *body* of Divinity'" (Hester, "'this cannot be said,'" 369). Donne thus equivocates, Hester argues, rendering his position indeterminate by yoking together contrary terms associated with two opposed theological systems. But such a reading, while certainly correct in detecting a punning allusion to the Eucharist, goes too far in trying to classify and codify the denominational implications of the words Donne uses. The phrase "survayed and digested" does not yoke two discrete contraries, for the debate over the sacraments was not simply bipolar, nor were certain key vocabulary words firmly established as the property of one side or another. Thus, though Hester links *surveying* to Protestant reading and *digesting* to Catholic Eucharist, the terms and the concepts they signify could as easily be assigned quite the opposite associations— insistence on the reception and digestion of the Eucharist being a hallmark of Protestant writing on the subject, while Catholic treatises allowed for participation in the sacrament through devout surveying or gazing upon the consecrated Host.[8] One cannot simply identify certain keywords or images as hinting at "Catholic" sympathies and certain others as alluding to "Protestant" discourse.

As Donne well knew, moreover, theological controversy over the sacraments was very far from being a clearly defined matter of Catholic dogma versus Lutheran or Calvinist consensus. Long before the Council of Trent, Thomist and Scotist scholastics disagreed about how—exactly—the sacraments convey grace.[9] And in the sixteenth and seventeenth centuries, intramural debates continued; not only did various Protestant theologians disagree vehemently with one another on various points of doctrine, but counter-Reformation Catholic writers of the same period continually parted ways in their interpretations and defenses of the dogmas promulgated at Trent. Thus, it is no surprise to find that Donne's statements about and reflections on the sacraments in his *Sermons* often involve a richly eclectic synthesis of conflicting theologies.[10] He speaks often in terms that reflect the English Church's emphasis on reception, portraying the sacraments as human works made effectual through the "cooperation"—as Hooker puts it—of divine power. But he is also concerned with a question much debated by the medieval scholastic theologians: the question of *how* sacraments convey grace. And though he rejects the Tridentine teaching that grace is conveyed "ex opere operato" (that a sacrament's effect is wrought by the performance of the sacramental action itself), he nevertheless stresses the efficacy of the sacramental *opus*, mentioning and adapting the Latin phrase in explaining how sacraments work.[11]

– i.e., mechanical efficacy.

Donne's beliefs about the Eucharist in particular reflect his sense of himself as a man who—as he put it in *Pseudo-Martyr*—"dares not call his Religion by some newer name then Christian" (fol. B3r). Even in the sermons he preached as Dean of St. Paul's, his various statements about the Lord's Supper fit no ready-made denominational category. Certainly, his stance on Eucharistic doctrine (though not always on other teachings and controversies) clearly resembles that of men like Andrewes and Laud, who defined what came to be called the High Church "Anglican" position. And thus one might say, as Eleanor McNees does, that "By treading a fine line between Roman Catholic transubstantiation and Lutheran consubstantiation on the one hand and Calvinist Virtualism on the other, Donne maintains an orthodox Anglican stance toward the doctrine of Real Presence in the Eucharist" (*Eucharistic Poetry*, 67).[12] But the term "Anglican" is somewhat anachronistic when used in such a way, and the category is deceptive, since (as my appendix on the doctrine of Eucharistic sacrifice demonstrates) Donne was capable of combining Calvinist formulations and Catholic-sounding language in a way distinct from the methods of men such as Andrewes and Laud. Donne does not so much tread the "fine line" of the *via media* as forge a synthesis that is distinctly his own.

The question of how literally Christ may be said to be present in the Eucharist is a case in point. Cranmer said that "Figuratively [Christ] is in the bread and wine, . . . but really, carnally, and corporally he is only in heaven" (Cranmer 2:401; quoted in Booty, "History," 364). To this and similar Protestant formulations, the Council of Trent responded by affirming that "in the Sacrament of the most Holy Eucharist are contained truly, really and substantially the body and blood together with the soul and divinity of our Lord Jesus Christ" (Thirteenth Session, "Canons on the Most Holy Sacrament of the Eucharist," Canon 1). Donne, for his part, sounds closer to Trent than to Cranmer when he insists that Protestants "require no figure, we beleeve the body of Christ to be in the Sacrament as literally, as really as [Roman Catholics] doe" (*Sermons* 7:193).[13] In this assertion, which attempts to dissociate the Protestant Eucharist from the figurative and poetical, Donne takes a Calvinist articulation and stands it on its head. For, in the *Institutes*, Calvin objects to the "unsavory scoffings" of those who call Protestants "Tropistes"; but he goes on to make clear that his Eucharistic theology depends very much upon the trope or "figure" of metonymy, which he calls "the common use of the Scripture" (*Inst.*

4.17.21). In 1 Corinthians 10:4, for example, St. Paul speaks figuratively of the rock Moses struck in the wilderness to provide water for the Israelites: "[They] did all drink the same spiritual drink; for they drank of that spiritual Rock that followed them: and that Rock was Christ." According to Calvin, Christ's statement that "This is my body" is no more to be taken literally than Paul's statement that "that Rock was Christ." The stone struck by Moses

> was Christ, because it was a visible signe, under which that spirituall drinke was truely in dede but not discernably to the eie perceived: so bread is at this day called the body of Christe, forasmuche as it is a sygne whereby the Lorde offereth to us the true eatyng of his bodye. Neither dyd Augustine otherwyse thynke or speake . . . If (sayeth he) the Sacramentes hadde not a certaine likenesse of those thynges whereof they are Sacramentes, they should not be Sacramentes at all. And of this likenesse oftentimes they take the names of the things themselves. (*Inst.* 4.17.21)

Thus, though he stresses that "Christ is the mater, or (if thou wilte) the substance of all sacramentes" (*Inst.* 4.14.16), Calvin strictly maintains the Augustinian distinction between the substance and the outward sign, the *res sacramenti* and the *sacramentum*, the signified and the signifier.[14]

Donne tends to blur that distinction just a bit more than Calvin does; in one sermon, he reworks Calvin's assertion about Christ as "substance" of the sacraments in such a way as to make it sound (despite the quotation from Luther) like a defense of Transubstantiation:

> This Sacrament of the Body and Blood of our Saviour, *Luther* calls safely, *Venerabile & adorabile*; for certainly, whatsoever that is which we see, that which we receive, is to be adored; for, we receive Christ. He is *Res Sacramenti*, The forme, the Essence, the substance, the soule of the Sacrament. . . . (*Sermons* 7:320)[15]

In this formulation, the Sacrament is a metaphor in which the tenor is infinitely more important than the vehicle; but the ambiguous phrase "whatsoever that is which we see" hints at the possibility—so important to poetic meaning—that the vehicle may be modified by the tenor and vice versa, that it may not be possible to maintain a clean distinction between signifier and signified. Indeed, Donne goes on to assert that one's reverence for the sign may be a fair measure of one's reverence for its substance: "he that feels Christ, in the receiving of the Sacrament, and will not bend his knee, would scarce bend his knee, if he saw him" (*Sermons* 7:320).[16]

Like many English Protestant thinkers, however, Donne also emphasizes that the communicant must not dwell overmuch on *how* Christ is received in the Sacrament.[17] This eschewal of speculation reflects Calvin's own insistence that the Lord's Supper is a mystery beyond the reach of both "witt" and "woordes" (*Inst.* 4.17.32) and his portrayal of Roman Catholic theologians as overblown poets, "caried above . . . with their excessive speches," who "darken the simple and playne truth" (*Inst.* 4.17.32).[18] Such theologians are, in Calvin's view, essentially Sidneyan artificers gone bad: in having "invented" the adoration of the Eucharist, they "have not only dreamed it of themselves," but have "framed" an idol modeled upon the fore-conceit, making for "themselves a God after the wil of their own lust" (*Inst.* 4.17.36).[19]

In a 1626 sermon, Donne draws a similar denigratory parallel, defining theologians as deranged wordsmiths:

> [T]he Roman Church hath catched a *Trans*, and others a *Con*,
> and a *Sub*, and an *In*, and varied their poetry into a Transub-
> stantiation, and a Consubstantiation, and the rest, and rymed
> themselves beyond reason, into absurdities, and heresies, and
> by a young figure of *similiter cadens*, they are fallen alike into
> error. . . (*Sermons* 7:296)

One of Donne's goals as a devotional poet is to avoid this sort of rhyming, to reject the intellectual hubris and artistic presumption of those who would "imprison Christ *in Opere operato*" and "conclude him so, as that where that action"—the sacramental "work" or "opus"—"is done, Christ must necessarily bee, and necessarily work" (*Sermons* 7:267).

But how was he to accomplish such a delicate task? As an alternative to the *ex opere operato* theory of grace, most Protestants relied upon a theology that stressed God's covenant with man and the faith of the receiver. Donne invokes covenant theology when he says in a sermon that we receive grace, "[N]ot *ex opere operator* [sic], not because that action is performed, not because that sacrament is administred, yet *ex pacto*, and *quando opus operamur*: by Gods covenant, when soever that action is performed, whensoever that sacrament is administred, the grace of God is exhibited and offered" (*Sermons* 2:258).[20] The sacramental covenant is made effective, Calvin stresses, by "the secrete workyng of the Spirite, whiche uniteth Christ hymself unto us" (*Inst.* 4.17.31).[21] Hooker, too, asserts that "sacraments . . . as signs" would be nothing but pictures, stimulants to faith that provide the mind with instruction through sensible means, except, "in that by God's own will and ordinance they are signs assisted always by the Holy Ghost," the "elements and words have power of infallible signification . . ." Thus, "they are called seals of God's truth; the spirit affixes unto those elements and words, power of operation within the soul, most admirable, divine, and impossible to be exprest" (*Laws* 6.6.10).[22]

However impossible it might be to express fully the nature of the Sacrament's efficacy, the Thirty-Nine Articles of the English Church stressed—as Calvin did—that "the meane whereby the body of Christ is receaued and eaten in the Supper, is fayth" (Article 28). And the effect of this reception upon the "worthy receiver," the communicant who consumes the sacramental signs in a spirit of faith, is the transformation of his or her soul: "There is the true Transubstantiation, that when I have received [the Sacrament] worthily, it becomes my very soule; that is, My soule growes up into a better state,

and habitude by it, and I have . . . the more deified soule by
that Sacrament" (Donne, *Sermons* 7:321).

Donne comes very close to Calvin, moreover, in associating the verbal ministry of preaching with the sacramental
ministry of Baptism and Eucharist.[23] For Donne, preaching is
itself one of the "sensible, and visible means" by which God
conveys himself in the Church (*Sermons* 2:319–20, 323–24).
Indeed, Donne sees Baptism, the Lord's Supper, and preaching
as a sacred triad of ministries which convey God to the Christian soul. He explains the idea with particular eloquence—
and at great length—in an undated christening sermon on
1 John 5:7–8 ("For there are three which beare record in heaven;
the Father, the Word, and the Holy Ghost; . . . and there are
three which beare record in the earth; the Spirit, and the
water, and the Bloud"). Explaining that "spirit . . . here is,
Spiritus oris, the word of God, the *Gospell*; and the preaching,
and ministration thereof," Donne proceeds to describe the co-
operative efficacy of the three earthly witnesses:

> [T]hese . . . he will always heare, if they testifie for us, that Jesus
> is come unto us; for the *Gospell*, and the *preaching* thereof, is
> as the deed that conveys *Jesus* unto us; the *water*, the *baptisme*,
> is as the *Seale*, that assures it; and the *bloud*, the *Sacrament*, is
> the *delivery* of Christ into us; and this is *Integritas Jesu*, the
> entire, and full possession of him. (*Sermons* 5:145, 149)

In this passage, three physically tangible signs convey, seal,
and deliver Christ to devout receivers; in order to have "full
possession of him," the believer must receive not only the
sacramental elements of water and wine, but also the spoken
words of the preacher. Indeed, like such Calvinist divines as
Thomas Cartwright and William Perkins, Donne stresses that
preaching is necessary to salvation. As he declares in his fourth
Prebend Sermon (28 January 1626/7), "There is no salvation
but by faith, nor faith but by hearing, nor hearing but by preaching . . . . Absolution is conferred, or withheld in Preaching"

(*Sermons* 7:320).[24] He is nearly as vehement in a sermon preached at the Spittle on Easter Monday, 1622 (only a few months before his sermon defending James's restrictive *Directions for Preachers*):

> [T]hen does God truely shine to us, when he appears to our eyes and to our ears, when by visible and audible means, by Sacraments which we see, and by the Word which we heare, he conveys himself unto us. . . . God hath joyn'd them, separate them not: Upon him that will come to hear, and will not come to see; will come to the *Sermon*, but not to the *Sacrament*; or that will come to see, but will not come to hear; will keep his solemn, and festival, and Anniversary times of receiving the *Sacrament*, but never care for being instructed in the duties appertaining to that high Mystery, God hath not shin'd. They arc a powerful thunder, and lightning, that go together: Preaching is the thunder, that clears the air, disperses all clouds of ignorance; and then the *Sacrament* is the lightning, the glorious light, and presence of Christ Jesus himself. (*Sermons* 4:105)

In his preaching, then, Donne seeks the inspiration of the Holy Spirit in order to write and speak efficaciously, affecting the souls of his audience. And this ambition, I will argue, helps to shape his sacred poetry as well. John Milton hoped that the works he wrote would achieve the status of God's Word, that they would be no less divinely inspired than those of Moses in Genesis or David and Solomon in the Psalms.[25] But John Donne hoped that the words he wrote—both as a preacher and as a poet—would achieve the status of God's Works, that they would share in the power of God's "effectuall signes of grace" (Article 25) and prove spiritually efficacious for those who received them with faith. This hope is especially apparent in "The Crosse," in which the text itself is set up both as a visible sign of invisible grace and as a sacramental sermon, an effectual preaching of Christ crucified. The sacramental emphasis is even stronger in *La Corona*, a poetic celebration of the Eucharist, designed to make both the poet's own soul and that of the faithful reader/receiver "the more deified . . . by that sacrament" (*Sermons* 7:321). In other divine poems, including "I am a little world" and "Goodfriday, 1613," Donne tests the limits of such a poetics, exploring the danger of spiritual reliance on what Calvin calls "the worke wrought"[26] even as he continues to explore the analogy between text and sacrament.

In his secular poetry, too—and particularly in his various adaptations of the Petrarchan mode—Donne plays upon the connections between the function of poetry and the function of sacraments. He distinguishes between efficacious inscription, capable of moving or persuading or teaching the reader, and futile verse in which the practitioners of "whining Poëtry" (*Triple* 3)—like the word-juggling theologians of Donne's sermon—"[rhyme] themselves beyond reason" (*Sermons* 7:296). In some of his love lyrics and verse epistles, Donne defines the relation between the Petrarchan lover and his beloved as insufficient, portraying the words of Petrarchan poetry as ineffective signs, the poetic equivalent of a "bare" Zwinglian sacrament; in other poems, he uses various strategies to invest his poetry with a secular equivalent of sacramental efficacy.

"The Canonization" is an example of Donne's ability to draw simultaneously on conflicting models of sacramental and literary reception. This lyric seems on one level to invite a formalist reading based on "Catholic" ideas of signification; the lovers of the poem, like the bread and wine of the Catholic sacrament, are transformed by a power beyond the ken of worldly men: "Call us what you will," the speaker says, "wee'are made such by love" (19). They "prove / Mysterious"—the word puns on "mysterion," which is the Greek word for "sacrament"—"by this love" (26–27).[27] The "ridle" of their union (23) is, like the miracle of transubstantiation, a sacred enigma that the secular mind cannot fully comprehend.[28] And like the tabernacle in which the Blessed Sacrament is reserved or the monstrance in which it is raised up for the adoration of the faithful, the "well wrought urne" of the poem will contain the lovers and inspire the prayers of the devout.[29]

But the poet who is writing "The Canonization," the poem itself makes clear, does not rest securely in the idea of "verse" as love's tabernacle; on the contrary, he is a writer concerned with audience, with the search for what the theologians called "worthy receivers." The speaker of the poem claims (in terms that appeal to New Critical aesthetics and Roman Catholic spirituality) that he and his beloved will "build in sonnets pretty roomes" and that "by these hymnes," their literary relics, "all shall approve" them *"Canoniz'd* for Love." But he undermines these claims by turning dramatically outward, first to pursue an argument with an interlocutor or implied reader of his own time and place, and then to predict the response that a future audience will have to "these hymnes." The invocation he foresees in stanza 5 is, moreover, a somewhat supercilious projection: this is how they will pray to us, he says (though not necessarily how they ought to).[30] He does not go as far as the speaker of "The Relique," who makes a Protestant-like effort to instruct and disabuse the superstitious men and women of a (seemingly Catholic) "time, or land, / Where mis-devotion doth command" (12–13) and "miracles are sought" (20); but he does invest the pleading invocation of the future-lovers with overtones of what Donne elsewhere calls "credulous pietie."[31] As is often the case with Donne, "The Canonization" defies categorization. It is neither simply Catholic nor simply Protestant, neither the perfect example of iconicity nor a poster child for the theory of self-consuming art nor the manifesto of a reception-aesthetic. Indeed, as Judith Scherer Herz argues, "The Canonization" (and Donne's poetry generally) is consistent only in its inconsistency. As Herz points out, Donne refused to settle; he avoided embracing any stable authorial identity, and his personae (insofar as they can be identified at all) often shift gears in mid-poem ("'An Excellent Exercise'").[32]

But he did demonstrate a persistent concern with audience and with the dynamics of literary reception; he did not publish much, and tried to monitor the distribution of his work even in manuscript.[33] He expressed his exasperation with those who misunderstood his work when he did "descend" to print it;[34] and he used various devices to announce that he would admit to his poetry, as the Church admits to the sacrament of the Eucharist, only those "who are instructed and presum'd to understand" (*Sermons* 5:127). In the Epistle to *Metempsychosis*, for example, Donne urges his readers to recall what they already know about the teachings of Pythagoras: "I will bid you remember, (for I will have no such Readers as I can teach)" (20–21).[35] In short, he does not wish to *inform*, but to engage those who are already informed. The qualified readers Donne seeks will enter into the experience of his poetry already prepared, already catechized in the doctrine that is a prerequisite for active participation.

Donne's early readers were quite sensitive to this element of the exclusive in Donne's poetry. Many of those who contributed commendatory poems to the 1633 edition, for example, stressed the sublimity and difficulty of Donne's verse, declaring that Donne's capacity to perplex is a function of his greatness. For Henry Valentine, Donne's soul "flew / A pitch of all admir'd, known but of few" (*Poems*, 381).[36] Arthur Wilson's elegy addresses the deceased in similar terms: "for in thy Fancies flight / Thou dost not stoope unto the vulgar sight, / But, hovering highly in the aire of Wit, / Hold'st such a pitch, that few can follow it" (*Poems*, 397). And Jasper Mayne holds forth on the same theme: "[W]ho hath read thee, and discernes thy worth, / That will not say, thy carelesse houres brought forth / Fancies beyond our studies[?]" (*Poems*, 394). The poetry of Donne is for initiates, these initiates declare, for those who are no longer "vulgar" in their perceptions but who—like the hypothetical observer in "The Extasie"—grow wiser through what they peruse and part far purer than they came; the reader "of purer mould" (Valentine) "discernes [the poet's] worth" (Mayne) even if he cannot hope to write on such a level himself.

"Discerne" is a key word here. It is a term favored by Donne in his sermons on the Eucharist and on the necessity of preparing oneself properly to receive it. "[T]his Sacrament," he explains in one sermon, "is accompanied with *precepts*, which can belong onely to *Men of understanding*, (for they must doe it in *Remembrance*, and they must *discerne* the Lords body) therefore the necessity lies onely upon such, as are come to those *graces*, and to that understanding. For they that take it, and doe not *discerne it*, (not know what they do) they take it dangerously" (*Sermons* 5:148). Donne's emphasis here on the receiver's "understanding" recalls a similar emphasis in the Elizabethan "Homilie of the worthy receiuing and reuerend esteeming of the Sacrament":

> . . . then may we see those things that be requisite in the worthy receiuer, whereof this [is] the first, that we have a right understanding of the thing it selfe. As concerning which thing, this we may assuredly perswade our selues, that the ignorant man can neither worthily esteeme, nor effectually use those marueylous graces and benefits offered and exhibited in that Supper . . . (*Homilies*, 198–99)[37]

Indeed, the homily goes on to note, Saint Paul's criticism of the Corinthians [1 Cor. 11:29] "for the prophaning of the Lords Supper, concludeth that *ignorance* both of the thing it selfe, and the signification thereof, was the cause of their abuse: for they came thither unreuerently, not *discerning* the Lords Body" (*Homilies*, 198–99; emphasis added). But as the *Book of Common Prayer* makes clear in an exhortation designed to be read "when the curate shall see the people negligent to come to the Holy Communion" (*BCP*, 254), it is no less a profanation to refuse the invitation to partake than to eat unworthily: "When God calleth you, be you not ashamed to say you will not come?" (*BCP*, 255).

In light both of the *Homilies'* emphasis on understanding and discernment as crucial to worthy reception, and the Prayer Book's attempt to shame noncommunicants into participation, one may more fully appreciate the strategy used by John Marriot, the printer of the 1633 edition of Donne's poems, in his prefatory epistle to the volume. Marriot addresses himself not (as is usually the case in such epistles) "To the Reader," but "To the Understanders," which he does "in hope that very few will have a minde to confesse themselves ignorant" (*Poems*, A1r). In so doing, the printer's epistle declares understanding to be—as the *Homilies* put it—"requisite in the worthy receiuer" (*Homilies*, 198) and counts on the challenge thus presented to entice readers eager to prove that they are indeed worthy and capable of such understanding. Like the *Homilies* and the Prayer Book exhortation, the printer's epistle is meant to inspire awe at the preciousness of the corpus it offers for general consumption while at the same time shaming any hesitant receiver/reader into participation: "I should profane this Peece," Mariott says, by "applying" to it any of the standard marketing devices; for this is, he insists, "A Peece which who so takes not as he findes it, in what manner soever, he is unworthy of it, sith a scattered limbe of this Author, hath more amiablenesse in it, in the eye of a discerner, then a whole body of some other" (*Poems*, A1v). The challenge and the burden here, as in the communicant's decision about whether or not to receive the Eucharist, lie upon the receiver; he must prove that he is not "unworthy" by "tak[ing]" the broken body of Donne's work as it is offered to him and appreciating it as a true "discerner."

The strategies used in the posthumous publication of his work notwithstanding, Donne does not always insist so intimidatingly upon the worthiness of the reader. On the contrary, much of Donne's poetry involves compromise and concession—compromise with his own doubts about the nature of sacramental signs and about poetry's capacity to be sacramentally efficacious, and concession to the role the reader plays in determining the efficacy and meaning (be it sacred or secular) of a poem.

In "The Extasie," for example, the hypothetical eavesdropper who would be capable of comprehending and appreciating the "dialogue of one" (74) would be one "so by love refin'd, / That he soules language understood, / And by good love were growen all minde" (21–23). This ideal listener would not need to see "souls language" inscribed in visible signs. He would not ask, as doubting Thomas does, to see and touch physical evidence; rather, he would be one of those "blessed . . . that have not seen, and yet have belicved" (John 20:29). The message he hears would, moreover, transform him; he would "thence a new concoction take, / And part farre purer then he came" (27–28). But like Calvin, who strongly emphasizes that God provides the sacraments as visible signs in order to bolster the feebleness of man's faith (*Inst.* 4.14.1), the speaker of "The Extasie" does not insist that all men be such refined disciples. Instead, he insures that "Weake men on love reveal'd may looke" (70) when it is inscribed in the "booke" of "the body" (72), incarnated in the visible sign of the poem. The reader who "marke[s]" this visible sign (75) will—the speaker implies—"see" (75) as much as the "refin'd" initiate has "heard" (74). That reader will embrace what is "reveal'd" (70) in Donne's poems even as she notes the "Small change" (76)— small but significant—that takes place in Donne's transitions from the audible and spiritual to the visible and physical, from spoken words to written texts.[38] My goal in this study is to be such a reader.

Chapter 1 is a reading of Donne's "The Crosse" (c. 1608). In this poem, Donne confronts the objections of "*purifying Puritans*" (*Sermons* 1:189) to representations of the Cross (including not only crucifixes, but the practice of making the sign of the cross on the child's forehead during baptism).[39] "The Crosse" argues passionately for the sacramentality of crosses; it is a celebration of Christ's own cross and of its representations in art, in ritual gesture, in physical and spiritual suffering. Donne explores the possibility that "th'image of his Crosse" (2) may be an effectual image of Christ; and in so doing, he works toward making his own representation of the cross—the poem itself—both a sacramental sermon and a grace-conveying sign. A study of "The Crosse" thus provides an excellent introduction to his ideas about the sacramental role poetry can play.

Chapter 2 focuses on *La Corona* (also written c. 1608); in this sonnet-cycle, Donne celebrates a poetic Eucharist, using language liturgically to make a sacramental offering to God. With an English Protestant idea of the Lord's Supper in mind, Donne insists that his poetic sacrament will be efficacious only if the "holy Spirit, [his] Muse did raise" (*Cor7*, 13). But he proceeds with trust in that spirit, presenting his work as a memorial sacrifice that—like the Eucharist itself as he would later describe it in his *Sermons*—cuts through space and time, uniting the communicants' self-oblation to Christ's redemptive offering of his body and blood upon the altar of the cross. Donne takes care to ensure, moreover, that the offering will not be his alone; through manipulation of form and genre, he invites the believing reader/communicant to unite his or her own voice with that of the poet/speaker and, in so doing, to experience the saving power of Christ's Eucharistic body.

Donne is not always comfortable, however, with the idea that his works are divinely assisted. Chapter 3 discusses two poems in which he considers the spiritual dangers of sacramental art: the Holy Sonnet "I am a little world" and "Goodfriday, 1613. Riding Westward." In "I am a little world," sonnet form itself is at issue; and in the cunningly-made microcosm of the poem, Donne's poet/speaker must negotiate the pitfalls of sacramental poetics. He crafts an analogy that terrifies him with the certainty of damnation, but he goes on to reinterpret his own trope; consecrating the elements of his analogy and making active use of the multivalence with which God invests language, the poet/speaker finds that the response to fire is fire, the answer to fears about sacramentality is sacrament, and poetic utterance remedies the despair that was spoken into being through poetry. In the "Goodfriday" poem, the poet/speaker goes so far as to consider surrendering all spiritual agency, leaving the work of redemption entirely to Christ; but his language makes clear that such resignation will be difficult for artistic as well as spiritual reasons. Playing upon the perennial dichotomy between Art and Nature, the poet/speaker demonstrates the tension between human artifice and the super-Natural act of generation that gives birth to redemption. He compares and contrasts his own making of an artificial day, the poem called "Goodfriday, 1613," with Christ's "beget[ting]" of "endlesse day" (12) on the first Good Friday. The human poet's highly wrought 42-line work is a compressed sequence of three sonnets, self-consciously *made* rather than begotten, while the work of redemption, the "endlesse day" born of Christ's blood, is—like Christ himself—begotten, not made. The poem thus casts doubt on whether any human action, including poetry as sacramental *opus*, can prove a reliable means of grace.

In his secular poetry, too, Donne often insinuates a link between the function of sacraments and the function of poems; and this link influences his sense of the love lyric's efficacy as a means of persuasion, his approach to literary reception, and his "reformation" of the Petrarchan mode, which he often associates with those aspects of Roman Catholic theology and devotion for which he had least sympathy. Part 2 of this book, consisting of four chapters, analyzes specific secular works—including one prose letter and selected verse letters and love lyrics—that turn upon the analogy between text and sacrament.

Chapters 4 and 5 focus on those lyrics and verse epistles in which Donne defines the relation between the Petrarchan lover and his beloved as insufficient or pernicious, differentiating efficacious inscription from the futile practice of "whining Poëtry" (*Triple*, 3). These poems—including "Aire and Angels," a verse letter to the Countess of Huntingdon ("That unripe side of earth"), "Loves Deitie," "The Funerall," and "Twicknam garden"—struggle toward a reformation of the love lyric, portraying Petrarchan speakers as the ultra-conservative Catholics of love-religion.

Chapter 6 investigates the strategies of a speaker not committed to that religion, though willing to use its language in the pursuit of his desires. In "The Flea," Donne's speaker makes ambivalent use of both Catholic and Reformed theological language, inviting his lady—and the reader of the poem—to participate in a theologically-charged erotic disputation and, ultimately, to partake of a sexual sacrament. In this debate, the signs and verbal gestures are as polyvalent and as open to interpretation as the signs and gestures of the Eucharist, but the goal is erotic fruition and literary pleasure rather than spiritual grace.

Chapter 7, "Ways of Having Donne," begins by exploring Donne's poetic practice in two epistolary poems to male friends, each of which demonstrates further his desire for an alternative to the definitively noncommunicative and reflexive art of Petrarchan love. In a sonnet-shaped verse letter to Thomas Woodward, Donne actually calls his own work a "bare Sacrament," wittily insisting upon its quasi-Petrarchan failure to convey his love; but in "Sir, more then kisses," a poem addressed to Sir Henry Wotton, he makes clear that he relies upon letters, which he elsewhere calls "friendships sacraments," as conduits of fraternal grace.

The chapter then proceeds from the analysis of the verse letters Donne wrote for men to consideration of two love lyrics that project a woman as implied receiver: "A Jeat Ring sent" and "A Valediction forbidding mourning." Both lyrics are circular in structure, and both play upon the idea that poems—like rings—may serve as sacramental pledges of love and fidelity only when they are offered to and accepted by "worthy receivers," to use the phrase many English Protestants favored in their discussions of the Eucharist. These two love lyrics—one bitter and sarcastic, the other reverent and hieratic—proceed from a sacramental poetics compatible with that of *La Corona*, itself an unbroken circle in which the poet's self-offering depends upon the cooperation of the receiver.

In chapter 8, "Equivocal Devotion," I turn to two verse letters directed to specific female readers: "Man to Gods image," which Donne addressed to the Countess of Huntingdon, and his incomplete verse letter "To the Countess of Bedford. Begun in France but never perfected." Donne makes ambivalent use of Roman Catholic sacramental imagery in the composition and presentation of "Man to Gods image," which he enclosed in a remarkable prose letter to his friend Henry Goodyer. The equivocal and reader-oriented quality of the poem and the prose letter proceed from Donne's conception of the written text as sacrament, the effect of which depends both upon who the reader is, and upon how he or she responds. Finally, in the incomplete verse letter to Lucy, Countess of Bedford, Donne draws an analogy between confession—one of the five Catholic sacraments reclassified and redefined by Protestants—and his poem of apology to his patroness; and in his failure to complete that "confession," he confirms his commitment to a distinctly nonconfessional art.

The first fruits of my study are, then, new readings of specific poems, fluid interpretations that recognize the flexibility of the poetics from which the works proceed and acknowledge that, as Judith Scherer Herz points out, Donne's poems resist attempts "to impose a unity, to make [them] yield single, albeit complex readings" ("'An Excellent Exercise,'" 14). To read Donne's poetry in the context of the Reformation debate over the sacraments is not to impose a unity, but to discover the shaping effect of a context as shifting, as multivocal, as various and unpredictable as Donne's texts themselves. And because that context helped to shape Donne's audience as well as his texts, the study of Donne's sacramental poetics sheds new light on literary reception in late sixteenth and early seventeenth century England, revealing a theory of reading that differs from anything to be found in classical rhetoric, a theory available to Donne and his contemporaries through the theology of sacramental reception and applied by Donne to the exchange between author and reader.

I

Devotional Poetry

ONE

ᶼ☙

Sacramental Crossing

In "The Crosse," Donne argues for and demonstrates the sacramental efficacy of crosses. The poem is a celebration of
Christ's own cross and of its "image" or representation in art,
in ritual gesture, and in the physical and spiritual sufferings of
Christians. Donne explores the possibility that an encounter
with "th'image of [Jesus's] Crosse" (2) may be an effectually
redemptive encounter with Christ; and in so doing, he works
toward making his own representation of the cross—the poem
itself—a sacramental seal, a grace-conveying sign.[1] A study
of "The Crosse" thus provides an excellent introduction to
his ideas about the sacramental role sacred poetry can play
for readers who receive divine poems as "visible means and
seals of grace" (Donne, *Sermons* 2:254).[2]

Donne's effort to create a literary sacrament begins with
his choice of subject matter: the Cross of Christ has always
figured centrally in sacramental theology. According to a
patristic commonplace based on John's Gospel, the sacraments
have their origin in the crucifixion, for they flow from the
side of Christ as he hangs upon the cross. As Donne explained

29

to his congregation, the elements of blood and water that pour
forth from the "pierced one" are the elements of the Eucharist and of Baptism respectively: "[U]pon his Death flowed
out from his side, those two *Elements of the Church, water*
and *bloud;* The Sacraments of *Baptisme,* and of the *Communion* of himself" (*Sermons* 6:288).[3] Both the Cross of Christ itself and the sign of the cross have, moreover, been considered
sacramental signs. According to Leo the Great (c. 400–461),
whom Donne cites with some frequency in his sermons, "the
Cross of Christ . . . is both a sacrament and an example"
(*Patrologiae Cursus Completus, Series Latina* 57:390; trans.
Toal 2:236). And St. Augustine lists the sign of the cross with
Baptism and the Eucharist, as one of the means by which the
faithful "have Christ" (*PL* 35:1763; trans. Gibb and Innes 282).[4]

Donne's poem thus takes a sacramental sign as its subject;
and beyond that, it presents itself *as* a sacramental sign, "a
visible word" that seals and confirms the faith of the believing reader.[5] In Donne's own time, however, the sacramental
status of the cross was disputed; "The Crosse" can thus define and establish its own sacramental function only by
entering into the debate and defending the sacramentality of
the cross in all its forms: pictorial and gestural, physical and
spiritual.

*The Context of "The Crosse": The Debate over the Cross in
Baptism*

In her notes on "The Crosse," Helen Gardner discusses the
subject matter of the poem: "At this period a cross on an altar
would be very rare, except in royal chapels" (92). She then
cites King James's words to the "Puritan" divines at the 1603
Hampton Court conference, as recorded in William Barlow's
summary of the proceeedings: "the materiall *Crosses,* which
in the time of Popery were made, for men to fall down before
them . . . are demolished as you desire" (Barlow, 74). Donne

is, Gardner concludes, "defending the cross as a pious and proper personal possession" (Gardner, 92).[6] In fact, however, Donne is addressing a controversy that endured well into the seventeenth century: the debate over whether or not the priest ought to make the sign of the cross upon the forehead of the new Christian (or over him) during the baptismal rite.[7]

It was this baptismal ritual that King James was defending (by contrasting "materiall crosses" with the sign of the cross) in the passage Gardner quotes from William Barlow's 1604 book, *The Summe and Substance of the Conference.* And Donne himself defended the practice throughout his career in the pulpit. Preaching before the Earl of Exeter in a 1624 sermon, for example, Donne uses the word "seal"—Calvin's favorite synonym for "sacrament" and a term that Donne himself often uses in that capacity—to refer to the sign of the cross as it is traced on the new Christian's forehead during baptism:

> These two seales then hath God set upon us all, his *Image* in our soules, at our *making*, his *Image*, that is his *Sonne*, upon our bodies and soules, in his *incarnation.* . . . He sets another seale upon us . . . in the Sacrament of *Baptisme*, when the seale of his *Crosse*, is a testimony, not that Christ was *borne*, (as the former seale was) but that also he *dyed* for us; there we receive that seale upon the *forehead*, that we should conforme our selves to him, who is so sealed to us. (*Sermons* 6:160)[8]

According to the sermon, the *Imago Dei* is the quintessential sacrament, the original "seale" of God upon man; but because sin has marred the divine image in man, Christ has become incarnate as a more perfect embodiment of that image. Christ has, in turn, instituted the Sacrament of Baptism as a seal or sacrament of redemption; and the sign of the cross made during the baptismal rite is a sacramental marking, an effectual seal that calls Christians to become, in their own right, perfect images of Christ.

Thus, when Donne begins "The Crosse" by asking "Since Christ embrac'd the Crosse it selfe, dare I / His image, th'image of his Crosse deny?" he is asking not only whether one may dare reject the use of the crucifix, that "picture" of the cross (7) so despised and mistrusted by Reformers, but also whether one ought to reject what Barlow refers to as "*the Crosse in Baptisme*" (65, 72). Donne addresses the issue directly in the rhetorical question of lines 15–16: "Who can blot out the Crosse, which th'instrument / Of God, dew'd on mee in the Sacrament?" In these lines, the "instrument of God" is both the sacrament of baptism and the priest who administers it.[9] The verb "dew'd" suggests that the cross traced on the new Christian's forehead "in the Sacrament" is metonymically linked to the sacred moisture of sacramental grace itself: "God raises up men," Donne explains in a sermon, "to convey to us the dew of his grace, by . . . visible sacraments" (*Sermons* 2:242). The poet cannot allow anyone to "blot out the Crosse" that is "dew'd" on him in baptism, for to do so would be to eradicate the visible seal that bears witness to his reception of grace.

In Donne's choice of the verb phrase "blot out," moreover, the reader may catch a glimpse of the implications this controversy has for Donne as a poet. The cross that is "dew'd" on man in baptism descends in the form of water, but one does not "blot out" water-marks; one blots out inscriptions made in ink. By asking "Who can blot out the Crosse . . .?" Donne is defending "The Crosse"[10]—his sign of the cross inscribed in ink—even as he defends the baptismal sign of the cross. Both, he implies, are effectual "image[s] of [Christ's] crosse" (2), sacramental inscriptions that one ought not to "deny" (2).[11]

The analogy between making the sign of the cross in ritual gesture and making an artistic image of the cross in words or pictures was by no means Donne's invention. On the contrary, the parallel between the graven images of art and the gestural images of ritual has a place at the very heart of

Protestant arguments against images and ceremonies in general and against the baptismal sign of the cross in particular. Theologians arguing for more stringent, "Puritan" reforms in the English Church often cited Colossians 2:14 as the point of departure for their arguments against ceremonial worship and the use of sacred images; in this verse, St. Paul declares that Christ has forgiven all sin, "Blotting out the handwriting of ordinances that was against us, . . . nailing it to his cross." Redemption is here defined as an erasure or cancellation of man's deadly pact with the devil, which is referred to figuratively as a piece of handwriting or—as the Vulgate renders it—a "chirographum." As many strict Calvinists read the passage, all human productions—including the ceremonies of the church and man's works of art in paint, pencil, and ink—were invalidated along with the original sinful inscription.

Thus, when Thomas Cartwright argued against the baptismal sign of the cross, he specifically portrayed it as a kind of inscription. His opponent, Richard Hooker, summed up Cartwright's argument thus: "Seeing God hath nowhere commanded to draw two lines in token of the duty which we owe to Christ, our practise with this exposition publisheth a new *gospel*, and causeth another *word* to have place in the Church of Christ, where no voice ought to be heard but his" (*Laws* 5.65.5). For Cartwright, as this paraphrase makes clear, the crossing gesture is not a holy seal, but an image devised by human hands; he characterizes it as an artful rendering, *drawn* like the lines on an engraver's plate or *published* like a book and no less dangerous than any other graven image. Thus, for the "Puritan" polemicist who opposes the practice, no less than for Donne who defends it, the sign of the cross in baptism is an imprinted image or handwritten text. But for Cartwright, it is an impiously original publication passed off as the work of the Almighty, whereas for Donne, it is God who authors and authorizes the inscription.

Indeed, in a sermon preached at St. Dunstan's, Donne cites

Colossians 2:14 as a call to writing rather than a prohibition against it:

> Beloved, the death of Christ is given to us, as a *Hand-writing*; for, when Christ naild that *Chirographum*, that first hand-writing, that had passed between the Devill and us, to his Crosse, he did not leave us out of debt, nor absolutely discharged, but he laid another *Chirographum* upon us, another Obligation arising out of his death. His death is delivered to us, as a *writing* ... in the nature of a Copy, to learne by; It is not onely given us to read, but to write over, and practise. (*Sermons* 10:196)[12]

In this passage, of course, "to write over" is not to compose a poem but to "practise" one's handwriting. Like scribes learning secretary hand, Christians must learn to "write over," to produce a fair copy of Christ's original.[13] Still, Donne's portrayal of this *imitatio Christi* as a "practise" of inscription, and of Christ's death itself as an inscription, opens up the possibility that poetic writing, too, may be an effectual *imitatio Christi*, that a poem called "The Crosse" may help to implement its author's and readers' participation in the cross of Christ.

The poem suggests its status as a sacramentally efficacious inscription in at least three ways. First, the poem underscores the definition of sacraments as *visible* signs and strongly evokes the ways in which *visual* experience may be sacramental; in so doing, it invites the reader to consider that the experience of reading "The Crosse"—a visible image of Christ's cross—may prove an occasion of grace. Second, the poem plays upon the figurative definition of a "cross" as a tribulation, an experience of physical, emotional, or spiritual suffering. The poet/speaker insists that the crosses of affliction are themselves sacraments, and he invites the reader to experience the poem as a sacramental cross of this sort. Finally, the poet preaches to his readers and to himself, countering possible abuses and sinful tendencies in himself and in them, and teaching the right use of sacramental signs. But even as he does so, Donne relies upon the idea that sermons themselves, including "The Crosse" as his poetic sermon, may also be sacraments. All three of these strategies help to define Donne's sense of his poem's sacramental function.

Sacrament as Visible Sign: Looking At The Cross and Reading "The Crosse"

Donne begins "The Crosse" by stressing the spiritual importance of visual orientation. Through a series of meditative rhetorical questions, he emphasizes the idea of the cross as a visible "image" or "picture," a sign accessible to the "eye" and essential to the spiritual well-being of the gazer:

> Since Christ embrac'd the Crosse it selfe, dare I
> His image, th'image of his Crosse deny?
> ....
> Who from the picture would avert his eye,
> How would he flye his paines, who there did dye?
>
> (1–2, 7–8)

Looking away from the image of the cross implies a rejection of the Christian's duty to be crucified with Christ.[14]

Though the poem goes on to urge that human beings must cross all of their senses, the poet insists that vision is the most powerful faculty and thus the most important one to control:

> And crosse thy senses, else, both they, and thou
> Must perish soone, and to destruction bowe.
> For if the'eye seeke good objects, and will take
> No crosse from bad, wee cannot scape a snake.
> So with harsh, hard, sowre, stinking, crosse the rest,
> Make them indifferent; call nothing best.
> But most the eye needs crossing, that can rome,
> And move; To th'others th'objects must come home.
>
> (43–50)

The rhetoric of this passage is characteristic of Protestant emphasis on the perils of visual sensation; indeed, the assertion that "the eye . . . can *rome*" may invite the reader to recall the Reformed church's association of the Roman Church with an overemphasis on the eye over the ear, on spectacle over preaching.[15] But that invitation is, nevertheless, issued to the eye; for the ear cannot perceive any difference between "roam" and "rome." The lines about the "snake" thus maintain a conservative position on the value of visual stimuli, insisting that a person who refuses to see evil will not be able to avoid it. And the image has a deeper theological resonance as well; for, though the snake in Genesis is Satan's instrument, the bronze serpent that Moses set up in the desert is a type of the crucified Christ.

In the book of Numbers, the Israelites murmur against God and are punished by a plague of "fiery serpents" whose venomous bites kill many of the people. When they repent and beg for help, God provides them with what Calvin calls one of the sacraments of the Old Testament (*Inst* 4.18.20). Following Yahweh's instructions, "Moses made a serpent of brass, and put it upon a pole, and it came to pass, that if a serpent had bitten any man, when he beheld the serpent of brass, he lived" (Numbers 21:9). Jesus himself establishes the analogy between the image of the snake and himself when he tells Nicodemus that, "as Moses lifted up the serpent in the wilderness, even so must the Son of man be lifted up: That whosoever believeth in him, should not perish, but have everlasting life" (John 3:14–15).

Donne found the bronze serpent typology both powerful and provocative. In at least one sermon, he linked it directly to the Eucharist, speaking of "The crucified Serpent [who] hath taken our flesh, and our blood, and given us his flesh, and his blood for it; . . . the Communion of the blood of Christ Jesus" (*Sermons* 10:190).[16] In "The Crosse," then, it is the sacramental image of the crucified serpent that Christians will see if they learn to discipline their eyes. The snake that they will "scape" by consenting to look on a "bad" object (46) is none other than Sin itself in the most fundamental sense. The cross of Christ, the object that saves those who gaze upon it, is no more pleasing to Christians' eyes than was the bronze serpent, a representation of the very evil from which they sought relief, to the eyes of the Israelites in the desert. Gazing upon the serpent that Moses set up meant staring at the plague that their own wrongdoing had brought upon them; and contemplating the cross means the very same thing for Donne and his readers. For, when he says that it "bore all . . . sinnes" (5), he is alluding to what he sees as the real source of radical objections to crucifixes and other representations of the cross: looking on the crucifix, one sees a horrible scenario of one's own making. The spectacle is a torture precisely because of the personal guilt a sinner must feel in knowing that "every sin is a Crucifying of Christ" (*Sermons* 1:196). But, as in the story of the bronze serpent, one must look upon the emblem of one's guilt in order to escape destruction.

By phrasing the problem of sin and salvation in terms of visual orientation, the maker and speaker of "The Crosse" presents as vital (one might say *crucial*) the choice of whether or not to look at the image of Christ's cross, which is also the choice of whether or not to read a poem on the cross. Just as averting one's eyes implies a damnable scorn for the sacrifice it represents, so crossing one's own desire to look away or to stop reading implies a willingness to participate sacramentally in Christ's passion, to be joined—as St. Paul says that Christians are through Baptism—to "the likeness of his death" (Romans 6:5).

By making positive use of the Brazen Serpent image, moreover, Donne asserts his position in the contemporary controversy over the sign of the cross; for Protestants arguing against the ceremony often invoked the serpent negatively, as a cautionary example of a sacred image that had to be destroyed once it was abused.[17] In 2 Kings 18:4, good King Hezekiah "brake the images, and . . . brake in pieces the brazen serpent that Moses had made: for unto those days the children of Israel did burn incense to it." At the Hampton Court Conference, the divine who raised objections to the sign of the cross in baptism specifically cited Hezekiah's action, asserting that the sign of the cross, no less than the serpent, must be abolished because of its use in idolatrous worship. Citing Romans 14 and 1 Corinthians 8, he expressed concern lest the continued use of a tainted ceremony be an occasion of scandal for "*Weake Brethren*." King James would hear none of it, for, "quoth his Maiestie, what resemblance is there, betweene *the Brasen Serpent*, a materiall visible thing, and the signe of *the Crosse* made in the ayre?" (Barlow, 65, 73).

Though James may have seen no resemblance between one sacred sign and another, "The Crosse" illustrates that Donne saw the likeness very clearly. He includes both the brazen serpent and the cross "dew'd on [him] in the Sacrament" among those "image[s]" of the cross from which he must not "avert his eye"; and he directly answers the "Puritan" objection that the "*Weake Brethren*" may be scandalized:

> From mee, no Pulpit, nor misgrounded law,
> Nor scandall taken, shall this Crosse withdraw,
> It shall not, for it cannot . . .
>
> (9–11)

Indeed, the refusal to be daunted by "scandall" is central to Donne's point. Explaining the nature of scandal in a sermon, he says that the word has a "double signification": "[T]he active scandall . . . is a malice, or at least an indiscretion in *giving* offence, and . . . the passive scandall, . . . is a forwardnesse, at least an easinesse in taking offence" (*Sermons* 3:171). Though Donne believed that the Roman Catholic Church was guilty of active scandal, that it had offended by tainting many religious practices with idolatry, he objected also to scandalous irreverence among Protestants: "[W]hen because they abuse the Crosse, we will abhor the Crosse," Donne warned his auditory (*Sermons* 3:175), we are guilty of active scandal, for we fail to heed Paul's warning against offending either Jew or Greek (1 Corinthians 10:31–32).

In the poem, Donne is making an even stronger point; refusing to be deterred by "scandall taken," he invokes the spirit of 1 Corinthians 1:23: "[W]e preache Christ crucified: unto the Jewes even a stumbling blocke" or—as it is rendered in the Vulgate—"*Scandalum Judæis*, a scandal to the Jews" (*Sermons* 3:181). Those overscrupulous Protestants who are offended by the sign of the cross are, "The Crosse" implies, guilty of the *passive* scandal attributed to the Jews in 1 Corinthians; they are offended by the Gospel itself.

In the face of nonconformist resistance, then, the poet insists upon a visual embrace of the visible sign of the cross as it is inscribed in countless objects and actions, both natural and of human origin:

> Swimme, and at every stroake, thou art thy Crosse,
> The Mast and yard make one, where seas do tosse.
> Looke downe, thou spiest out Crosses in small things;
> Looke up, thou seest birds rais'd on crossed wings;
> All the Globes frame, and spheares, is nothing else
> But the Meridians crossing Parallels.
>
> (19–24)[18]

This passage offers the text of the physical world itself as a series of visual encounters with the cross. The enormous number of cruciform things and patterns invests fleshly creatures, manufactured objects, even human motion itself with the holiness of Christ's Cross.[19]

The text of Donne's poem, too, is by design a cross-filled visible universe. Donne uses the word "cross," in various noun and verb forms (crosse, crosses, crossing, crosse[']s) 31 times in 64 lines, ensuring that when readers of the poem "Looke

downe" they will indeed "sp[y] out Crosses in small things"
(21); that is, they will see the cross in the print on the page.
They will see it in the frequent repetition of the word "crosse,"
and they will also see it in the individual cruciform letters x
(which appears at the poem's center—line 32—in the word
"Crucifixe") and t (which appears either in lower case or,
as a Tau cross—uppercase T—at least once in every line of
the poem).[20] Donne ensures that readers' eyes will gaze continually on crosses as they scan the lines of his poem; those
who read it reverently are demonstrating that they do not
"avert [their] eye[s]" from the cross's "picture" (7), that they
do not despise "the chosen Altar" (4) of Christ's Eucharistic
self-offering.

The act of reading "The Crosse" devoutly thus confirms—
just as a devout reception of Baptism or the Eucharist would—
that such readers share in the benefits of Christ's cross, that
they "profit by the sacrifice" (3). Like the cross received upon
the forehead in Baptism, the poem is a sacramental "seale of
[Christ's] *Crosse*, . . . a testimony . . . that . . . he *dyed* for us"
(*Sermons* 6:160). The poem, like the outward signs of a sacrament as they were understood by English Protestants, does
not in itself convey grace.[21] But, the poem's conclusion suggests, by faithfully and ardently receiving the visible signifier,
readers will feel the effects of the invisible grace it signifies:
"Then doth the Crosse of Christ worke fruitfully / Within
our hearts, when wee love harmlessly / That Crosses pictures
much" (61–63). These lines recall the description of sacramental efficacy in the Elizabethan Homily on "Common Prayer
and the Sacraments," which says that a sacrament "setteth
out to the eyes and other outwarde sense, the inward *working*
of Gods free mercy, and doeth (as it were) seale in our *hearts*
the promises of God" (*Homilies*, 133–34; emphasis added).
Evoking this passage with his choice of the words "worke"
and "hearts" in the concluding lines of "The Crosse," Donne
confirms the analogy between sacraments (signs that present

"to the eyes" the "working" of God in men's "hearts") and "pictures" of the Cross (including the poem itself), which provide an occasion for Christ's cross to "worke fruitfully / Within our hearts."

Sacramental Suffering: Loving "our Crosses" and Reading "with more care"

Donne, I have argued, presents the reading of "The Crosse" as an experience that is sacramental because it is visual; the poem is a grace-conveying sign that presents itself to the eye of the Christian reader. Imprinted with Christ's seal, the "Materiall crosses" of the created universe—including the text of the poem—are "good physicke" (25), physical things that work as medicine for the soul.[22] As such, the crosses inscribed in the material world resemble the ecclesiastical sacraments of Baptism and Eucharist, the "medicinall institutions of Christ in his Church" (Donne, *Sermons* 2:193). God has always provided such institutions, Donne the preacher stresses, in order to "succor the infirmity of Man, with sensible and visible things" (*Sermons* 1:283).[23]

But as Donne the poet points out, punning on the word "cross" as a synonym for "suffering" or "affliction," physical representations of Christ's cross are important precisely because they help us to see the inestimable value of our own crosses, our own sufferings:

> . . . the losse
> Of this Crosse, were to mee another Crosse;
> Better were worse, for, no affliction,
> No Crosse is so extreme, as to have none . . .
>
> (11–14)

The Christian's afflictions, Donne insists often in the sermons, conform him or her to the crucified Christ. Indeed, the crosses of tribulation are essential to salvation precisely because they can themselves be sacraments: "[A]ll our fiery tribulations fall under the nature, and definition of *Sacraments*, . . . they are so many *visible signs of invisible Grace*" (*Sermons* 8:71).[24] Thus, though "The Crosse" declares and demonstrates that "Materiall Crosses . . . good physicke bee" (25), the poet insists that "yet spirituall have chiefe dignity" (26):

> These for extracted chimique medicine serve,
> And cure much better, and as well preserve;
> Then are you your own physicke, or need none,
> When Still'd, or purg'd by tribulation.
> For when that Crosse ungrudg'd, unto you stickes,
> Then are you to your selfe, a Crucifixe.
>
> (27–32)

The most efficaciously sacramental crosses, these lines insist, are the purgative crosses of "tribulation" (30). Christians are transmuted by their afflictions, the alchemical words "Still'd" and "purg'd" suggest, in that they are purified by them; their base elements are turned into something more refined.[25]

The lines also stress, as do both Catholic and Protestant texts on the Eucharist, that the disposition of the receiver is all-important.[26] Those "spirituall" crosses that are patiently accepted, "ungrudg'd" (31) by their receiver, make him into his own "Crucifixe"; he becomes, that is, a perfect image or reflection of Christ crucified. As Donne explains in a sermon:

> [W]hen I am come to that conformity with my Saviour, as to *fulfill his sufferings in my flesh* [Colossians 1:24], . . . then I am crucified with him, carried up to his Crosse: . . . I put my hands into his hands, and hang upon his nailes, I put . . . my mouth upon his mouth, and it is I that say, *My God, my God, why hast thou forsaken me*? and it is I that recover againe, and say, *Into thy hands, O Lord, I commend my spirit.* (*Sermons* 2:300)

The end of rectified suffering is a merging of the believer's identity with that of the crucified Jesus, a sacramental transformation of the self into Christ.[27]

In "The Crosse," Donne specifically defines this transformation as a work of *art* carried out by crosses:

> As perchance, Carvers do not faces make,
> But that away, which hid them there, do take.
> Let Crosses, soe, take what hid Christ in thee,
> And be his image, or not his, but hee.
>
> $(33-36)$[28]

According to these lines, the crosses Christians endure are sculptors; they work upon latent potential, seeking to restore and uncover in men and women the divine likeness that should characterize souls made in God's image but that is obscured by a stony coating of sin.[29] As Donne stresses in his sermon on the redemptive effects of suffering, tribulations do not work to wholesome effect upon confirmed sinners; their suffering serves only to "stone and pave them, obdurate and petrifie them" (*Sermons* 2:300).[30] By contrast, one who recognizes the spiritual preciousness of crosses and testifies to that recognition in a devout study of crosses provides substantial evidence that his heart is not obdurate, that a true image of Christ lies just beneath the stony surface.

Donne is asking readers to make such a study by reading "The Crosse." In urging them to "Let Crosses" carve and shape them, he is asking them to let all crosses—including not only the spiritual crosses one bears and crosses carved of wood or stone, but also the literary "Crosse" they now hold in their hands—work on them and make them into living works of art, living images of Christ and his cross. To read the poem aright, the poem itself implies, will be to "take up the cross, and follow" Christ (Mark 10:21), to renew one's baptism. Just as in the sacrament, Christians "receive that seale [of Christ's cross] upon the *forehead*, that [they] should conforme [them] selves to him" (*Sermons* 6:160), so in reading the poem, they receive "The Crosse" again and further their likeness to the crucified savior, becoming not "his image, . . . but hee" (36).[31]

If the experience of reading "The Crosse" is to be a literary exercise in sacramental suffering, however, Donne cannot afford to make the poem too enjoyable. In a verse epistle to the Countess of Huntingdon, he dissociates himself from the rhetorical extravagance of Petrarchan love poetry by declaring that he will not "vexe [her] eyes to see / A sighing Ode, nor crosse-arm'd Elegie" (21–22); but in "The Crosse," he must vex his readers' eyes, insuring that they do not take too much pleasure in any cross—literary or spiritual.

There is little chance that the poem will prove delightful for readers who object to the sign of the cross. For them, Donne's ostentatiously witty poem will most certainly be vexing; and as a test of their willingness to endure vexation patiently and humbly, it will provide them with a decisive opportunity to demonstrate their likeness to Christ. Indeed, insofar as it is addressed to those who object to crosses, the poem stands as something of a dare: if you can patiently endure this image of the cross, which will surely be offensive to you, then you will be demonstrating that you truly are Christ-like.

Donne the preacher issues just such an implicit challenge in a pun-filled christening sermon that directly addresses what he calls "*schismaticall*" objections to the cross in baptism:

> [I]f we had rather *crosse* one another, and *crosse* the Church, then *crosse* the *child*, [then,] as God shewed *Moses, a tree,* which made [bitter] waters . . . sweet, when it was cast in, so [let us] remember that there is the *tree of life,* the *crosse of Christ Iesus,* and his Merits, in this water of baptisme[.] [A]nd when we all agree in that, that all the vertue proceeds from the *crosse of Christ* . . . let us admit any representation of *Christs crosse,* rather then admit the true *crosse of the devill,* which is a bitter and *schismaticall* crossing of Christ in his Church . . . (*Sermons* 5:108–09)

This barrage of cross-puns—so strongly reminiscent of those featured in "The Crosse"—must surely have provoked Donne's more "schismatically" inclined listeners to a reaction like the one recorded in Richard Brathwayte's elegy on Donne: "As fine words [truly] as you would desire, / But [verily,] but a bad edifier" (*Poems*, 401).

The "beetles"—as Brathwayte calls them—who said such things about Donne's sermons would no doubt have found the "fine words" of "The Crosse" at least as "bad." And they would have had a point: the witty language of the christening sermon and the poem is undeniably less edifying than it is provocative. But in each case, the provocation is functional. Forcing the listener or reader to confront repeated verbal representations of Christ's cross and defining the rejection of such representations as the embrace of another, more pernicious kind of cross, the preacher and the poet both create situations in which neither listeners nor readers can avoid a decisive choice. They may persist in "the sinne of scorning" Christ's cross (Donne, *Cross*, 6), holding to what the sermon calls a "bitter and *schismaticall* crossing of Christ in his Church," in which case they condemn themselves by failing to demonstrate Christ-like docility. Or they may consent to "admit any representation of *Christs crosse*" (*Sermons* 5:109), to "love harmlessly / That Crosses pictures much" (*Cross*, 62–63), in which case their encounter with the sermon or poem will be a sacrament according to the Calvinist definition: an "outwarde signe, wherewith" they "testifie [their] godlinesse as well before [God] and the Angels as before men" (Calvin, *Inst*. 4.14.1).[32]

But what, one must ask, if the readers are not inclined to object to ceremonies and images? What if they are (as seems more likely) comfortable conformists all too ready to mock "Puritan" sensitivity to the peril of idolatry?[33] Insofar as it delights them, wittily embracing a symbol of which they approve, "The Crosse" cannot prove a sacramentally efficacious trial for them. On the contrary, it may prove to be an occasion of self-indulgent excess, a gluttonous surfeit of "joy in crosses" (42). To counter that possibility, Donne includes in his poem a cautionary homily on the dangers of pride and immoderation.

"The Crosse" as Sacramental Sermon

"The Crosse" begins in the first person singular with a series of meditative rhetorical questions that counter the poet/ speaker's own tendencies even as they answer "Puritan" objections to crosses. In asking, "dare I /. . . th'image of his Crosse deny?" (1–2), he implies his own reluctance to gaze on the Crucifixion. The first 18 lines of the poem thus model the act of self-crossing, of countering the sinful desire to "avert" one's "eye" (7) from Christ's suffering by redirecting one's gaze and one's will toward the "chosen Altar" (4). But with the introduction of the word "thou" in line 19, at the same moment that the poem shifts from the interrogative to the imperative, Donne moves from making a demonstration (which readers of the poem are allowed to witness) to preaching a sermon (which is directly addressed to the reader). The reader is not likely to notice this shift at first because the poet/preacher is urging, not penitent introspection, but an exuberant embrace of the visual universe. Where the preacher in the pulpit would urge his "auditory" to listen, the poet—"preaching" in the silent medium of writing—tells his readers to be attentive spectators, to "Looke" at what he is showing them: "Looke downe, thou spiest out Crosses in small things; / Looke up, thou seest birds rais'd on crossed wings" (21–22).

The poem begins to sound more like a sermon from the pulpit, however, when the preacher turns from the celebration of physical and spiritual crosses to a cautionary homily on the dangers of pride and excess:

> But, as oft Alchimists doe coyners prove,
> So may a selfe-dispising, get selfe-love.
> And then as worst surfets, of best meates bee,

> Soe is pride, issued from humility,
> For, 'tis no child, but monster; therefore Crosse
> Your joy in crosses, else, 'tis double losse.
>
> (37–42)[34]

These lines use three interrelated tropes to condemn false humility and the pride it masks. First, the "selfe-love" that arises from excessive "selfe-dispising" is defined as an alchemist-turned-counterfeiter. Since man is the base metal that can be "Still'd, or purg'd" into the substance of Christ by the alchemy of "tribulation" (30), spiritually efficacious crosses are true "Alchimists" (37), devoted to the quest for metallic purity. But Pharisaical displays of self-crossing—like those Jesus dismisses in Matthew 6:16—turn the divine alchemy of those crosses into the fraudulent art of the coiner, who mints money that merely appears to be gold.[35] Secondly, the poet/preacher defines the hypocritical "selfe-love" of spiritual "coyners" as a deformed offspring of their virtuous "self-dispising." The one "get[s]" or fathers the other (38); yet the sinful progeny of the virtue is "no child, but monster" (41). Finally, the idea of a virtue begetting a vice suggests a third trope, a potentially eucharistic analogy between pride and gluttony: "as worst surfets, of best meates bee, / Soe is pride, issued from humility" (39–40). Too much of a good thing is not only bad for a person, it causes the very "worst" sort of surfeit. As 1 Corinthians 11 makes clear, human beings can be made ill even by the very best "meat" of all, the Eucharistic bread, if they consume it unworthily.[36] Similarly, the sacramental crosses that can—like the Eucharist—restore man's likeness to Christ, may, if used self-indulgently, be as dangerous to the soul as a surfeit is to the body. One must thus, the preacher insists, "Crosse / [One's] joy in crosses" (41–42).

As Donne moves from celebrating the cross to warning his readers of its possible abuse, then, the poem becomes increasingly homiletic. The poem's sermon-like qualities serve to ballast its status as a poem, shifting the balance of the Horatian formula from delight toward edification; and as a sermon, "The Crosse" can carefully define the conditions of its own reception as a sacrament, for as Donne tells his congregation, "Ceremonies have their right use, when their right use hath first beene taught by preaching" (*Sermons* 8:228). The poem thus "crosses" the errors both of "schismatics" who reject the sign of the cross and of conservatives who devalue preaching; for the poet insists that the former look upon "The Crosse" as visible sign, and that the latter listen to it as sermon. "The Crosse" challenges "Puritan" readers by presenting them with a visible sacrament they ought not to spurn; but it also reins in the more conservative churchman's fondness for visual sign and ceremonial.[37]

In another sense, however, the poem's sermon-like qualities reinforce its author's bid to produce a sacramental artifact; for sermons themselves, as Donne saw them, have an efficacy like that of the sacraments. In his sermons, Donne specifically associates preaching and Holy Communion by portraying the sermon as an indispensable prelude to the Eucharistic banquet: "[T]he first course (that which we begin to serve in now) is Manna, food of Angels, plentifull, frequent preaching; but the second course, is the very body and blood of Christ Jesus, shed for us, and given to us, in that blessed Sacrament, of which himselfe makes us worthy receivers at that time" (*Sermons* 6:223).[38] Both sermon and Eucharist, moreover, are able to effect redemptive change:

> Now, as the end of all bodily eating, is Assimilation, that after all other concoctions, that meat may be made *Idem corpus*, the same body that I am; so the end of all spirituall eating, is Assimilation too, That after all Hearing, and all Receiving, I may be made *Idem spiritus cum Domino*, the same spirit, that my God is.... (*Sermons* 6:223)

According to this formulation, the function of both sermon and sacrament is to transform the receiver into that which he receives, to make him one with Christ. That transformation, as we have seen, is precisely the function that "The Crosse" claims for crosses and—by implication—for itself as both sermon and sacrament.

In acknowledging the poem's status as sermon, one may better appreciate the rationale underlying its highly figurative language. As Dennis Quinn demonstrates in a study of Donne's sermons, Donne's practice as a preacher was modeled on the Augustinian "conception of Christian eloquence" (276), according to which the "preacher cooperates in the sacramental application of Christ's merits to men's souls by imitating the divine process visible in scripture" (284). Preaching is thus a sensible incarnation of the Word rather than a kind of rhetoric: "as the Son was made flesh in Christ, and . . . as He was incorporated in the Bible, so He is once more incarnated in preaching the words of the Bible" (282). According to this conception of the Word reincarnate in the pulpit, "Men are saved by vision, not by persuasion. . . . The text is seen not as a verbal or rhetorical communication but as a likeness" (291). As a sacramental sermon, then, "The Crosse" seeks to present Christ incarnate in vivid, palpably sensuous human language, to transform readers by confronting them with the redemptive spectacle of the crucified Savior.

Very interesting

Crossing "concupiscence of witt"

Despite its reliance on the visual, "The Crosse" stresses that one must continually "Crosse and correct" (58) both the "eye" (49) and the poetic imagination or "witt" (58); but the poet/preacher does not entirely heed his own warnings. By the time he warns his readers against excess—telling them solemnly to "Crosse / Your joy in crosses" (41–42)—he has opened himself to charges of precisely the over-indulgence he urges them to avoid. The poem/sermon itself, with its rich layers of cross imagery and its profuse displays of wit, seems to intensify rather than "Crosse" its maker's "joy in crosses." Suggesting as he does that the work of his own hands is a sacramentally efficacious sign, the poet himself is in danger of proving a false alchemist, of flashing gilded lead and calling it gold.

The irony is especially apparent when he moves from instructions about crossing the senses (lines 43–50) to advice about a more interiorized self-discipline:

> And crosse thy heart: for that in man alone
> Points downewards, and hath palpitation.
> Crosse those dejections, when it downeward tends,
> And when it to forbidden heights pretends.
>
> (51–54)

Who, these lines encourage the reader to ask, is more likely to fly "to forbidden heights" than the poet, the Sidneyan maker who, "lifted up with the vigour of his own invention, doth . . . freely rang[e] only within the zodiac of his own wit" (Sidney, 216)? The most dangerous excess in "The Crosse"'s witty display is—after all—the intemperance of the poetic imagination, the power that "pretends" (54) not only in the sense of aspiring or laying claim to "forbidden heights" (54) but also in the sense of *feigning* or creating *fictions* (*OED* def. 15).

Donne does not shrink from addressing the issue of poetic wit quite directly:

> And as thy braine through bony walls doth vent
> By sutures, which a Crosses forme present,
> So when thy braine workes, ere thou utter it,
> Crosse and correct concupiscence of witt.
>
> (55–58)

But whatever the poet's reservations about the exhalations of a witty mind, his "braine workes" another cross-pun into the warning itself, even as he "utter[s] it"!

Elsewhere, Donne testifies to the idea that wit—like the crosses as he defines them in "The Crosse"—may have an alchemically transformative power. In his sonnet "To E. of D.

with six holy Sonnets," he asks the inspirer of his verses to read them and to exert his judgment,

> As fire these drossie Rymes to purifie,
>   Or as Elixar, to change them to gold;
> You are that Alchimist which alwaies had
> Wit, whose one spark could make good things of bad.
>
> (11–14)

It is no wonder, then, that "The Crosse," as a poem aspiring to treat a sacramental object in a sacramentally efficacious way, will be filled with wit. Its sacramental power is in large part due to the transfigurations that wit's "Elixar" can effect.

As Donne notes in line 39 of "The Crosse," however, "worst surfets, of best meates bee"; and if wit is the poem's great strength, it is also its most dangerous ingredient. In order to make "The Crosse" a working example of the Cross's sacramental power, Donne has, it seems, disregarded his own advice to "Crosse and correct concupiscence of witt" (58). One must wonder, when one reads lines 59–60—"Be covetous of Crosses, let none fall. / Crosse no man else, but crosse thy selfe in all" (59–60)—whether the poet, who is so prodigal in his verbal expenditures, letting crosses "fall" into his poem whenever he can, has not practiced the very opposite of what he preaches. Indeed, the pride implicit in his lofty instructional pose would seem to be out of control, for he holds to the second person imperative even as he gives his readers orders that might well apply to him as an author: avoid pride, beware of wit's excesses, let no crosses "fall."

Does Donne, in fact, allow "The Crosse" to "fall" by idolizing the sacrament of his own making? Are the poem's sacramental aspirations simply too monumental? It is, without doubt, a close call. Part of Donne's point throughout, however, is to illustrate—rather than merely address—the danger of idolatry that he sees inherent in all sacramental actions; and as he draws the piece to a close, Donne reinforces his belief that things sacramental are, despite the dangers involved in their use, too valuable to discard. In the process of concluding the poem, he reinforces the idea that "The Cross," like the other sacramental crosses represented within it, is itself a valid seal, to be received with due reverence and solicitude.

He does so by leaving behind the commands which have characterized so much of the poem and switching back to a first-person stance. This time, however, he uses not the singular "I," but an all-inclusive plural:

> Then doth the Crosse of Christ worke fruitfully
> Within our hearts, when we love harmlessly
> That Crosses pictures much, and with more care
> That Crosses children, which our Crosses are.
>
> (61–64)

These, the last four lines of the poem, do much to buttress and enhance the poem's homiletic force. The inclusiveness of the first person plural is an antidote for any presumption that may have crept into the poet's tone as he lectured to the reader. Its subtle suggestion of shared experience is a signal that Donne has not forgotten his own need—evoked in line 3—to "profit by" Christ's "sacrifice." Indeed, his return to first person marks an ongoing commitment to the self-denial, the penitential crossing and questioning of self, that is displayed in the poem's opening series of rhetorical questions. Insofar as he speaks now in the plural, however, the poet extends the sacramentality of the poem to others. The poet-priest will not attempt a private Eucharist, that "false and preposterous imitation" of the Sacrament attacked by Calvin (*Inst.* 4.18.8). Rather, he will recognize that his utterances and gestures are truly sacramental only when they are made in a corporate context, received and shared by a community of readers.[39]

Donne calls his Christian audience to recognize that it participates in the "fruitfull" effects of the Cross he venerates. Looking upon Christ's sign has brought him both joyfully to identify with the crucified Christ and humbly to recognize his own distance from the Savior; by referring to "our" experience as one with his, Donne urges readers to believe that they are themselves completing—and benefitting from—the sacramental act of contemplating the crucifix. He insists that the poem must be "our" "Crosse" as well as his.

And "our Crosses," Donne insists in the last two lines of the poem, are the "children" of the Cross that Jesus embraced. By casting all human crosses—including the devotional poem he has made—as the legitimate offspring of Christ's cross, Donne counters the earlier image of pride as "no child, but monster" (41). That misbegotten sin is to be shunned; but the poem, as one of "our Crosses," is a child to be loved and received "with . . . care" (63). Our love for our own, personal crosses is accompanied by care partly because they are difficult to carry; they cause us "care" in the sense of burdensome anxiety. But the pun on "care" calls the reader to bring to all crosses—including "The Crosse"—not so much that negative kind of "care," but the positive "care" of painstaking attention. We must be alert to the pitfalls of wit even as we submit ourselves to that wit's sacramental power. We must study "The Crosse" as Donne studied the sign that begot it, reaping all the sacramental benefits that it conveys, yet careful of the dangers—of idolatry on the one hand and irreverence on the other—that, for Donne, surround the reception of every sacrament.

The prayer Donne makes in stanza 21 of "A Litanie" provides a particularly valuable gloss on his ambitious undertaking in "The Crosse":

> When plenty, Gods image, and seale
>   Makes us Idolatrous,
> And love it, not him, whom it should reveale,
> When wee are mov'd to seeme religious
> Only to vent wit, Lord deliver us.

(185–89)

Certainly Donne must have feared, in writing "The Crosse," that he was committing the very sin he describes in these lines; for in making the connection between worldly plenty, which men too often put in God's place, and the witty abundance of rhetorical *copia*, he identifies wit as itself a potential idol. But at the same time, by pointing out that the wealth of good things which God bestows upon us should be taken as a sacramental seal of God's presence in our lives, a visible sign of the grace that works inwardly, Donne testifies to the sacramental value of all plenty: of copious wit as well as of material abundance. Rather than reject God's seal, we must make use of it, and pray to be delivered from the sin that its use might occasion. In "The Crosse," then, Donne is highlighting the risks involved even as he celebrates both Christ's cross and the verbal seal which is the celebration.

Dying Upon This Theme: Lucius Cary's Response to "The Crosse"

Whether or not "The Crosse" succeeds as a sacramental text, whether or not it proves spiritually efficacious, is—of course—a question that will be answered differently by each reader of the poem. For C. A. Patrides, who contrasts Donne's poem with Browne's treatment of the quincunx in *The Garden of Cyrus*, "The Crosse is merely clever" (41). But at least one of Donne's seventeenth century readers thought quite the opposite. In his elegy on Donne in the 1633 edition of Donne's poems, Lucius Cary[40] alludes admiringly to "The Crosse":

> His Poetrie
> It selfe was oftentimes divinity,
> Those Anthemes (almost second Psalmes) he writ
> To make us knowe the Crosse, and value it,
> (Although we owe that reverence to that name
> Wee should not need warmth from an under flame.)

Creates a fire in us, so neare extreme
That we would die, for, and upon this theme.

(Poems 390)

The lines seem to refer to more than one poem—perhaps Cary has "Goodfriday, 1613" or "Upon the Annunciation and the Passion" in mind as well—but "The Crosse," which specifically defends the use of crosses against those who would abolish them, is clearly one of the works he is praising. What Cary values in these poems is their power to move readers, to ignite devotional fervor. His parenthetical remark about how "Wee should not need" them to inspire us recalls Calvin's description of sacraments as concessions to the weakness of man's faith (*Inst.* 4.14.3); and by calling them "Anthemes"— that is to say, hymns, he classifies them as belonging to a liturgical genre.[41] Indeed, by adding the phrase "(almost second Psalmes)," he affords them a status little below that of scripture, the Psalter being, of course, an integral part of the English Church's liturgy. As his tribute to Donne continues, Cary also compares Donne's "Litany" and cross poems to preaching, declaring "that but for the name, nor this, nor those / Want any thing of Sermons, but the prose." For Cary, in short, Donne's divine poems act as means of salvation; they are both liturgical and homiletic, both a form of worship and a discourse of instruction. They teach men to "value" the cross, and they "make us know" it experientially.

For Cary as for Donne, then, the function of a sermon (or of a sermon-like poem) is not simply instructive. Indeed, from the start of his poem, he celebrates both Donne's ministerial vocation and his sermons themselves as essentially sacramental. Cary applies the traditional idea of the sacraments as conduits of grace to Donne himself, saying that he was "the voice of Truth, / Gods Conduit-pipe for grace" (*Poems*, 389). In preaching the Word, Cary asserts, Donne "victual'd with that blest food" the hearts of his listeners, giving them in verbal form the same Christ whose flesh they received by eating the bread of the Eucharist (*Poems*, 390). Those who heard him preach, Cary insists, must not "forget that heavenly Eloquence, / With which he did the bread of life dispense" (*Poems*, 389). Indeed, Dean Donne was, as Cary saw him, a living sacrament whose audible words and visible works were both means of salvation: "No Druggist of the Soule bestow'd on all / So Catholiquely a curing Cordiall. / Nor only in the Pulpit dwelt his store, / His words work'd much, but his example more" (*Poems*, 390). God provides man with both Word and Sacrament, both audible preaching and visible signs; Donne, Cary feels, incarnated both in himself.

Interestingly, it is the tribute to Donne as a man who preached as much by example as by the spoken word that leads Cary to his praise of Donne as poet:

> Nor only in the Pulpit dwelt his store,
> His words work'd much, but his example more,
> That preach't on worky dayes, His Poetrie
> It selfe was oftentimes divinity . . .
>
> (*Poems*, 390)

The contrast in these lines is not only between words and works, but between the holy milieu of "the Pulpit" and the secular world of "worky days"; poetry, Cary implies, falls within the realm of the profane. It may be made of words, but it is "worky." Only Donne, whose work-a-day deeds "preach't" as effectively as his sermons, could pull his poetic *works* (no less than his other exemplary actions) into the realm of "divinity." The challenge, Cary's organization makes clear, was not only to make something secular into something holy, but to produce visible, written works no less powerful and redemptive than the audible, preached Word.

In his cross poems, Cary insists, Donne met this challenge, presenting his readers with a means of redemption. Playing upon the resemblance between the words "Antheme" and "theme" Cary insists that Donne's "Anthemes" of the cross make readers willing to "die, for, and upon this theme"; that is to say, a poem like "The Crosse" makes them willing to die not only *for the sake of Christ's cross* or *upon a cross*, but also upon "The Crosse," upon their literary encounter with the "theme" of that powerful "Antheme."[42] The poetry of "The Crosse," this formulation insists, succeeds in a sacramental office; like baptism or the eucharist, it brings those who receive it into conformity with the crucified Christ. They die "upon" the theme of "The Crosse" as Jesus did upon his Cross.

Cary's reading of "The Crosse" is, I would argue, a response that the poem itself invites. And while Cary may have exaggerated his own emotional and spiritual response to Donne's writing, it is nevertheless instructive that at least one contemporary reader chose to praise "The Crosse" by assenting to the work's definition of itself as a sacramental text.

Two

⁂

"Deigne at My Hands"

"God made us with his word," Donne says in one of his undated Trinity-Sunday sermons,

> and with our words we make God so farre, as that we make up
> the mysticall body of Christ Jesus with our prayers, with our
> whole liturgie, and we make the naturall body of Christ Jesus
> appliable to our soules, by the words of Consecration in the
> Sacrament . . . (*Sermons* 3:259–60)

In his sonnet cycle *La Corona*, Donne relies upon this conception of liturgical language in order to become a poetic maker
of Christ; through the poem, he seeks to "make the . . . body
of Christ appliable to" his own soul and to the souls of readers
who unite their voices with his. Provided that the "holy Spirit,
[his] Muse did raise" (*Cor*7, 13), the poet/speaker can hope
that his poetry will achieve a sacramental "power of operation within the soul, most admirable [and] divine" (Hooker,
Laws 6.6.10). Donne presents his work to God as a sacred
offering that, like the Eucharist, cuts through space and
time, uniting the self-oblation of each Christian with Christ's

redemptive offering of his body and blood upon the altar of the cross. Thus, through Donne's *"crown of prayer and praise"* (*Cor1*, 1), as through the prayers and praises of the Communion liturgy, the receiver/reader is to experience the saving power of Christ's Eucharistic body.[1]

The connections between *La Corona* and the Eucharist have been largely neglected, though twentieth century readers have explored the poem's relation to Roman Catholic meditational handbooks and to the cycle of the liturgical year. In exploring these sources of inspiration, scholars originally focused largely on the ways in which the work reflects Donne's recusant upbringing. Louis Martz (105–08) clearly demonstrates the relation between *La Corona* and English manuals for saying the rosary; and in her introduction to Donne's *Divine Poems*, Helen Gardner preserves this emphasis, discussing the sonnet cycle in the light of Donne's "devotional conservatism" and venturing the opinion that, while Donne himself may not have "felt there was anything particularly Catholic" in the piety of *La Corona*, it is "doubtful whether anyone who had been brought up as a Protestant would have" concentrated on the Mysteries of the Faith or addressed Saint Joseph and the Virgin as Donne does in his sonnet cycle (xxii).[2] More recently, due to the realignment of emphasis attending Barbara Lewalski's theory of Protestant poetics, many scholars have immersed themselves in Reformation theology, neglecting Catholic source materials and concentrating on Protestant devotional manuals and treatises. In this climate, even *La Corona*, which once seemed so "Catholic," has been read—inaccurately, I would argue—as an essentially Calvinist work of art.[3]

The most sensitive criticism of the work remains that of A. B. Chambers, who has convincingly demonstrated *La Corona*'s relationship to the endless cycle of the liturgical year, the basic structure of which is the same in the Roman and English Churches. For *La Corona* is—like most English devotional poetry of its time—eclectic. As R. V. Young points out, "though generally Protestant," the religious poets of seventeenth century England "are not, *in their poetry*, so much militant proponents of the Reformation as Christians confronting God." These poets, including Donne, "draw upon a number of Christian resources—Catholic and Protestant, Medieval and Renaissance" ("Donne's Holy Sonnets," 38). Thus, Young urges, critics should attend to "marks of the strains exerted by competing versions of grace and salvation" in poems such as Donne's Holy Sonnets; they should appreciate the ways in which the power of this poetry is often generated by the poets' "sensitivity to the theological tensions of the era" ("Donne's Holy Sonnets" 39).

La Corona, too, despite its relatively serene liturgical mood (as compared with the Holy Sonnets' atmosphere of anguished spiritual struggle) demonstrates such sensitivity. The work defies oversimplified theological categories; for the poet offers it to God as a poetic Eucharist that is neither strictly Roman nor strictly Calvinist but distinctively English (resembling in many respects the Communion rite of the *Book of Common Prayer*) and Donnean (incorporating those elements of the Catholic Mass that he did not reject as a Protestant and reflecting beliefs about the Eucharist that he would later express in his sermons). As the poet presides over his poetic liturgy, he is as alert as the writers of the Elizabethan *Homilies* to the perils of excess, presumption, and idolatry, the dangers he so narrowly evades in "The Crosse"; but he does not lose touch with the deep reverence for the Sacrament instilled in him during his Catholic childhood and youth. *La Corona* thus draws upon energies both devotional and polemical; it is at some points charged with the vigor of Eucharistic and ecclesiastical controversy, and at others infused with the quiet awe of liturgical worship. The result of this powerful mixture is, as Chambers has argued, a "major" work: "subtle, dense, intricate, polished, and one of the superior examples of its kind" ("Uses of Time," 168).

Poem as Sacramental Offering

Like the Eucharist, *La Corona* is an offering to God. The phrase with which it opens—*"Deigne at my hands"*—recalls the response "Suscipiat Dominus sacrificium de manibus tuis" in the Tridentine Mass (*Roman Liturgy*, 101).[4] The priest says, "pray that my Sacrifice and yours may be acceptable to God the Father almighty" and the server responds, "May the Lord receive the Sacrifice from thy hands" (*Missal*, 635–37). There is a key distinction, however, between the Catholic Sacrifice of the Mass and Donne's Eucharistic offering in *La Corona*. In the Mass, the priest prays that God will "Accept . . . this unspotted host, which I, Thy unworthy servant, offer unto Thee, . . . for my innumerable sins, offenses, and negligences, and for all here present: . . . that it may avail both me and them for salvation unto life everlasting" (*Missal*, 631).[5] But Donne's poem, like the English Protestant Eucharist, carefully distinguishes itself from an offering that "may avail . . . for salvation."

In his sermons, Donne rejects what he calls the "blasphemous over-boldnesse" of those "who constitute a *propitiatory Sacrifice, in the Church of Rome*" (*Sermons* 7:429). He stresses what was to become the high-church Anglican doctrine: that the Eucharist is a *commemorative* sacrifice, in which the priest

> *offers up* to God the Father, (that is, to the *remembrance*, to the contemplation of God the Father) the *whole body* of the *merits of Christ Jesus*, and begges of him, that in contemplation of that *Sacrifice* so offered, of that Body of his merits, he would vouchsafe to return, and to apply those merits to that Congregation. . . . [T]he *whole body* of *Christs actions* and *passions*, we sacrifice, wee represent, wee offer to God (*Sermons* 7:429–30).[6]

La Corona is a commemorative sacrifice modeled on precisely this conception of the Eucharist, an oblation in which the poet re-presents "the *whole body* of *Christs actions* and *passions*" from the moment of his conception to his ascension into heaven, offering that body up to the "Antient of dayes" (*Cor1*, 4).' The offering is presented, moreover, not as a work that is in itself effectual (since "our workes" can serve only our mortal purposes or "ends" [*Cor1*, 9]), but rather as a prayer that God himself will make something of those purposes, that he will "[crown] our ends" (*Cor1*, 9) and "with [his] owne blood quench [his] owne just wrath" (*Cor7*, 12).

The opening sonnet of the cycle is particularly important in defining the nature of *La Corona* as offering. The poet/speaker begins by stressing his awareness that God alone is the source of all good. In addressing the Deity as "Thou which of good, hast, yea art treasury" (3), he plays upon the fact that, since God declares his name to be the first person form of the verb "to be"—"I am" (Exodus 3:14), his name in the second person is "Thou art." When the artistically self-conscious poet/speaker corrects "hast" to "art," he draws attention to the more powerful meaning in that second verb and hints that it may also serve as a noun. God not only *has* the "treasury" of all "good," he *is* the treasury of all good "art"; indeed, the speaker hopes that God will consent to be called "Thou art," to *be* "art," to incarnate himself in the words of the offered poem as he does in the bread and wine of the Eucharist, which is the one perfect offering that God "Deign[s]" to receive "at [man's] hands" (1).

The poet/speaker prays, "doe not, with a vile crowne of fraile bayes, / Reward my muses white sincerity" (5–6), for he knows that such a "vile" payment is the only one his poems, insofar as they are his alone, can merit; "But," he begs Christ, instead of "Reward[ing]" me, "what thy thorny crowne gain'd, that *give* mee, / A crowne of Glory, which doth flower alwayes" (7–8; emphasis added). He foregoes reward and seeks God's free gift because, as he says, "The ends crowne our workes, but thou crown'st our ends" (9): only Christ himself is a corona worth wearing. It is the Lord himself who is the heavenly "crowne of Glory," and it is with him that the saints will be crowned when they reach the "ends" God has in store for them.

In contrasting this heavenly crown with the "vile" laurel, the sonnet alludes to Isaiah 28, which foretells the downfall of the wicked and the salvation of the just:

> The crown of pride, the drunkards of Ephraim, shall be trodden under feet: And the glorious beauty, which is on the head of the fat valley, shall be a fading flower. . . . In that day shall the Lord of hosts be for a crown of glory, and for a diadem of beauty, unto the residue of his people . . . (Isaiah 28:3–5).[8]

Donne's sonnet, which implicitly contrasts the poet/speaker's own "sober thirst" with the inebriate folly of those poets who seek the "vile crowne of fraile bayes" (5), shares in the prophetic nature of Isaiah's vision. Donne seeks to set himself apart from the "drunkards" who seek the laurel crown of poetic fame; and his insistence that he is "zealously possest, / With a strong sober thirst" (11–12) plays up the contrast between himself—a poet of God—and profane poets, whose inspiration is so frequently compared to the influence of wine. Secular artists have, like "the priest and the prophet" whom Isaiah decries, "erred through strong drink, . . . they err in vision" (28:7). But the "strong sober thirst" of the poet/speaker is for Christ, "the Lord of hostes" who is himself, as the Isaiah allusion confirms, the "crowne of Glory" which crowns our ends (*Cor1*, 8–9). It is this "first last end" (*Cor1*, 11)—Christ, the Alpha and the Omega, the beginning and the end (Revelation 1:8, 11)—who can slake the thirst of the poet/speaker.

Christ's means of satisfying the parched soul, Donne's poems and sermons stress, is the gift of the Eucharist by which he conveys himself to Christians. Thus, it is the Eucharistic logic of Psalm 116:12–13 that informs *La Corona*: "What shall I render unto the Lord for all his benefits toward me? I will take the cup of salvation, and call upon the name of the Lord."[9]

The only way man can *offer* an appropriate oblation to God, the psalm verses stress, is to *accept* Christ's thirst-quenching sacramental gift. The poet who would quench his thirst even as he offers God a poetic *"crown of prayer and praise"* must therefore model that crown on the Church's greatest act of prayer and praise, the Eucharist, the acceptance of Christ's "cup." In the first sonnet of *La Corona*, the poet/speaker thus prepares for a Eucharistic event; as Advent prepares for and looks forward to both Christmas and to the Second Coming, so this sonnet—which, as Gardner observes, "might well be called 'Advent'" (57)—prepares for and looks forward to Christ's advent within *La Corona*: a verbal incarnation in the Eucharistic language of the poem.

Lines 11–12 describe the preparation in particularly rich terms: "The first last end, now zealously possess, / With a strong sober thirst, my soule attends." The lines may be understood in several different ways. Gardner explains that "'Possest' qualifies the soul, which is 'wholly occupied' by its thirst" for "the expected Saviour" (59). According to this reading, Donne is awaiting Christmas; for in preparing to write a Eucharistic poem, he is preparing for Christ to enter into poetry even as he entered into the world on the first Christmas and continues to enter into each Christian through the Eucharist. When Christians receive the Sacrament, he says in a sermon, they have "another Christmas-day, another manifestation and application of Christ to [them] selves" (*Sermons* 7:280); in receiving *La Corona*, readers are to experience just such a Christmas, just such a coming of Christ to them. One may also, however, interpret "possest" to mean "taken possession of" (*OED* def. 1) and read the phrase "now zealously possest" as modifying "end"; if one reads the lines this way, they refer to a present enjoyment of Christ, the "first last end" which the soul already possesses insofar as it "attends"— "waits upon" (*OED* def. 7) or "pays heed to" (def. 2)—Christ in the Eucharist.

The paradoxical combination of waiting for an event still to come while attending to a present event reflects the dual nature of Donne's sonnet, which, as a part of *La Corona*'s endless circle, is no less the sonnet following the work's seventh sonnet, "Ascention," than it is the one preceding the second, "Annunciation." In repeating the fourteenth line of "Ascention" as its first line, *"Deigne at my hands"* becomes, as A. B. Chambers puts it, *La Corona*'s "first-last poem" ("Uses of Time," 166). Because the work is, like the liturgical year, an endless cycle, "Donne's soul already has possessed itself of the first-last end of the poem," even in what appears to be its opening sonnet, "for he is repeating an experience, a devotional act, previously incorporated within himself and described to others in his verse. His soul can therefore attend—give attendance to—the Christ, who has ended, does end, and shall end all thirst" (A. B. Chambers, "Uses of Time," 166–67).

But as every Christmas is preceded by an Advent season, so every celebration of the Eucharist is preceded by a penitential rite. In his Christmas sermon for 1626, Donne says that, "as the Church prepares our devotion before Christmas-day, with foure Sundayes in Advent," so each communicant is made ready for the Sacrament, another "birth of Christ" which takes place in his soul, "by that which [is] said before" (*Sermons* 7:280).[10] Donne is referring here to the "general confession" that the *BCP* Communion rite provides to be pronounced either by one of the congregation or by one of the presiding clergymen "in the name of all those that are minded to receive the Holy Communion" (*BCP*, 259). This penitential prayer, like the penitential season of Advent, prepares the faithful to receive Christ. The opening sonnet of *La Corona* has a similar function: in order to present his work as a Eucharistic offering, the poet/speaker must first present himself "kneeling humbly upon [his] knees" (*BCP*, 259): that is, in a posture of "low devout melancholie" (*Cor1*, 2).[11]

Once he has done so, he can turn from humble dejection to joy. In the *Book of Common Prayer*, the confession and general absolution are followed by consolation; the priest quotes several New Testament passages illustrating "what comfortable words our Savior Christ saith, to all that truly turn to him" (*BCP*, 260); with these words in mind, the priest urges, "Lift up your hearts" and the people respond, "We lift them up to the Lord."[12] Line 13 of *La Corona*'s opening sonnet recalls this liturgical exchange: "'Tis time that heart and voice be lifted high," the poet/speaker proclaims; and in line 14, we hear his uplifted voice announce the "comfortable words" which make it possible for men to lift their hearts: "*Salvation to all that will is nigh.*"

This final line recalls a number of scriptural verses used in the liturgies of Advent.[13] Particularly relevant to the poem's Eucharistic function is Romans 13:11, "now is our salvation nearer." For, according to Donne's sermon on that text, the Sacrament is the means by which our salvation draws nigh; in the sermon, Donne emphasizes the importance of the word "now," explaining that it "denotes an Advent, a new coming, or a new operation, otherwise then it was before: And therefore doth the Church appropriate this Scripture to the celebration of the *Advent*, before the Feast of the Birth of our Saviour" (*Sermons* 2:250).[14] He goes on to insist that the term "Salvation" as it is used in Romans 13:11 refers to "outward means of salvation" (2:253) and to the grace received through them:

> [When] Grace works powerfully in thee, in the ways of sanctification, then is this Salvation neer thee; . . . If this Salvation be brought to this neerness . . . thou shalt find it . . . in those organs wherein thy soul uses thy body, in thy senses, and in the sensible things ordain'd by God in his Church, Sacraments and Ceremonies. (*Sermons* 2:262)

And, the poet of *La Corona* would add, in the "sensible" medium of sanctified poetry. As he anticipates the work's second sonnet, "Annunciation," which proclaims Christ's conception in the womb of the Virgin, Donne makes known to "all that will" the availability of Christ's saving grace in the poetic sacrament he "now zealously" administers (11): "*Salvation . . . is nigh,*" he announces (14), to all communicant/readers who "will" seek it in the "sensible" form of his poetry.

The Poet as his Maker's Maker: "Annunciation"

Because the poet/speaker of *La Corona* is sure that he is performing his "bounden duty" (*BCP*, 264) as a Christian by offering a Eucharistic sacrifice to God, the first sonnet of *La Corona* ends confidently. Like the exhortation used to call the faithful to Communion—"You that do truly and earnestly repent of your sins, . . . Draw near, and take this holy Sacrament to your comfort" (*BCP*, 259)—the concluding line of *Cor1* tells readers that the refreshment of the Eucharist is available to "all that will" join in "heart and voice" with the priestly poet/speaker.

His voice is no longer sunken in the depths of "low devout melancholie" (*Cor1*, 2), but is elevated with a ring of authority as he summons "all" to salvation. The alteration bears witness to the fact that God is indeed the "All changing" force (*Cor1*, 4) who can effect a Eucharistic transformation of "our workes" (*Cor1*, 9) into sacramentally efficacious offerings. It is the Eucharistic sacrament of that "All changing" God, Donne stresses in a sermon, that can bring the believer to a "transmutation, which admits no re-transmutation, which is a modest, but infalible assurance of a final perseverance, so to be joyned to the Lord, as to be one spirit with him" (*Sermons* 1:164).[15]

Thus, as the second sonnet of *La Corona* begins, Donne illustrates God's ability to change not just the poet/speaker, but "all" men, by making them one with Himself:

> *Salvation to all that will is nigh,*
> That All, which alwayes is All every where,
> Which cannot sinne, and yet all sinnes must beare,
> Which cannot die, yet cannot chuse but die,
> Loe, faithfull Virgin, yeelds himselfe to lye
> In prison, in thy wombe . . .
>
> *(Cor 2, 1–6)*

Through the Incarnation of Christ, the plurality of a human "all" is united with the perfect singularity of the divine "All." In a sermon passage that puns on "all" as an end-rhyme, Donne stresses that the "*naturall* union" of the Divine and the Human "(that Christ hath taken our *Nature*,)" is confirmed in "a *Sacramentall union*" when we receive the Eucharist: "we are so washed in his bloud, as that we stand in the sight of his Father, as cleane, and innocent, as himselfe, both because he and we are thereby become one body, and because the garment of his righteousnesse covers us all" (*Sermons* 5:173).[16] The meeting of "all" and "All" in the poem on Christ's conception similarly initiates a verbal conflation of Christ and man; and in the "Resurrection" sonnet, that conflation will allow the poet/speaker to feel that his own flesh is Eucharistically one with Christ's, that he can write of Christ's resurrection as his own.

As he introduces the union of God and man through the play on "all" and "All," Donne also continues to draw upon the structure and language of the English communion rite. In the 1559 *Book of Common Prayer*, the *sursum corda* is followed by a prayer and "the proper preface, according to the time." The Preface "Upon Christmas Day, and Seven Days After" speaks of the Annunciation and its implications:

> [T]hou didst give Jesus Christ, thine only Son, to be born as this day for us, who by the operation of the Holy Ghost, was made very man of the substance of the Virgin Mary his mother, and that without spot of sin, to make us clean from all sin. (*BCP*, 261)

The "Annunciation" sonnet of *La Corona* places similar stress upon the sinlessness of Christ's incarnation and on his taking his human "substance" from the Virgin Mother. The divine "All," the speaker tells the "faithfull Virgin,"

> yeelds himselfe to lye,
> In prison, in thy wombe; and though he there
> Can take no sinne, nor thou give, yet he'will weare
> Taken from thence, flesh, which deaths force may trie.
>
> (2–8)[17]

In the succeeding lines, the metapoetic implications of Christ's Incarnation become clear. As a "maker" privileged to be the vessel of divinity, the Virgin is the poet's model; as she "conceiv'd" Christ in the "little room" of her womb, he will seek to conceive a Eucharistic reincarnation of Christ in his sonnets' little rooms: "Whom thou conceiv'st, conceiv'd; yea thou art now / Thy Makers maker, and thy Fathers mother" (11–12). In imitating the Virgin's creative role, the poet assumes a sacerdotal function of the sort Herbert celebrates in "The Priesthood":

> . . . th'holy men of God such vessels are,
> As serve him up, who all the world commands:
> When God vouchsafeth to become our fare,
> Their hands convey him, who conveys their hands.[18]

Like the priests whose "hands convey" the Lord, the poet of *La Corona* asks God to "Deign at my hands" (*Cor1*, 1) a Eucharistic poem.

His prayer is, however, marked by an effort to avoid presumption. In "Crucifying," Donne will present Christ's death as a crime engineered by scribes—writers—who would "prescribe a Fate" to the creator of Fate itself (7); the poet must not crucify Christ anew by a similarly *presumptuous* attempt to in*scribe* Christ's presence in his poetry. In "Annunciation," therefore, Donne presents the Virgin as her "Makers maker" (12), providing himself with a positive creative paradigm as an alternative to the crucifiers' gall. He stresses that the Virgin's conception of Christ, which corresponds to the poet's ability to conceive Christ anew in his poetry, is possible only because he "Whom thou conceiv'st, conceiv'd" (*Cor2*, 11); Christ "yeelds himselfe to lye" in the "little roome" of the Virgin's womb (*Cor2*, 13) just as he binds himself with the promise to be present in the Eucharist.[19] And if the little rooms of the corona-maker's sonnets are to be a Eucharistic response to Christ's sacrifice rather than a profane bid for "a vile crown of fraile bayes" (*Cor1*, 5), it must be because Christ will "Deigne" (*Cor1*, 1 and *Cor7*, 14) to put on the crown he offers, to wrap himself in the apparel of language even as he once consented to "weare / . . . flesh" (*Cor2*, 7–8) and still consents to be "apparell[ed]" in those "*outward things*"—including sacraments and sacramental poems—that "beare witnesse of . . . faith" (*Sermons* 3:368).[20]

"kisse him in the Sacrament": "Nativitie"

The next sonnet of *La Corona*, "Nativitie," compresses into 14 lines the speaker's meditations on a series of events including Christ's birth, the Wise Men's Epiphany, the slaughter of the Innocents, and the flight into Egypt.[21] It concludes with the poet/speaker's apostrophe to his own soul:

> Seest thou, my Soule, with thy faiths eyes, how he
> Which fils all place, yet none holds him, doth lye?
> ....
> Kisse him, and with him into Egypt goe,
> *With his kinde mother, who partakes thy woe.*
>
> (9–10, 13–14)

The exhortation to "kisse" the child makes a particularly effective contribution to *La Corona*'s Eucharistic theme and function. In a sermon on Psalm 2:12—"Kisse the son, lest he be angry"—Donne speaks of the kiss in sacramental terms: it is "the band and seale of love" (*Sermons* 3:313) without which

Christ will not receive us; indeed, it is an emblem of Real Presence: "he hath invited us, enabled us to kisse him, for he is presentially amongst us" (*Sermons* 3:314).[22] In the person of Christ himself, Donne explains, "the Divine and the humane nature have kissed each other" (*Sermons* 3:320); and Christians can participate in that embrace through the Eucharist: "Confesse to God . . ., Reconcile thy selfe to him, and kisse him in the Sacrament, in the seale of Reconciliation" (*Sermons* 3:322). Thus, when the poet/speaker of *La Corona* tells his soul to kiss the infant Jesus, he is urging and enacting a Eucharistic oneness with the divine child.

The command, "Kisse him," as it appears in line 13 of "Nativitie" recalls not only Donne's interpretation of Psalm 2, but also his Eucharistic reading of a scriptural event that occurred during the period of time covered in the "Nativitie" sonnet: old Simeon's embrace of the child Jesus at his presentation in the temple. The Gospel of Luke tells the story of how "it was revealed" to Simeon "by the Holy Ghost, that he should not see death, before he had seen the Lord's Christ" (2:26). When Mary and Joseph came to the temple for her purification, and to present their first born son according to the law, Simeon saw the child:

> Then took he him up in his arms, and blessed God, and said, Lord, now lettest thou thy servant depart in peace, according to thy word: For mine eyes have seen thy salvation. . . . And Simeon blessed them, and said unto Mary his mother, Behold, this child is set for the fall and rising again of many in Israel; and for a sign which shall be spoken against; (Yea, a sword shall pierce through thy own soul also,) . . . (Luke 2:28–30, 34–35)

Simeon's embrace of the child, his reference to the vision he beholds, and his prophecy of Mary's woe are all reflected in "Nativitie," where Donne tells his soul to see Christ "with . . . faiths eyes," to kiss him, and to go into Egypt with the sorrowful mother.

And as McNees notes, the story of the presentation had Eucharistic implications for Donne: "In his Christmas sermon of 1626," McNees explains, "Donne compares the epiphany of Christ to Simeon in the temple with the epiphany of Christ within man's soul in the Sacrament" ("John Donne," 100). The text for the sermon is the "Nunc dimittis" of Luke 2:29–30; and Simeon's declaration, "Mine eyes have seen thy salvation," provide an occasion for a long discourse on Eucharistic controversy. According to Donne, Simeon saw Christ not as Abraham did, only "with the eye of faith"; rather, he beheld his Salvation "with his bodily eyes," as can the Christian communicant:

> Beloved, in the blessed, and glorious, and mysterious Sacrament of the Body and Blood of Christ Jesus, thou seest *Christum Domini*, the Lords Salvation, and thy Salvation, and that, thus far with bodily eyes; That Bread which thou seest after the Consecration, is not the same bread, which was presented before; . . . it is severed, and appropriated by God, in that Ordinance to another use. (*Sermons* 7:293, 294)

The words of *La Corona*, the signs visible on the page, are also consecrated signs, "severed" from the ordinary, profane use of poetic language, the pursuit of the "vile crowne of frail bayes" (*Cor1*, 5). Language thus consecrated is still human language, as Donne in his sermon says that the consecrated bread "is bread still" (*Sermons* 7:294); but in it, as in the sacrament, Christian readers may say—with Simeon—that they embrace Christ and that their "eyes see his salvation" (*Sermons* 7:296).[23]

The poet/speaker of "Nativitie" thus asks himself a sacred riddle that may be solved only through the paradox of the Eucharist, in which an ubiquitous deity makes himself present and visible in a particular sign: "Seest thou, my Soule, with thy faiths eyes, how he / Which fils all place, yet none holds him, doth lye?" (9–10). The stress on spiritual rather than physical vision in this awe-filled question insists—as both Catholic and Protestant Eucharistic poetry often does—that where the senses fail, "sola fides sufficit": faith alone suffices.[24] At the same time, the poet/speaker's careful phrase "yet none holds him" distinguishes his riddle from what Donne would later call the "hereticall Riddle" of transubstantiation (*Sermons* 7:294; in the Christmas sermon on Simeon). He thus distinguishes *La Corona*'s sacramental evocation of Christ's presence from any hubristic attempt to "imprison Christ *in Opere operato*" (*Sermons* 7:267) or to "mold him up in" the poetic equivalent of "a wafer Cake, or a peece of bread" (*Sermons* 5:135).

"all which should be writ": "Temple"

In "Nativitie," Donne evokes the idea of Eucharist and of Eucharistic poetry as a new incarnation, a sacramental participation in the mystery of Christmas. But the Lord's Supper is even more deeply linked to the events of Holy Week, when Christ instituted the Eucharist and offered up his Body on the altar of the Cross. In *La Corona*, Donne makes the transition from "Nativitie" to "Crucifying" through a sonnet entitled "Temple." In it, he reflects further both on the nature of Christ as God Incarnate and on *La Corona* as a sacramental locus for Christ's ongoing self-revelation.

"Nativitie" ends with the Holy Family's flight into Egypt, and "Temple" opens with lines that at first seem to urge their return to Palestine: *"With his kinde mother who partakes thy woe, / Joseph* turne backe" (1–2). In Matthew 2:19–20, Joseph hears a similar exhortation: "[A]n angel of the Lord appeareth in a dream to Joseph in Egypt, Saying, Arise, and take the young child and his mother, and go into the land of Israel: for they are dead which sought the young child's life." In the context of the ensuing lines, however, the exhortation takes on a second meaning as an allusion to the moment,

narrated in Luke 2:41–45, when Mary and Joseph thought
that Jesus was lost:

> Now his parents went to Jerusalem every year at the feast of
> the passover. And when he was twelve years old, they went up
> to Jerusalem, . . . And when they had fulfilled the days, as they
> returned, the child Jesus tarried behind in Jerusalem, . . . And
> when they found him not, they turned back again to Jerusa-
> lem, seeking him.

This turning back is, as the lines in *La Corona* stress, one in
which Mary "partakes" or shares Joseph's "woe": for when
they finally find Jesus in the Temple, Mary says to him, "Son,
why hast thou thus dealt with us? behold, thy father and I
have sought thee sorrowing" (Luke 2:48).

The poet/speaker of "Temple" is also seeking Christ, whose
"liberall dole" (*Cor5*, 13) will be Eucharistically distributed
in "Crucifying"; he will "partake" of—sacramentally consume—that woeful "dole" just as Christ's "kinde mother . . .
partakes" the "woe" of the devout soul in the final line of
"Nativity" (*Cor3*, 14) and the "woe" of her husband Joseph in
the opening line of "Temple" (*Cor4*, 1). Donne also shares in
Mary's and Joseph's awe; when they find Jesus in the Temple,
his dual nature is revealed:

> see where your child doth sit,
> Blowing, yea blowing out those sparks of wit,
> Which himselfe on the Doctors did bestow;
> The Word but lately could not speake, and loe
> It sodenly speakes wonders . . .
>
> (2–6)

Christ is here both the "child" of human parents and the
divine creator of human "wit," both helpless *infans* and all-
powerful "Word." Through the traditional paradoxes of these
lines, Donne's "Temple"—like the Temple where Christ's
parents found him—becomes the locus for a manifestation of
Christ as God-Man.[25] Indeed, at the very heart of *La Corona*,

in the central lines (7–8) of the central sonnet (fourth of seven), is the head that wears the corona, the *theanthropic* mind of Christ, possessed of both "Godhead" and "manhood" (9) and inspiring awed amazement "That all which was, and all which should be writ, / A shallow seeming child, should deeply know" (7–8).[26] Though the poet/speaker asks "Whence comes" this wonder, his question implies an acknowledgment that the Christ child did know, not only the prophecies that were and the Gospels that would be written of him, but all texts, all writing "which should be"—including *La Corona* itself. If it is Christ himself who is "Blowing . . . those sparks of wit, / Which himselfe . . . did bestow" (3–4) on the poet/speaker, then the sonnet "Temple" (and *La Corona* as a whole) is a "Temple" for the "Word" (5), a text which "should be writ" (7).

Moistening the Soul: "Crucifying" And "Resurrection"

The concluding line of "Temple," which refers to miracles as evidence of Christ's divinity, gives Donne his opening for the crucifixion sonnet. Though miracles are the means by which the incarnate Word engenders "faith in some" (*Cor5*, 2), they are politically dangerous; the learned authorities of the Temple were once "astonished at his understanding, and answers" (Luke 2:47), but the leaders of the people now resent his wondrous abilities:

> By miracles exceeding power of man,
> Hee faith in some, envie in some begat,
> For, what weake spirits admire, ambitious, hate:
> In both affections many to him ran,
> But Oh! the worst are most, they will and can,
> Alas, and do, unto th'immaculate,
> Whose creature Fate is, now prescribe a Fate . . .
>
> (1–7)

The perverse "will" of Christ's enemies (5) violently negates for them the *"will"* to salvation underscored in line 14 of *La*

Corona's opening sonnet; and their attempt at "Measuring ... infinity" (*Cor5*, 8)—crushing the immeasurable into the narrow numbers of "ambitious" human craft or artifice (*Cor5*, 3)—perverts the Virgin's role as her "Makers maker" (*Cor2*, 12).

Because she was "faithfull" (*Cor2*, 5), God begat his Son upon her; and she was humbly willing to provide herself as the vessel that shut "*Immensity*" in "little roome" (*Cor2*, 14, 13). By contrast, Christ "begat" only "envie" in those without "faith" (*Cor5*, 2). These "ambitious" spirits are the "worst" of men (*Cor5*, 3, 5), and in their cruelty they negate the work of "*his kinde mother*" (*Cor3*, 14). The Christ whom the "Annunciation" sonnet says "cannot sinne" (*Cor2*, 3) remains "th'immaculate" (*Cor5*, 6); "and yet all sinnes must beare" (*Cor2*, 3) when "hee / Beares his own crosse, with paine" (*Cor5*, 9–10). He who "cannot die, yet cannot chuse but die" (*Cor2*, 2–4) will find that he "must beare more and die" (*Cor5*, 11) when his prerogative is usurped by the wicked determinists who "prescribe a Fate" to Fate's creator (*Cor5*, 7).[27]

The language of "Crucifying," so precisely gauged to overturn that of "Annunciation," thus provides a cautionary negative exemplum that further defines the Eucharistic poetics of *La Corona*: the Virgin is a model for the priest (or priestly poet) who presides meekly in his administration of the Eucharist (or the Eucharistic poem), who acknowledges that if Christ still consents "into our world to come" (*Cor3*, 4), it is because he "yeelds himselfe" (*Cor2*, 5), not because his presence can be conjured by human language. In contrast, Christ's enemies "will and can, / Alas, and do, unto th'immaculate, / Whose creature Fate is, now prescribe a Fate" (4–6); these men are presumptuous scribes and priests who usurp divine prerogative.[28] They would impose necessity on God, proceeding "as they proceed in the Romane Church *Ex opere operato*, to tye the grace of God, to the action of the man" (*Sermons* 6:92). According to "Crucifying," the scribes and Pharisees

[handwritten margin note: Definitely Calvinist]

(condemned by Jesus in Matthew 23) were an intellectual elite who envied Christ's ability to work *"miracles exceeding power of man"* (*Cor5*, 1); their latter-day counterparts, Donne declares in a sermon, are the Scholastic theologians who teach the "Pharisaicall, and carnall" doctrine of transubstantiation (*Sermons* 7:289), fostering the belief that "every day, every Priest can miraculously change bread into the body of Christ" (*Sermons* 3:370).[29] In the Gospel, the "chief priests, and the scribes" (Matthew 26:3) resolve to "prescribe a Fate" to God by killing Jesus (*Cor5*, 7); so the Roman priests claim, with "blasphemous over-boldnesse," that they have the ability "to *make* a Christ, and then invest the malice of the Jews, and *kill that Christ*, whom [they] have made; for [Eucharistic] *Sacrifice*, Immolation, (taken so properly, and literally as they take it) is a *killing*" (*Sermons* 7:429–30).

Like those who crucified Christ, the proponents of transubstantiation are "Measuring selfe-lifes infinity to'a span, / Nay to an inch" (*Cor5*, 8–9). On Golgotha, the infinite reach of those "hands which span the Poles, / And turne all spheares at once" (as Donne puts it in "Goodfriday, 1613") is reduced to the narrow arms' span of a human body and "measured" by the torture of crucifixion.[30] But Christ's tormenters do not stop there; for as Protestants saw it, transubstantiation was the Roman priesthood's attempt to contract the Lord's body even further, "to an inch" (*Cor5*, 9): that is, to the miniscule dimensions of the consecrated host.[31] The poet/speaker must avoid such presumption; he must not be the kind of priest or scribe who tries to "prescribe" Christ's presence and to force him (rather than welcome him) into the "little roome" (*Cor2*, 13) of his sonnets.

He thus concentrates, as English Protestant theologians so often did, upon reception rather than consecration, Eucharistic *experience* rather than priestly *opus*. As "The Crosse" makes clear, the oneness of the communicant with the crucified Christ is, for Donne, the consummate expression of sacramental experience.[32] In order to receive the Eucharist on Easter Sunday, one must pass through the fasting and self-mortification of Lent; for before Christ's Resurrection "comes the day of his crucifying," and a communicant must approach Easter by "a crucifying of [himself]"; if he does so, he will receive complete satisfaction in the Eucharist: "his soule shall be satisfied as with marrow, and with fatnesse, in the body and bloud of his Saviour" (*Sermons* 2:362). This view of the Eucharistic event is the key to Donne's meaning at the climax of *La Corona*, the crucial juncture between the fifth sonnet, "Crucifying," and the sixth, "Resurrection." In this transition, Donne's poet/speaker cries out as a communicant experiencing soul-nourishing union with the crucified Christ.

"Crucifying" begins in the past tense but moves to the present in order to describe the crucifixion itself:

> they will and can,
> Alas, and do, unto the'immaculate,
> Whose creature Fate is, now prescribe a Fate,
> Measuring selfe-lifes infinity to'a span,
> Nay to an inch. Loe, where condemned hee
> Beares his owne crosse, with paine, yet by and by
> When it beares him, he must beare more and die;
> Now thou art lifted up, draw me to thee,
> And at thy death giving such liberall dole,
> *Moyst, with one drop of thy blood, my dry soule.*
>
> (5–14)

The tense of these lines evokes the Passion as an event that the poet/speaker and the reader can experience "now" (7, 12); in Donne's theology, that experience is made possible by the Eucharist.[33] At every celebration of the Eucharist, Donne explains in a sermon preached at Lincoln's Inn in 1619, "that very body of Christ, which offered himself . . . upon the cross, once for all, that body, and all that that body suffered, is offered again" (*Sermons* 2:256). In the poem, too, Christ's sacrifice is a present-tense experience; for *La Corona*, like the

Eucharist, transcends time and allows the speaker and the reader to *"partake"* of Christ's *"woe"* (*Cor3*, 14 and *Cor4*, 1), to share in the eternal "dole" of the crucifixion (*Cor5*, 13).

The sonnet's final lines evoke most richly the Eucharistic nature of Christ's sacrifice. The speaker calls Jesus' death a "liberall dole" (13), a generous distribution of food and drink as a charitable gift to poor *"dry soule[s]"* (14); and his prayer for refreshment proceeds from his belief that the blood shed on the cross is still available to man in the Eucharist, through which Christ continues "applying his blood unto us . . . to the worlds end" (*Sermons* 2:319–20). When the "liberall dole" of bread and wine is received, Christ "draw[s]" the communicant up to his cross, for the Eucharist makes available in the present the nourishment which was provided by the sacrifice on Golgotha. Indeed, the phrase "lifted up" as Donne uses it here evokes the belief—shared by Protestants and Catholics alike—that the "mysteries" of the Eucharist "do as nails fasten us to [Christ's] very Cross, that by them we draw out . . . the blood of his gored side, in the wounds of our Redeemer we there dip our tongues, . . . our hunger is satisfied and our thirst forever quenched" (Hooker, *Laws* 5.67.12).[34]

For a Protestant reader, the poem's wording reflects the belief that Christ lifts the communicant up to himself through the sacrament rather than descending from heaven to become present in the bread and wine: Christ promises "that his fleshe is verily meate, and his blood is drink," Calvin explains, and the sacramental words and signs "sende us to the crosse of Christ, where [his] promise hath ben truely performed and in all pointes fulfilled" (*Inst.* 4.17.4). Roman Catholics, Calvin charges, "thinke not Christ present, unlesse he come downe to us. As though if he did lift us up to him, we should not aswel enjoy his presence" (*Inst.* 4.17.31).[35] The speaker of "Crucifying" thus prays to Christ as he is "Now . . . lifted up" (12) in heaven, having ascended to his Father, even as he prays to the crucified Lord "lifted up" on the cross.

From another perspective, the speaker's prayer that Jesus will "draw mee to thee" (12) suggests the idea of sacramental suffering so powerfully expressed in "The Crosse"; and for a reader with a recusant background, the idea of sharing Christ's crucifixion by being *drawn* to him might evoke the barbaric form of torture used during Donne's lifetime in the public executions of Catholic priests who were hanged, *drawn*, and quartered for treason.[36] From such a reader's perspective, the speaker's prayer would seem to plead for a Eucharistic approximation of martyrdom; if Christ will "draw" Donne up to the cross, the poet will—like a priestly martyr—be tortured along with his Savior, hanged on the scaffold of the Cross and drawn into sacramental union with the Crucified. Thus joined to his Savior, the poet/speaker's "dry soule" will need only "one drop" of the sacred blood to be wholly "Moyst" (14).[37]

The poetic expression of sacramental experience takes place, however, less in the words of "Crucifying" itself than in the difference between the words of its last line and those same words, reapplied, at the start of the next sonnet. In this transition, Donne taps the energies of English Protestant Eucharistic doctrine with particular specificity. As Eleanor McNees demonstrates in her discussion of Donne's Eucharistic poetics, English Protestant theology of the Eucharist in the early seventeenth century stressed (among other principles) the idea of a change in the *use* to which the elements of bread and wine are put.[38] As Donne explains,

> That Bread which thou seest after the Consecration, is not the same bread, which was presented before; . . . it is severed, and appropriated by God, in that Ordinance to another use; It is other Bread, so as a Judge is another man, upon the bench, then he is at home, in his owne house. (*Sermons* 7:294)

Yet this change is, Donne goes on to say, a true transformation:

... this transforming, cannot be intended of the outward form and fashion, for that is not changed; but be it of that internall form, which is the very essence and nature of the bread, so it is transformed, so the bread hath received a new form, a new essence, a new nature, because whereas the nature of bread is but to nourish the body, the nature of this bread now, is to nourish the soule. (*Sermons* 7:295)[39]

Between "Crucifying" and "Resurrection," then, Donne does to a word what the Consecration does to the bread and wine— he changes its nature by changing its use.

Each of the poems in *La Corona* is linked to the one before it through the repetition of the former sonnet's fourteenth line as its first; but as witty as Donne is, he forgoes much wordplay in the working out of this scheme. Each linking line acquires a subtly different sense as it appears in a new context, but we must wait until the first line of "Resurrection" to see a dramatic shift in the use of a particular word, a pun that plays upon the possibility of the "same" word being used as either a verb or an adjective. In "Crucifying," the word "Moyst" is a verb in the imperative mood: *"Moyst, with one drop of thy blood, my dry soule,"* Donne begs. In "Resurrection," the power of the risen Christ is manifested in the transformation which the application of his blood effects in Donne's soul. As the bread becomes Christ's body, the wine his blood, the suppliant verb becomes an adjective, and the spirit is refreshed with hope:

> *Moyst with one drop of thy blood, my dry soule*
> Shall (though she now be in extreme degree
> Too stony hard, and yet too fleshly,) bee
> Freed by that drop ...
>
> (1–4)

Just as in the Eucharist, bread and wine are invested with a new use, so here the word "Moyst" is given a new function.[40] It no longer asks for something, but instead modifies the word "soule"; and the modification or alteration of the soul itself is, for Protestants and Catholics alike, one of the most important fruits of Eucharistic participation.[41] He no longer fears the "first" death (that of the body) or the "last" (the soul's damnation); for having come to the "conformity" with Christ that is necessary for a true participation in the Sacrament, he undergoes "that transmutation, which admits no re-transmutation, which is a modest, but infalible assurance of a final perseverance, so to be joyned to the Lord, as to be one spirit with him" (*Sermons* 1: 164). The shift from verb to adjective, which reflects the change in the Eucharistic elements and Donne's "modest but infalible assurance" of a change in his soul, is—as we have seen that he stressed in his sermon—an inward transformation. The outer appearance of the word, like that of the Eucharistic bread or of the devout communicant himself, remains unaltered; but it is given, as are the bread and the believer, a new existence.

In her study of George Herbert, Asals explains the verbal act of equivocation—punning—as a breaking of the word which recreates poetically the breaking of the holy bread (*Equivocal Predication*, 11). McNees explains the idea in a way that applies even more clearly to the Eucharistic climax of *La Corona*: "The function of the Prayer of Consecration— to separate the bread and wine from a profane to a spiritual use, not to transubstantiate the elements—provides an analogy for Donne's use of divisive poetic figures, particularly pun and paradox" ("John Donne," 103). Indeed, I would argue that, in the space between the "Crucifying" and "Resurrection," Donne's pun on "Moyst" enacts a poetic consecration and reception of the Sacrament "whereupon there ensueth"—to use Hooker's description of the Eucharist's effect—"a kind of transubstantiation in [him], a true change both of soul and body, an alteration from death to life" (*Laws* 5.67.11).

As Donne explains in a sermon, the Holy Communion is "a *Sacramentall union*" through which Christians are "so washed in [Christ's] bloud, as that we stand in the sight of his Father, as cleane, and innocent, as himselfe" (*Sermons* 5:173); as he puts it in another sermon, "Those who are worthy receivers of his flesh here, are the same flesh with him" (*Sermons* 3:113). It is just such a sense of sacramental oneness with Jesus's risen body that operates at this crucial transition point in *La Corona*; for the poet/speaker does not begin the "Resurrection" sonnet by describing the events of the first Easter morning. Rather, he now feels that he can speak of Christ's Resurrection by envisioning his own. And the image of moistening makes clear that Christ's blood is what makes his resurrection possible; he is "Freed by that drop" (*Cor6*, 4) that falls upon him in the Eucharist.[42]

Death is, in fact, the only way to resurrection, as Donne asserts when he says that "Flesh" cannot "by other meanes be glorified" (*Cor6*, 9, 11). Through Christ's death, remembered and reenacted in the Eucharistic feast, death is itself— like the elements of bread and wine—consecrated, given a new use. Thus, in line 10 of *La Corona*'s resurrection sonnet, Donne says that, in the grave, flesh is "made that . . . of which, and for which 'twas." Gardner notes that this line comments on the dual function of death. It returns our bodies to the dust of which they were originally fashioned; but because of God's mercy, it also has another use: "[M]an having induced and created death, by sin, God takes death, and makes it a means of the glorifying of his body, in heaven" (Donne, *Sermons* 6:72; quoted in Gardner, 63).

The resurrection of the body at the end of time is, moreover, prefigured in our resurrection from sin in this life: "May then sinnes sleep . . . soone from me passe, / That wak't from" it—as I will eventually be waked from "deaths sleep"— "I . . . may / *Salute the last, and everlasting day*" (*Cor6*, 12–14). These lines reflect the attitude attendant upon the "worthy receiver" of the Eucharist; for as Donne insists in an Easter sermon, the Sacrament—which both the Fourth

Lateran Council and the *Book of Common Prayer* specifically insisted be received at Easter—ought to be the communicant's own Easter:

> [L]ay hold upon the gracious promises, which by our Ministery [God] lets fall upon the Congregation now; and gather the seales of those promises, whensoever, in a rectified conscience, his Spirit beares witnesse with your spirit, that you may be worthy receivers of him in his Sacrament; and this . . . shall be your resurrection. (*Sermons* 7:116–17)

The hope Donne feels in the "Resurrection" sonnet is, then, theologically dependent upon his reception of the Sacrament, enacted in the Eucharistic pun that links "Resurrection" to "Crucifying."

Also dependent on that sacramental moment is the poet/speaker's sense of himself as an active subject: when he declares at the end of "Resurrection" that "I againe risen may / *Salute*" (13–14), it is the first appearance of the word "I" in *La Corona*. Up until this point, the poet/speaker uses only the possessive and objective forms of the first person singular, referring to *"my hands"* (*Cor1*, 1), "my low devout melancholie" (*Cor1*, 2), "my muses white sincerity" (*Cor1*, 6), "my soule" (*Cor1*, 11) or *"my dry soule"* (*Cor5*, 14); asking Christ to "draw mee to thee" (*Cor5*, 12) and declaring that "to mee / Feare" will not "bring miserie, / If in thy little booke my name thou enroule" (*Cor6*, 6–8). Only through the celebration of Christ's death and resurrection can a dynamic subject, an "I" that is "risen" from the dormancy of sleep, enter into the work.

La Corona itself—like Christ in the womb of the Virgin or the consecrated bread of the Eucharist—is thus a child able to redeem its own parent, a work able to bestow redeemed identity on its maker. Once his "I" arises, the poet/speaker is a confident subject, addressing Christ as the "Bright Torch, which shin'st, that I the way may see" (*Cor7*, 11); but he reaches this clear sense of assurance only through a work that is both his and not his, *"this crown . . . /* Weav'd in my low devout melancholie" (*Cor1*, 1–2), but not—the ambiguious "this" and the passive verb "weav'd" suggest—simply the crown of sonnets that *I* have woven.

"Resurrection" as Ars Moriendi

When the poet/speaker identifies himself as "Freed" from the "Feare of . . . death" (*Cor6*, 4, 7), he testifies that *La Corona*, insofar as it is a Eucharistic poem, is also a calming *ars moriendi*. When "In the Sacrament our eyes see his salvation," Donne says in a sermon, "in that light wee depart in peace" (*Sermons* 7:296; alluding to Luke 2:29–30). For the communicant, like Simeon, may be content to die:

> [T]o a deliberate desire, to be dissolved here, and to be united to Christ in heaven, . . . a godly, a rectified and a well-disposed man may safely come. . . . Neither can a man at any time be fitter to make and obtain this wish, then when his eyes have seen his salvation in the Sacrament. (*Sermons* 7:297)[43]

The poet/speaker of *La Corona* is just such a "well-disposed" communicant; once he has enacted his poetic reception of the Eucharist, expressing the confident belief that his soul shall be *"Moyst"* with *"one drop"* of Christ's blood, he can profess a freedom from anxiety; he is "Freed by that drop, from being starv'd" (4)—since Holy Communion has fed his spiritual hunger—"hard" (4)—since the sacrament testifies to a receptive heart rather than a sin-hardened one—"or foule" (4)— since in the Eucharist "our souls" are "washed through [Christ's most precious blood" [*BCP*, 263]).[44] His "life" is "abled" (5) by the Eucharistic dole of Christ's death; he is made *able*, "empowered," as Shawcross observes, by being a-*bled*, "given blood" (*Complete Poetry*, 337). And thus "abled," he feels his courage rising: "nor shall to mee / Feare of first or last death, bring miserie, / If in thy little booke my name thou'enroule" (*Cor6*, 6–8).

The "If" of the speaker's prayer is a reminder that there is no perfect guarantee of salvation in the fallen world; and yet his fearless and authoritative tone as he continues—"Flesh in that long sleep is not putrified / But made there, of which, and for which 'twas" (9–10)—testifies that he *has* been a worthy receiver, that he is ready for death. As Donne argues in the sermon on Simeon, the believer's calm willingness to die is itself a sign that the Sacrament has had a redemptive effect upon him:

> At least, make this an argument of your having beene worthy receivers thereof, that you are *in Æquilibrio*, in an evennesse, in an indifferency, in an equanimity, whether ye die this night or no. . . . [Y]et if thou now feare death inordinately, I should feare that thine eyes have not seen thy salvation to day; who can feare the darknesse of death, that hath had the light of this world, and of the next too? (*Sermons* 7:297, 298).

The poet/speaker of *La Corona* clearly does not "feare death inordinately"; for he looks beyond it with confidence to the light of "*the last, and everlasting day*" (*Cor6*, 14). And as he makes the transition from "Resurrection" to "Ascension," he prays that he may be "wak't" from the sleep of sin and the sleep of death (*Cor6*, 12, 13) in order to greet Christ, "the light of this world, and of the next too"—as he calls Him in the sermon—or the "Sunne" who "Lightens the darke clouds"— as he calls him in *La Corona* (*Cor7*, 2, 6). Christ is the "*last and everlasting day*" (*Cor6*, 14, *Cor7*, 1) whom he invites all penitent men and women to "*Salute*" in the present even as they will in the future.

"Ascention" as Ending and Beginning

In "Ascention," as in "Crucifying," the poet/speaker evokes a timeless moment:

> *Salute the last and everlasting day,*
> Joy at th'uprising of this Sunne, and Sonne,

Yee whose just teares, or tribulation
Have purely washt, or burnt your drossie clay;
Behold the Highest, parting hence away,
Lightens the darke clouds, which hee treads upon,
Nor doth hee by ascending, show alone,
But first hee, and hee first enters the way.

(1–8)

As he envisions the moment when Christ "was taken up on high, and a cloud received him" (Acts 1:9), the poet/speaker looks back to the moment described in the first chapter of Acts; but he also celebrates the present moment. In that present, devout men and women reading the sonnet are called, not only to "Behold" the Ascension as though it were happening at this moment, but also—like communicants listening to the Preface for Ascension in the Communion rite of the English Church—to realize that the Lord's ascent is a preparation for their own. Just as the Preface says that Christ ascends "to prepare a place for us, that where he is, thither might we also ascend" (*BCP*, 262), so the sonnet declares: "Nor doth hee by ascending, show alone, / But first hee, and hee first enters the way" (7–8).

It is in the Eucharist—the visible sign of his blood—that the "Milde lambe" has "with [his] blood . . . mark'd the path" to heaven (*Cor7*, 10). The readers whom the poet/speaker addresses, "Yee whose just teares, or tribulation / Have purely washt, or burnt your drossie clay" (*Cor7*, 3–4) are thus communicants, receivers of the poetic Eucharist he has just ministered. It is their penitent reception of that sacrament that has made them one with the Apostles who first beheld "th'uprising of this Sunne, and Sonne" (*Cor7*, 2); for, Donne explains in a sermon, the saints of Revelation, "those . . . who have *already washed their long robes, and made them white in the blood of the Lambe*" are those "who have already by teares of repentance, become worthy receivers of the seale of reconciliation, in the Sacrament of [Christ's] body, and bloud" (*Sermons* 5:178).[45]

In this same present-tense moment, moreover, the poet/ speaker begs Christ "if thy holy Spirit, my Muse did raise, / *Deigne at my hands this crowne of prayer and praise*" (13– 14). With these lines, he recalls the reference to his "muses white sincerity" in the opening sonnet (*Cor1*, 6) and further reinforces the analogy between *La Corona* and the English Communion service, which begins with a prayer that the Holy Spirit will cleanse and inspire all who celebrate the Eucharist. Addressing God as the One "unto whom all hearts be open, all desires known," the priest says:

> Cleanse the thoughts of our hearts by the inspiration of thy Holy Spirit, that we may perfectly love thee, and worthily magnify thy holy name. (*BCP*, 248).[46]

This prayer is a request that the "inspiration" of the divine Spirit will ensure the "white sincerity" (*Cor1*, 6) of each worshiper's heart. In asking that God accept the work only if his muse has been "raise[d]" by God's Spirit, the poet/speaker of *La Corona* similarly acknowledges his muse's dependence on God for any "white sincerity" she may possess. He recognizes that the words of *La Corona* can be sacramental only if they, like the sacraments as Hooker defines them, are "signs assisted . . . by the Holy Ghost" (Hooker, *Laws* 6.6.10). But "Ascension" radiates confidence that they are so assisted; indeed, with his reference to the "holy Spirit" (*Cor7*, 13), Donne evokes not just the Ascension, but the next feast of the liturgical year: Pentecost or Whitsunday, when the Spirit descended to inspire the Apostles. In the *Book of Common Prayer*, the Collect for the Sunday between Ascension and Whitsunday calls upon Christ to "send . . . thine Holy Ghost to . . . exalt us unto the same place whether our Savior Christ is gone" (*BCP*, 167), thus linking the Ascension to Pentecost as Donne does in lines 7–8 of "Ascension" when he says that Christ does not "show alone, / But first . . . enters the way" that the redeemed will follow. In the Epistle assigned for Whitsunday itself, moreover, the Apostles' speech is described as divinely inspired: "And they were all filled with the Holy Ghost, and began to speak with other tongues, even as the same Spirit gave them utterance" (Acts 2:4; *BCP*, 169). It is with a true Whitsunday whiteness, then, the poet/speaker of *La Corona* is inspired to pray, *"Deigne at my hands this crowne of prayer and praise"* (*Cor7*, 14; *Cor1*, 1).

Indeed, the images of "Ascension" look not only into the past when Christ was raised into heaven and at the present, when the poet prays that the "holy Spirit, [his] Muse did raise" (*Cor7*, 13), but also forward to the *Parousia* when the world "shall see the Son of man come in a cloud, with power and great glory" (Luke 21:27). And in this way, the poet/speaker returns to the Advent theme with which he began in the first sonnet of *La Corona*; for Luke 21 is one of the Gospel readings for Advent, and as Chambers points out, the season of Advent "does not limit itself . . . to Christ's humble coming years ago. It also anticipates his last coming in glory" ("Christmas," 115).[47]

The Advent sonnet is also, as I have stressed, an anticipation of and preparation for Christ's sacramental coming, his entry into *La Corona* as a poem of Eucharistic celebration. Indeed, the past, present, and future advents of Christ, his nativity, his sacramental presence, and his return in Glory, were, for Donne, inseparable: "[C]onsider," he says in one sermon, "that in that receiving his body, and his bloud, every one doth as it were conceive Christ Jesus anew; Christ Jesus hath in every one of them, as it were a *new incarnation*, by uniting himselfe to them in these visible signes" (*Sermons* 2:223). And, in Apocalypse 7:3, he explains in another sermon, the redemptive "seale of the living God" that the angels are to set upon the foreheads of God's servants may be identified as "The Sacraments of the New Testament, . . . by which . . . [the] Priest, [God's] Minister, seals . . . Reconciliation between God and his people" (*Sermons* 10:55). Ink, no less than bread or wine, is "a visible thing"; as Donne notes in the sermon on Apocalypse, the Angel of Ezekiel 9:4, who was *"to set a marke upon the foreheads of all them that mourned* . . . had a visible thing, *Inke*, to marke them withal" (10:53). In *La Corona*, as in "The Crosse," ink is the visible sign, the sacramental element that seals the poet/speaker's reconciliation with God and celebrates—for and with participating readers—a new incarnation of Christ that takes place not in the poetry itself so much as in the souls of those who receive it.

The Priestly Poet and the English Church as Ideal Reader

But who were the readers Donne had in mind as he composed *La Corona*? In a letter to Henry Goodyer discussing his liturgical poem "A Litanie," Donne comments on how it may seem presumptuous for "a Lay man, and a private" to give "divine and publique names, to his own little thoughts"; but he defends himself by citing precedents, litanies written privately by medieval monks but later canonized by the Pope and appointed "for publike service in their Churches." "[M]ine," he concludes, "is for lesser Chappels, which are my friends" (*Letters*, 33). His ambitions for *La Corona* seem subtly less humble; for though the author of that work remains "a Lay man, and a private," his voice in the sonnet-cycle is that of a poet-priest whose words summon "all that will" to a literary Eucharist. As Gardner stresses, Donne's "crown of prayer and praise" is "inspired by liturgical prayer and praise— oral prayer; not by private meditation and the tradition of mental prayer" (xxii). And while "A Litanie" "is an elaborate private prayer, rather incongruously cast into a liturgical form," appearing to be "impersonal" when it "is, in fact, highly personal" (Gardner, xxviii, xxiv), *La Corona*'s "peculiar excellence" is, as Anthony Low rightly observes, its "impersonality," which renders the sonnets "more durable as devotional exercises or poems read repeatedly" and ensures that, "Though intended for private use," the work is "close to public discipline and communion of feeling" (*Love's Architecture*, 51).

Some twentieth century scholars have, however, found the poet/speaker of *La Corona* less than fully engaged with the spirit of community. Chanoff calls the work "a private sacramental offering . . . consciously patterned after public worship" (157). Anne Ferry argues that the speaker's claim to "white sincerity" (*Cor1*, 6) definitively separates him from communal prayer (*The "Inward" Language*, 225).[48] And as Julia Walker sees him, "Donne's speaker was never part of a congregation"; rather, "Donne's use of the public liturgical form with the private singular pronoun is intended to emphasize [the speaker's] separateness" ("Religious Lyric," 41). Clearly, such arguments cannot be ignored; the speaker of *La Corona* is a poet who alludes within the work to his own activity in weaving it as a devotional offering; the phrases "Reward my muses white sincerity" (*Cor1*, 6) and "if thy holy Spirit, my Muse did raise" (*Cor7*, 13) are not prayers that a reader can (even silently) utter in unison with him. But such phrases do not, I would argue, undermine the work's status as a Eucharistic offering that includes the reader; for the poet/speaker is to readers as a presiding priest is to the congregation.

The question of whether the poet/speaker of Donne's sonnet-cycle is an isolated "I," engaged in a private meditation, or a priestly celebrant speaking for, with, and to the communal Body of Christ bears directly on *La Corona*'s Eucharistic character. For, as the term "Holy Communion" suggests, the Eucharist is communal by definition. It is, as the Council of Trent asserts in its "Decree Concerning the Most Holy Sacrament of the Eucharist," "a symbol of that one body of which He is the head and to which He wished us to be united as members by the closest bond of faith, hope, and charity, that we might *all speak the same thing and there might be no schism amongst us* [1 Corinthians 1:10]" ("Decree Concerning the . . . Eucharist," chapter 2).[49] The deep divisions occasioned by the Reformation-era Eucharistic debate were thus exquisitely ironic, and the irony was a painful one for devout Protestants and Catholics alike, particularly those—like Donne—who were ecumenically inclined. But some of the most serious objections to the Catholic Mass on the part of Reformers had to do with their contention that the Roman doctrine of Eucharistic sacrifice violated the corporate character of the sacrament, separating the sacrificing priest from the congregation. Particularly offensive, from the Protestant perspective, were those Masses in which the priest alone took communion: "For what hath the Lord commaunded us," asks Calvin, was it "not to take, and divide it among us [Luke 22:17]? . . . Therefore when one taketh it without distributing, what likenesse is there?" (*Inst.* 4.18.8).

The Council of Trent answered this objection by insisting that "masses in which the priest alone communicates sacramentally . . . ought to be considered as truly common, partly because at them the people communicate spiritually and because they are celebrated by a public minister of the Church, not for himself only but for all the faithful who belong to the body of Christ" (Twenty-second Session, "Doctrine Concerning the Sacrifice of the Mass," chapter 6).[50] This explanation relies, in turn, upon the idea that there are "three ways of receiving" the Eucharist: "some receive it sacramentally only, as sinners; others spiritually only, namely those who eating in desire the heavenly bread set before them, are by a lively *faith which worketh by charity* [Galatians 5:6] made sensible of its fruit and usefulness; while the third class receives it both sacramentally and spiritually, and these are they who so prove and prepare themselves beforehand that they approach this divine table clothed with the wedding garment" ("Decree Concerning the . . . Eucharist," chapter 8).

For English Protestants, these explanations were insufficient; purely spiritual reception was not an option, except in the case of sick persons unable to consume the bread and wine.[51] Thus, a rubric in the Communion rite of the *Book of*

Common Prayer specifies that "there shall be no Communion, except four, or three at the least, communicate with the priest" (267). In keeping with this requirement, the prayer for sincerity and purity of heart said at the opening of the communion rite (quoted above, p. 88) is phrased in the first person plural. So, too, are the Prayer of Humble Access ("We do not presume . . ." [*BCP*, 263]), the priest's prayer over the bread and wine ("grant that we receiving these thy creatures" [*BCP*, 263]), and the prayer of Oblation said after Communion. The Oblation, moreover, offers to God not the consecrated Host and chalice, but "*our* sacrifice *of praise and thanksgiving*" and "*ourselves, our souls and bodies*, to be a reasonable, holy, and lively sacrifice" (*BCP*, 264; emphasis added).[52]

There is much less emphasis on the first person plural in *La Corona*. Instead, the language of the poet/speaker mingles first person singular ("*Deigne at my hands*" [*Cor1*, 1]; "*my dry soule*" [*Cor5*, 14]) with the first person plural ("*our* ends" [*Cor1*, 9]; "*our* world" [*Cor3*, 4]) and the imperative second person plural ("*Salute the last and everlasting day, / . . . / Yee whose just teares . . . / Have purely washt, or burnt your drossie clay*" [*Cor7*, 1, 3–4]). This grammatical mixture is less reminiscent of the English Communion rite than of the Tridentine Mass. In that liturgy, the Roman Catholic priest offers the Eucharistic sacrifice both for himself and for the people; he thus alternates between first person singular petitions that ask God to accept and render efficacious his priestly offering, and first person plural prayers that speak for the whole congregation:

> Accept, O holy Father, . . . this unspotted host, which *I*, Thy unworthy servant, offer unto Thee, *my* living and True God, for *my* innumerable sins, offenses, and negligences, *and for all here present: as also for all faithful Christians* . . . *We* offer unto Thee, O Lord, the chalice of salvation. . . . Accept *us*, O Lord, . . . and grant that the sacrifice which *we* offer . . may be pleasing to Thee. . . . Let *my* prayer, O Lord, be directed as

incense in Thy sight: *the lifting up of my hands* as an evening sacrifice. . . . Receive, O holy Trinity, this oblation which *we* makc to Thee, in memory of the Passion, Resurrection and Ascension of our Lord Jesus Christ . . . (*Missal*, 632–35; emphasis added).

Immediately before the *sursum corda*, moreover, the priest addresses the people in a second person imperative: "Brethren, pray that *my* Sacrifice and *yours* may be acceptable to God the Father almighty," and the response (which may be spoken by the server) is, "May the Lord receive the Sacrifice from *thy* hands, to the praise and glory of His Name, *to our benefit and that of all His holy Church*" (*Missal*, 635, 637; emphasis added). Thus, though Donne specifically excludes any hint that his offering in *La Corona* is a propitiatory sacrifice on the model of the Catholic Mass, his grammar indicates that he conceives of his role as poet and speaker of the work in terms much influenced by the Roman Catholic liturgy. The poet/speaker in *La Corona* resembles the Catholic priest in that he speaks neither as a man praying in isolation nor as a layman in a congregation, but as a presiding celebrant who offers for himself and others—with due recognition of his own unworthiness—an "oblation . . . in memory of the Passion, Resurrection and Ascension of . . . Christ" (*Missal*, 635).

As Donne sees it, however, English priests do not differ in this respect from the Roman clergy. They, too, offer up a "*Sacrifice peculiar to the Priest, though for the People*" (*Sermons* 7:429) and though they do not claim the power to transubstantiate the Eucharistic elements, they are nevertheless called to "work upon the reall body of Christ, since [God] hath made [them] Dispensers . . . of that, to the faithfull, in the Sacrament" (*Sermons* 10:129).[53] Thus, though Donne's language in *La Corona* is in some ways strongly reminiscent of the Tridentine liturgy, it defines the priestly role of the poet/

speaker in terms that Donne found applicable to the Protestant clergy, and it carefully avoids excluding the reader from that speaker's celebration of a poetic Eucharist.

Donne uses several different means to establish that the words of his poem are inscribed and offered to God in communion with participating Christian readers rather than in isolation from them and the Church (as Calvin claimed that Catholic priests were in their offering of the Mass as Sacrifice). First, in drawing on both the Roman Mass and the English Communion rite, he joins his private meditations to the communal act of Eucharistic worship and at the same time blurs the lines of demarcation separating two different congregations claiming membership in the Body of Christ. By uniting in its language the compatible elements of Roman and English theology and liturgy, *La Corona* thus fulfills poetically the Eucharist's function as the symbol of Christian unity.[54]

Second, Donne underscores emblematically his own desire to participate in communal worship by choosing to write in the *corona* genre. As Donne explains in a sermon, "a congregation that compasses the Preacher, was ordinarily called a Crown, *Corona*" (3:346).[55] By making his work a *corona*, then, the poet/speaker of Donne's sonnet cycle identifies with an ecclesiastical congregation or *corona*; he speaks from within that communal crown. Using the language of liturgy and weaving his sonnets into the shape of a crown/congregation, Donne offers up the completed *corona* as a woven emblem of this ecclesiastically empowered voice.

In addition, though the first person poet/speaker of *La Corona* speaks as the priest and preacher whose voice leads the rest of the congregation, his inclusion of phrases in the first person plural and his direct address to a community of Christians in the "Ascension" sonnet invite readers to make the poet/speaker's prayers their own. Through these invitations,

Donne's poem evokes the sacramental conception of voice and writing that English devotional poets found in Augustine's *Ennaratio in psalmos*. As Asals explains, Augustine stresses "the relationship between the voice of David, the divinely inspired Poet of the scriptures and the sacramental *Corpus Christi*" which is the Church. Augustine argues that the

> speaker of the Psalms . . . is a Man "extended throughout the whole world, of which *the Head is above, the lims below*: We need not then dwell long on pointing out to you, who is the speaker here: let each one of us be a member of Christ's Body; and he will be the speaker here." (*Equivocal Predication*, 42, quoting the commentary on Psalm 43 in Augustine 2:198–99).

If the Christian reader of *La Corona* approaches Donne's poetry in a similar spirit, he or she will not have to wonder who the speaker is; he or she will know that, as a member of Christ's Body, he or she "is the speaker here."

According to the Augustinian poetics Asals finds at work in Donne's poem "Upon the translation of the Psalmes," the words of a devotional poem as they appear written or printed on paper are the visible sign of the communal Body's voice; and as such, they are a "means for establishing sacramental contact with the . . . head of that body," Christ ("*Davids Successors*," 31, 34). In *La Corona*, declarations such as "*Salvation to all that will is nigh*" (*Cor1*, 14, *Cor2*, 1) and exhortations such as "Joy at the'uprising of this Sunne, and Sonne, / Yee" (*Cor7*, 2–3) invite each Christian reader—each member of Christ's Body, whether Catholic or Protestant—to read *La Corona* as an offering by the poet/speaker not only for himself but "for all here present: as also for all faithful Christians" (*Missal*, 631).

But the ideal reader of *La Corona* is the English Church herself, for it was in that Church that Donne found the blending of reformed and Catholic doctrine closest to the ecumenical synthesis he achieved in *La Corona*.[56] In presenting his work to a human audience, therefore, Donne may have sought something of an ecclesiastical endorsement for his poetic sacrament by placing it in the care of a woman whom he and his contemporaries hailed as an incarnation of the English Church: George Herbert's mother, Magdalen.

As Asals explains, both Herbert and Donne were fascinated by Mary Magdalen and drew powerful parallels between the saint and her seventeenth century English namesake. Donne's memorial sermon on Magdalen Herbert is—as Asals puts it— "the portrait of a lady as the Anglican Church, defining the path of the 'middle way'" (*Equivocal Predication*, 94). And that portrait is based upon a long tradition surrounding what Asals calls "Magdalene: The Place." Saint Mary Magdalene, Asals explains,

> had been throughout the Middle Ages an image of the Church: her name, we are told, *magdalus*, signifies "tower." And Odo of Cluny for one "elaborates on the significance of the tower, explaining that *magdalus* or *tower* signifies the Church and that mystically 'this blessed woman' Mary Magdalene herself signifies the Church. . . ." Catherine of Siena, Johannes Smeaton observes in 1617, gave Magdalene the title of "Mother" . . . For their own Mother the seventeenth-century Anglican Church chose a Magdalene of *Now*, Magdalene Herbert: other men "Want her for their own mother," Herbert tells us in *Memoriæ Matris Sacrum*. (*Equivocal Predication*, 97–98).[57]

Given this conception of Magdalen Herbert, Donne may have turned to her as the person best able to endorse and confirm *La Corona* as a valid Eucharistic offering. In his sermons, he stresses that the Church is God's "*Ubi*, his place, . . . he re-turnes to us in this place, as often as he maketh us partakers of his flesh, and his bloud, in the blessed Sacrament" (*Sermons* 5:368); and almost as often as he mentions sacraments and things sacramental, he speaks of them as "in" the Church: "there are [God's] offices fixed: there are his provisions, . . . his precious bloud, and body: . . . there is grace for prevention of future [sins] in his Sacraments" (*Sermons* 2:221). Thus, if *La Corona* is truly to be a sacramental poem, it—like all things sacramental—must be "in" the Church, harbored by Magdalen.

The evidence that Donne presented *La Corona* to Magdalen Herbert is conjectural but compelling. In his 1670 *Life of Herbert*, Izaak Walton presents a sonnet by Donne headed with the title "To the Lady Magdalen Herbert, of St. *Mary Magdalen*":

> Her of your name, whose fair inheritance
>   *Bethina* was, and jointure *Magdalo*;
> An active faith so highly did advance,
>   That she once knew, more than the Church did know,
> The *Resurrection*; so much good there is
>   Deliver'd of her, that some Fathers be
> Loth to believe one Woman could do this;
>   But, think these *Magdalens* were two or three.
> Increase their number, *Lady*, and their fame:
>   To their *Devotion*, add your *Innocence*;
> Take so much of the'example,'as of the name;
>   The latter half; and in some recompence
> That they did harbour *Christ* himself, a Guest,
>   Harbour these *Hymns*, to his dear name addrest.

According to Walton, this sonnet was enclosed in a letter that reiterates its plea for safe "harbour":

> I commit the inclosed *Holy Hymns* and *Sonnets* . . . to your judgment, and to your protection too, if you think them worthy of it; and I have appointed this inclosed *Sonnet* to usher them to your happy hand. (Quoted in Gardner, 55).

Could some of the poems sent to Magdalen Herbert for her perusal and "protection" be the sonnets of *La Corona*? According to Gardner, Grierson was the first to propose that theory. But the association between *La Corona* and the Magdalene sonnet seems to be hinted at by Walton himself in his elegy on Donne.[58]

At any rate, the Magdalen sonnet addresses Mrs. Herbert
in terms that define her as the ideal audience for *La Corona*.
Gardner notes that in the sonnet, "Donne accepts . . . the tradition of the Western Church . . . which identifies the woman
who was a sinner (Luke 7) with Mary of Bethany and with
Mary Magdalene, the demoniac (Mark 16, Luke 8), who stood
by the Cross and appears in the Resurrection narratives. . . .
Mrs. Herbert is to add to the number of Mary Magdalenes,"
imitating the saintly second half of the Magdalen's life and—
most specifically—emulating Mary of Bethany, who with her
sister Martha welcomed Christ into her home as "a Guest"
(Gardner, 56). Donne entrusts his literary offering to the namesake of the saint who sheltered the Lord, insisting that she
provides an ideal resting place for a work that—as we have
seen—not only addresses God, but begs him to incarnate himself anew in its language.

The last two and a half lines of the dedicatory sonnet are
tellingly ambiguous. The request that Magdalen Herbert harbor the hymns "in some recompense / That they did harbour
Christ himself, a guest" may, as Gardner assumes, refer back
to the Marys, "they" who—in the person of Mary of Bethany—
offered hospitality to Jesus (56); or "they" may refer to the
Hymns themselves, those poems which propose to house
Christ, as did the Virgin's womb, in the "little roome" they
have to offer.[59] The ambiguity is important because it is only
insofar as Christ is present in the work, even as he is present
in the Eucharist, that *La Corona* can be said to have achieved
sacramental status.

The decision on this matter, as Donne acknowledges by
entrusting his sacred poetry to Magdalen Herbert, belongs to
the Church. The Church of England defines for her children
the nature and number of the sacraments, and determines
which "sacramental and ritual, and ceremonial things" shall
be preserved in worship as "the bellows of devotion" (*Sermons*
2:258–59). If, as the type of the English Church, Magdalen

determines Donne's ecumenically eclectic sonnet-cycle worthy to be "harboured" and enshrined by her possession, it gains the approval of God himself "as he speaks by his Church" (*Sermons* 2:258). The presentation of *La Corona* to Magdalen Herbert may thus have been Donne's ultimate offering of his Eucharistic garland, a gesture that completed and reinforced his petition: *"Deigne at my hands this crowne of prayer and praise."*

THREE

ॐ

Cunning Elements and Artful Turns

The sonnet is a problematic form for post-Reformation English poets because of the idolatrous implications of its history as the Petrarchan poets' verse-form of choice. As Ernest Gilman points out, Sidney uses the "the language of Protestant iconoclastic polemics" to define Astrophil's folly in Sonnet 5: "What we call *Cupid's* dart, / An image is, which for our selves we carve; / And fooles, adore in temple of our hart" (Gilman, 12–13, quoting *Astrophil and Stella* 5:5–7). As suggested in Sidney's phrase "which for our selves we carve," the problem with poetry is not simply that sonnets are put to work in the service of idolatrous desire. Rather, the peril lies in the making of the iconic, highly wrought artifact itself, in the carving of verbal images, regardless of the sort of love or desire those images express.[1]

In *La Corona*, therefore, Donne takes care to dissociate the art of sonnet-making from the sin of presumptuous self-reliance; the delayed appearance of the word "I" in the work is one safeguard against the futile subjectivity and idolatrous self-absorption that are a sonneteer's Petrarchan birthright.[2] *La Corona*'s liturgical language also helps deflect the danger attending the sonnet form, distinguishing Donne's work as that of a poet whose words proceed from a sense of spiritual community and rely upon the Spirit of God for inspiration; the poet of *La Corona* thus carefully avoids claiming to effect his own salvation through "the worke wrought."[3]

Many of Donne's *Holy Sonnets*, however, step dangerously closer to the Petrarchan edge: in "O Might those sighes," the speaker feels that he has "spent" (2) all of his eloquence—troped as the "sighes and teares" (1) of Petrarchan love poetry—on the worldly "griefs" (6) of his "Idolatry" (5), and that he has no poetic resources left to express the "holy discontent" (3) of repentance; in "Oh, to vex me," he parallels his "humorous . . . contritione"(5)—which is "ridlingly distemperd, cold and hott" (7)—with the oxymoronic "contraryes" (1) of Petrarchan poetry; and in "What if this present were the worlds last night?" he imagines Christ as the mistress whose "picture" he holds in his heart (3), relying—rashly, if Petrarch's experience is any guide—on the argument that his beloved's "beauteous forme assures a pitious minde" (14).[4]

In most of the Holy Sonnets, moreover, and in "Goodfriday, 1613," the poet/speaker is a man alone. His voice—like that of Petrarch in the *Rime sparse*—rings out in a desolate space inhabited only by himself and the projected image of his Beloved; and, like Petrarch, he often speaks as much to himself as to the object of his devotion. He is cut off from that sense of shared liturgical experience that affords *La Corona* its sacramental power; he must therefore rely upon his own invention, his own *concetti*, his own skill as a sonneteer.

In a sermon on the Apostles' Creed, Donne draws a sharp contrast between private and communal prayer that illuminates the differences between the "Holy Sonnets" and *La Corona*:

I lock my doore to my selfe, and I throw my selfe downe in
the presence of my God, . . . and I bend all my powers, and faculties upon God, as I think, and suddenly I finde my selfe scattered, melted, fallen into vaine thoughts, into no thoughts; I
am upon my knees, and I talke, and I think nothing; I deprehend
my selfe in it, and I goe about to mend it, I gather new forces,
new purposes to try againe, and doe better, and I doe the same
thing againe. *I beleeve in the Holy Ghost*, but doe not finde
him, if I seeke him onely in private prayer; But *in Ecclesia*,
when I goe to meet him in the *Church*, when I seeke him where
hee hath promised to bee found . . . in his Ordinances, and
meanes of salvation in his Church, instantly . . . not a dew, but
a shower is powred out upon me, and presently followes . . .
The Communion of Saints, the assistance of the Militant and
Triumphant Church in my behalfe; And presently followes . . .
The remission of sins, the purifying of my conscience, in that
water, which is his blood, Baptisme, and in that wine, which
is his blood, the other Sacrament; and presently followes . . .
A resurrection of my body . . . and . . . *Life everlasting* . . . (*Sermons* 5:249–50)

In the phrases from the creed, the expression of communal
belief recited in the first person singular by the whole congregation at Morning and Evening Prayer, Donne finds the words
that bring peace to the human soul. As in *La Corona*, refreshment and hope spring from the established forms and patterns
of the Faith. Indeed, in another sermon, Donne portrays the
avoidance of raw spontaneity as a bid for the very highest
kind of creative achievement: "Of God himselfe, it is safely
resolved in the Schoole, that he never did any thing in any
part of time, of which he had not an eternall pre-conception,
an eternall Idea, in himselfe before. . . . And therefore let him
be our patterne for that, to worke after patternes . . ." (*Sermons* 7:60–61). In *La Corona*, Donne takes the liturgy and
ordinances of the Church as his pattern—and the creative
achievement of the work cannot be separated from its status
as a formal prayer.

In sharp contrast to such efficacious language is the meaningless succession of half-distracted, idiosyncratic prayers which, in Donne's sermon on the Creed, dissolve into "vaine thoughts, into no thoughts." These failed private devotions are strongly reminiscent of the "Holy Sonnets," works filled with spurious arguments, false starts, unresolved questions, and sudden reversals. We are faced, then, with Donne's own doubts concerning the kind of prayer represented in the "Holy Sonnets"; and yet the impact of those works—their success as art—is no doubt partly a function of the degree to which they express the experience of personal insufficiency, of tortured subjectivity, of divine absence rather than Eucharistic presence, of an ongoing frustration reminiscent of Astrophil's Petrarchan anguish rather than joyful fruition of the sort that characterizes love lyrics like "The Good Morrow" and "The Sunne Rising." As Gardner puts it, "The flaws" in the Holy Sonnets' "spiritual temper are a part of their peculiar power" (xxxi).

It is still useful, however, to discuss the Holy Sonnets in terms of sacramental function; for Donne's desire to write sacramentally efficacious poetry, as demonstrated in "The Crosse" and *La Corona*, also bears upon the inward turn of his "Divine Meditations."[5] In "Wilt thou love God," one of the sonnets that Martz links to a specific Ignatian meditation, Donne's speaker interiorizes the Eucharistic meal, playing upon the idea of mental communion familiar to Protestants and Catholics alike. He presents the subject matter of the poem as spiritual food that effects his likeness to the deity: "Wilt thou love God, as he thee! then digest, / My Soule, this wholsome meditation" (1–2). As in *La Corona*, the thoughts that feed the poet/ speaker of this sonnet are characterized by his sense of wonder at the interwoven mysteries of Incarnation and Passion, and even his vocabulary recalls the Eucharistic sonnet cycle; a reference to man's gaining, through Christ, the "endlesse rest" of the heavenly Sabbath (8) echoes line 10 of *La Corona*'s first sonnet. Although the piece begins as a solitary meditation in which the poet/speaker addresses his own soul, it moves in line 12 from the second person to the first person plural "Us," effectively confirming the speaker's status as a part of redeemed humanity, of the "man" (13, 14) Christ died to save.

The speakers of Donne's divine poems do not always feel so peacefully capable of mental communion, however; in "Since she whome I lovd, hath payd her last debt," as I have argued elsewhere, Donne portrays himself as prone to idolize the sacramental woman who has been his Eucharistic conduit of grace ("Ambivalent Mourning," 184–91). In other poems, the poet/speaker feels himself altogether cut off from the sacramental, denied the purgative waters of baptism and unable to look upon the visible signs of Christ's Body and Blood. This is the case in the Holy Sonnet "I am a little world" and in "Goodfriday, 1613," which is a highly compressed sequence of three sonnets that leads, as most Petrarchan sonnet sequences do, only to ongoing desire and irresolution.[6]

In "I am a little world," Donne resolves the problem of spiritual sickness and wrests a sacramental conclusion from the poem's fire imagery; but in the Goodfriday poem, one too many "turns" make for a conclusion that recalls the last-minute reversals in many of the sonnets of *Astrophil and Stella* and that leaves the poet/speaker alone with his conceit, a conceit that does far more to win the human reader's admiration than to effect the poet's or reader's sacramental union with Christ crucified.

The Cunning Elements of "I am a little world"

In "I am a little world," the speaker combats a nearly desperate fear of damnation with a desire to be purged, either by

water or by fire. He declares himself "a little world made cunningly / Of Elements, and an Angelike spright" (1–2), but he
feels certain that his microcosm is doomed:

> But black sinne hath betraid to endlesse night
> My worlds both parts, and (oh) both parts must die.
> You which beyond that heaven which was most high
> Have found new sphears, and of new lands can write,
> Powre new seas in mine eyes, that so I might
> Drowne my world with my weeping earnestly,
> Or wash it if it must be drown'd no more:
> But oh it must be burnt; . . .
>
> (3–10)

Gardner (76) has explained that the sonnet's movement
from flood to fire is based upon two scriptural passages. Recalling God's rainbow covenant with Noah—that there shall
never again be "a flood to destroy the earth" (Genesis 9:11)—
the speaker reasons that his microcosm, too, "must be drown'd
no more." A watery apocalypse thus ruled out, he concludes
with St. Peter that the end will be a conflagration, "the day of
God, wherein the heavens being on fire, shall be dissolved,
and the elements shall melt with fervent heat" (2 Peter 3:12).
These biblical glosses clarify the reasoning behind the sonnet's turn at line ten, but they do not sufficiently explain
either the psychological dynamics or the sacramental poetics
at work in the poem.

In order to appreciate the emotional force—and, ultimately,
the metapoetic implications—of the parallel Donne is making, we must recognize the typological relation between the
Flood and baptism: the water of the Deluge is a "figure" of
baptism (1 Peter 3:20–21). In a sermon preached at a christening, Donne stresses that the sacrament does for individual
Christians what the Flood did for the earth: "it destroyes all
that was sinfull in us" (*Sermons* 5:110). Thus, the speaker's
"little world" has, like Creation itself, been drowned once
already; and the connection between the macrocosmic and

microcosmic events is made clearer by the fact that baptism, like the Flood, is never to be repeated. There is, as the Nicene Creed declares, "one baptism, for the remission of sins" (*BCP*, 251).[7]

According to Christian teaching, God has made ample provision for sins committed after baptism, but Roman Catholics and Protestants disagree sharply about the nature of that provision. Catholics find the remedy for such sin in the sacrament of Penance; repentance thus includes "not only . . . *a contrite and humble heart* [Psalm 51:17], but also the sacramental confession of those sins, . . . sacerdotal absolution, as well as satisfaction by fasts, alms, prayers and other devout exercises of the spiritual life" (Council of Trent, "Decree Concerning Justification," chapter 14). But for Protestants, who recognize only two sacraments (Baptism and the Eucharist) and who reject the idea that penitents must confess to a priest, the contrite sinner is to find assurance of forgiveness in the memory of his or her baptism. Thus, in a christening sermon, Donne stresses that "all the *actuall sinnes* [in the infant's] future life, shall be drowned in this baptisme, as often, as he doth religiously, and repentantly consider, that in *Baptisme* . . . he received an *Antidote* against all poyson, against all sinne" (*Sermons* 5:110).[8]

Such assurances notwithstanding, however, Donne's sermons often betray the fact that—having lost access to the Catholic sacrament of Penance—he was preoccupied with the desire for a second baptism. He speaks of martyrs as having "found a lawfull way of Re-baptizing, even in bloud" (*Sermons* 5:66) and—in one early sermon—goes so far as to define tears of repentance as the "souls rebaptization" (*Sermons* 1:245). In "I am a little world," the speaker wishes to weep such sacramentally potent tears; but he has set up his typological analogy between baptism and the Great Deluge, and having done so, he feels that his "little world," like the earth itself, "must be drown'd no more" (9). Seeking to solve the problem he has thus posed for himself, he first considers what seems to be a valid alternative to drowning, suggesting that his world may be "wash[ed]" in tears even if it can no longer be drowned. Such a cleansing would seem to be the perfect completion of the typological comparison he has drawn: the earth, though it is never again to be utterly destroyed by water, is refreshed by gentler rains; and Christ provides not only baptism, but "another Water," as Donne explains punningly in a sermon: the "Ablution . . . [of] Absolution from actuall sins, the water of contrite teares, and repentance" (*Sermons* 9:329).

In the poem, however, the speaker's state is one of near, if not complete, despair. In declaring from the start of his analogy that his "worlds both parts . . . must die" (4), the speaker has testified to a horrifying conviction: he will suffer, not only the physical death of his "Elements," but also "the second death" (Revelation 21:8)—that of the "Angelike spright" itself.[9] And the poem's form reflects his spiritual state. The line in which he considers washing as the alternative to drowning is the sonnet's ninth line; in a conventional Italian sonnet, it would be the turn. But here, it extends the water imagery of the octave into what ought to be the sestet, disrupting the relation between the sonnet's "both parts," only to make a far more decisive turn by resorting to fire imagery in line 10: "But oh it must be burnt."[10] In his dark state of mind and soul, the speaker cannot rest with the thought of cleansing tears, and the poet cannot rest with a neatly shaped Italian sonnet. The poem's desperate logic is clear; since the macrocosm "must be drown'd no more" after Noah's flood, it will instead be destroyed by fire. 2 Peter 3:7 declares that, just as the world was once destroyed by water, so "the heavens and the earth, which are now, . . . are kept in store unto fire against the day of judgment and perdition of ungodly men." And if the fate of the macrocosm is thus fixed, must not the microcosm, too, be destined for a fiery end?

It would seem that the speaker—who, as the self-destructive

inventor of the sonnet's ruling conceit, cannot be neatly distinguished from Donne, the maker of the distorted sonnet itself—has analogized himself into a furnace. He is trapped by the parallels that his own wit has generated; as we have seen, "The Crosse" warns against just such a danger: "when thy braine workes, ere thou utter it, / Crosse and correct concupiscence of witt" (57–58). But here, even the crossings and corrections—as in the careful substitution of washing for drowning—help to seal the speaker/sonneteer's fate. According to the artful parallel he has established, both parts of his "little world" are "reserved unto fire" (2 Peter 3:7) just as are the earth and sky of the macrocosm. He finds himself hedged by the flames he himself has fanned. Playing out the apocalyptic implications of his own trope, he finds that he must remain faithful to the poetic correspondence between sinful world and sinful self.

The irony of this suicidal commitment to analogy is that it springs from the poet/speaker's near-despairing sense that he has been *un*faithful to the commitment he made in baptism. For it is just such apostasy which—on the microcosmic level—may lead to the fires of spiritual destruction. The Novatian heretics of the third century considered any breach in the baptismal covenant to be completely irreparable; they "denied that any man could have [grace] again, after he had once lost it, by any deadly sin committed after Baptisme" (*Sermons* 5:86). Many of Donne's sermons argue against such harsh doctrines and the despair they inspire.[11] But those pastoral efforts reflect the Dean's own preoccupations; he was haunted by the specter of an unforgivable sin, a transgression that would wipe out the effects of his baptism once and for all.[12]

Several passages in the scriptures fed Donne's fears. As he points out in a sermon on Christ's declaration that "the blasphemy against the Holy Ghost shall not be forgiven unto men" (Matthew 12:31), the concept of unforgivable sin is "grounded in evident places of Scriptures" (*Sermons* 5:91). One of these is Hebrews 6:4–6, a passage that sheds significant light on the emotional logic of "I am a little world":

> [I]t is impossible for those who were once enlightened, and have tasted . . . the good word of God, . . . [i]f they shall fall away, to renew them again unto repentance: . . . For the earth which drinketh in the rain that cometh oft upon it, and bringeth forth herbs meet for them by whom it is dressed, receiveth blessing from God: But that which beareth thorns and briers is rejected, and is nigh unto cursing; whose end is to be burned.

This passage specifically invokes the image of earth that takes no benefit from having been watered. Those who bear no fruit when they are blessed by God's rain of grace will meet a fiery doom. No wonder, then, that the speaker of the sonnet should feel the threat of flaming death for "both parts" of his microcosm. Having acknowledged that his "little world," though it was once covered by the waters of baptism "must be drowned no more," he must fear that his wrongdoing has ruled out the possibility of being "renew[ed] . . . again" (Hebrews 6:6) and that, by sinning willfully after he has "received the knowledge of the truth," to quote another verse from Hebrews chapter 10, he has doomed himself to "the violent fire which shal devoure the adversaries" (Hebrews 10:26–27).[13]

Donne's anxiety about the impossibility of repeating one's baptism must surely have been fed by his status as a convert from Catholicism to Protestantism—which is to say, from the Catholic perspective, as an apostate. Even in a sermon in which he affirms the ecumenical belief that "we must be . . . far, from straitning salvation, to any *particular Christian Church*, of any subdivided name, *Papist* or *Protestant*" (*Sermons* 10:169–70), Donne stresses that it is a grave matter to depart from the Church into which one was baptized. "[T]he *Ego te baptizo* I can heare but once," he says, consciously or unconsciously recalling his own recusant roots through the use of Latin rather than the English of the *Book of Common Prayer*:

and to depart from that Church, in which I have received my baptism, and in which I have made my Contracts and my stipulations with God, and pledged and engaged my sureties there, deserves a mature consideration; for I may mistake the reasons upon which I goe, and I may finde after, that there are more true errours in the Church I goe to, then there were imaginary in that that I left. (*Sermons* 10:161)[14]

As the sermon continues, however, it becomes clear that this disconcerting passage introduces the possibility of a negative biographical interpretation only to reinforce Dean Donne's "mature consideration" that he and his auditory ought to cling to the Church of England and her sacraments. He recounts a satirical anecdote about a French Protestant who converted to Catholicism for monetary gain and then, in a far more serious tone, tells two stories of English Protestants who gave themselves "leave, to thinke irreverently, slightly, negligently of the *Sacraments*, as of things . . . *indifferent*" or even "*impertinent*" (*Sermons* 10:161). His bowels, he says, "earn'd and melted" at the story of a woman who thought it unimportant to have her dying child christened; and he was moved with "sorrow" and "holy indignation" at the attitude of a man who refused the Eucharist when Donne brought it to him on his deathbed because he felt he had *"not lived so in the sight of [his] God, as that [he] need[ed] a Sacrament"* (*Sermons* 10:161, 162).[15]

Donne's own feelings were the exact opposite of those expressed by the dying man. In an Easter sermon, he tells his congregation that the Church has provided an ongoing source of hope and renewal: just as "from the losse of our Spikenard, our naturall faculties in originall sin, we have a resurrection in baptisme," Donne explains, so "from the losse of the oyntment of the Lord . . . and the falling into some actuall sins, . . . we have a resurrection in the other Sacrament" (*Sermons* 7:112). In "I am a little world," then, the speaker leaves behind the fears inspired by his meditation on one

sacrament—Baptism—to find hope in the thought of another—
the Lord's Supper. He seeks a Eucharistic renewal in the very
flames with which, according to his typological analogy, he
"must be burnt" (10). Having acknowledged the fiery guilt of
his sins, the speaker prays: "Let their flames retire, / And burne
me ô Lord, with a fiery zeale / Of thee'and thy house, which
doth in eating heale" (12–14). The lines refer not only to the
purgative fires which—as in "Goodfriday, 1613"—may restore
God's image in the poet, but also to the Eucharist, through
which the zealous believer is healed and strengthened "in eating." As Docherty points out, "The ambiguity here concerns
who is eating what. The fire of the zeal consumes the poet
certainly; but more importantly the poet also eats the Lord,
and it is this eating which heals him" (226).[16]

As long as one does not reject the Eucharist, Donne feels,
one has a means of being restored to God; for the Epistle to
the Hebrews characterizes the relapsed sinner as one who
"hath trodden under foot the Son of God, and hath counted
the blood of the covenant, wherewith he was sanctified, an
unholy thing" (Hebrews 10:29). In a sermon, Donne interprets
this passage from Hebrews as applying only to "a falling
away . . . from Christ in all his Ordinances"; for, he explains,
"as it is impossible to live, if a man refuse to eat, Impossible
to recover, if a man refuse Physick, so it is Impossible for him
to be renewed" if he rejects the "conveyance of [Christ's] merits" through preaching and the sacraments (*Sermons* 7:112).
The sonneteer is at pains to demonstrate that he is no such
man. Begging to be burnt by the fire "which doth in eating
heale" (14), he declares that, far from rejecting nourishment
and restorative medicine, he embraces both.

In the *Devotions*, Donne associates the ninth verse of Psalm
69, "*For the zeal of thine house hathe eaten me*," with his
feverish desire to be recalled from the "excommunication" of
bodily sickness which forbids him to go to Church: "*Lord,
the zeale of thy House, eats me up, as fast as my fever; It is*

not a *Recusancie*, for I would come, but it is an *Excommuni-cation*, I must not" (*Devotions*, 17; Expostulation 3).[17] He is unable to worship in God's temple not only because he is phys-ically sick in his bed, but also because he is himself no longer a holy place, having been—as he puts it in another Holy Son-net—only "till I betray'd / My selfe, a temple of [the] Spirit divine" (*HSDue*, 7–8). In "I am a little world," his adaptation of the psalmist's cry serves a similar purpose; for here, too, he is praying to be healed. He hopes that, "in eating" the sacra-ment of Holy Communion, he will be restored to the house of God. Moreover, by partaking of the Eucharist and thus receiv-ing Christ into his own body, he himself can become God's temple once again; for, when Christ enters into him, he will drive out all evil as he did the merchants and moneychangers from the Temple. As the passage from the Gospel of John re-counts it, Jesus "made a scourge of small cords, [and] he drove them all out of the temple . . . And his disciples remembered that it was written, The zeal of thine house hath eaten me up" (John 2:15, 17).

The allusion to this Gospel passage is particularly signi-ficant in light of Donne's conversion from Catholicism to Protestantism, for his hope in the sonnet is to be restored to a cleansed temple, a reformed Church, and to be characterized by that hallmark of reformed piety, zeal.[18] Young argues that "what is always sought but always doubtful" in Donne's Di-vine Poems "is the confident assurance of the Real Presence of Christ in the Sacrament of the Altar" and that "the ambi-guity of Eucharistic doctrine in the Church of England must have been a source of anxiety for Donne" ("Donne, Herbert," 173). In this poem, however, as in *La Corona*, Donne is com-forted precisely by the doctrine of the Eucharist as he found it expressed in the English Church, with its insistence upon the experience of divine Presence not in the transubstanti-ated elements but in the act of receiving, "in eating."

But how can the essentially excommunicate sinner, bedridden in his sins, participate in the eating that heals? The English Church's service for "The Communion of the Sick" provides an answer. According to the rubrics in the *Book of Common Prayer*, the rite exists so that, "if the sick person be not able to come to the church, and yet is desirous to receive the communion in his house," he may do so (*BCP*, 307). The Epistle read during this service, taken from Hebrews 12, reminds the ailing communicant of sickness's purgative function: "My son, despise not the correction of the Lord. . . . For whom the Lord loveth, him he correcteth, yea, and he scourgeth every son whom he receiveth" (*BCP*, 308). The same book of the Bible that fuels Donne's burning fear thus provides as well for Christ's restorative, Eucharistic entry into His defiled temple.

As the closing line of the sonnet suggests, it is not so much the body of the believer, as his soul—moved by devout zeal—that consumes the sacrament. This idea, too, is supported by the prayer book rubrics, which explain that a Christian may communicate spiritually if "by reason of extremity of sickness" he cannot physically consume the consecrated elements: "[T]he curate shall instruct him, that if he do truly repent him of his sins, and steadfastly believe . . ., he doth eat and drink the Body and Blood of our Savior Christ, profitably to his soul's health, although he do not receive the Sacrament with his mouth" (*BCP*, 308).[19]

Relying upon the doctrines articulated in the rite for the "Communion of the Sick," "I am a little world" remedies private desperation with liturgically informed belief. The poet does not stop, despairingly, at the seventh verse of 2 Peter 3, which prophesies the fiery end of the world, but proceeds to the consoling words found in verse 13 of the same chapter: "Nevertheless we, according to his promise, look for new heavens and a new earth, wherein dwelleth righteousness" (2 Peter 3:13). This verse looks forward to the perfecting of the macrocosm, not to the renewal of an individual's body and soul. But because the logic of Donne's sonnet is built upon the microcosm/macrocosm analogy, Donne can hope that the heavens and the earth of his microcosm—his spirit and his body—will also be transformed by purgative flame.

It is important to note that the sonnet's world analogy is complete only when Donne, realizing that no lesser power can help him, looks to the "new heavens and new earth," burnt into being by God himself.[20] Invoking other powers only helps to advance the self-destructive course of the analogy he has set up:

> You which beyond that heaven which was most high
> Have found new sphears, and of new lands can write,
> Powre new seas in mine eyes, that so I might
> Drowne my world with my weeping earnestly . . .
>
> (5–8)

These lines address not only heroic Renaissance scientists and explorers, but also the saints, the heroes of the Church Triumphant.[21] The speaker is, however, following a false lead when he asks those who have traveled beyond the old world to supply him with waters drawn from the oceans they have discovered; for the saints have not yet seen the "new heavens and new earth" that will be fired into being at the end of time. On that day, their "Angelike sprights" will be reunited with the perfected elements of their own little worlds, their resurrected bodies. But until then, Donne stresses in a sermon on 2 Peter 3: 13, no one really knows the nature of the "new heavens and new earth" which are to be. In the sermon, Donne compares charts of New World discoveries to the works of various commentators explicating that verse:

> [I]n these *discoveries* of these new *Heavens*, and this new *Earth*, our *Maps* will bee unperfect. . . . [W]hen wee have travell'd as farre as wee can, with safetie, that is, as farre as *Ancient*, or

> *Moderne Expositors* lead us, . . . wee must say at last . . . that
> wee can looke no farther into it, with these eyes. . . . We limit,
> and determine our consideration with that *Horizon*, with which
> the *Holy Ghost* hath limited us. (*Sermons* 8:81–82)[22]

God, then, is the only author who "of new lands can write"
in such a way that the text becomes an aid to salvation;
and with Donne's concluding prayer for the zeal "which
doth in eating heal," it becomes clear that only the words
of the divine Author can provide an escape from the typological cul-de-sac that the human sonneteer has constructed
for himself.

Yet the poet cannot throw down his pen. Even as he calls
upon the Lord to burn him, he phrases his prayer in terms
that, on every level, maintain a delicate tension between divine action and human response.[23] In evoking the Eucharistic
encounter, the petition for the "fiery zeale . . . which doth in
eating heale" involves the penitent's willingness to "take and
eat" even as it implies that he is a helpless object of the Lord's
corrosive flames, a man "now zealously possest"—to cite the
expression in *La Corona* (*Cor1*, 11)—by a God who *is* zeal.[24]
The phrase "zeale / Of thee'and thy house" is, moreover, ambiguous with regard to possession; the zeal with which Donne
wishes to be burned is, in one sense, *of* God and his house in
that it is a characteristic of Christ and his Church, an expression of their great love for each man. From that perspective,
the allusion to Christ's furious assault on the temple merchants supports the poet's view of himself as a temple awaiting the zealous savior's whip of knotted cords. Yet the prayer
is also a request that he himself be imbued with zeal of—that
is, for—the Lord and his house; and zeal is the hallmark of
the embattled Christian, himself active and eloquent on be-
half of God and his Church.[25]

Human response remains a factor in the process of redemption as "I am a little world" portrays it; and for Donne as the

maker of this highly wrought conceit, human response takes the form of poetic act. The artist must exert himself to heal his work—the poem—if he is to call upon God to heal and redeem *him*, the divine artist's own "cunningly" made work.[26] Though Donne crafts the first ten lines of the poem to reflect in deliberately dangerous trope the precarious state of his soul, it is also through a poetic act that he finds the way to make his final prayer. He can ask for the "fiery zeale . . . which doth in eating heale" only insofar as he can reinterpret the fire which threatens him with destruction; and doing so means enacting a Eucharistic change. The element's function is redefined— flames are interpreted as instruments, not of annihilation, but of medicinal nourishment—in an enactment of the moral choice by which the afflicted man turns from despair to repentance.

As I have stressed in my reading of *La Corona*, the English Protestant definition of Eucharistic transformation involves a change in the use of the elements: in the sacrament, the bread and wine ordinarily used to nourish the body are appropriated for a sacred function and become nourishment for the soul. Here, threatened by hellfire and in danger of utter despair, the poet/speaker must avail himself of the Eucharistic flexibility of poetic language and transform the element of fire. He must rework the image of burning, relying on the fact that flames—like the bread and wine of the Lord's Supper— have more than one use. Fire may destroy, or it may be an agent of purgation and digestion.[27]

The poet's Eucharistic consecration of the fire imagery redefines and transforms the sonnet itself. As we have seen, its turn may be said to occur in line 10's desperate shift away from water imagery to that of fire; but from another perspective, the real turn does not take place until line 12, when the poet/speaker rejects the fevered fires of lust and envy, and addresses God directly, praying for restorative fire. While this

twice-turned shape dramatizes the speaker's tormented fluc-
tuation between hope and despair, the resonant confidence of
the final couplet—with its strong masculine rhyme—bears
witness to the resolution of that conflict.[28]

The resolution is anticipated, moreover, in the sonnet's
own testimony that it is no spontaneous effusion, poured—
unpremeditated—from the heart. "I am a little world made
cunningly," it says in its opening line, testifying to its status
as a completed artifact, carefully crafted and revised, already
"made" even as it begins.[29] Here, no less than in *La Corona*,
the poet has taken seriously the belief that human beings
should, like God, "worke after patternes" (*Sermons* 7:61), that
a maker's art must be based upon a fore-conceit.

"I am a little world" demonstrates, moreover, that the peril
and the efficacy of such making are inseparable. For according
to the sacramental poetics that underlies the sonnet, conceits
are either truly deadly or truly redemptive, like the sacrament
of Eucharist itself. A man who receives the Eucharist unworthily is damned (1 Corinthians 11:29) or, as Donne puts it, he
"*makes* Christ Jesus . . . his damnation" (*Sermons* 7:321; emphasis added). Similarly, to doubt one's salvation is, as Donne
sees it, to weave a kind of dark Faustian conceit:

> [T]o doubt of the mercy of God . . . goes so neare *making* thy
> sinne greater then Gods mercy, as that it *makes* thy sinne
> greater then daily adulteries, daily murthers, daily blasphe-
> mies . . . could have done, and though thou canst never *make*
> that true in this life that thy sinnes are greater then God can
> forgive, yet this is a way to *make* them greater, then God will
> forgive. (*Sermons* 2:333; emphasis added)

In the sonnet, too, the poet makes a metaphor that threatens
its inventor with perdition.

But he also finds his way out of the deadly trope, consecrating the elements of his analogy, making active use of the
multivalence with which God invests language, and giving
sacramental form to the fire of tribulation:

[I]f *we* can say . . . [t]hat all our fiery tribulations fall under the nature, and definition of *Sacraments*, That they are so many *visible signes of invisible Grace*, . . . If I can bring this *fire* to . . . conforme it selfe to mee, and doe as I would have it; that is, concoct, and purge, and purifie, and prepare mee for God . . . [then] I shall finde, that . . . [t]hough we can doe nothing of our selves, yet as we are in *Christ*, wee can doe all things. (*Sermons* 8:71–72)

Guided by the Spirit, the poet makes what he will of the element of fire, saying such things as to put it to a new and spiritually profitable use. In "I am a little world," the healing flames of a Eucharistic fire save Donne from a burning fear that he has lost the grace of Baptism: the response to fire is fire, the answer to fears about sacramentality is sacrament, and poetic utterance remedies the despair that was spoken into being through poetry.

The Three Sonnets of "Goodfriday, 1613"

"Goodfriday, 1613," like "I am a little world," ends with a prayer for burning purgation; in the longer poem, however, the fires remain corrosive, and the poet/speaker discovers no sacramental trope that can unite his own work with that of the savior.[30] The poem's powerfully irresolute conclusion arises, I would argue, from its ominously Petrarchan form: 42 lines in length, "Goodfriday, 1613" is a highly compressed sequence of three sonnets in which the speaker can never quite bring himself to surrender entirely to grace or to rely on God instead of the "opus operatum" of his own poetic work.[31] Like Astrophil in Sidney's *Astrophil and Stella*, he becomes less and less capable of restraining either himself or his art.

Indeed, in order to understand the spiritual and artistic implications of the final "turne" in "Goodfriday, 1613," I would first turn briefly to Sidney's sonnet sequence, a work that offered a biting critique of Petrarchan poetics even as it provided Donne and his contemporaries with the definitive example of English Petrarchism. In *Astrophil and Stella,* of course, Astrophil thinks that his problem is the competition between virtuous love of Stella and the base promptings of carnal desire; and up to a point, he is quite right. But an even more dangerous problem is posed by the nature of his medium, by the Petrarchan sonnet itself in all its self-defeating, self-referential self-sufficiency.

Early in the sequence, Astrophil tries very hard to dissociate his poetry from the slick beauty and rich, aureate artificiality of conventional Petrarchan sonnets that, he insists, show their authors' lack of sincerity: they "bewray a want of inward touch" (*Astrophil and Stella* 15:10).[32] He claims that he has no desire to load his verse with the "living deaths, dear wounds, fair storms, and freezing fires" that burden the imitators of Petrarch (*A&S* 6:4). He is a plain-spoken fellow: "I can speak what I feel, and feel as much as they, / But think that all the map of my state I display, / When trembling voice brings forth, that I do Stella love" (*A&S* 6:12–14).

But as the sequence continues, both the reader and Astrophil discover that Astrophil's simple declaration of love does not map his state quite so perfectly as he intends. For the shaky-voiced conclusion of Sonnet 6 sounds rather euphemistic and insincere when compared with the raw imperative at the end of Sonnet 71: "Give me some food" (14). This expression of unvarnished physical need is a metaphor (food = sexual satisfaction) couched in a personification (it is "desire" that "still cries: 'Give me some food'"), but it taps a deeper level of honest self-expression than does the literal assertion "I do Stella love." Lust will have its say.

The sonnet that ends with desire's cry is, however, a nearly successful attempt to keep it silent. Until desire bursts into the poem in the fourteenth line, Sonnet 71 presents a morally edifying definition of Stella that resembles the Horatian definition of poetry in Sidney's *Defense.* She is a "fairest book" that both delights and teaches (*A&S* 71:1). In Stella, as in a good poem, there is no conflict between beautiful form and ethical content; the two work together. Her "fair lines . . . true goodness show"; indeed, "while [her] beauty draws the heart to love, / As fast [her] virtue bends that love to good" (*A&S* 71:4, 12–13). And if Stella is an ideal poem, Astrophil's sonnet through line 13 is a work dedicated to her Horatian aesthetic. This dedication falls apart, however, in an abrupt *volta* or turn between lines 13 and 14. The "desire" that speaks up in line 14, shattering the good intentions of the previous 13 lines, may thus be understood not only as the untamed force of Astrophil's lust, but as the unruly desire of the sonnet itself: as a 14-line poem in a Petrarchan sequence, it does not want to serve the purposes of an "erected wit" (*Defense of Poesy*, 217) but to be itself, a sonnet, a self-contained ball of witty self-consciousness and unfulfilled erotic longing.

In the first line of the next sonnet, Astrophil confronts this rogue aesthetic directly by punning on the second person form of the verb *to be*: "Desire, . . . thou my old companion *art*" he says, addressing "Desire" *as* art (*A&S* 72:1). Like Petrarch himself, who cannot separate his art from his love, his pursuit of Laura from his pursuit of the Laurel, Astrophil finds that he cannot keep the artless sincerity of pure love separated from the artful designs of lust. He begins by telling his desire that "though thou . . . oft so clings to my pure love, that I / One from the other scarcely can descry," yet "Now from thy fellowship I needs must part" (*A&S* 72:1–3, 5); he maintains this stance for 13 and one-half lines, making it almost to the end of the sonnet: "thou desire, because thou would'st have all, / Now banished art," he says (*A&S* 72:13–14); but his effort collapses in the last half line with a plaintive rhetorical question: "Now banished art—but yet, alas, how shall?" (14). Desire—both for sexual satisfaction and for an artful wit that serves itself rather than "virtue"—intrudes itself at the last, turning the poem from ethical declaration to Petrarchan sigh at what is nearly the last possible point in its structure, with only three metrical stresses to go. Astrophil's entrapment in Petrarchan poetics is, I would argue, an object-lesson in the dangers of sonneteering, a demonstration of the sonnet's persistent tendency to part company with any ethically or spiritually "erected" poetics and to turn inward on itself.

In "Goodfriday, 1613," Donne does not forget Sidney's lesson. Though his speaker, like Astrophil, thinks that his problem is the competition between true "devotion" (2) and more carnal impulses (the "Pleasure or businesse" [7] by which his soul is "whirld" [8]), the most dangerous kinds of turn are for him—as for Astrophil—the cunningly-delayed turns of his own sonnets. And there are exactly three sonnets—14 lines + 14 lines + 14 lines—in the 42 lines of the poem.[33]

The first 14 lines of "Goodfriday, 1613. Riding Westward" are both an attempt to explain away the speaker's impious motion and a piece of material evidence that he remains intent on secular "Pleasure or businesse" (7), including the pleasure and business of poetic composition. It is the definitively artificial form of his strained analogy, no less than his worldly journey to the West, that continues to divide him from artless "devotion"—which he calls man's "naturall forme" (6).[34] For eight lines, he develops his complex analogy between the tendencies of the human soul and the whirlings of the planets; and at that traditional turning point or *volta*, he reaches his first period. Then, in what amounts to the sestet of the poem's first sonnet-like section, he "bends" (10) away from his analogy even as he completes it: "Hence is't," he says "that I am carryed towards the West / This day" (9–10) when the greatest of celestial and spiritual motions takes place in the "East" (10): there, the "Sunne" rises (11) and the Son is raised on the cross. What may be termed the first "sonnet" of the work ends as he reaches another period, asserting the central truth of Redemption with ringing certainty: "But that Christ on this Crosse, did rise and fall, / Sinne had eternally benighted all" (13–14). The art of the speaker, so strongly evident in the octave's long, complex analogy between planetary and spiritual motion, is thus made supernumerary in the sestet, subsumed in the supernatural creativity of the savior who—himself "begottcn, not made" (Nicene Creed; *BCP*, 250)—"beget[s]" rather than makes the "endlesse day" that is man's salvation (12).

The half-hidden sexual innuendo in these lines, which present Christ as the hanged God whose erection or "rising" spills life onto the parched dryness of a sin-blasted world, is carried forward in the second sonnet-like section of the poem, lines 15–28.[35] In this section, the poet/speaker meditates on the Atonement, which he depicts as the Christian equivalent of the primal scene, the moment of his own begetting as a redeemed soul: "Yet dare I'almost be glad," he says, "I do not see / That spectacle of too much weight for mee" (15–16). It is unthinkable to "see God dye" (19), to watch him in the act of pouring out his vital fluids, mingling "that blood which is / The seat of all our Soules" (25–26) with the "dust" of the ground in order to "Make durt" (27) and remake the creature first "formed . . . of the dust of the ground" (Genesis 2:7).[36] This remaking of man is no art, the sexual analogy suggests, but a super-natural version of natural reproduction.

In lines 21–22 of the poem, which form the midpoint of "Goodfriday, 1613" as a whole and lines 7–8 of the work's second sonnet-like section, the poet/speaker concludes that sonnet's octave with a definitive *volta*, an image of the crucified Christ as the *primum mobile* whose hands "turne" not the little world of a sonnet, but the entire cosmos:

> Could I behold those hands which span the Poles,
> And turne all spheares at once peirc'd with those holes?

In these lines, positioned at the center of "Goodfriday, 1613," Donne marks the crucifixion as the turning point in Christ's work of redemption and implicitly contrasts that mighty undertaking with his own artistic effort as he crafts the "turne" of his work's second 14-line section.[37]

As he moves from the octave to the sestet of the poem's central sonnet, he does not speak of his own conversion or turning; rather, he forges on in a series of rhetorical questions that mingle spiritual awe with theological reflection:

> Could I behold that endlesse height which is
> Zenith to us and to'our Antipodes,
> Humbled below us? or that blood which is
> The seat of all our Soules, if not of his,
> Make durt of dust, or that flesh which was worne
> By God, for his apparell, rag'd, and torne?
>
> (23–28)

These lines reflect upon an essentially sacramental mystery, pondering not only the hypostatic union of God and Man in Christ, but the substance of Eucharist, Jesus's Blood and Body, which is the point of sacramental contact between the human and the divine. The poet/speaker's rhetorical questions invite a negative answer but do not pronounce a definitive "No, I cannot behold his Body and Blood."[38] McNees comments on his perplexity:

> . . . Donne still appears reluctant to assert a eucharistic Real Presence. . . . Intellectually, his questions echo the Puritan difficulty of realizing Christ simultaneously on earth and in heaven. Yet the emotional vividness with which Donne catalogues the crucified Christ's physical traits is . . . reminiscent of the first step of the Ignatian meditational method—composition of place. The carnal imagery suggests that Donne is conjuring up Christ's physical presence . . . to identify himself with Christ's sacrifice and thereby become worthy of partaking in the eucharistic meal. Yet this process is backward. To achieve true conformity with the crucified Christ, the speaker must first suffer his own internal crucifixion through penance. (*Eucharistic Poetry*, 57–58)

The speaker's problem, considered from this perspective, is that he has not prepared himself or—rather—that he has not *been prepared* (with an emphasis on the verb's passivity) by the gift of sacramental tribulation that Donne celebrates in "The Crosse." He cannot experience Christ's sacramental presence without receiving that gift.

It is with a prayer for purgative punishment, then, that Donne will end "Goodfriday, 1613"; but before he reaches that petition, he asks a fifth rhetorical question focusing on the Blessed Virgin rather than on Christ. This query, which begins the poem's third 14-line section, introduces the subject of the final "sonnet" of "Goodfriday, 1613": the challenge that the crucifixion poses to the human poet as maker.

> If on these things I durst not looke, durst I
> Upon his miserable mother cast mine eye,
> Who was Gods partner here, and furnish'd thus
> Halfe of that Sacrifice, which ransom'd us?
>
> (29–32)

These lines present the Blessed Virgin as a grief-stricken maker who now beholds the destruction of her beloved work. Mary as she is described here no longer provides the poet with a precedent for devout making and divinely sanctioned poesis (as she does in *La Corona*, where her womb is a model for the "little roome" of a sonnet). Instead, the "miserable mother" at the foot of the cross models a maker's willingness to submit to the will of God and to stand by meekly while the perfect fruit of her labor is immolated by her divine collaborator. The Virgin "furnish'd . . . / Halfe of that Sacrifice, which ransom'd us" (31–32) but can be a "partner" to God—both sexually and artistically—only by allowing him to destroy the work they have made together.[39]

The poet/speaker of the last "sonnet" in "Goodfriday" thus does not want to look on the human "mother" of the sacrificed Christ; he knows that her example would call him to sacrifice his own work. He goes on to acknowledge that both she and her dying Son "are present yet unto my memory, / For that looks towards them" (34–35) in an act of anamnesis that might, if further developed, involve the poet/speaker in a Eucharistic meditation like the one Donne carries out in *La Corona*. But he does not develop that brief allusion to memory; instead, he concludes that what matters most is not *his* vision, but that of Christ: "and thou look'st towards mee, / O Saviour, as thou hang'st upon the tree" (35–36). Unlike the fearful yet desiring gaze of the subject that, in a Petrarchan sonnet, merely reflects back from the "murderous mirrors"[40] of his love-object's unpitying eyes, the gaze of the "Goodfriday" speaker is met with an answering look that redeems rather than kills.

Having acknowledged Christ's gaze, the speaker believes himself ready to surrender to grace; and at the traditional turning point (that is, at line 37 of "Goodfriday, 1613" which is line 9 of the work's third sonnet) he tries to do just that, to make an artful turn in his poem that reflects a spiritual turn toward submission: "I turne my backe to thee, but to receive"—that is, but to take what you will give to me, to eschew attempts at offering worthy works of my own. Indeed, this "turne" will—the ensuing lines imply—be a turn to utter receptivity, passivity, and submission; Christ, he insists, must do all:

> I turne my backe to thee, but to receive
> Corrections, till thy mercies bid thee leave.
> O thinke mee worth thine anger, punish mee,
> Burne off my rusts, and my deformity,
> Restore thine Image, so much, by thy grace,
> That thou may'st know mee . . .
>
> (37–42)

Whether the action is intellectual ("thinke" and "knowe"), corrosive ("punish" and "Burne"), or constructive ("Restore"), only Christ and his grace can perform it. The speaker ("mee") and his qualities ("my rusts, and my deformity") can only be objects of these verbs. Indeed, if "mans Soule be a Spheare" (1), only the "hands" of Christ—which, in lines 21–22, "span the Poles / And turne all spheares at once"—can "turne" him. Only the redemptive force of Christ's sacrifice as evoked in that "turne" can "Restore [Christ's] Image" (41) in the poet/ speaker; he can rely on no other "turne." Or so it seems, at any rate, until the last three feet of the poem's final line: ". . . and I'll turne my face."

In the last three stresses of "Goodfriday, 1613," the redemptive movement of the third sonnet and of the entire three-sonnet sequence is called into question; for there the poet inserts another kind of "turne." With the phrase "and I'll turne my face," he reasserts his own presence as subject and doer of action; and though his action is deferred to a future when Christ's "mercies" will "bid [him] leave" or cease the scourging that the poet has begged for in the preceding 5 and 2/5 lines, it nevertheless makes the final outcome of the redemption process dependent upon his own action, upon a final (and perhaps too artful) "turne" that is the work of the poet rather than of Christ. Lacking the ambiguity of "I am a little world"'s conclusion, in which "eating" is an action both performed by the speaker and done to him by the divine fire for which he prays, the conclusion of "Goodfriday, 1613" proposes a contractual sequence: first, you do this for me; then, I will "turne." First, grant my prayer; then I will undertake the process of conversion.[41]

If one compares the language of "The Crosse," in which the speaker urges himself and others to "Let Crosses . . . take what hid Christ in thee" so that one may "be his image, or not his, but hee" (35–36), one can see the distinction between a freely chosen act of surrender to the shaping force of God's corrections and a human "turne" that is definitive and final. One must not, as Sherwood rightly complains that some critics do, "minimize [Donne's] regard for human powers" ("Conversion Psychology," 110). "Goodfriday, 1613" certainly does not proceed from those versions of Protestant doctrine that, as Sherwood puts it "denied human initiative" (111). Indeed, Sherwood rightly emphasizes the difference between "Donne's initiative in turning his back" in line 37 as a "free spiritual movement" and the "turne" of line 42, which is projected into the future (111, 110). But it does not follow that Donne's work maps "free human movement towards the boundaries of man's limits, then a clear recognition of those boundaries, then a willing request for God's aid" in which "Donne looks *for the will to be turned* after his free request for God's necessary correction" (Sherwood, "Conversion Psychology," 111; emphasis added). The poet/speaker does not look for his will "to be turned" but promises—on certain conditions—to "turne" it himself.

Sherwood glosses the conclusion of "Goodfriday, 1613" with a number of Old Testament penitential texts that evoke "turning as an activity assimilating human and divine motions" (119). But in a passage like Zechariah 1:3—"Thus saith the Lord of hosts; Turn ye unto me, . . . and I will turn unto you"—the order is exactly the opposite of that described in Donne's poem, where the speaker/poet reserves his "turn" for last. The most relevant scriptural gloss on the conclusion of "Goodfriday, 1613" is, I would argue, the refrain line that occurs three times in Psalm 80: "Turn us again, O God, and cause thy face to shine; and we shall be saved" (verse 3).[42] The prayer at the conclusion of "Goodfriday, 1613" revises the psalmist's prayer, inverting its emphasis: the Psalm speaks of *God's act of turning man*, presenting a sequence in which salvation follows from that turning and from the shining of the divine face;[43] the poet/speaker of "Goodfriday, 1613" speaks of his own face and his own act of turning.

The power of "Goodfriday, 1613"—and particularly of its conclusion—thus arises from the work's status as the sacrament of its author's perilous spiritual state. It—no less than *Astrophil and Stella*—is the outward and visible sign of a poet's unsuccessful struggle to turn away from Petrarchan subjectivity, self-referentiality, and ambition. He who made me, the poem declares, cannot cease to craft his own turns.

The Reader and the Sonneteer in "Goodfriday, 1613" and "I am a little world"

A poet/speaker like that of "Goodfriday, 1613" is, it would seem, in no position to provide his reader with a sacramentally efficacious text. A number of twentieth century interpreters of the poem have, however, credited the poem with such spiritual efficacy. O'Connell, for example, arguing that the speaker achieves "identification with Christ" in the final lines, proposes that this identification

> universaliz[es] the poem; it makes the final prayer available to all who share this identity. By letting go of his self-centered individualism, the speaker is united both to Christ and to members of the community of faith.... ("'Restore Thine Image,'" 26)

It is just such a Eucharistic unity that *La Corona* seeks to effect; but where, exactly, is such a communion evoked in "Goodfriday, 1613"? If anything, the poet/speaker seems closer to a sense of shared humanity in the poem's opening conceit, where he speaks in general terms of "man's Soule" (1) and "our Soules" (7), than at the conclusion, in which the entire universe is concentrated into the I/thou relationship between Donne and Christ.

Indeed, despite the scattered appearance of a few more first person plural pronouns in lines 24–30, where the poet is reflecting on Christ's nature in relation to human nature,[44] a sense of isolation dominates the work. As Carey points out,

> Warwickshire and Shropshire, with their rivers, birds, trees and sizeable populations, have been obliterated.... It is no earthly terrain he passes across. The poem's geography is surreal. He

moves like a planet away from a giant crucifix, the landscape's only feature, which he dare not look at, and on which Christ hangs, watching him. In all the two counties, Donne and Christ are the sole figures. (121)

Though a reader may—as O'Connell does—take the Christian conviction that "the reader . . . too is, or is called to be, 'thine image'" as an invitation "to participate" in the experience of Donne's poet/speaker ("'Restore Thine Image,'" 26), the text of Donne's "Goodfriday, 1613" in itself does not issue that invitation.

As Friedman argues compellingly, however, it does present a powerful dramatization of its own insufficiency, demonstrating "the specious appeal of rationalizing intelligence and the creations of verbal artifice" (437) even as it uses those means to take the poet/speaker as far as they can take him. As Friedman concludes, the poem grapples with and "come[s] very close to solving the problem of devotional poetry" by using "the powers of reason and imagination to reveal their incompleteness for the tasks of faith" (442). But it does not follow, I would argue, that this dramatization is, as Friedman also argues, "a vehicle of conversion for Donne's audience" (424).[45]

If we can trust the headnote that replaces the poem's title in the Dobell manuscript, the very first member of that audience may have been Donne's friend, Henry Goodyer. The headnote explains that "Mr. J: Duñ goeing from Sr H: G: on good fryday sent him back this Meditaon, on the Waye" (*Complete Poetry*, 488). It would not have been the first time that Donne composed a work intended for Goodyer's eyes while riding from one place to another. In one of Donne's prose letters to Goodyer (probably dating from 1608), he speaks of "the high way, where I am contracted, and inverted into my self" as one of his "two ordinary forges of Letters to" his friend (the other being his "poor Library, where to cast [his] eye upon good Authors kindles or refreshes sometimes meditations not unfit to communicate to near friends" (*Letters*, 137). Certainly, if Donne did send "Goodfriday, 1613" back to Goodyer at Polesworth while still "on the Waye" to his destination, he must have thought of the work as a meditation "not unfit" for such a reader as Goodyer. But is the poem designed as "a vehicle" for his friend's "conversion," to use Friedman's phrase?

In the prose letters he sent to Goodyer, Donne was often gently critical of his friend, including admonitions and advice; the same is true of the one extant verse letter Donne addressed to Goodyer, which, like "Goodfriday, 1613," begins with a generalization about human experience:

> Who makes the Past, a patterne for next yeare,
>   Turnes no new leafe, but still the same things reads,
> Seene things, he sees againe, heard things doth heare,
>   And makes his life, but like a paire of beads.
>
>   (1–4)

The image Donne uses here is that of a rosary meditation, a circular and repetitive devotion which he characterizes as unproductive, urging instead the benefits of "travaile" (31), by means of which the soul may insure "That she returnes home, wiser then she went" (32). The poem goes on to urge that Goodyer "love [God] as now, but feare him more, / And in your afternoones thinke what you told / And promis'd him, at morning prayer before" (38–40). It would seem that this verse letter, at least, is intended to convert and perfect Goodyer; but Donne pulls back from such a project as he concludes, admitting that his advice can make no significant contribution to Goodyer's spiritual development: "But why doe I touch / Things, of which none is in your practise new, / And Tables, or fruit-trenchers teach as much" (42–44). Goodyer can be as morally edified by observing the natural consequences of overindulgence as he can by reading Donne's poem; the real purpose of the verse letter is, then, to benefit the author, not the reader:

> But thus I make you keepe your promise Sir,
>   Riding I had you, though you still staid there,
> And in these thoughts, although you never stirre,
>   You came with mee to Micham, and are here.
>
> (45–48)

In these lines, the poem identifies itself as one that is, like "Goodfriday, 1613," written from the road as a meditation intended to make an absent addressee present to the poet.

As in "Goodfriday, 1613," however, the work's effect on that addressee remains indeterminate. For, though Donne feels that the composition of the poem has allowed him to bring Goodyer with him to Mitcham, the advice proffered in the earlier stanzas is that Goodyer should travel much further afield, to "outlandish ground" (22) where he will be a "stranger" (25); and the poet cannot be certain that his work will convince the reader to undertake such a journey. Indeed, he admits that his addressee has in actuality "still staid" (46) where he is and that he will perhaps "never stirre" (47). Thus, unable to ensure the conversion of his reader, Donne settles for the good that writing the poem can do for him, its author. His final emphasis is on the benefits he receives through writing's power to evoke an absent presence, rather than on any real attempt to move his addressee through rhetorical persuasion.

"Goodfriday, 1613" resembles the verse letter to Goodyer in that it neither settles definitively upon an effort to move an addressee (Christ) nor resolves to depend on that addressee's response. Though he struggles to hand himself and his text over to a divine reader's interpretive act of "know[ing]" (42), Donne ends "Goodfriday, 1613"—as he does the verse letter to Goodyer—with an emphasis on his own action as turner and maker of himself and of his poetry. And this emphasis on the speaker's role as writer is unalloyed by any call (like *La Corona*'s "*Salvation to all that will is nigh!*" [*Cor1*, 14]) for the participation of human readers; the writerly self-consciousness of the poem thus problematizes the idea that "Goodfriday, 1613" might serve as a vehicle for its readers' conversion. Indeed, the poem's emphasis on Christ as the only reader whose response can determine its final turn implies that Donne's sending the work to Goodyer was yet one more turn away from, rather than toward the poem's all-important divine reader.[46]

In "I am a little world," Donne addresses the role of human readers more directly, only to insist upon their supernumerary status as bystanders or observers, restricting them to a place outside the text where they can watch but not participate in the poet/speaker's encounter with the divine. For, as we have seen, the only reader on whom the poet/speaker of "I am a little world" can rely is the "Lord" he addresses in the last two and one half lines of the sonnet; only He, the maker of Donne's microcosm, can "burne" Donne's body and soul in the healing fires of purgation (13) and thus prevent "both parts" (4) of his "world" (8) from being "burnt" (10) in the destructive fires of hell.

As the maker of the sonnet, of course, Donne himself must decide whether his cunningly made artificial world will be burnt—tossed into the embers on the hearth—or will survive as a living work, circulated and read. And insofar as he chooses the latter course, he testifies that the sonnet is designed not as a wholly private microcosm, but as art, as a world meant for the delectation and/or edification of human readers. In his love lyric "The triple Foole," Donne deals with the problem that such a choice raises: the conflict between a poem's therapeutic function, operative during its composition, and its aesthetic function, which enters in when the work is presented to an audience. In "The triple Foole," a frustrated lover tries to use poetry to alleviate his pain, but finds that his work's artistic success interferes with the purgative effects of poetic composition:

> . . . as th'earths inward narrow crooked lanes
> Do purge sea waters fretfull salt away,
>   I thought, if I could draw my paines,
> Through Rimes vexation, I should them allay,
> Griefe brought to numbers cannot be so fierce,
> For, he tames it, that fetters it in verse.
>
>   But when I have done so,
> Some man, his art and voice to show,
>   Doth Set and sing my paine,
> And, by delighting many, frees againe
>   Griefe, which verse did restraine.

(6–15)

The speaker complains about the actions of a performer he refers to as "Some man" other than himself; but there can be little doubt that he is putting his "art and voice" on display in the text of the poem itself and that he himself may thus be held responsible for frustrating his own emotional agenda by producing verse that is capable of "delighting many." In "I am a little world" and "Goodfriday, 1613"—as in devotional poetry generally—the tension between art's aesthetic and nonaesthetic function is more problematic still, for it is the soul's redemption rather than the speaker's emotional state that is at stake.[47]

The poet/speaker of "I am a little world" confronts the problem by deliberately turning away from all addressees but God. The plural "you" whom he addresses in lines 5–8 are, I have noted, heroic achievers in both the secular and sacred realms; more specifically, they are Sidneyan makers, writers "lifted up with the vigour of [their] own invention, [who] . . . grow . . . another nature, in making things either better than nature bringeth forth, or, quite anew, forms such as never were in nature" (*Defense of Poesy*, 216). Those who "beyond that heaven which was most high / Have found new sphears and of new lands can write" (5–6) are visionaries, and because they "can write," the poet/speaker turns to them for a transfusion of "new" inspiration, troped in Petrarchan terms as tears: "Powre new seas in mine eyes," he begs (7), so that I can continue "weeping earnestly" (8). In making this request, he associates the inspiration such writers might provide with the weepy creativity of "whining Poëtry" (*Triple*, 3), implying that any divine poetry flowing from what these addressees "Powre" into him will be the religious equivalent of Petrarchan lyrics. As he puts it in another Holy Sonnet: "O Might those sighes and teares returne againe / Into my breast and eyes, which I have spent, / That I might in this holy discontent / Mourne with some fruit, as I have mourn'd in vaine" (*HSSighs*, 1–4).

As long as he is addressing himself only to other writers, however, the sonneteer finds that he cannot write poetry that bears "fruit" in winning the approval of the Beloved. Sidney's Astrophil, who tries to break free from "turning others' leaves" (*A&S* 1:7) but who repeatedly slips back into the absurd postures convention imposes upon the Petrarchan sonneteer, learns this lesson about poetic originality the hard way. The flames that still envelope him at the end of *Astrophil and Stella* are not the healing fires of purgation; on the contrary, he is trapped in his "own fire's might" and his "boiling breast" is a lover's hell, a "dark furnace" in which a ray of hope leads only to ongoing "despair" (*A&S* 108:1, 2, 3, 7).

The poet/speaker of "I am a little world" emerges from both the Christian hell and the Petrarchan inferno by placing his trust in a creative power that is not tied to tears and does not rely upon the contributions or judgments of other human writers. In doing so, however, he leaves the reader of his sonnet without a role to play. Insofar as that reader is herself a

writer—an active reader engaged in interpretive exploration—
she will identify with the "you" of lines 5–8 and will be left
behind, as they are, when the poet/speaker turns to God
in lines 12–14. She may, of course, produce her own account
of the sonnet, choosing to play God and to pass judgment on
the speaker, deciding whether or not his Eucharistic trope is
an aesthetic or spiritual success. But even as she does so, her
inability to answer the poem's concluding prayer must force
her to admit that her critical judgment of the *speaker* and the
"little world" of the poem has no bearing upon the spiritual
judgment faced by the *poet* and by his "little world" of body
and soul. She cannot make the "flames" of lust and envy
"retire" from John Donne, nor is her critical judgment the
Final Judgment that so terrifies the poet. Indeed, the ultimate
effect of Donne's sonnet, with its strong emphasis on its own
artificiality, is to call to the reader's attention both that the
poet cannot write his own way to salvation and that she, the
reader, is not the God who can save him.

What sort of readerly megalomania could make such a reminder necessary? It is not only, I would stress, some twentieth century Reader-Response-Critic-gone-mad who needs to
be told that she is not God; for in a patronage culture, a noble
reader's power over a poet extends well beyond the boundaries of the reading experience, and the godlike influence of
a lord might well prove a strong temptation to the religious
poet to concern himself with pleasing someone other than
the Lord.

In the sonnet to Magdalen Herbert, "Her of your name . . .,"
Donne asks his reader/addressee to identify with the saint(s)
whose name she shares and, assuming that she has quasi-eccle-
siastical (if not quasi-divine) authority, asks the lady to "Harbour" poems that are "addresst" (14) to God rather than to
her. The terms of the poem keep the distinction between saint
and divinity quite clear. This is not always the case, however.
In Donne's "To E. of D. with six holy Sonnets," we catch a

glimpse of how Donne proceeded in presenting examples of his divine poetry to another aristocratic reader:

> See Sir, how as the Suns hot Masculine flame
> > Begets strange creatures on Niles durty slime,
> > In me, your fatherly yet lusty Ryme
> (For these songs are their fruits) have wrought the same;
> But though th'ingendring force from whence they came
> > Bee strong enough, and nature doe admit
> > Seaven to be borne at once, I send as yet
> But six, they say, the seaventh hath still some maime . . .
>
> (1–8)

Donne sends to the Earl (either of Dorset or of Derby)[48] six "strange creatures" while withholding a seventh sonnet, which some other readers (the ambiguous "they" of line 8) have judged imperfect. Whoever "they" are, the readers Donne trusts to review the sonnets before he sends them to the Earl must be critics of some discernment, for his decision to withhold the seventh is based on their criticism. But "they" are not able to do for the other six sonnets what the "E. of D." can do for them; for Donne goes on to say that he submits the six he does send in order that they may be further improved. The Earl's "judgement" (9) and "invention" (10) are, he says, "As fire these drossie Rymes to purifie, / Or as Elixar, to change them to gold" (11–12). Calling the Earl the creative force whose "fatherly yet lusty Ryme" has inspired him, and naming him the all-powerful "Alchimist" (13) who possesses the quintessence—"Wit, whose one spark could make good things of bad" (14), Donne invites his reader to play God. Thus, when the poet tells his noble addressee, "I choose your judgement" (9), one must wonder Whose judgment he is avoiding.

If Shawcross's informed speculations are correct, "I am a little world" is not one of the seven sonnets mentioned in "To E. of D." (*Complete Poetry*, 338). But the Earl's role in the sonnet addressed to him does cast light on the spiritual danger that attends Donne's address to nondivine reader/

writers in lines 5–8 of "I am a little world." If the final prayer of that sonnet is to be a devout and sacramentally efficacious prayer—"burne me ô Lord, with a fiery zeale / Of thee'and thy house, which doth in eating heale"—the poet must rely on the equivocal nature of fire and of the word "eating"; but he must, at the same time, hope to suppress the equivocal potential in the words "Lord" and "thy house"—both of which might be read by a noble patron (whether the Earl of Dorset or of Derby) as if addressed to him instead of God.

The potential for such idolatrous elision is nowhere more amply demonstrated than in a prose letter Donne wrote to the notorious Robert Carr, Viscount Rochester to thank him for his favor and assistance. Donne's nineteenth and twentieth century admirers have always been embarrassed and dismayed by the poet's epithalamion celebrating Rochester's scandalous marriage to the Countess of Essex, Frances Howard, by Donne's willingness (expressed in a letter to Goodyer [*Letters*, 179–81]) to write a prose defense of the marriage annulment that cleared the way for the Countess's union with Rochester, and by his reliance upon Rochester's patronage.[49] The language of Donne's letter to Rochester, which Hester estimates to have been written in the summer of 1613, is particularly disturbing when read in conjunction with the Holy Sonnets:

> After I was grown to be your Lordships, by all the titles that I could thinke upon, it hath pleased your Lordship to make another title to me, by buying me. . . I know there may be degrees of importunity even in thankfulnesse: but your Lordship is got above the danger of suffering that from me, or my Letters, both because my thankfulnesse cannot reach to the benefits already received, and because the favour of receiving my Letters is a new benefit. And since good Divines have made this an argument against deniers of the Resurrection, that it is easier for God to recollect the Principles, and Elements of our bodies, howsoever they be scattered, then it was at first to create them

of nothing, I cannot doubt, but that any distractions or diver-
sions in the ways of my hopes, will be easier to your Lordship
to reunite, then it was to create them. (*Letters*, 290–91)

How, one must ask, would the reader of this letter have read
the Holy Sonnet beginning "As due by many titles I resigne /
My selfe to thee, O God . . ."? To the Divine Lord addressed in
the sonnet, the poet declares, "first I was made / By thee, . . .
and when I was decay'd / Thy blood bought that, the which
before was thine"; and though Rochester did not spend his
own blood "in buying" Donne, the poet nevertheless declares
in his letter that the Viscount will never find "any thing which
[he] may call [his] more absolutely and intirely" than Donne.
Though the sonneteer, in addressing God, gives himself the
title "Thy servant, whose paines thou hast still repaid" (6), he
is just as ready to sign his letter to Rochester with the protes-
tation that "if it agreed with your Lordships purposes, I should
never wish other station, then such as might make me still,
and onely / *Your Lordships* / *Most humble and devoted servant* / J. Donne" (*Letters*, 291).[50] In the letter to Rochester, the
analogy Donne draws between God and the unsavory royal
favorite is mere convention, a mode of courtly compliment
not to be cited as evidence that their author was guilty of idolatry; indeed, the constraints of convention may even extend so
far as to make charges of sycophancy inappropriate. As text,
then, the letter to Rochester is not necessarily remarkable;
but as a context for the reception of "As due by many titles,"
it is a revealing gloss on how the inherently problematic genre
of the devotional lyric becomes all the more problematic in a
patronage culture.

The letter's allusion to the reassembly of scattered bodies
on Judgment Day also invites a rereading of Donne's sonnet
on that subject, "At the round earths imagin'd corners," which
begins by addressing the "Angells" of the apocalypse (1–2)
and urging them to sound their trumpets. The speaker of the
sonnet moves next to address the "numberlesse infinities /

Of soules" that will "arise / From death" in response to the angels' summons (3–7), as well as those who will be living at the time of the Second Coming (7–8); but in the sestet, the speaker turns to address one he calls "Lord" (9). Revising the ringing imperatives of the sonnet's octave, he begs for more time, "a space" in which that Lord may "Teach" him "how to repent; for that's as good," he concludes, "As if thou'hadst seal'd my pardon, with thy blood" (13–14). Any Christian reader must, of course, find this conclusion ironic, since the most essential tenet of Christian belief is that Christ *has* sealed man's pardon with his blood. But if the reader of the sonnet is a lord to whom the poet is indebted for "buying" him with some less sanguine currency, the irony is all the deeper.

The question before us here, however, is not so much how Donne allows dangerous ambiguities to cloud the question of the implied reader's identity in "As due by many titles" and "At the round earths imagined corners," as how he takes steps to eliminate such ambiguity in "I am a little world." In that sonnet, at least, the poet/speaker makes clear that no human reader—whether noble or common, whether a Jacobean contemporary of John Donne or a denizen of future "sphears" and "new lands" he cannot yet envision—can mistake himself or herself for the poem's true addressee. On the contrary, the poem insists that human readers acknowledge their limits; whatever they "Powre" (a visual pun on "pour" and "power") into the poem, their watery contribution cannot do what God's fire can. Readers of "I am a little world" are told in no uncertain terms that they remain bystanders and onlookers; they are allowed to watch as the poet wrestles with his Maker and with his own tropes, but he makes it quite clear that their response is not, in the final analysis, what matters to him. They cannot save him; they cannot answer his prayer.

It is in other, more secular forms—the love poem, the seduction lyric, the verse letter—that the human reader's response truly matters, not only to the poet as an individual—

insofar as the reader's reception of his poem determines something in his relationship with that reader—but also within the world of the text, in the production of its meaning. As Donne sees it, it is God who will choose whether to *"Deigne at [his] hands"* the crown of *La Corona* and whether to grace the fiery tropes of "I am a little world" with Eucharistic presence; but in secular poems to friends and patronesses, poems in which the implied reader or projected auditor is a man the speaker knows or a woman he hopes to know better, the poet's project is directed toward shaping the responses of a human being. It is to those poems that I—as one such reader—now turn my face.

II

Secular Poetry

FOUR

ॐ

Toward An Anti-Petrarchan Love-Religion: "Aire and Angels"

Donne's divine poetry is—as we have seen—shaped by his response to Sidney, who portrays Petrarchan lyric as idolatrous. Many other devotional lyricists of the seventeenth century, both Protestant and Catholic, also object to secular Petrarchism; but they often express their disapproval by baptizing Petrarchan poetics, redirecting the familiar conceits and oxymora of the Petrarchan lover towards a divine Beloved, or portraying Jesus's sufferings in Petrarchan language. The latter is Robert Southwell's strategy in "The Burning Babe," where the supremely loving Christ child is "scorched by excessive heat" and "floods of tears did shed / As though his floods should quench his flames which with his tears were fed" (5–6). Christ is here the *true* Petrarchan lover, compared with whom men like Astrophil are mere lustful imposters. But he is still a Petrarchan; his suffering love is an oxymoronic

145

blend of fire and flood. Similarly, George Herbert objects to Petrarchan verse forms and conceits only insofar as poets use them in pursuit of profane love. "Why are not *Sonnets* made of thee?" (5), he asks God in the sonnet, "My God, where is that ancient heat"; and in another sonnet, "Sure Lord, there is enough in thee to dry / Oceans of *Ink*," he argues that, since "Roses and Lillies speak thee; . . . to make / A pair of Cheeks of them is thy abuse" (6–7). Neither Southwell nor Herbert finds Petrarchan images or attitudes particularly problematic in and of themselves; they are acceptable and even serviceable when applied to the worship of God.[1]

But Donne is concerned less with the gap between the sacred and the profane than with the gap between the effectual and the ineffectual, between sacramental inscription and self-defeating sigh. For him, Petrarchism is problematic even in a sacred context precisely because it is the poetics of an eternally suffering, definitively frustrated longing, rather than of love's fruition. Thus, his divine poems are less concerned to reject profane love-poetry in favor of sacred verse, than to illustrate the hazards and disadvantages of using Petrarchan poetic strategies in any context.

For a Petrarchan speaker like the one who begins his sonnet with the cry, "O Might those sighes and teares returne againe," the irony is double: a repentant Petrarchan lover, having spent the days of his "Idolatry" (5) "mourn[ing] in vaine" (4), does not even have the "remembrance of past joyes, for reliefe" (11); and insofar as he retains a Petrarchan pose—writing a sonnet with a Petrarchan rhyme scheme, beginning with a sighing "O," adorning his verse with "showres of raine" (5), and meditating on his "vehement griefe" (13) rather than addressing his Beloved, he remains the ineffectual suitor—the "(poore) me" (12) who once failed to win his lady's grace and now wallows, in spite of the fact that he does "repent" (7), in a "holy discontent" (3) that does not even mention God's grace, much less call upon him for relief.[2]

The Holy Sonneteer's desire to stop what he is doing and to "Mourne with some fruit" (4) reflects an impulse repeatedly expressed in Donne's secular love lyrics. Donne's lovers, no less than his repentant personae, long to turn away from the Petrarchist's self-defeating moans; they repeatedly express the desire that they may turn lyric laments into conduits of erotic grace, that they may convert Petrarchan frustration into emotional communion. Whether or not they succeed in their flight from poetic Tradition, however, is often ambiguous. Indeed, Donne's *Songs and Sonets* demonstrate that, as complicated as the spiritual transition from Recusancy to Protestant priesthood must have been for Donne, it was no less difficult—in aesthetic terms—for an English poet of the late sixteenth century to "reform" the poetics of unconsummated desire and become a post-Petrarchan lyricist.

In "Aire and Angels," the reader can hear one speaker's account of his conversion from Petrarchan adoration to belief in reciprocal devotion. He began, he explains, by loving an abstract notion, an ideal "thee" without any specific identity:

> Twice or thrice had I loved thee,
> Before I knew thy face or name;
> So in a voice, so in a shapelesse flame,
> *Angells* affect us oft, and worship'd bee . . .
>
> (1–4)

Before he came to love any one lady in particular, these lines suggest, the speaker was in love with his own lyricality, his own poetic "voice" (3); indeed, like Petrarch in the highly self-referential and metapoetic *Rime sparse*, he idolized and "worship'd" (4) the "shapeless flame" (3) of poetic inspiration itself. And though he has now progressed beyond that stage of his history, the speaker does not condemn his former Angel-worship; on the contrary, he seems as casually comfortable with the memory of his abstract love as a libertine would be with the hazy recollection of just how many times he had slept with a particular woman. In fact, the first line of the poem, "Twice or thrice had I loved thee," seems deliberately crafted to sound like the opposite of what it is; the reader is prompted to expect an account of carnal experiences past, rather than a recollection of idealism past. But perhaps the suggested resemblance between the Petrarchan idealist and the Don Juan is part of Donne's point: the realm of sheer imagination is the Petrarchan lover's playground, no less than the court or the city is the libertine's; and though he worships rather than fornicates, he finds later that the specifics of his love are no less cloudy and difficult to recall with precision.[3]

As he recounts his gradual conversion from idealized love to his present love for the woman whom he addresses, the speaker of "Aire and Angels" presents the stages of his progress in terms that correspond to Theseus's condescending account of poetic composition in *A Midsummer Night's Dream*: "[A]s imagination bodies forth / The forms of things unknown," the skeptical Duke informs his Amazon bride Hippolyta, "the poet's pen / Turns them to shapes, and gives to airy nothing / A local habitation and a name" (5.1.14–17).[4] Like Theseus' poet, the speaker of "Aire and Angels" began (so he says, using the past tense) by dealing in the realm "of things unknown." He loved a "shapelesse flame" (3) or disembodied, abstract "voice" (3) that "affect[ed]" him (4) even though he had no knowledge of its owner's identity; he did not know her "face or name" (2). He began to give form to his original abstract ideal, however, when he came into the presence of the woman to whom the poem is addressed; but, he tells her, she was at first nothing more than what Theseus would call the "local habitation" of his imagination's "airy nothing": "Still when, to where thou wert, I came, / Some lovely glorious nothing I did see" (*Air*, 5–6). Thus, the speaker explains, he proceeded to give his "airy nothing . . . a name"—to use Theseus's terms once again; that is, he made sure to learn "what" and "who" she was, and thus came to practice a full-fledged Petrarchan adoration of one fair lady in particular. Rounding out the first stanza of "Aire and Angels" at the sonnet-like length of 14 lines, Donne's persona describes his surrender to the Petrarchan convention of the Lady's features as Cupid's dwelling places: "now / That [Love] assume thy body, I allow, / And fixe it selfe in thy lip, eye, and brow" (12–14).

In the second stanza of the poem, however, the speaker—like Sidney's Astrophil—finds that a Petrarchan lover with a "Laura" of flesh-and-blood will never find satisfaction as long as he merely worships an unresponsive beauty. In "allow[ing]" love to "fixe it selfe in" the lady's "lip, eye, and brow," the lover of "Aire and Angels" has made the mistake that the speaker of "Elegie: Loves Progress" warns against when he tells men not to be diverted from "the right true end of love" (2) by "set[ting] out at the face" (40) and fixating on such distracting "Ambushes" as the "hair" (41), "brow" (43), "Nose" (46), and "lips" (53). It is of no use to a lover if love inhabits the lady's features, for such an incarnation is mere surface penetration, and it leaves the lady herself emotionally untouched. Indeed, in sonnet 11 of *Astrophil and Stella*, the love that sets traps in Stella's cheeks and plays "bo-peep" in her décolletage is, Astrophil fumes, a "fool" who, "Playing and shining in each outward part" of Stella, does not even try "to get into her heart" (11–14). In Donne's poem, as in Sidney's sequence, the Petrarchan lover realizes that he has become helplessly fixated on what his eyes perceive and that he has thus failed to receive the erotic and emotional grace that the lady might bestow.[5] Her enchanting beauty, thus reified and idolized, is a sacrament empty of meaning, an outward sign that corresponds to no inward grace; and in failing to grasp the full significance of "the visible signe," the lover has, to borrow a phrase from Calvin, "stode amasedly gazing at it" (*Inst.* 4.14.4).[6] He has been stupefied.

But now he realizes his mistake:

> I saw, I had loves pinnace overfraught,
>   Ev'ry thy haire for love to worke upon
> Is much too much, some fitter must be sought;
>   For, nor in nothing, nor in things
> Extreme, and scattring bright, can love inhere. . . .
>
> (*Air*, 18–22)

As Achsah Guibbory points out, stanza two introduces a tense shift; the speaker moves from a present tense "now" at the end of stanza one (when the speaker "allow[s]" love to "assume" the lady's features) to a past tense formulation when he says that he "saw [he] had loves pinnace overfraught" (18) in affording love that liberty ("Donne, the Idea of Woman," 106). Guibbory argues, moreover, that "the bawdy innuendoes of 'take a body' [10] and 'assume thy body' [13]" imply that, in the interim between the "now" of stanza one and the rueful hindsight of stanza two, "the speaker and his mistress have had sexual relations" (106). But this seems to me too hasty a conclusion; the speaker's image of "loves pinnace overfraught" (18) recalls quite tellingly Petrarch's nautical portrayal of erotic frustration and despair in *Rime sparse* 189, "My ship laden with forgetfulness."[7] And in Donne's poem, the lover's problem seems to arise from the fact that he has as yet gained no access to what the speaker of "Loves Progress" calls "the Centrique part" of his lady.[8] Though it might be true that his phallic "love" *could* "inhere" (22) in that female "nothing" (21), the speaker of "Aire and Angels" has experienced only the "lovely glorious nothing" (6) of neo-Platonic idealism and the "overfraught" fixation (18) of Petrarchan blazoning, which "allow[s]" love to inhere, not in the "Centrique part," but in the extremities and excrescences of the body, "things extreme and scattring bright," like the hands and hair.[9]

Thus, as Slights observes, the speaker has grown weary:

> Although his dissatisfaction with this phase of love's progress
> is usually explained either as the degeneracy of love into lust

or the overwhelming of love by admiration, . . . [a] simpler, and more obvious explanation of the ship of love sinking under the demands of female beauty is boredom. Rather like Andrew Marvell's lover who does not have a hundred years to praise his mistress's eyes, Donne's lover thinks that "Ev'ry thy haire for love to worke upon / Is much too much" (19–20). (102)

Like Marvell's speaker, moreover, the lover of "Aire and Angels" realizes—or comes to realize—that he will never be physically requited as long as he remains trapped in the poetics of the blazon, devoted to "things extreme and scattring bright." In rejecting such "things," Donne's lover makes clear his conviction that the reified, jewel-like images strewn through works like Petrarch's *Rime sparse* cannot serve as effectual instruments to unite male and female; they float free of that correspondence between signifier and signified that—according to Augustinian sacramental semiotics—must be maintained if signs are to function sacramentally as means of grace (which is to say, in the case of a love lyric, as a means of attaining the beloved's favor).

Thus, with the "Then . . ." that begins the octave of his second "sonnet," the speaker of "Aire and Angels" proposes a new model of love, in which "Angells" (27) are male, not female, and "womens love" (28) is the "spheare" (25) or "pure" body (24) of "Aire" (27) in which the even purer angelic spirit of "mens" love (28) incarnates itself. What purposes does this concluding lesson in angelology serve? Though the speaker hints at sweet intimacy in line 25—"So thy love may be my loves spheare"—the sense of mutuality that the poem would have if it ended there is strained, if not fully subverted, by the pontificating tone of the generalizations in the poem's last three lines.[10] These seem to speak less to the lady than to readers of the poem in general: "Just such disparitie / As is twixt Aire and Angells puritie, / 'Twixt womens love, and mens will ever bee" (26–28). The tone is that of a dispassionate lecturer, rather than of an ardent angel still seeking to work his way into the airy body he desires. As Herz points out, moreover, the "angelic sex change" in the poem—the unexplained shift from the idealized Petrarchan woman as angel to the requited male lover as angel—"should possibly provoke more unease than it seems to have" ("Resisting," 30). As Herz asks, "If there is no clearly differentiated he and she, then just what is this disparity all about?" (30)

At least one of the things that it is about, I would suggest, is the lack of clear differentiation between lover and beloved in an essentially narcissistic Petrarchan poetics, where the female beloved reflects and is generated by the male lover's own mind, where the words "my love" may interchangeably refer either to the poet's feelings or to the woman that his poetic imagination has invented and defined.[11] Donne's speaker inverts his own conceits in order to insist on a "disparity" between lover and beloved, male and female, precisely because he desires to escape the solipsism of his own imagination and to experience a love in which there really is a "thou" as well as an "I."[12] But that task, the poem reveals, is problematic. As Herz remarks earlier in the same essay, "Donne might mock the Petrarchan mode on the level of style (those sigh tempests and such heavy weathers), but in the construction of his subjectivity he is remarkably close to Petrarch" ("Resisting," 28.) I would add only that he is also remarkably conscious of and uncomfortable with this fact, and that many of his love lyrics are—to alter Shakespeare's phrase—sessions of unquiet thought about the matter; these poems critique, at a level deeper than that of stylistics, their makers' own tendency to Petrarchize. And in some of the best of them, Donne specifically associates Petrarchan love and poetry with Catholicism and the sacraments of the Roman Church.

Donne's Catholic Petrarchans

Donne establishes the ruling conceit for the first part of "Satyre III" when he praises "our Mistresse faire Religion" (5): men's denominational preferences are as various as their tastes in women. Crants the Calvinist (49–54) loves a "sullen" country girl; the conforming English Protestant, Graius (55–62), settles for the fiancée his "Godfathers" pick; and the non-commital Graccus (65–69) is "The Indifferent," who will commit himself only to variety.[1] Given these characterizations, one might expect the Roman Catholic, Mirreus, to be in love with a whore, a painted papal moll like Duessa; and indeed his mistress is clothed in the "brave" frippery to which Protestants "will not be inthrall'd" (49). But she is not much of a seductress; her lover is having trouble tracking her down:

> Mirreus
> Thinking her unhous'd here, and fled from us,
> Seekes her at Rome, there, because hee doth know
> That shee was there a thousand yeares agoe,

153

He loves her ragges so, as wee here obey
The statecloth where the Prince sate yesterday.

(43–48)

Mirreus's pursuit of an evasive mistress has distinctly Petrarchan overtones. His beloved has, like Daphne, "fled" the
place in which her beauties might have been profaned; and so
he is led "far astray . . . pursuing her who has turned in flight"
(Petrarch, *Rime sparse* 6:1–2). Like Petrarch, he fetishizes his
lady's apparel and adores an absent presence.[2]

The satire's parallel between Catholicism and Petrarchism
points to a related analogy in Donne's love poetry, where the
attitudes and utterances of unrequited lovers are often reminiscent of specifically Roman piety. Donne finds that the
religion of love has more than one denomination; and his
Petrarchan speakers—faced with the rejection of their faith
in favor of sexual pragmatism, jolly promiscuity, or mutual
devotion—speak in defensive Counter-Reformation accents.
Their discourses of desire uphold a creed of nonfulfillment,
assert the efficacy of erotic relics and sacraments, and pro-
claim invalid any love-doctrine that challenges the orthodoxy
of frustration. Indeed, some of the most stubbornly Petrarchan
personae in the *Songs and Sonets*—the speakers of "Loves
Deitie," "The Funerall," and "Twicknam Garden"—redefine
both love and desire in order to uphold the ways of their
tradition-bound "faith" and resist the temptation of requited
lovers' more expedient practice.

Petrarchism, Papacy, and Poetic Impotence in "Love's Deitie"

The speaker of "Loves Deitie" is in a mood to challenge
Petrarchan discourse on the most fundamental level; he wants
to redefine its vocabulary: "It cannot bee / Love, till I love
her, that loves mee" (13–14). His frustrated desire is defined
as "love," he argues, only since the perverse young "god of
Love" (2)—backed by "custome" (6)—imposed the "destinie"

(5) of unrequited passion upon him. Thus, he wishes to return to the practices of those who "dyed before" the bad little boy was born (2); "hee, who then lov'd most" never "Sunke so low, as to love one which did scorne" (3–4). If contemporary lovers rose up to "ungod" the willful Cupid, the speaker thinks, they could return to the nobler ways of the ancients (20). He no sooner proposes (19) that they overthrow the deity's "Tyrannie," however, than he recants his rebellious words. In the final stanza, he declares that he would be "loth" to see his lady requite him since she already loves another, and "Falshood is worse then hate" (26, 27).

Andreasen reads the poem as affirming the values Petrarch himself embraces at the end of the *Rime sparse*, when he acknowledges Laura's moral rectitude and admits that her acquiescence would have destroyed them both. Donne's speaker, Andreasen argues, "accepts traditional morality through his recognition that [the lady's] infidelity would be worse than rejection, however much he might long for reciprocity" (137, 138). The central contest of the poem, seen in these terms, is that between moral and immoral impulses. But Andreasen's discussion is rich with the language of Reformation controversy: the lover rebels against "tradition by appealing to the earliest era of love"; he will recognize "only the early apostolic era as the proper precedent" and maintains this "mood of iconoclasm" until the sudden reversal of the final stanza; the whole is "a contrast between . . . tradition . . . and reformation" (137–38). According to this reading—which is based upon the terms the poem itself establishes—the "custome" the speaker finally reaffirms is not "traditional morality," but traditional religion; and that, in a Protestant milieu, is not the same thing at all. The speaker has not struggled onto moral high ground; rather, he has made an unsuccessful attempt to abjure Petrarchan frustration, which is troped in the poem as love's Papistry.

Central to the speaker's un-Reformed love religion is the

spurious pontifical authority of the love god himself. The
speaker's indictment of the deity resembles Donne's Protestant analysis of papal history: the Pope's claims to universal
primacy are based upon the teachings of pious men who could
not realize how their doctrines would later be twisted; for "the
Ancients spoke of many . . . things controverted now . . . [and]
never suspected that so impious a sense would have been put
upon their words, nor those opinions and doctrines so mis-
chievously advanced, as they have been since" (*Sermons* 3:316).
In the poem, the speaker is "Sure, [that] they which made
[Cupid] god, meant not so much" (8) as to have him preside
over frustrated desire; but, with a display of pope-like ambition, this "moderne god will now extend / His vast prerogative,
as far as Jove" (15–16). Like the Bishop of Rome, the love god
does have a legitimate ecclesiastical role to play; and when,
"in his young godhead" he "practis'd" only his duly appointed
function (9), he fulfilled the same role as the legendary Bishop
Valentine, uniting male and female, lover and beloved: "[W]hen
an even flame two hearts did touch, / His office was indul-
gently to fit / Actives to passives" (10–12).[3] But now, having
brought under his rule many things which have nothing to do
with weddings—resentment, unconsecrated desire, letters sent
from afar, poetry of formal compliment and complaint, and
all courtly or Petrarchan situations which make men "rage . . .
lust . . . write . . . commend" (17)—this renegade Cupid is a
pope who grasps at secular authority and abuses the faithful.

Thus, when the speaker of "Loves Deitie" recants his protestations and renews his allegiance to the Petrarchan love
god, he is plunging back into erotic recusancy. Both he and
his lady ought, he feels, to persevere in the faith they currently profess:

> [W]hy murmure I,
> As though I felt the worst that love could doe?
> Love might make me leave loving, or might trie
> A deeper plague, to make her love mee too,

> Which, since she loves before, I'am loth to see;
> Falshood is worse then hate; and that must bee,
>   If shee whom I love, should love mee.

(22–28)

As the speaker sees it, a relationship founded on female infidelity would be a "plague" worse than either ongoing frustration or the quenching of his own ardor. And self-interest, no less than respect for the "moral order" determines his feelings; for, when considered in light of the speaker's fear that he has not yet "felt the *worst* that love could doe" (23), the thought "Falshood is *worse* then hate" (27) implies a concern lest he endure her infidelity rather than her disdain.

He is convinced that duplicity and betrayal "must bee" his lot if she requites him, for he assumes that if he is not her first paramour, he will not be her last. Implicit in his preference for unrequited passion is a smug logic: as long as one remains frustrated, one will never sprout the cuckold's horns. In "The Indifferent," a libertine Venus condemns to inevitable cuckoldry those "Heretiques" (24) who "thinke to stablish dangerous constancie" (25); the Cupid of "Loves Deitie" enforces a bitterly monogamous Petrarchan faith that is in some respects exactly opposed to his mother's religion of "sweetest . . . Variety" (*Ind*, 20). But mutual devotion is *anathema* in both erotic denominations, and the speaker of "Loves Deitie" is thus convinced that female reciprocity is a bad thing. Any "Rebell and Atheist" who tries to break free from the creed of nonfulfillment will, he concludes, get what is coming to him; the only way to avoid the "worst that love could doe" is to stay within the One True Church of frustrated desire.

The language of Petrarchan poetry helps to ensure that lovers will do just that; it is a discourse that perpetuates the dubious pleasures of unconsummated longing. In a verse letter to the Countess of Huntingdon, Donne promises Elizabeth Stanley Hastings that he will not "vexe [her] eyes" (*HuntUn*, 21) with a cruciform verbal icon, the "crosse-arm'd Elegie" of

Petrarchan suffering (22). For such utterances are, he insists, perversely effectual; they generate the very frustration they purport to lament: he "Who first look'd sad, griev'd, pin'd, and shew'd his paine, / Was he that first taught women, to disdaine" (35–36). This mock foundation-myth proposes that Petrarchan art is a self-fulfilling prophecy and identifies Petrarchan desire as "love . . . with such fatall weaknesse made, / That it destroyes it selfe with its owne shade" (33–34). The passive construction "love . . . made" punningly refers to love as poetic product ("made" weak in the sense of "badly composed"), as well as to ineffectual wooing as feeble lovemaking. Congenitally flawed, "made" weak from the start, the lover's murky discourse (the "shade" or shadow he casts) is reflexively fatal; his anguished state both originates in and is destroyed by its own utterance, "that thing [that] whispers it selfe away" (30). The inverse of seduction poetry, the Petrarchan lament ensures that no sexual persuasion will take place; so for those pursuing "The right true end of love" (*ElProg* 2), the faint moans of "whining Poëtry" (*Triple* 3) prove worse than useless.

But is any poetry worth writing? The speaker of "Satyre II" has his doubts:

> Though Poëtry indeed be such a sinne
> As I thinke that brings dearths, and Spaniards in,
> Though like the Pestilence and old fashion'd love,
> Ridlingly it catch men; and doth remove
> Never, till it be sterv'd out; yet their state
> Is poore, disarm'd, like Papists, not worth hate.
>
> (5–10)

The lines associate poverty stricken rhymers with both Catholicism and the maladies of Petrarchan desire; their self-defeating "sinne" weakens England and makes it vulnerable to the extravagant fashions and ultra-Catholic aggressions of Spain, while they themselves are afflicted with the plague-like disease of "old fashion'd love": pitiable and impotent, they suffer its "Ridlingly" paradoxical symptom of icy fire, fever and chills.

The speaker mocks every kind of poet, from the professional playwright to the dilettante lyricist; but most important as a guide to the *Songs and Sonets* is his comment on the writer who "would move Love by rithmes" (17). Such efforts are useless, he argues, for "witchcrafts charms / Bring not now their old feares, nor their old harmes" (17–18). Donne plays upon a popular Reformation theme—compare Corbett's "Faeryes Farewell"—that associated the Catholic past with a now-defunct magic. The writer of feeble Petrarchan pleas finds himself thwarted in the pursuit of sex because he trusts in the poetic equivalent of "hocus-pocus"; his superstitious mumblings make no impression on the women of the satirist's reformed and enlightened age.

Martyrdom, Idolatry, and Magic in "The Funerall"

"Satyre II" defines the art of the love lyric as an outmoded magic; but in "The Funerall," a Petrarchan nonetheless tries his hand at what the satirist calls "witchcrafts charms." The speaker's lady has denied him sexual grace; she has refused to "save" him from the death of frustration (*Fun*, 24); and although she has given her admirer a "subtile wreath" of her hair (3), he cannot be certain just "What . . . shee meant by'it" (17). He does, however, find his own use for the token: since the woven circlet is all that he has of the lady, he makes a fetish of it.[4] Calling it her representative, he insists that it be treated with all the reverence due to her:

> Who ever comes to shroud me, do not harme
> Nor question much
> That subtile wreath of haire, which crowns my arme;
> The mystery, the signe you must not touch,
> For 'tis my outward Soule,

Viceroy to that, which then to heaven being gone,
   Will leave this to controule,
And kccpc thcsc limbes, her Provinces, from dissolution.

                                                              (1–8)

In referring to the bracelet as the "viceroy" of his body's spiritual monarch, the lover proclaims it the absent presence both of his own soul and of the lady whose "controule" over him the bracelet signifies and exercises.

As the poem proceeds, his attitude becomes more and more recognizably idolatrous and, from the perspective established in "Satyre III," Romanist. Mirreus and his coreligionists call the Pope Christ's vicar and reverence him as the regent of the King who has "to heaven . . . gone." And from the Protestant perspective, they commit idolatry in adoring the Sacrament, for in doing so they "worshippe the giftes in steede of the giuer himselfe" (Calvin, *Inst.* 4.17.36). Similarly, this lover honors the inanimate "Viceroy," his beloved's gift to him, as he would the lady herself. Indeed, he deals with frustration precisely as does the Catholic of "Satyre III": he loves his mistress' "ragges so, as [subjects] obey / The statecloth where the Prince sate yesterday." But the speaker feels that his monarch has condemned him to death. By withholding herself from the speaker and granting him only an empty sign of the grace that might have saved him, the lady has killed him.

In the final stanza, then, he seeks revenge. He reinterprets the wreath of hair once more and, with insolent disregard for the lady's intended meaning, works his own will upon the sign:

What ere shee meant by'it, bury it with me,
   For since I am
Loves martyr, it might breed idolatrie,
If into others hands these Reliques came;
   As 'twas humility
To'afford to it all that a Soule can doe,

> So, 'tis some bravery,
> That since you would save none of mee, I bury some of you.
>
> (17–24)

At first, it would seem that the lover here develops Protestant scruples about the veneration of the bracelet. But his Reformation sentiments appear deeply ironic, given the idolatrous attitude underlying the opening stanza, where his reification of the sign allowed him to feel that he was reverencing the lady in reverencing it. In the final lines, that same literalism—what theologians would call a "carnal" understanding—makes him gloat over the violence he can do to the symbol that represents her.

Protestants accused the Roman clergy of a gross disregard for God's intentions in instituting the Eucharist, and they detected in the doctrine of Eucharistic sacrifice a hubristic desire to control the Giver of the sign: to make Him and then slay Him through the magic of the Mass, to entomb Him through the reservation of the Host.[5] The speaker of "The Funerall" is guilty of just such "bravery." The lady has given him a sign of herself, and "What ere shee meant by'it," he can use it to love her to death. His talisman will be wrapped into his winding sheet and lie with him forever in the grave.

The speaker hints at the emotional logic underlying his spite when he speaks of the wreath as something that can reproduce. He insists that the ring of hair be buried with him lest it "breed idolatrie" in others; it has already bred that semiotic sin in him. The spiritual adultery he has committed in his fetishistic relation with the signifier is the only kind of sex he has been allowed. But like most Renaissance lovers, he is uncomfortable with the idea that he might not be the only one. Thus, in taking precautions to insure that his beloved object does not "breed" with someone else, he is protecting, not the other men who might handle it, but himself. Their idolatry would give them as much of the lady as he has possessed, and he will brook no rivals.[6] This jealous concern to protect his prerogative reinforces the satirical parallel linking the speaker to the priesthood of the Roman Church. Not only does he parody the Eucharistic Sacrifice by imposing his own murderous will upon the sign his deity has left him, but he guards against the possibility that his "subtile . . . mystery" (3, 4) should fall into unconsecrated "hands" (20). "The mystery, the signe you must not touch," he insists (4), recalling the Tridentine insistence that the laity may neither administer the sacrament nor touch the vessels in which it is contained.[7]

Even more important in establishing an analogy between the speaker and the Roman Catholic clergy is the speaker's insistence that he dies as "Loves martyr" (19). This claim, and the manner in which he asserts it, illustrates "That there may be"—as Donne puts it in *Pseudo-Martyr*—"an inordinate and corrupt affectation of Martyrdome" (A1r).[8] In *Pseudo-Martyr*, his treatise on the Oath of Allegiance controversy, Donne argues that the "the Roman Religion doth . . . mis-encourage and excite men to this vitious affectation" and that "in the Romane Church the Jesuits exceed all others . . . in all those points, which beget or cherish this corrupt desire of false-Martyrdome" (A1r).[9] Thus, in "The Funerall," the speaker's Petrarchan dedication to an unrequited passion identifies him as the Jesuit pseudo-martyr of love; and by portraying Petrarchan love as a species of the Jesuits' "vitious affectation," Donne implies a rejection of Petarchism no less dramatic than his rejection of Jesuit doctrine in *Pseudo-Martyr*.

But the poet's evocation of Petrarchism as a cunningly erroneous and self-destructive religion remains equivocal; for Donne brings to the analogy between Petrarchan lover and Jesuit martyr a deeply ambivalent attitude toward the Society of Jesus.[10] In attacking the Jesuits' "corrupt desire of false-Martyrdome," *Pseudo-Martyr* condemns what Donne elsewhere calls his own "sickly inclination" and attributes to early contact with men who harbored such desire: at the beginning of *Biathanatos*, he explains his interest in the topic of justifiable suicide by noting that he had his "first breeding and conversation with men of a suppressed and afflicted religion, accustomed to the despite of death and hungry of an imagined Martyrdom" (*Biathanatos*, 39). In these lines, which describe propensities that he attributes to the Jesuits in *Pseudo-Martyr*, Donne maintains an equivocal stance toward the would-be martyrs he knew in his youth; his language is simultaneously sympathetic and denigratory. In saying that their Religion was "afflicted," he is on one level pointing out that it was subject to cruel persecution, and on another implying that it was diseased, plagued by its own tendency to self-destruction. And in what sense was the Martyrdom hungered for by the men in question "imagined"? Donne's modifier on one level mocks their aspirations, calling the martyrdom they longed for *imaginary* and arguing (as *Pseudo-Martyr* does) that it is suicide rather than true martyrdom. But the point of *Biathanatos* is to explore whether there may be a circumstance in which suicide is an act of piety rather than a sin, and the word "imagined" may also be interpreted to mean that the martyrdom longed for by Donne's priestly relatives and acquaintances was quite real, "imagined" only in that it was still vividly envisioned rather than accomplished. Donne sees it both ways; he anatomizes a tradition he knows from within, evoking his ambivalence both toward the policies of a government seeking to stamp out the "Old Religion" and toward the ultramontane dogmatism of men claiming to represent it as martyrs.[11]

The poetry of Petrarchan desire is also a tradition Donne knows from within; and when he impugns "old fashion'd love" by making the Petrarchan speaker of "The Funerall" a Jesuit-like martyr to unrequited love, his censure of Petrarchism is no less ambivalent. The persona—like the Catholics Donne spoke of in *Biathanatos*—is a man "of a suppressed and afflicted Religion, . . . hungry of an imagined Martyrdom"; and his Religion—Petrarchan love—is both his strength and his weakness, his virtue and his vice.

Petrarchan Envy and the Jesuit Threat in "Twicknam Garden"

If the speaker of "The Funerall" is the Jesuit pseudo-martyr of love, the "selfe traytor" of "Twicknam garden" (5) is his more aggressive fellow-priest, a man whose Petrarchan religion leads him—as the English feared that the Jesuits' religion led them—to commit acts of aggression against those who have rejected his beliefs. In "The Funerall," the lover's attitude toward other males is purely defensive; but the Arch-Petrarchan of "Twicknam garden" puts erotic recusancy on the offensive and offers successful lovers a Eucharist of suspicion. Like a Jesuit missionary seeking (as the English saw it) to disturb the peace of Protestant England, he seeks to drive a wedge between requited men and the women they love. Satisfying his own perverse desire by subverting consummated love, he pushes the doctrine of Petrarchan frustration to an alarmingly aggressive extreme and makes his poem into a sacrament of envious nonfulfillment.

In the first stanza, he attributes to his frustrated longing a perverse sacramental efficacy; the "spider love" which torments him is a priest performing poisonous magic: it "transubstantiates all, / And can convert Manna to gall" (6–7). Under the influence of such a powerful force, the speaker himself becomes an agent of corruption; the garden into which he has entered now "may thoroughly be thought / True Paradise," for he has "the serpent brought" (8–9). As both a phallic symbol and an emblem of primal envy, the snake image establishes an alarming affinity between ruthless *invidia* and frustrated masculine desire. The remainder of the poem plays upon the implications of that affinity.

In the second stanza, the lover objects to the joys of spring-time itself. His feeling that it would be "wholsomer" for him if "winter did / Benight the glory of this place" (10–11) is often compared with Petrarch's sensation in the well-known "Zefiro torna," and the parallels are valid as far as they go: in each lyric, the speaker contrasts his own emotional state with the sweetness of the season.[12] But in Petrarch, the poet's subjectivity is powerful enough to ruin the spring for him; objective reality is of no concern to him, and he does not desire to work quasi-magical alterations in the realm outside his own consciousness. Donne's speaker has a state of mind less powerfully detached, and he shows more aggression; still able to perceive the beauties around him, he *wills* that they might be marred. Petrarch feels that "the singing of little birds, and the flowering of meadows, and virtuous gentle gestures in beautiful ladies are a wilderness and cruel, savage beasts" (*Rime sparse* 310:12–14). His perceptions are utterly distorted, and social reality is flattened out into a backdrop for autonomous subjectivity; the ladies' gestures become a static part of the landscape upon which the author's feelings are projected. In Donne's poem, the process is reversed; the landscape is invested with quasi-social characteristics, and the trees become insensitive onlookers whose derision fuels the speaker's anger and resentment. He sees in the garden's beauty the laughing faces of others who have no sympathy for him, and he responds with the dark wish "that a grave frost did forbid / These trees to laugh, and mocke mee to my face" (12–13).

He is determined, however, not to "leave this garden" (15). Like the Jesuits whose martyrdom Donne questions in *Pseudo-Martyr*, he refuses to depart from "this place" (8, 11) in which he may betray himself as a "selfe traytor[ous]" witness to the power that "convert[s]" and "transubstantiates all" (7, 6)— all, that is, save the chaste "shee" who is *semper eadem* and whose version of "truth kills" him (24, 25).[13] Thus, in order that he "may not . . . Indure" the "disgrace" of the trees' mocking laughter, he asks that Love, that powerful transformer of substances, change him into "Some senslesse peece of this place" (16): "Make me a mandrake, so I may groane here, / Or a stone fountaine weeping out my yeare" (17–18). The request would at first seem to be a retreat from the petty malevolence in the first half of the stanza, a move toward a more conventional Petrarchism. For in the *Rime sparse*, metamorphosis is the ultimate effect of love's agonies; mythic transmutation allows the poet to express his emotion through richly significant forms.[14] Indeed, as a mandrake, the speaker of "Twicknam Garden" might be beneficial to other lovers, since the plant is traditionally believed to function as an aphrodisiac and fertility charm.[15]

It is on the fountain form that he settles, however, as he elaborates his fantasy in the final stanza:

> Hither with christall vyals, lovers come,
>> And take my teares, which are loves wine,
>> And try your mistresse Teares at home,
> For all are false, that tast not just like mine;
>> Alas, hearts do not in eyes shine,
> Nor can you more judge womans thoughts by teares,
>> Then by her shadow, what she weares.
> O perverse sexe, where none is true but shee,
>> Who's therefore true, because her truth kills mee.
>
> (19–27)

By choosing to become a fountain, the speaker completes an ironic analogy—first hinted at in the opening stanza—between himself and Christ. He has come, grief-stricken and anguished, to his own Garden of Gethsemane, and he now parodies the Savior's Eucharistic self-offering.[16] Like Jesus, the speaker would give "loves wine" to those seeking Truth; but his tears are the Eucharistic drink neither of Christianity nor of fulfilled eros. Shed in pain and possessed of magical properties, they are the sacramental outpourings of unrequited desire;

but their flavor, he insists, is that of authenticity itself. Thus, he can offer his lachrymal wine to requited lovers as a means of testing women's fidelity.

Men of reformed love-religion—those who have rejected Petrarchan superstition and embraced the joys of mutual desire—must resist jealous qualms. In "The good-morrow," the lovers' waking souls "watch not one another out of feare" (9); and the speaker of "The Anniversarie" aspires to a love stronger than any anxiety: "True and false feares let us refraine" (27). Donne's requited lovers are by no means blind to the possibility that a woman may be unfaithful—they forget it no more than Renaissance Protestants do the danger of idolatry; but they nevertheless confirm their faith in mutual truth, confronting head-on the spectral threat of infidelity. Such speakers treat both their ladies' tears and their own poetic utterances as sacramental witnesses or seals of commitment. Their ears are "fed with true oathes," and their eyes are nourished by the flow of "sweet salt teares" (*Anniv*, 15–16). But the speaker of "Twicknam garden" ministers bitter tears, and his wine feeds suspicion rather than faith; he encourages lovers to cater to their doubts. With the disruptive spirit that the English saw in Jesuit missionaries, he tries to disturb the faith of those who have entered into true love's communion and to replace it with the spurious sacramentalism of the old dispensation. He urges them to collect "loves wine" in "christall vyals" so that they may carry it home and use it as an elixir of truth.[17]

In a sermon preached at St. Paul's, Donne critiques Catholic churchmen who sell the "merchandises" of Rome, proclaiming "the value, and efficacy of uncertain *reliques*, and superstitious charms, and incantations." Such vendors are "Ambassadours to serve their own turns, and do their owne businesse." The English clergy, by contrast, offer free of charge "no other *reliques*, but the commemoration of [Christ's] Passion in the *Sacrament*" (*Sermons* 10:126–27).[18] Those who deal in trinkets and potions supplant the central mysteries of faith for their own gain, and that is precisely what the Twicknam lover does. For, in Donne's *Songs and Sonets*, consummated love has its own central mystery—the reflection of one lover's face in the other's eye, and the trust that "true plaine hearts doe in the faces rest" (*GoodM*, 15); the Twicknam lover discredits this core of emotional faith when he insists that "Alas, hearts do not in eyes shine" (23). In its place, he offers magical assurance: conveniently portable tears for fears. According to the telling logic of Donne's sermon, then, this charm-peddler must be an ambassador to serve his own turn; he must be making a profit of one sort or another.

So what does the Twicknam lover have to gain by offering a truth potion to fulfilled lovers? It would at first seem that he gets nothing more than the chance to vent his resentful feelings toward women: "O perverse sexe, where none is true but shee, / Who's therefore true, because her truth kills mee." His anger is generated by a refusal to perceive the true use of a thing—a refusal which, from a Protestant perspective, is characteristic of Roman sacramentalism.[19] The speaker insists upon defining feminine fidelity not as a positive expression of love for one man, but rather as a weapon of malice to be used against him. In the first stanza, he identifies the only "True Paradise" as that which harbors a serpent; here, he can conceive of no edenic lady, no woman who is one man's *hortus conclusus*, except by accounting for her behavior as an expression of malice. Thus, like "the spider love" itself, he "convert[s] Manna to gall." For in the horn-mad Renaissance, a lady's fidelity is the heavenly bread that sustains her lover; but with his perverse interpretation, the speaker flavors sweet devotion itself with bitterness.

The craving for certainty about a woman's truth—the fatal appetite of the "curioso impertinente," as Cervantes calls him—provides the speaker with a guaranteed market for his tearful wine.[20] It will be difficult for men to ignore the offer of an elixir which detects infidelity, for it nourishes a fear already latent in their hearts.[21] The speaker's assertion that "none is true but" the one he loves is, in essence, a challenge; he dares those who think themselves happy to test the validity of their contentment. And for one lover, the man to whom the Petrarchan's unattainable lady is true, the challenge is a particularly insidious trap. For according to the closing couplet, that man alone will find that his mistress is true; but in so doing, he will learn also that his lady is the object of the speaker's devotion and that she is faithful to him only out of spite toward another.[22]

The speaker's formulation redefines the Petrarchan love triangle in a way that marginalizes the requited male; it casts him as the sexually neutral catalyst of a chemical reaction in which the Petrarchan and his cruel fair are, ironically enough, the active ingredients. The overt misogyny of the closing stanza masks the speaker's real agenda: a redefinition of requited love that places it in the service of the Petrarchan nonrelationship and the poetry of frustration.

In "Twicknam garden," Donne puts Petrarchan metamorphosis to work as a disguised instrument of aggression; he recontextualizes in a social milieu Petrarch's insistence that he has lived "without any envy; for if other lovers have more favorable fortune, a thousand of their pleasures are not worth one of my torments" (*Rime sparse* 231:2–4). This claim, made in isolation from those whom it deflates, is fairly straightforward grandstanding. The disavowal of envy is part and parcel of the claim to infinite superiority of feeling; Petrarch dwells apart in a universe whose very structure differs from that of the worldly lovers of whom he has spoken in the third person. In Donne's poem, however, the speaker addresses requited lovers directly, song becomes social discourse, and the distance breaks down. Having precipitated an encounter between himself and those who have succeeded in love, the speaker must avail himself of new strategies. Uprooted from their self-absorbed and self-reflecting isolation, Donne posits, the utterances of Petrarchan frustration cannot sustain their gem-like perfection; in a direct confrontation with the fulfilled sexuality of requited love, the Petrarchan's claim to a suffering so sublime as to be beyond envy degenerates into a mean-spirited act of sabotage: the fox spreads a rumor about pesticide poisoning among those beasts who *can* reach the grapes.

The speaker's announcement that "all are false, that tast not just like mine" (22) has the ring of a dogmatic hubris which, Donne the preacher insists, Protestants must avoid. They must not, he explains, harbor a "peremptory prejudice upon other mens opinions, that no opinion but thine can be true, in the doctrine of the Sacrament." Rather, he tells his congregation, "exercise thy faith onely, here, and leave . . . disputation to the Schoole" (*Sermons* 7:291). The speaker of "Twicknam garden" gives lovers the opposite advice. Like a Roman Catholic dogmatist, he insists upon his sacrament as the only efficacious and valid alternative to a system of barren, even deceptive signifiers.[23] For, in order to impress upon requited lovers their need for his truth-telling tears, he declares that "hearts do not in eyes shine" (23) and that one can no more "judge womans thoughts by teares, / Then by her shadow, what she weares" (21–22). The speaker thus denies the sacramental validity of female tears, insisting that there is no correspondence between the outward signs and the inward reality which the woman would have her lover believe they represent. He urges his listeners to delve into the nature of the mystery he has impugned; and in so doing, he tempts them to that "Carnality in the understanding . . . concupiscence of disputation" (*Sermons* 2:84) which Donne sees as a characteristic fault of Roman Catholics.

In a sermon, Donne cites Saint Gregory's description of this masochistic inquisitiveness: "The mind of a curious man delights to examine itself upon Interrogatories, which, upon the Racke, it cannot answer, and to vexe it selfe with such doubts as it cannot resolve" (*Sermons* 2:84). In "The Blossom," Donne links such self-torture to frustrated sexuality when the speaker addresses his heart as "thou which lov'st to bee / Subtile to plague thy selfe" (17–18). But the sadistic Petrarchan of "Twicknam garden" satisfies his desire in a slyly complementary way: he facilitates the self-torture of requited hearts, finding his delight in making Iagoesque suggestions.

The poem is an exploration of Petrarchism's darker recesses. But Donne attacks only the things he knows well enough to turn inside out. The Jesuitical wit of *Ignatius His Conclave* fights Counter-Reformation fire with fire. The elaborate arguments of *Biathanatos* reveal suicidal preoccupations in the author of *Pseudo-Martyr*, and a poem like "Twicknam garden" tells us perhaps more than we would like to know about how a psyche prone to frustration and resentment anatomizes such feelings.[24] Years after Donne became a priest of the English Church, we can find him playing games with the many different levels of masculine jealousy. As a preacher, he uses precisely the same strategy as does his Twicknam speaker to warn the benchers of Lincoln's Inn about the dangers posed by—what else?—Jesuits:

> There is a snare laid for thy wife; Her Religion, say they, doth not hinder her husbands preferment, why should she refuse to apply her self to them? We have used to speak proverbially of a Curtain Sermon, as of a shrewd thing; but a Curtain Mass, a Curtain *Requiem*, a snare in thy bed, a snake in thy bosome is somewhat worse. I know not what name we may give to such a womans husband; but I am sure such a wife hath committed adultery, Spiritual Adultery, and that with her husbands knowledge; call him what you will. (*Sermons* 4:138–39)

What are we to make of such tactics? Like those employed in "Twicknam garden," they play less upon desires—sexual or spiritual—than upon fears.

In a much later sermon, Donne defines the preacher's role in terms of earnest and heartfelt wooing: "True Instruction is a making love to the Congregation, and to every soule in it; . . . Wee have no way into your hearts, but by sending our hearts" (*Sermons* 9:350). But this direct approach would not work if those most in need of "Instruction" were not present; and in the sermon on spiritual cuckoldry, addressed to the male professionals and students of Lincoln's Inn, that is precisely the case. Questioning the Protestant fidelity of the lawyers' crypto-Catholic wives, the preacher is faced with a distinctly Petrarchan problem: female absence. The women are, presumably, not on hand to hear the Protestant love-songs of Dr. Donne, and thus we find him resorting to the devious strategies of the Twicknam speaker.[25]

The discourses of frustrated desire turn out, then, to be inseparable from the aggressive maneuvers of envy; and Donne's Catholic Petrarchans have found but one of many ways to play out the drama of invidious sexuality. Throughout the *Songs and Sonets*, Donne explores the deep affinity between the bewitchment of love-longing and the voodoo strategies of malice. Even an apparently requited lover can fear that his mistress will work "Witchcraft by a picture," burning his image in the light of her eye or drowning it in the salt water of her tears.[26] It becomes clear that only the man who can "keep off envies stinging" (*SGo*, 6) can believe himself requited by "a woman true, and faire." In some of the greatest of Donne's love lyrics, couples achieve such confident unassailability; they choose—as do the lovers of "The Anniversarie"—to "refraine" from fears both "True and false." But there are also those like the Twicknam speaker, caught up in a frustrated, spider-like desire, who come to find envy itself erogenous and who satisfy their desire by pricking others with its sharp little sting.

Six

᠅

"The Flea" as Profane Eucharist

For the Petrarchan speaker of "Twicknam garden," love is a spider; but it's the small winged insect that gets the girl. In "The Flea," Donne's most notorious Ovidian seducer has no taste for the bitterly transubstantiated "Manna" and tearful "wine" of frustration; he is intent on sexual fruition. He finds, however, that a sacramental conceit can be applied as wittily to seduction as to Petrarchan complaint. Elevating a flea's consecrated blood, he celebrates a sexual Eucharist within the jet cloister of an insect's exoskeleton.

For at least one seventeenth century admirer of Donne, poems like "The Flea" seemed uniquely efficacious conduits of erotic grace; Jasper Mayne's funeral elegy on Donne in the 1633 edition of the *Poems* urges would-be lovers to take Donne's seduction poetry as their model:

> From this Muse learne to Court, whose power could move
> A Cloystred coldnesse, or a Vestall love,

> And would convey such errands to their eare,
> That Ladies knew no oddes to grant and heare.

(Poems, 394–95)

In these lines, Mayne praises the "power" of Donne's erotic verse partly through subtle allusion; specifically, the image of "Cloystred coldnesse" pays tribute to "The Flea" by recalling the speaker's argument that he and his lady are "cloysterd in these living walls of Jet" (15).[1] Mayne's allusion fails, however, to capture the wit with which Donne applies his religious imagination to the business of seduction. In "The Flea," the cloister image is of the seducer's own making, and he puts it to his own erotic uses; it is a weapon in his arsenal, not—as in Mayne's poem—a metaphor for the female chastity he has under siege. According to Mayne's rather conventional conceit, Donne's rhetoric is powerful enough to burst through the convent wall and melt the snowy virtue of a nun. Donne's speaker, however, addresses not a Carmelite in full habit, but an English girl who lives at home with her "grudg[ing]" parents; and his wit is too finely honed, too specific, to describe the chastity of a post-Reformation English virgin as "Cloystred coldnesse."

Indeed, as M. Thomas Hester argues, the denominational affiliations of the speaker and the lady help to determine the shape of the courtship drama. Consulting Reformation and Counter-Reformation treatises on the controversy over the Eucharist, Hester argues that the speaker in "The Flea" "appropriates the precise lexicon and paradigms of the current theological debate" in which Catholics and Protestants sought to define the word "This" (*Hoc*) as it functions in the all-important assertion, "*Hoc est corpus meum*" ("'this cannot be said,'" 377).[2] The speaker signals the analogy between his argument and the Eucharistic debate "by the reiteration of 'this' (six times in the first nine lines)"; and as the argument unfolds, the "'Catholic' exegete elevates before his 'Protesting' lady" a quasi-Eucharistic sign, telling her that, in essence, *Hoc est corpus nostrum*. For Hester, however, the lady's triumphant gesture upon killing the flea "*marks* . . . the death of the speaker's carnal hopes," for her purpled nail shows "the absence of mystery or miracle in his sexual metonymy," and she is thus able simply to deny "the real sacrifice" of her virginity (Hester, "'this cannot be said,'" 381). According to Hester's reading, then, the poem "traces its own failure" as sexual persuasion, "unless . . . she is to be seduced by the rigor of an erect wit" (377). This phallic image puts a Donnean edge on the Christian concept of redeemed reason (compare Sidney's reference to "erected wit" in the *Defense of Poesy* [217]); and the argument of "The Flea" does depend upon the keenness of that edge.

But Hester's metaphor remains insufficient, for the seductiveness of the speaker's theological wit is a function not of its rigor, but of its delightful flexibility. The poem, I would argue, functions simultaneously on each of several mutually contradictory levels; for, by inscribing the speaker's argument in Eucharistically-charged language, Donne has insured that his signs and verbal gestures will be as polyvalent and as open to debate as the signs and gestures of the sacrament. The Lord's Supper is for one Christian an efficacious sacrifice, for another a merely symbolic action, and for yet another a dynamic event that takes place in the heart of the individual receiver; in the same way, "The Flea" may be read as a Petrarchan tribute, a libertine entrapment, or a true lover's persuasion. The poet assigns a given set of responses to the lady in the white spaces between the stanzas and—in so doing—sets up the shifting strategies the speaker makes in response to "her." But it is the reader of the poem who decides the lady's final answer in the white space following the third stanza and—in so doing—defines the effectiveness and significance of the speaker's argument as a whole. In short, the outcome of the seduction is—as any undergraduate will testify—"left up to the reader."

Interpretations of the Eucharist are, nevertheless, guided

by theologians' readings of authoritative scriptural and patristic texts; indeed, they often allude to the importance of discovering Christ's authorial intention in the words of institution.[3] The options open to the reader of "The Flea" are similarly delimited by what John Shawcross calls the "author's text" (*Intentionality*, 3–4). In the poem, Donne directs reader response not only by using the language of theological debate, but also through his choice of the flea-poem subgenre and his reworking of that lyric type as seduction-poem (in which the speaker addresses a lady) rather than as envious apostrophe (in which the flea itself is addressed).[4]

In the analysis that follows, I explore two different ways of reading the seduction as successful; each depends upon a different reading of the images and arguments presented to the lady who is the "reader" within the text. The first is an anti-Petrarchan, libertine reading, based upon the principles of radical iconoclasm; the second is a response rooted in an English Protestant semiotic, and finds in the speaker's signs and gestures an invitation to genuine erotic communion. This second way of reading the poem helps to explain some intriguing parallels between the woman in the lyric and Anne More Donne as her witty husband constructs her in a prose letter.

However one approaches the text, the lover's strategy suggests from the start that he wishes to anticipate "reader response," for he tailors his approach to suit his lady's wit and temperament. Clearly, she is a resourceful and practical-minded opponent, not to be impressed by helpless longing or ingenious postures of despair. Thus, the speaker's opening gambit employs neither elaborate Petrarchan compliments—which many of Donne's speakers decry as inherently self-defeating—nor the despairingly lascivious alternative of the conventional flea poem, in which an unrequited lover fantasizes about being the flea in his mistress' cleavage.[5] Instead, Donne's speaker addresses the lady directly and attempts to dispense with at least one of her reasons for resisting his advances: the fear of pregnancy. As Hester points out, the lover jokingly alludes both to the Annunciation miracle and to Renaissance theories of conception when he points to the flea as the virgin womb in which "two bloods" are "mingled" with no "sinne, nor shame nor losse of maidenhead." Though *it* "swells with one blood made of two," she needn't fear that her own womb will, for "this, alas, is more then wee would doe" (9).[6]

The lady could, if she had a mind to, play along with this mock-Christian miracle of virginal conception; but she is not impressed. The flea and the argument are both pests; and in the white space between the first and second stanzas, she moves to crush them. The speaker intervenes quickly; but the way in which he does so seems to make matters worse. Leaving behind the argumentative stance and demonstrative terminology of the polemical theologian, the speaker adopts the pleading, prayerful accents of a worshiper:

> Oh stay, three lives in one flea spare,
> Where wee almost, yea more then maryed are.
> This flea is you and I, and this
> Our mariage bed, and mariage temple is;
> Though parents grudge, and you, w'are met,
> And cloysterd in these living walls of Jet.
>   Though use make you apt to kill mee,
>   Let not to that, selfe murder added bee,
>   And sacrilege, three sinnes in killing three.

(10–18)

The speaker here indulges in the Petrarchan hyperbole which he so carefully avoided in the first stanza; he claims to be slain by the lady's cruelty and defines his desire as a holy devotion.[7] At the same time, his phrasing and his choice of imagery lend that devotion a distinctly Catholic character. Indeed, the second stanza puts the erotic theology of the first into full-blown liturgical practice; the speaker consecrates and elevates the flea: "This flea *is*"—hoc est—"you and I"! The literalism of his hocus-pocus cannot but exacerbate the lady's irritation.[8] And as for the "living walls of Jet": what self-respecting Protestant lady would submit to being "cloysterd" anywhere? In Tudor England, the speaker's insistence that the flea is a monastery practically ensures that its walls will be razed, even as his pleading tone, his exaggerated reverence, and his tribute to her "killing" powers virtually solicit the "cruel" response that is *de rigeur* for ladies addressed in the Petrarchan mode.

But the speaker's shift in tone serves a purpose: he began by eschewing the self-defeating language of Petrarchan courtship which "destroyes it selfe with its owne shade" (as Donne puts it in a verse epistle "To the Countesse of Huntingdon" [34]); but if his insectile signifier is to die, he wants it to die as the embodiment of such definitively frustrated and frustrating discourse. Thus, speaking in the persecuted tones of what Donne elsewhere dubs "whining Poëtry" (*Triple*, 3), the speaker reifies and venerates the sign, insisting that violence done to it will be a "sacrilege" (18). The lady responds to his papistical-sounding nonsense with an iconoclast's righteous violence and acts upon the implicit dare; by the start of the third stanza, she has demolished the jet walls of the idolatrous "temple."[9]

In response to her action, he at first assumes a stance of shocked indignation: "Wherein could this flea guilty bee," he asks, "Except in that drop which it suckt from thee?" (21–22). But the lady is undaunted, flushed with the excitement of iconoclastic zeal. In his study of Renaissance iconoclasm, Gilman recounts the story of a Lancashire boy who, when urged by a radical Protestant schoolmaster "to mock the images in the chapel, seized a sword from the image of St. George and broke it over the saint's head, shouting, 'Let me see now how thou canst fight again!'" (8). The thrill of exposing an idol's impotence exhilarates the lady of the poem in much the same way, and the speaker can hear the ringing defiance and mockery in her voice: "thou triumph'st, and saist that thou / Find'st not thy selfe, nor mee the weaker now" (23–24).

At the very moment when she is sure that she has defeated him, however, he once again shifts ground. Though he previously identified the signifier with the signified, claiming that it would be "selfe murder" for her to kill the symbol which ~Excellent!~ represented her, he now admits—with Protestant care—that the reality is a thing separate from the sign; her violence destroyed only the signifier, not the thing it represented. If she wants to be an iconoclast, he goes on to stress, she must be consistent; for she too has been treating a sign as though it were the very thing it signified:

> thou
> Find'st not thy selfe, nor mee the weaker now;
> 'Tis true, then learne how false, feares bee;
> Just so much honor, when thou yeeld'st to mee,
> Will wast, as this flea's death tooke life from thee.
>
> (23–27)

A woman's honor, his analogy implies, is the reality for which sexual abstinence—physical chastity—is but a tangible sign. An intact "maidenhead" is not the "honor" with which tradition equates it; and because there is such a gap between signifier and signified, the destruction of the sign will not affect the underlying truth. The devil can quote scripture, and a lover Augustine: the sacrament is one thing, its virtue is another.[10]

Read this way, "The Flea" is a voluptuous worldling's "Theatre for Fastidious Mistresses"; its emblems exhort a virgin to break her own most precious icon. The lady (or the reader of the poem, deciding for her) may leave it at that. She may sleep with her suitor on the understanding that tangible seals mean nothing; agreeing that the flea's death is an empty occurrence, she need attribute no significance to the "death" of her virginity. As we have seen in Mayne's verse tribute to Donne, a seventeenth century reader was clearly capable of eliding the poet's success with the speaker's triumph. And for a significant number of twentieth century readers, too, the seduction seems a *fait accompli*. Critics who choose to eschew the role of resisting reader, who enjoy the sheer pleasure of surrendering to Donne's wit, afford the lady at least as much latitude and argue that she will indeed yield to the speaker's "irresistible conclusion that the loss of maidenhood is nothing more than a flea-bite" (Winny, 126).[11]

Other readers, however, see in the speaker's argument something beyond the desire for meaningless fun. As Marotti notes, Donne's lyric differs from most erotic persuasions in mentioning marriage at all (*John Donne, Coterie Poet*, 93). And the theological imagery, gamesome though it is, does more than teach a lesson in iconoclasm. Rather, the speaker's blasphemous analogies preach a sexual-salvation-history with a Protestant flavor. The flea is set up as the incarnate union of the lover and his lady even as Jesus is the incarnate union of God and Man. And if the speaker offers it to be a sign of their oneness, the covenant between them can be fully accomplished— as in the case of Christ's Atonement—only through the *shedding* of the "one blood made of two" (8). The killing of Jesus was the consummate sin, yet it was the only means to reconcile God and man. Similarly, it is "sacrilege" (18) for the lady to "[Purple her] naile, in blood of innocence" (20) yet that nail of crucifixion proves instrumental in the lover's Plan to make her his own.

It is here that a distinctly Protestant appeal comes into play: the Reformers rejected the Catholic conception of the Mass as a sacrifice offered by the priest because they held that Jesus' death on Calvary was the only sacrifice and could not be repeated or continued in the Eucharist.[12] Similarly, the flea has served as Paschal-erotic Victim, and its spilt "blood of innocence" (20) cancels all guilt: "[This is] the effect of his bloodshed, that sinne be not imputed unto us" (Calvin, *Inst.* 2.17.4).

When the innocent victim in which they "are met" (14) is slain, the guilt of the speaker and his lady is cancelled once and for all. Thus, her yielding to him will be no sacrifice, no holocaust in which her honor "Will wast" (26) and be consumed, but a sinless *communion*, a mutual partaking.

The analogy between sexual yielding and Protestant communion is set up by the poem's movement: it starts with static gazing upon an elevated sign and shifts to the un"wast"ed use of that sign; this sequence recalls the Protestant response to visual adoration of the Eucharist, which for many Catholics had replaced the taking of communion.[13] The Elizabethan "Homilie of the worthy receiving and reuerend esteeming of the Sacrament" urges believers not to hold back from participation in the meal "although it seeme of small vertue to some" but rather to seek the "fruition and union" of the Eucharistic banquet in which they may "sucke the sweetnesse of everlasting salvation" (*Homilies*, 197, 200):

> To this, his commandement forceth us. . . . To this, his promise entiseth. . . . So then of necessity we must be our selves partakers . . . and not beholders. (*Homilies*, 198)

The speaker of the poem also feels "enticed" to do more than just look. Though Neoplatonic lovers may vilify sexual "partaking" as an act of "small vertue," he presses forward to "sucke the sweetnesse" of a "fruition and union" which can save him from the death of frustration conventionally suffered by Petrarchan lovers. He wishes to avoid the folly of stupefied gazing—so mockingly repudiated in "Elegy XIX"—and become one of those who "taste whole joyes," as the speaker of the elegy puts it.

The lady moves things in the right direction by handling the sign (none too gently) rather than merely "Marke[ing]" it as the speaker first asked her. But physical violence done to outward signs does *not*, he hopes to convince her, destroy what they represent. Renaissance Protestants stressed that Christ's body is not chewed up, swallowed, and digested along with the bread; the homily on the Sacrament explains that it is "a ghostly substance" that believers "receive . . . with the hand of [the] heart" (*Homilies*, 200–01). The speaker of "The Flea" wants the lady to think in the same way of her "honor"—that "ghostly" or intangible signified which she has so closely identified with the tangible signifier called "maidenhead." Though he never directly promises to receive her honor into his keeping, he hopes to convince her that its substance will not be lost and "wast"ed when her hymen breaks. Thus, the ambiguous syntax of the penultimate line gives the impression that "yeeld'st" is a transitive verb with "honor" as its direct object: "Just so much honor, when thou yeeld'st to me," he says, and we expect to hear next what will happen after she has yielded "just so much honor" to him. Of course, "honor" turns out to be the subject of the completed sentence, "yeeld'st" intransitive, and the "when . . ." clause parenthetical, but even after we hear the speaker's statement in full, the impression remains: her honor will not be *wasted on him* because it will not be wasted *by* him when she yields.[14] He may want to consume her virginity, but as a semiotic sophisticate, he knows the difference between sign and signified, between defloration and dishonor, between giving over and giving in.

Thus, if the lady of the poem wishes to be married in fact as well as in flea, she may grant her lover's request on conditions his own imagery suggests. She may insist that he receive her Eucharistic virginity—and the honor it signifies— with the reverence and faithfulness of a devout communicant who receives "with the hand of the heart." If she does so, she will be committing herself to him. For in conveying himself through the Eucharist, Christ confirms that he will never abandon the faithful believer; as Calvin puts it, he "doth . . . so communicate his body to us, that he is made throughly one with us" (*Inst.* 4.17.38). In the same way, the lady who conveys her honor as she yields her body assures the lover to whom she entrusts them that she will never absent herself from him. The female speaker of another Donne poem makes the point eloquently: "I faine would stay," says the woman in "Breake of day," for "I [love] my heart and honor so / That I would not from him, that had them, goe" (10–12).

But it is a very worried lady who speaks those lines, and her "aubade" reminds us of the dangers involved in yielding. Having surrendered body, heart, and honor to her lover, the Renaissance mistress must fear that he will abandon her and take everything *but* her body with him. Will the lady of "The Flea" risk such danger? Clearly, she still has the option of refusing altogether; she can point out that what the speaker says about his spurious private symbol has no bearing on the socially determined relation between the sign of virginity and the substance of honor.[15] Will she allow her lover to consume that sign? Will she convey to him that substance?

If she is anything like the woman Donne married, she may. The lady's scruples and anxieties do not necessarily imply that the speaker's love is unrequited. "Though parents grudge, and you, w'are met," he says (14); and as Marotti points out, "the progression from 'parents' to 'you' to 'we' . . . places the woman rhetorically, emotionally, and morally between the disapproving parents and the importunate suitor" (*John Donne, Coterie Poet*, 94).[16] This is precisely the situation in which Anne More, Donne's own beloved, found herself; and as Edward LeComte argues, Anne may have escaped the impasse by consummating her relationship with Jack before the clandestine ceremony in which they took their vows. LeComte consults two key documents: a letter Donne wrote to his irate father-in-law on 2 February 1602 [New Style], in which he claims that their wedding took place "about three weeks before Christmas" 1601, and a record of the court's decision on the secret marriage's validity, dated 27 April 1602. Noting the vagueness and inconsistency of the dates cited in these documents, and considering seventeenth century attitudes toward clandestine marriage, LeComte speculates on the actual "sequence of events":

> Ann and John, after a separation of many months, found each other irresistible when at last they met again several times in the fall of 1601. They had made solemn promises to each other, and looked forward to marrying. Physical union was not an evasion of, but a way into, marriage: it strengthened their legal claims on each other. So, with the dissolution of Parliament on 19 December, Ann was taken back by her father to Loseley, neither a virgin nor a bride. In January, it probably was, the girl sent word to her lover in London that she had reason to believe she was pregnant. Thereupon, . . . she escaped from her father long enough for a secret ceremony. [Donne], when at last he had to inform Sir George More, predated the marriage so that the couple's first child, Constance, would be born nine months afterwards, not seven or eight. (20)[17]

The marriage did not stay secret for long—a pregnancy would help explain that fact—and Donne found himself in very serious trouble: disgraced, sacked, and imprisoned, he composed the aforementioned letter to his father-in-law. In it, he confesses that he and Anne married in December, but claims that they had committed themselves to one another even before the ceremony. His spurious argument in the letter recalls the one advanced in "The Flea." Comparing the lovers' precontract to a building with a strong foundation, Donne argues that their private engagement was—like the flea as "marriage temple"—too holy to be torn down: "So long since as her being at York House this had *foundacion*, and so much then of promise and contract *built* upon yt, as withowt violence to conscience might not be shaken" (*Selected Prose*, 113; emphasis added). He then intercedes for Anne as the poem's speaker does for the flea, begging "that she may not to her danger feele the terror of your *sodaine* anger"; Donne fears that his father-in-law will, like the lady of the poem, react with "cruell and sodaine" violence. But he can't leave it at that; with the same saucy impudence displayed by the speaker of the poem, he goes on to stress that, "Though parents grudge, . . . [they] *are* met":

> I know no passion can alter your reason and wisdome, to which I adventure to commend these particulers; that yt is irremediably donne; that if yow incense my Lord [Egerton, Donne's employer] yow destroy her and me; [and] that yt is easye to give us happines . . . (*Selected Prose*, 113).

"[I]t is irremediably donne"; the marriage is consummated, and Anne More is now, quite irreversibly, Anne Donne. Like the speaker of the poem, the bridegroom argues that the union he defends is a *fait accompli* and points out "How little" it would take for the addressee to make him happy. But he does so, like the speaker of the poem, partly to keep the potential benefactor from "killing three": himself, his spouse, and—if LeComte is right—their unborn child.

Surely Janet Halley is right to caution readers against the hope that they can know the "real" Anne More Donne through the textual constructions of her husband.[18] But the parallels between these two texts—one a dramatic lyric and the other a petitionary letter—give us a clearer appreciation both of the lady who speaks silently but eloquently between the stanzas of "The Flea" and of the poet's intentions in devising her. The intention of Donne's letter to George More is clear: he wants his father-in-law's blessing (and with it his financial assistance); he wishes to defuse More's anger, to persuade him to endorse the union. He thus describes and defends Anne as a young woman who has, heroically, risked everything for the sake of mutual commitment: "We both knew the obligacions that lay upon us, and we adventurd equally" (*Selected Prose*, 113). In the poem, Donne invites the reader to view the exchange between the speaker and the lady in a similar light, to see that, if the young lady of "The Flea" chooses to take seriously the quasi-Eucharistic signs which her lover offers, she, too, will "adventure equally" and convert what "wee would *doe*" to an act "irremediably *donne*." She will embrace her lover's sacramental imagery and insist that the gift of her virginity be considered no less binding than a precontract.

As critics of the poem, we can insist on no one reading, no one way of taking the sacrament; readers will continue to decide for themselves.[19] But we cannot avoid envisioning a range of specific outcomes from chaste denial to playful submission or reasoned acquiescence, and the speaker does seem set on excluding the possibility of outright refusal. As Baumlin notes, the poem "erects logically and morally specious arguments that the skeptical reader, taking the addressee's part, must seek to refute" (242); but it "cannot be fully defeated, for its arguments resist a reader's resistance, refusing to deconstruct" (244).

Calvin explains the effectiveness of sacramental grace in terms that may explain such stubborn persistence: a sacrament is like a rhetorical persuasion, he asserts, and the operation of the Holy Spirit ensures that its rhetoric cannot fail. It guarantees that the signs presented to the faithful *will* take effect, for it prepares their hearts to receive them (*Inst.* 4.14.9–10). In the sacramental persuasions of erotic love, a successful seduction presupposes the influence of another inward flame: the spirit of mutual desire. If that is present, it will—to borrow Calvin's wording—"truely bring to passe that the hearer . . . will obey the selfe same counsels which otherwise [s]he would have laughed to scorne" (*Inst.* 4.14.10). Such predestinate wooing, such preaching to the converted, is—Donne argues in one of his verse epistles—the only kind a man should attempt: "Man's better part consists of purer fire, / And findes it selfe allow'd, ere it desire," he says (*HuntUn*, 59–60). Perhaps it is this logic that underlies "The Flea," with its confident allusion to a future "when"—not "if"—the lady yields.

SEVEN

&

Ways of Having Donne

For Donne, Petrarchism is the Roman Catholicism of love; but where can a secular poet of the English Renaissance go to escape the Babylonian captivity of Petrarchism? For students of Donne, the oldest answer to this question is "Ovid"; and, indeed, the Ovidian sexuality of Donne's *Elegies* and of poems like "The Flea" is one avenue of escape from the sighs and tears of frustrated desire. But Donne's interest in the sacramentality of language leads him to consider another alternative as well: poetry modeled on the personal letter, which—for Donne as for many Renaissance humanist writers—is a truly sacramental genre, a form of writing that effects the presence of the absent writer and brings about his union with the reader. Interestingly, the only poem in which Donne makes explicit the analogy between poem and sacrament is a verse epistle cast in the quintessentially Petrarchan form of a sonnet. It is to this poem—one of several sonnets addressed to Thomas Woodward—that I would turn next, as a means of introducing the more complex representations of literary reception in Donne's verse letter to

Henry Wotton, "Sir, More then kisses," and in several of the love lyrics.

Sonnet as "bare Sacrament": Donne's Verse Letters to "T. W."

Three of the four poems Donne addressed "To Mr. T. W." (identified by Shawcross as Thomas Woodward, younger brother of Donne's friend Rowland Woodward) are sonnets in which the addressee is portrayed in Petrarchan terms as the poet's beloved.[2] Donne equates being deprived of Woodward's presence with the pains of hell; he calls him "My pain, and pleasure," and begs for a letter that will assure him of T. W.'s love. Within this Petrarchan framework, poetry is the lover's only contact with the beloved; and Donne uses the language of sacrament to underscore that fact:

> . . . though I languish, prest with Melancholy,
> My verse, the strict Map of my misery,
> Shall live to see that, for whose want I dye.
>
> Therefore I envie them, and doe repent,
> That from unhappy mee, things happy'are sent;
> Yet as a Picture, or bare Sacrament,
>   Accept these lines . . .
>
> (7–13)

The lines of the poem go to Woodward; but their speaker, the poet who made them, most definitively does not. For in referring to the sonnet as a "bare Sacrament," Donne is making a technical distinction between his poem and an efficacious sign.[3]

Hooker stresses in his *Laws* that the Church of England takes the sacraments not "for bare *resemblances* or memorials of things absent, nor for *naked signs* and testimonies of grace received before, but . . . for means effectual whereby God . . . delivereth [grace] into our hands" (*Laws* 5.57.5). The poem, then, is limited in precisely the way that Hooker says a true sacrament is not: it serves only as a resemblance or token of memorial. Donne is emphasizing his melancholy absence from T. W. by sending him a poem that is only a "Picture" (12), an artistic rendition of the sender that cannot effect real presence. Indeed, though Donne's verse is devised as a "strict Map of [his] misery" (8), it will not even represent his feelings accurately; for the lines of poetry—once they "see" T. W.—become "things happy," signifiers so thoroughly separated from their intended referent (the "unhappy" sender), that he can feel envy towards them as toward another person (10–11). In taking on a life of its own, the poet/speaker's Petrarchan lyric ceases to function as valid communication; it can do nothing for the one whom it is meant to represent, whether he thinks of himself as the quasi-divine figure who institutes the "Sacrament" or as the worshiper who offers it up as a Eucharistic self-oblation.

Having characterized his sonnet as a "bare Sacrament," Donne further accentuates its impotence by asking—in language reminiscent of Roman Catholic ideas of Eucharistic sacrifice—that it may function as a true and effectual sacrament, able to occasion the bestowal of T. W.'s grace and favor: "Accept these lines, and if in them there be / Merit of love, bestow that love on mee" (13–14). From an English Protestant perspective, the speaker is jumbling together two erroneous extremes as he constructs the analogy between poem and sacrament: first, he calls his poem a mere naked sign; then, he asks that it be accepted as a worthy oblation. The English Church's view, as Hooker expresses it, is that there is no merit *in* the sacrament itself, but rather that it *conveys* the merit of that which it represents: "what *merit, force or virtue soever there is in [Christ's] sacrificed body and blood, we freely, fully, and wholly have it by this sacrament*" (*Laws* 5.67.7). In the sonnet, the problem is that, as a "bare Sacrament," a Petrarchan exercise in absence, it neither has nor conveys merit of love. The poet/speaker's prayer is rendered void by the very mode of expression he has chosen. The song of the abject

Petrarchan lover grows out of absence and takes its very meaning from his failure to bring himself into contact with the
beloved.

The sonnet is not, of course, functioning in the classic
Petrarchan context of frustrated heterosexual love; and as a
move in the game of witty repartee which occasions the exchange of poems among young courtiers and law students,
the "failure" is really a coup.[4] Indeed, it seems that it was the
young Thomas Woodward himself who prompted Donne's use
of theological wit; for as becomes clear in George Klawitter's
discussion of all four poems to T. W., the first—"All haile sweet
Poet" does not make use of religious metaphors or similes,
but Woodward's response to that piece does. In his poem answering "All haile sweet Poet," Woodward questions whether
"the nimble fyer" (5) of Donne's creative imagination is "fyre
of heaven or . . . of hell" (6). For, Woodward explains,

> It doth beget and comfort like hevens ey
> And like hells fyer it burnes eternally.
> And those whom in thy fury & iudgment
> Thy verse shall skourge like hell it will torment.
>
> (7–10)

It would seem to have been partly in answer to this hellfire conceit, then, that Donne introduced into his next poem
("Hast thee harsh verse") a more theologically sophisticated
twist on Woodward's imagery. Addressing his own work,
Donne bids it tell Woodward that

> . . . all questions, which men have defended
>   Both of the place and paines of hell are ended;
> And 'tis decreed our hell is but privation
>   Of him, at least in this earths habitation . . .
>
> (7–10)

Since one popular definition of hell is the soul's pain at being
deprived of the Beatific Vision, Woodward is here afforded
quasi-divine status. Having been thus inspired to theological
wit, moreover, Donne infuses the sonnet with a number of

related conceits, playing upon the idea of himself as being at the same time God the Father, the divine "Creator" of the poem, and Sinful Man, the human soul in need of the grace that the poem (as his "Saviour") can obtain for him; "by thine and my labour," he says to his poem, "I am thy Creator, thou my Saviour" (5–6).

The theological language continues in the third poem from Donne to T. W., "Pregnant again with th'old twins Hope, and Feare," in which a letter from T. W. is portrayed as a life-giving charitable meal like the "liberall dole" Christ distributes at the Eucharistic climax of *La Corona*:

> And now thy Almes is given, thy letter'is read,
> And body risen againe, the which was dead,
> And thy poore starveling bountifully fed.
>
> After this banquet my Soule doth say grace,
> And praise thee for'it, and zealously imbrace
> Thy love . . .
>
> (7–12)

T. W.'s letter has, these lines assert, the Eucharistic power not only to nourish, but to infuse life. When Donne compares his work to a "bare Sacrament" in his fourth poem to T. W., then, he is building upon a series of theologically oriented conceits first suggested by Woodward's images of hell.

Though no other verse letters from Woodward to Donne are extant, and it is thus impossible to ascertain how the original reader of the "bare Sacrament" sonnet received the Zwinglian Eucharist sent to him by Donne, it is clear that in that poem—as in Petrarch's sonnets—the display of poetic imagination is at least as important as the communication of desire. Indeed, the entire point of the "bare Sacrament" sonnet is that such poetry cannot effect the fulfillment of the poet's desire. The best it can do is to serve, as Petrarch says that his poetry serves him, as a sort of therapy.

Donne was not always willing, however, to settle for the accomplished failure of a "bare Sacrament" like the "T. W."

sonnet; in many of his verse epistles, he seeks to accomplish something more than witty futility. For, as he makes clear in his sermons, Donne believed in the power of epistles to defeat absence. In a 1618 sermon preached at Whitehall, he cites Saint Ambrose's explanation of that power:

> An Epistle is *collocutio scripta*, . . . Though it be written far off, and sent, yet it is a Conference, and *seperatos copulat . . .*; by this meanes wee overcome distances, we deceive absences, and wee are together even when wee are asunder. . . . (*Sermons* 1:285)[5]

Indeed, as Cameron argues, Donne "conceived of the letter, whether in prose or verse, as a dynamic and efficacious form of discourse" (370). The word "efficacious" is, I would stress, particularly appropriate, for it is one of the words most commonly used to describe the unique effectiveness of the sacraments; and as Marotti points out (*John Donne, Coterie Poet*, 121), Donne once called letters "friendships sacraments."[6] By writing verse letters, then, Donne determines to bring the sacramental power of epistles into the realm of poetry.

Verse Letter as Self-Offering: "Sir, more then kisses"

One of the most remarkable results of this effort is a piece addressed to Donne's friend, Henry Wotton; probably written during the summer of 1598, the poem opens with a passionate statement on the power of epistles: "Sir, more then kisses, letters mingle Soules; / For, thus friends absent speake."[7] This verse letter is designed to function as an efficacious utterance that bridges distance and makes the absent present by effecting a eucharistic oneness between the sender and the receiver. Just as God makes himself present to Christians by enabling them to "kisse him in the Sacrament" (*Sermons* 3:322), so Donne's letter is to facilitate and seal the friends' spiritual intimacy; just as the Eucharist makes a man *"Idem spiritus cum Domino,* the same spirit, that [his] God is" (*Sermons* 6:223), so by the power of a letter in verse, Donne and Wotton's souls are to be conjoined or merged.[8] The giver and the recipient are to be made one.

In the opening lines of his poem to Wotton, Donne stresses that, for him, letters to and from friends are not only welcome respites from the weariness of everyday existence, but necessary means of maintaining life and virtue:

> This ease controules
> The tediousnesse of my life: But for these
> I could ideate nothing, which could please,
> But I should wither in one day, and passe
> To'a bottle'of Hay, that am a locke of Grasse.
>
> (2–6)

In these lines, letters are the only thing that stands between Donne and spiritual atrophy. The sweet "ease" of correspondence is the vital moisture that preserves him from the fate of the wicked as it is prophesied in Psalm 37:2: "For they will soon fade like the grass, and wither like the green herb."[9]

As Pebworth and Summers point out, moreover, lines 2–6 of the poem are particularly significant and poignant when one recognizes "Sir, more then kisses" as the third verse letter in an exchange that begins with Donne's "Here's no more newes" and continues with Wotton's "'Tis not a coat of grey" ("'Thus,'" 365–73). Wotton's poem, as Pebworth and Summers demonstrate, tactfully rejects the unsought advice that Donne had proffered in "Here's no more newes," and gently schools the author of that somewhat smug and sententious poem in the finer points of virtue and friendship. In "Sir, more then kisses," then, Donne expresses a chastened attitude and modifies the argument of his earlier verse letter in accordance with the ideas expressed in Wotton's "'Tis not a coat of grey." As Pebworth and Summers explain:

> "But for" the letters of friends, "I could ideate nothing which
> could please" (lines 3, 4) is a graceful acknowledgment that
> he failed to please Wotton in "Here's no more newes" and an
> implicit promise that now—with Wotton's letter to inspire
> him—he intends to do better. ("'Thus,'" 370)

The operative word in this analysis is, I would argue, "grace-
ful"; for, given Donne's use of the psalm verse to describe the
dire consequences of epistolary deprivation, it is clear that
the poet wishes to portray both the reception and the production of letters as means of grace. In saying that "This ease"
relieves the weariness of his life and in insisting that "But for
these," he would "wither" like the wicked of Psalm 37, Donne
leaves the referent of "This ease" and "these" deliberately
ambiguous; the words may refer to the letters he has received
from friends and the pleasure he has taken in reading them, or
to his own epistles. He relies both upon reading letters and
upon composing replies to keep him from "wither[ing]" (5).
In short, Donne here defines epistolary exchange itself as
able—like divine grace—to lift him out of dryness and make
him capable of good that he would not otherwise be able to
"ideate" or conceive of, much less perform.

As Donne explains in the same 1618 sermon in which
he discusses the power of epistles, God restores man's "dead
will"

> by his Grace precedent and subsequent, and concommitant:
> for, without such Grace and such succession of Grace, our
> Will is so far unable to pre-dispose it selfe to any good, as
> that . . . we have no interest in our selves, no power to doe any
> thing of, or with our selves, but to our destruction. (*Sermons*
> 1:293)[10]

Without grace, which is conveyed by the sacraments, the "external and visible means and seals of grace" (*Sermons* 2:254),
man would be incapable of doing anything pleasing to God;
without receiving sacramentally efficacious letters from

friends, including Wotton's "'Tis not a coat of grey," Donne would be incapable of the subsequent grace he receives through his own good works, including his present effort at an epistolary sacrament, "Sir, more then kisses." Together, the reception of Wotton's letter and the writing of his own work of grace redeem Donne from creative and intellectual desiccation.

The argument of Donne's verse letter, which seems rather impersonal and aphoristic when read outside of the context Pebworth and Summers establish, appears much more delicately nuanced in light of that context.[11] Discussing the "knottie riddle" of country, town, and court ("of all three /... each is worst equally" [19–20]), and counseling his friend to choose none of them, Donne advises, "Be thou thine owne home, and in thy selfe dwell" (47). This exhortation harmonizes with Wotton's "'Tis not a coat of grey," which declares that "It is the mynde that makes the mans estate, / For ever happy, or unfortunate" (5–6). If Donne's answering letter is really to exceed the power of a ritual kiss, however, if it is to be a sacramental utterance that "mingles souls," Donne must do more than simply embrace and elaborate upon his friend's wisdom. Thus, as he ends his epistle, Donne effects a more complete communion with his friend through a gesture that redefines both of their identities and purports to make the poem itself an enactment (rather than simply a declaration) of their oneness.

First, Donne claims Wotton as the source of his own poem's wisdom, acknowledging the degree to which "Sir, more than kisses" is indebted to Wotton's discourse; he then declares his love for his friend, enumerating the qualities he admires in him:

> But, Sir, I'advise not you, I rather doe
> Say o'er those lessons, which I learn'd of you:
> Whom, free from German schismes, and lightnesse
> Of France, and faire Italies faithlesnesse,
> Having from these suck'd all they had of worth,

> And brought home that faith, which you carried forth,
> I throughly love.
>
> (63–69)

These lines ensure that Wotton, identified as the original author of the "lessons" Donne's poem presents, will receive "Sir, more then kisses" as a permanent record of his own virtuous identity, as a voice-print that will remind him of who he is. Donne's poem is not, of course, a mere restatement of Wotton's "'Tis not a coat of grey"; rather, as Pebworth puts it, Donne "conflates his earlier stance [in "Here's no more newes"] with Wotton's [in "'Tis not a coat of grey"]" ("Sir Henry Wotton," 290). But by enumerating the qualities he cherishes in his friend, Donne defends the claim that "Sir, more then kisses" "Say[s] o'er" the "lessons" (64) he has learned from Wotton. For the man he says he loves, the discriminating English traveler, would indeed have been able to articulate the argument at the core of "Sir, more than kisses"; indeed, the Englishman who has avoided the spiritual pitfalls of three foreign lands has precisely the wisdom necessary to pass judgment on the similarly unsavory trio of country, town, and court.

And that man—the grammar of the lines implies—is Donne no less than Wotton. Wotton, the "you" of line 64, is described in an adjectival clause four and a half lines long, within which four descriptive lines separate the direct object ("Whom" [65]) from the subject and verb ("I throughly love" [69]). The descriptive lines specify that the Wotton whom Donne loves is a man unadulterated by the flaws of German, French, and Italian religion, one who has absorbed the good things of Europe and come home with his native faith and personal identity intact.[12] But by sandwiching the phrases "free . . ." (65f.) and "Having . . ." (67f.) between "Whom" (65) and "I" (69), Donne leaves open the possibility that those phrases may refer to either or both of the two pronouns. If the two friends are in agreement, their souls "mingle[d]" by their letters, Donne

is—even as Wotton is—"free from" the various diseases of
continental Protestantism and Catholicism and distinguished
by "Having . . . suck'd" the best out of Europe while retaining
an English faith.

Insofar as the lines imply a claim about Donne's own religion, they declare him to be Wotton's coreligionist. There is
irony in such a declaration; for in the late 1580s, Donne had
traveled to Europe as a Catholic rather than as an English Protestant. As Flynn argues in *John Donne and the Ancient Catholic Nobility*, Donne's Jesuit uncle Jasper Heywood probably
arranged for his 12-year-old nephew to sojourn in Europe in
order to prevent the young Catholic from being forced to take
the Oath of Allegiance. During his travels, Flynn argues, Donne
visited Paris, fought with Parma's troops in the siege of
Antwerp, and traveled to Spain and Italy in the company of
William Stanley, the son of the Earl of Derby (131–46).

As Flynn also demonstrates, however, English Catholics
like Donne and the Stanleys perceived many conflicts between
the "Old Religion" of their English Catholic tradition, and the
ultramontane Catholicism of Europe as it emerged after the
Council of Trent ("'*Annales* School'").[13] After he entered
the English Protestant priesthood, Donne would construct in
his sermons what Shami aptly characterizes as "a broadly-
conceived and tolerant spirituality" not easily classified with
labels such as "Laudian" or "Puritan," "Royalist" or "Calvinist" ("'Stars,'" 11). An early version of that spirituality is demonstrated, I would argue, in the conclusion of "Sir, more then
kisses," where the "faith, which [Wotton] carried forth" from
England is left unnamed, and the ambiguous descriptive
phrases attached to the pronoun "Whom" (65) may also be
read as modifying "I" (69). Given the ambiguity, lines 65–68
not only praise Wotton; they also assert that Donne himself,
"Having . . . suck'd all they had of worth" (67) from the Euro-
pean lands he visited some ten years earlier, has "brought
home that faith, which [Wotton] carried forth" (68) in his later

travels: an English faith sharply distinct from any continental religion and not readily identifiable with any one faction
within the Church of England.[14]

In fact, the closing lines of "Sir, more then kisses" implicitly recognize Wotton as the author of *The State of Christendom*, a broadly ecumenical work composed about four years
earlier, in 1594. As Dennis Flynn notes, Wotton wrote *The
State of Christendom* from the point of view of a fictional
persona whose experience resembles Donne's, a politically
loyal Englishman of the "Old Religion" who has been (as
Donne was for a time) an exile forced to travel in Europe for
reasons of conscience.[15] Since the narrator of *The State of
Christendom* has so much in common with Donne, then,
Donne confirms his own identity in "Say[ing] o'er the lessons,
which [he] learn'd" from the author of that book. He may be
echoing; but he is echoing a voice that, in its turn, sounds
remarkably like his own.

Donne can thus cast his verse letter as the means by which
he defines and takes control of his own identity:

> But if my selfe I'have wonne
> To know my rules, I have, and you have
>
> DONNE: (69–70)[16]

These final two lines declare that "DONNE" possesses his
own name and completes "Sir, more then kisses" successfully,
only insofar as the poem is able to "Say o'er" what Wotton
has taught its author of himself and his own "rules." And the
DONNE/done pun helps to define the poem as a whole in
sacramental terms. First, it refers to the poem not as a solo
utterance but as a shared action, not as something said, but
as something done—and done by Donne only insofar as Wotton, too, has performed it. Second, it associates Donne's and
Wotton's mutual doing, or having done, with the double "having" of the poet's identity, the shared possession of "DONNE"
that the poem itself brings about. Donne claims that, by means

of the self-teaching action of the poem, Wotton possesses as his own the man who echoes him. And once Donne has effected Wotton's possession of him, he has achieved a sense of true *self*-possession; he, too, has "DONNE." He has himself insofar as he knows who he is: a writer one with the man who first said these wise things and thus "wonne" by the rules which are both his own and his friend's. To be "DONNE" is to be "wonne" is to be one with Wotton. The poem both effects this victorious union and stands as its visible sign or seal.

As the efficacious sacrament of Donne's and Wotton's shared identity, "Sir, more then kisses" confirms the friends' place in a community of shared values. In *La Corona*, the eucharistic transformation of an individual soul takes place only within the context of a prayer offered in a communal voice. The sacramental event involves not only the poet's communion with the crucified Lord, but his unity with a congregation of Christian readers who constitute the Body of Christ. Neither relationship comes first; each is a condition for the other. Similarly, the soul-kiss which Donne and Wotton exchange through Donne's verse letter can take place only in the context of the fraternal body or community of values that, paradoxically, it both depends upon and generates.

In a discussion of Ben Jonson's poems, Stanley Fish argues that they eschew "representation . . . in favor of the instantaneous recognition, in another and in the work of another, of what one already is" (31). Donne's strategy in "Sir, more then kisses" is in some ways very similar to Jonson's as Fish describes it; yet it is also subtly different. Both Donne and Jonson present the reader with himself, but Jonson's works are "gathered and enclosed: . . . rather than presenting a positive ethos in a plain style, they labor to present nothing at all and to remain entirely opaque" (39). In the Wotton poem, Donne does not eschew representation of the virtuous and self-sufficient man, but turns from that description to cite

Wotton as its source. Jonson's poems, Fish says, "generate the community . . . not by creating its members (who are already what they are), but by providing a relay or network by means of which they can make contact with and identify each other" (40); a Jonson poem is thus neither "communication" nor "exhortation," but "testimony" (42). Donne's poem, however, is not only a "testimony" to the existence and identity of a community, but a means of establishing his and his reader's identities as members thereof. The verse epistle to Wotton is thus, like a sacrament of the English Church, a sign or seal that determines the sender's and receiver's shared identity even as it generates the community that unites them.

Though he does not discuss the verse epistle to Wotton, Thomas Docherty's observations on the issue of identity in Donne and Montaigne are pertinent to "Sir, more then kisses":

> The self is always a part of a social relation; that is, it is constituted by social dialogue. . . . The self, then, derives from an anterior community; and the moment of discovery of self-awareness or of self-nomination is also the moment at which the self discovers her or his exchangeability, mutability and mutuality. (194)

Indeed, Donne's text "becomes a scene of mutual recognition, the producer of *ecclesia*. . . . [T]he reader discovers or 'hears' herself or himself in the voice of the Other, and a corporate identity is produced" (Docherty, 197).[17] At the end of his poem, Donne can offer himself to be "had" by Wotton only insofar as he has received Wotton, sucking from him all he has of worth (consuming the best of Wotton's writing just as Wotton has consumed the best of Europe) and digesting his friend's wisdom in order to write it out anew. The reader—Wotton himself, as well as subsequent readers—can thus see in the poem's conclusion precisely why letter writing is, as Donne said at the start, essential to his existence: it is in this activity, in writing sacramental verse that unites him with his reader, that the word DONNE finds its meaning.

The Lover's Mass in "A Valediction of my name, in the window"

Between man and man, friend and friend, the verse letter to Wotton suggests, there can be true communion; and a verse letter can be the poetic sacrament that seals that communion. But what of the relation between man and woman? And what of the love lyric? Is there any way in which it may serve as a seal of mutual love?

In at least one of the *Songs and Sonets*—"A Valediction of my name, in the window"—Donne uses a technique similar to that employed at the end of the verse letter to Wotton, "signing" his name to the poem both metaphorically (through the image of his name engraved in the window pane) and numerologically, through a system of gematria that ascribes the same numerical value to the letters of the words "my name" as to those of the words "John Donne."[18] "My name engrav'd herein, / Doth contribute my firmnesse to this glasse," says the poet/speaker in the opening lines of the "Valediction," suggesting that the poem itself, no less than the window that bears his "scratch'd name" (20), is a "glasse": both a "through-shine" opening that presents the writer's self to the reader and something "more" (with a possible pun on his wife's maiden name), a mirror or looking-glass for that reader:

> 'Tis much that Glasse should bee
> As all confessing, and through-shine as I,
>   'Tis more, that it shewes thee to thee,
>   And cleare reflects thee to thine eye.
> But all such rules, loves magique can undoe,
>   Here you see mee, and I am you.
>
> (7–12)

As Julia Walker points out, this passage neither presents "woman as . . . man's image—'you are me'" nor argues, "even more traditionally, 'you are mine.'" On the contrary, "The line ["Here you see mee, and I am you"] is free of the element of possession and becomes a statement of conflated identity"

("Anne Donne," 101).[19] But this conflation comes near the beginning of the poem rather than at the end, as the merger of identities does in Donne's verse letter to Wotton; and as the "Valediction" continues, the poet/speaker makes clear that the text of his poem, like the name in the window, stands as a hedge against female infidelity, rather than as a seal of perfect mutuality.

Nevertheless, "A Valediction of my name, in the window" defines even this less exalted function in quasi-sacramental terms. The sacraments are, according to Calvin, provided "for our weaknesse": "our faith, as it is smal and weake, unlesse it be stayed on every side, and be by al meanes upholden, is by and by shaken, wavereth, staggereth, yea and fainteth." Thus, "God vouchesaveth even . . . in the fleshe it selfe to set fourth a mirror of spirituall good thinges" (*Inst.* 4.14.3). In the same way, the speaker of the "Valediction" engraves his name in brittle "glasse" (2) in order to prop up the faithfulness of his lady; marked with the poet/speaker's name, the "glasse"—and by extension the poem—is both a "throughshine" window (8) that reveals and partakes of the poet/speaker's "firmnesse" (2) and a mirror that will reflect to the lady a firmer, more faithful version of herself.

But the sacrament the speaker of the poem offers is no Calvinist seal; it is a parody of the Catholic Mass. As Hester explains, the speaker of the "Valediction," like many of his counterparts in Donne's other dramatic love lyrics, "uses the terms and arguments of the current Recusant position concerning the hermeneutics of the Sacraments":

> [T]he doctrinal vocabulary used to present his outrageous metonymies transfers the terms identified with the warring parties in the controversy about the Sacrament . . . to the speaker's defense of . . . his (libertine) amatory creed of sexual incarnation. The "lesson" of love which Donne's outrageous lover reads and explicates is not just Spenser's Easter defense by which we love "*like as* we ought" (*Amoretti*, 68), but it is blasphemously

analogous to the canon of the Catholic Mass by which . . . we
engage in the . . . "substantiall," "daily" descent of the real
body's "dying" . . . ("'this cannot be said,'" 373, 374).[20]

There is a telling contrast between Spenser's delicate and dec-
orous simile and Donne's "outrageous" insistence on the real
presence of the body in love and in poetry. For, in describing
the function of the engraved glass, the poet/speaker of the
"Valediction" evokes a triple analogy between his inscribed
name, the text of the poem, and his body as Eucharistic *corpus*. And in so doing, as Hester notes, "the lover challenges
his beloved" to recognize their love as "'substantiall'—the
term identified [by Protestants] as 'the hallmark of Popery'"
("'this cannot be said,'" 375).[21]

But the language Donne's poet/speaker uses does not so
much evoke the Roman Catholic Mass itself as Protestants'
hostile and mocking portrayals of it. Beginning in stanza four,
his phrasing links his inscriptions (both the engraved name
and the poem) to what Protestant polemicists represented as
the Catholic Church's necrolatrous theology of *Corpus Christi*:
"thinke this ragged bony name to bee, / My ruinous Ana-
tomie," he commands (23–24), insisting that the visible sign
of his "ragged" inscription *is* his dead and broken body. He
then promises that the skeletal self-representation he sets up
will ensure his second coming: "The rafters of my body, bone /
Being still with you, the Muscle, Sinew, and Veine, / Which
tile this house, will come againe" (28–30). The curious roof
imagery of these lines warps and parodies a key moment in
the Mass; for the prayer of the priest shortly before receiving
the Host in the Tridentine liturgy is that adapted from the
words of the Centurion to Christ: "Domine, non sum dignus
ut intres sub tectum meum"; "Lord, I am not worthy that
Thou shouldst enter under my roof" (*Roman Liturgy*, 179;
Missal, 661). In the liturgy, the body of the communicant
is the unworthy house/roof under which the Body of Christ
will enter. In the poem, the speaker twists the metaphor,

implying that "this house" (30) roofed in his absence by the bare rafters of his name's "ruinous" corpus (24), and to be covered upon his return by his living flesh and blood, is the delectable body of the woman (in which all his "soules bee, / Emparadis'd" [25–26]). In his absence, the speaker says, his mistress is to attend to the remnant of himself that he has left her, and in so doing, "Till my returne, repaire / And re-compact my scatter'd body" (31–32) and "till I returne, / Since I die daily, daily mourne" (41–42). These lines evoke the alleged Catholic belief that "Christ died not once, but dieth daily" (Rogers, 301).[22] They recall Spenser's satiric portrait of the Roman Catholic Mass as evoked by "Fidessa" (a.k.a. Duessa) when she tells Redcrosse of the slain spouse for whom she "shall . . . euer mone" and whose "blessed body spoild of liuely breath" she seeks for everywhere (*The Faerie Queene* 1.2.23:9; 1.2.24:1).[23]

The poem's final stanza, however, pulls back from this quasi-satiric use of eucharistic language:

> But glasse, and lines must bee,
> No meanes our firme substantiall love to keepe;
> ....
> Impute this idle talke, to that I goe,
> For dying men talke often so.
>
> (61–62, 65–66)

The "lines" of the poem are, according to this concluding stanza, mere "idle talk"—which is to say, Hester explains, "the sort of 'idol' talk of which the Protestant Establishment accused Catholics" ("'this cannot be said,'" 374).[24] And the implication for the sacramental potential of the love lyric is clear. As Baumlin puts it: "Writing . . ., both the name and the poem itself, cannot guarantee the lady's faith. . . . And the poet of 'A Valediction: of my Name in the Window' is [thus] unable to claim for his language the power . . . of sacramental presence" (183, 184).[25]

Sacramental Rings: The Controversial Context for Donne's Circular Lyrics

In "A Valediction of my name, in the window," Donne cannot or will not attempt to invest the heterosexual love lyric with the sacramental power he claims for poetry in his verse letter to Wotton. But this is by no means true of all his love lyrics. In many of the *Songs and Sonets*, Donne represents the love of man and woman itself as a means of grace. As Achsah Guibbory observes,

> Donne's sense of love as sacramental . . . might be seen as expressing a Roman Catholic understanding of marriage as a sacrament . . . constituted by the agreement between the loving partners rather than by any officiating priest. ("Fear," 205)[26]

Indeed, even after he became a priest in the English Church, Donne maintained a sense of the sacramental in married love. In a 1627 marriage sermon, he explains:

> [F]or Mariage among Christians, *Sacramentum hoc magnum est*, saies the Apostle, *This is a great secret, a great mystery.* Not that it is therefore a *Sacrament*, as *Baptisme*, and the *Lords Supper* are Sacraments. . . . But Mariage among Christians, is . . . A Sacrament in such a sense; a mysterious signification of the *union of the soule* with Christ. . . . [B]y the *Civill* union, common to all people, they are made *Eadem caro*, The same flesh with one another; By this mysterious, this Sacramentall, this significative union, they are made *Idem Spiritus cum Domino*; The same Spirit with the Lord. (*Sermons* 8:103–04)

This passage insists upon marital union as a means of grace, a sign that does not only signify the soul's union with Christ, but that actually effects it. In defining marriage this way, Donne goes much further than the English Prayer Book, which ventures only as far as the basic Pauline doctrine that in matrimony "is signified and represented the spiritual marriage and unity betwixt Christ and his Church" (*BCP*, 296). Donne, by contrast, sees marriage as transforming the two-made-one, divinizing them and making their spiritual substance one with that of Christ.

In his secular love poems, too, Donne insists upon what Guibbory calls "a kind of transmutation or transubstantiation through human sexual love" ("Fear," 206). Indeed, many of the poems of consummated love evoke what amounts to a religion of love. In poems like "The Canonization," "The Extasie," and "The Sunne Rising," Guibbory argues, "the lovers . . . become the locus of value in the world as their love assumes a sacramental, incarnational, mysterious significance, and . . . the private experience of love takes the place of institutionalized religion" ("Fear," 206); but she notes as well that

> even in the celebratory poems, there are traces of doubts and uncertainties about the value of love. The problem of tone in the "The Extasie" and "The Canonization" and the outrageous flirtation with blasphemy in the latter poem leave readers uncertain how seriously to take the claims for the sacramental value of sexual love. ("Fear," 207)

It is no wonder, then, that the status of the love lyric itself, as a visible, readable seal of mutual love, should often remain ambiguous or indeterminate in Donne's poetry. In "A Valediction of my name, in the window," the poet/speaker ends by dismissing completely the idea of a sacramental inscription that can seal and confirm love, ensuring the presence of the lover even in absence. But in two poems that play upon the analogy between a ring and a love lyric—"A Valediction forbidding mourning" and "A Jeat Ring sent"—Donne's language suggests that a poem may indeed be a sacrament of eros, an effectual seal either of fidelity or (ironically) of infidelity.

The meaning of these lyrics emerges from a context of controversy about the meaning and sacramentality of rings; for, in Elizabethan and Jacobean England, the use of wedding bands was much debated. In Roman Catholic practice, the ring as used in the marriage ceremony, like holy water and the crucifix, is and was a "sacramental," a sacred sign that does not in itself convey grace, but that helps to prepare a person for the reception of grace. Though the noun "sacramental" was not retained by the English Church, the use of many such symbols and ceremonies was; and the psychology underlying that use is Hooker's point of departure in the fourth book of his *Laws of Ecclesiastical Polity*:

> [I]n every grand or main public duty which God requireth at the hands of his Church, there is, besides the matter and form wherein the essence thereof consisteth, a certain outward fashion whereby the same is in decent sort administered. . . . Now men are edified, when either their understanding is taught . . . or when their hearts are moved with any affection suitable thereunto; when their minds are in any sort stirred up unto that reverence, devotion, attention and due regard, which in those cases seems requisite. . . . From hence have risen not only a number of prayers, readings, questionings, exhortings, but even of visible signs also; which being used in performance with holy actions, are undoubtedly most effectual to open such matter, as men when they know and remember carefully, must needs be a great deal the better informed to what effect such duties serve. (*Laws* 4.1.2–3)

It is not until late in book 5 that Hooker comes to his discussion of matrimony and the particular ceremonies surrounding it, but his comments in book 4 are directly relevant to his later defense of the wedding ring: "Touching significant ceremonies," Hooker urges, "some of them are sacraments, some as sacraments only" (*Laws* 4.1.4); he thus maintains the analogy between sacrament-like signs and true sacraments even as he distinguishes between them. He explains that "Sacraments are those which are signs and tokens of some general promised grace, which always really descendeth from God unto the soul that duly receiveth them; other significant tokens are only as Sacraments, yet no Sacraments" (*Laws* 4.1.4).[27] In his role as a preacher, Donne went a step further in defining the role of such "tokens." The "evidence" or "manifestation" of grace, he says in his 16 June 1619 sermon preached before the Prince and Princess Palatine in Heidelberg, "is not only, (though especially) in the sacraments, but in other sacramental and ceremonial things, which God (as he speaks by his Church) hath ordained, as the cross in baptism. . . . [T]hese sacramental and ritual, and ceremonial things, . . . are the bellows of devotion" (*Sermons* 2:258–59).

For many English Protestants, however, the ring—no less than the cross—was a remnant of "popery" that they wished to see abolished; indeed, the debate over the use of the wedding ring inspired almost as much passion and sarcasm as the controversy over the sign of the cross in baptism. "As for matrimony, that also hath corruptions too many," noted the authors of the 1572 *Admonition to Parliament*: "It was wont to be counted a sacrament, and therefore they use yet a sacramental sign to which they attribute the virtue of wedlock, I mean the wedding ring, which they foully abuse" (quoted in Hooker, *Works* 2:431, n. 2). In answering the *Admonition*, Bishop John Whitgift denied any such abuse. The ring, he insisted,

> is not of the substance of matrimony; neither yet a sacramental sign, . . . but only a ceremony of the which M. Bucer . . . saith on this sort; . . . 'This ceremony is very profitable, if the people be made to understand what is thereby signified. . . . [T]he roundness of the ring doth signify, that the wife ought to be joined to her husband with a perpetual band of love, as the ring itself is without end.' (Quoted in Hooker, *Works* 2:431, n. 2)[28]

Thomas Cartwright found this explanation absurd and, in his answer to Whitgift, scoffed at the allegorical interpretation Whitgift had attributed to Bucer:

> [I]f it be M. Bucer's judgment which is here alledged for the ring, I see that sometimes Homer sleepeth. For first of all I

have shewed that it is not lawful to institute new signs or sacraments, and then it is dangerous to do it, especially in this
which confirmeth the false and popish opinion of a sacrament.
And .. to make such fond allegories . . . of the roundness of the
ring . . . is (let me speak it with good leave) very ridiculous and
far unlike himself. (Quoted in Hooker, *Works* 2:431, n. 2)

Despite Cartwright's disdain for "fond allegories," however,
both Hooker and Donne found uses for them.

"A Jeat Ring sent": An Outward Sign of Inward Disgrace

It is in the context of the religious debate over the meaning
and status of rings that Donne wrote his witty lyric, "A Jeat
Ring sent." This is not to say, of course, that religious controversy is the only relevant context. The poem works as it does
partly because it plays upon the bawdy humor (like that of
the later acts of Shakespeare's *Merchant of Venice*) in which
rings symbolize female genitalia; the zero-shaped ring is the
outward sign of a woman's pledge to keep her "nothing" for
her husband alone. Indeed, this level of meaning is the most
obvious one in "A Jeat Ring." The final lines of Shakespeare's
play—Gratiano's "Well, while I live I'll fear no other thing /
So sore, as keeping safe Nerissa's ring" (5.1.306–07)—might
well serve as a gloss for Donne's poem, in which the speaker
feels that he can keep his mistress's ring "gladly safe" (11)
only by taking it into his own keeping; as he says to the ring,
it is not safe with the woman, since "She that, Oh, broke her
faith, would soon breake thee" (12). But the symbolic link
between rings and female sexual fidelity accounts for only one
level of wit and significance in this poem. As is clear in "The
Flea," Donne does not neatly separate the bawdy implications
of an image or symbol and its more serious, quasi-sacramental meaning. In "A Jeat Ring," too, Donne's wit blends the
sacred, the sexual, and the textual.[29]

In the first stanza, the speaker addresses the ring itself,
setting up a twofold analogy between the ring and each party

in his failed relationship: the ring reflects both his and his beloved's characteristics, since it is "black" (signifying both melancholy and constancy) and "endlesse" as he, but also "brittle," like "her heart" and easily "broke" like her faith. Beyond this analogy, both the form and the content of the lines suggest a further parallel between ring and *poem*. Donne creates a ring of words—a posey almost short enough to be inscribed in a ring—in the poem's first couplet. The lines begin and end with the punningly metapoetic words, "Thou art": "Thou art not so black, as my heart, / Nor halfe so brittle, as her heart, thou art" (1–2). This circular posey, written in black ink on the ephemeral surface of a sheet of paper, is a "brittle" ring of jet. It, like the ring to which it refers, is a sign that declares both the speaker's qualities and those of the lady.[30] "What would'st thou say?" the speaker asks the ring/posey, "shall both our properties by thee bee spoke . . .?" (3), and with this question, he opens up the possibility that the poem's meaning, no less than the ring's, is less than fully determined.

In breaking her faith and presenting a ring to mark the occasion, the lady has set up a significant sign for her erstwhile lover to read, but its meaning is ambiguous, open—as are the "living walls of Jet" in "The Flea"—to a range of possible interpretations. Indeed, the conceit of "A Jeat Ring sent" is an inversion of the one that operates in "The Flea." The lady, sexually and semantically active, is able to present her own "Figure" (7) to the lover; she no longer is confined to response, as is the virginal lady/reader of "The Flea," whom the speaker of that poem commands to "Marke" the sign he presents to her. In "A Jeat Ring," the lady actively presents her own sign, challenging the lover either to continue in his "endlesse" devotion despite her infidelity or to fling the ring/her away and thus set her free. His question "What would'st thou say?" is thus addressed, through the ring, to the ambiguous lady it represents.[31] The distinction between the ring and its sender thus becomes very blurry in stanza 2, where Donne makes it difficult to determine whether the speaker's addressee is the ring or the "cheap" woman who has given it to him; sign and signifier are essentially one:

> Marriage rings are not of this stuffe;
>   Oh, why should ought lesse precious, or lesse tough
> Figure our loves? Except in thy name thou have bid it say,
>   I'am cheap, and nought but fashion, fling me'away.
>
> (5–8)[32]

The wit of these lines relies in part upon the idea that the jet ring, precisely because it is cheap and easily broken, is a no less perfect symbol or seal of broken faith than a golden ring would be of true love.

In this implication, the second stanza picks up where the first leaves off, with its negative emphasis on superlative appropriateness: "Nothing more endlesse, nothing sooner broke" (4). The line certainly has bawdy implications; the lady having proved untrue to her constant lover, "Nothing" can better figure forth her wayward honor and her promiscuous vagina (referred to in Elizabethan slang as the female "no-thing" that corresponded to the male "thing") than a brittle ring of jet. But the line also recalls Hooker's solemn defense of the wedding ring as an appropriate symbol for Christian marriage. Hooker says that there is "Nothing more fit to serve as a token of our purposed endless continuance" than a wedding ring (*Laws* 5.73.6); Donne's speaker says that there is "Nothing more endlesse, nothing sooner broke" (4) than the jet ring his unfaithful lady has given him.

Hooker's comments on wedding rings provide a helpful gloss for the interpretation of Donne's poem; for they stress that a gold ring is not only a token of fidelity, but also a sign of the husband's authority and control over his wife:

> The ring hath been always used as an especial pledge of faith and fidelity. Nothing more fit to serve as a token of our purposed endless continuance in that which we never ought to

revoke. This is the cause wherefore the heathens themselves did in such cases use the ring, whereunto Tertullian alluding saith, that in ancient times "No woman was permitted to wear gold saving only upon one finger, which her husband had fastened unto himself with that ring which was usually given for assurance of future marriage." (*Laws* 5.73.6)

Central to Donne's irony in the poem is the contrast between gold and jet, between fastening a woman to one's self and flinging her away,[33] between a relationship in which a man decides what a woman is "permitted" to wear and one in which a woman makes her own choices and "bid[s]" signs "say" what she would have them say (7).

Indeed, Donne's witty inversion of all that the wedding ring might signify confirms Hooker's comment on how easy it is for men to mock solemn and ceremonial things:

The cause why the Christians use it, as some of the fathers think, is either to testify mutual love or rather to serve for a pledge of conjunction in heart and mind agreed upon between them. But what rite and custom is there so harmless wherein the wit of man bending itself to derision may not easily find out somewhat to scorn and jest at? (*Laws* 5.73.6)

Hooker's remarks, though originally directed at polemicists like Cartwright, who used words like "fond" and "ridiculous" to mock conservatives' allegorical interpretations of the ring, might equally well be applied to Shakespeare's "wit" in *The Merchant of Venice* or Donne's in "A Jeat Ring sent."[34] For in stanza 3, the speaker returns (circle-wise) to the bawdy implications of the "Nothing[s]" in the opening stanza.

Addressing the ring, he puts it on "this fingers top" (10); thrusting a phallic finger into the symbol that signifies his wayward mistress, he continues to use her as his own, to make her "stay with" him, and to keep the outward sign of her sexual organ unbroken even if she breaks the real thing, "her faith"

(12). Whereas the woman in "The Flea" tries to foil that poem's speaker by breaking his sign, the lover in "A Jeat Ring" foils the woman by accepting her token/sign and imposing on it the meaning he wishes to give it: he will neither love her nor fling her away, he will just wear her as the cheap piece of jewelry she is. The speaker's gesture completes the meta-poetic conceit first hinted at in the opening couplet's ring-like circularity. "A Jeat Ring sent" is "top[ped]" with the circular posey of the opening couplet, "Thou art . . . thou art"; and the puckish deixis "this fingers top" (10)—like a finger pointing from the margin at the text of the poem—identifies the text as a rigid extension of the hand that made it.

The poem thus functions as a ring-finger, while the opening couplet that "top[s]" it functions as a ring, one of those "significant tokens" that, though they are not sacraments, are "as Sacraments" (Hooker, *Laws* 4.1.4). But whereas a woman's golden wedding band is one of those "sacramental and ritual, and ceremonial things" that foster "devotion" (Donne, *Sermons* 2:258–59), the black ring-posey that tops the male "finger" of "A Jeat Ring sent" both signifies and fortifies disdain. And whereas a wedding ring figures forth the graces of a wife's chaste fidelity, the poet/speaker of "A Jeat Ring" wears a posey on his finger/text to signify the dis-grace of his own unchaste resolve. Readers who look at the finger/poem are invited to see the posey/ring upon it and to appreciate its significance; the circular opening couplet is the definitive outward sign both of the defiant male's scorn and of his claim to continued ownership of a "cheap" bit of "stuffe." Insofar as the implied reader is the unfaithful woman herself, the finger/text will be an effectual thrust at and into her. The speaker of "The Flea" claims that his addressee is already deflowered, that he and she "are met" (will she, nil she) in the "jet" enclosure of the insect. Likewise, the poet/speaker of "A Jeat Ring" claims that—whatever his reader/addressee may do—his dubious relations with her are ongoing in and through the brittle blackness of the posey/ring that tops his finger/poem.

Eucharistic Love and Lyric Circularity in "A Valediction forbidding mourning"

In "A Jeat Ring sent," the brittleness and faithlessness of woman are figured in the brittleness of the posey/poesy. In "A Valediction forbidding mourning," by contrast, the speaker attributes to the "firmnes" of the implied female reader both his ability to return faithfully to her, and the perfect circularity of his inscription. In 36 lines, the poet/speaker traces a 360-degree conceit, linking the image of beaten gold to the idea of an unbroken circle and thus presenting the "Valediction" itself as both golden and circular.

But the status of the text as sacramental ring is not made apparent from the start in "A Valediction forbidding mourning." Like most of the *Songs and Sonets,* the poem is a dramatic lyric that implies the immediate presence of the addressee. The "Valediction" thus does not begin, as does "Sir, more then kisses," by defining itself as an epistle that *"seperatos copulat"* (Donne, *Sermons* 1:285); rather, it presents itself as an utterance anticipating and preparing for a parting that is soon to take place, and it insists that the love between the speaker and the addressee, rather than any written text, is the "meanes" by which they may "overcome distances, ... deceive absences, and [remain] ... together even then when [they] are asunder" (*Sermons* 1:285, describing the function of epistles).

As the "Valediction" unfolds, however, its dependence upon a sacramental poetics analogous to that of *La Corona* becomes clear. Like that cycle of sacred sonnets, "A Valediction forbidding mourning" ultimately defines itself as a circular inscription (a 360-degree conceit rendered in 36 lines); and like *La*

Corona, it presents that inscription as sealing and confirming a sacramental communion. As Baumlin points out, the
"Valediction" proceeds from "a linguistic theology that claims
for the poet-priest's language a power of sacramental presence, of invoking the poet and his beloved within the textual
space" (17). And yet it does not present the poet's power as
free-standing; rather, the "Valediction," like *La Corona*, is
modeled on the English Church's definition of a sacrament.
It calls for the active participation of the reader/recipient in
order to effect and perpetuate a literary communion. The poet,
"A Valediction" makes clear, is as dependent upon his reader
as the speaker of the poem is upon the woman he addresses;
neither can call his "circle just" (35), neither can call his conceit effectual, without the "firmnes" (35) of the receiver's faithful participation.[35]

In "A Valediction" no less than in *La Corona*, Donne
defines that participation in Eucharistic terms. As Anne
Barbeau Gardiner has demonstrated, the love poem focuses
on the very question that dominated theological debate over
the Sacrament:

> How could the body of Jesus Christ be Present at the Lord's
> Supper when he had ascended bodily to the right hand of the
> Father? Or, how could the lover still abide intimately, as he
> had pledged to do, with his beloved spouse the Church when
> he had departed to an inconceivable distance till his Second
> Coming? . . . John Donne also raises this momentous question
> when he has the lover pledge . . . that he will remain—all the
> while he is on a journey—Really Present with his beloved. (113)

He can achieve an absent presence, "A Valediction" implies,
both through the sacramental power of the love that binds
them together and through the written text that is the visible
sign and celebration of that love. As such a text, "A Valediction forbidding mourning" is neither a Jesuitical Petrarchan
Mass ("Twicknam garden") nor an erotic Calvinist's seduc-
tive Communion ("The Flea") nor a brittle black knockoff of

the wedding ring as sacramental token ("A Jeat Ring sent"). Instead, it is the poetic Eucharist of a requited poet/lover and the ring of gold that signifies his ongoing commitment to his beloved.[36]

As a poetic Eucharist, it is—like *La Corona* and the Lord's Supper itself—an *ars moriendi*. The poet/speaker of the sonnet cycle emerges from his literary communion with the Crucified as a man free from "Feare of first or last death" (*Cor6*, 7); and in a sermon, Donne tells communicants that they will know they have "beene worthy receivers" if they "are *in Æquilibrio*, in an evennesse, in an indifferency, in an equanimity, whether [they] die this night or no" (*Sermons* 7:297). It is just such a holy *apatheia*, such a gentle indifference to the parting of soul and body, man and woman, that the speaker of "A Valediction forbidding mourning" urges upon the implied receiver of his sacramental poem:

> As virtuous men passe mildly away,
>   And whisper to their soules, to goe,
> ....
> So let us melt, and make no noise . . .

> (1–2, 5)

These lines set the scene for a dramatic lyric, evoking the moment of parting between the speaker and his lady. At the same time, however, they hint at an act that is the very opposite of parting, at the idea of merging identities, of two metals dissolving alchemically into one fluid substance as they "melt" together in noiseless liquefaction (Freccero, "Donne's 'Valediction,'" 298). As in the Eucharist, participation in a holy death is, at the same time, an experience of mystical communion.

The alchemical implications are further developed in the fifth stanza:

> But we by'a love, so much refin'd,
>   That our selves know not what it is,

Inter-assured of the mind,
   Care lesse, eyes, lips, and hands to misse.

(17–20)

In these lines, though the phrase "so much refin'd" turns out to modify "love" (the love being so much refined that it cannot be defined), the strained word order and deceptive punctuation of the stanza at first suggest that the phrase modifies "we," that the speaker and his lady are themselves "refin'd" by the love they share.[37] The refinement of the lovers is, as Freccero explains,

> exactly analogous to the refinement or sublimation practiced by the alchemists in their search for the philosopher's stone. The volatile 'spirit' of a metal is extracted by liquefaction, transmuted by sublimation and subsequently 'fixed' by settling. The all-important sublimation was considered to be a transmutation of the 'spirit' of a metal from one level of reality to another. ("Donne's 'Valediction,'" 296–97)[38]

In the *Sermons*, too, Donne uses the language of alchemy, speaking of God's refining souls through an alchemical process. According to Donne, both the sunshine of "temporal blessings" and the fire of tribulation purge and purify human beings, making them into a "more refined mettall"(*Sermons* 1:164, 163); and when believers are thus purified, they experience "that transmutation, which admits no re-transmutation, which is a modest, but infalible assurance of a final perseverance, so to be joyned to the Lord, as to be one spirit with him; for . . . they who are thus changed into him, are so much His, . . . nothing can separate them from him" (*Sermons* 1:164). In the "Valediction," love's refining of the couple has a similar confirmatory effect; it lifts them out of the "sublunary" sphere of change and mutability, giving them the purity and elasticity of "gold to ayery thinnesse beate" (24). Their minds "Interassured" (19), and their "two soules . . . one" (21), they can be physically divided and "endure not yet / A breach" (22–23).

The poem does not, however, end with this assurance. Rather, it goes on—through the alternative conceit of the compass—to confront the reality of separation as it must be experienced "If," in fact, their "two soules . . . be two" (21, 25) rather than one. In order to cope with this possibility, the speaker turns from aural imagery (the whispers and hushing of the opening stanzas) to the circular inscription made by the compass and, by implication, to the 36-line inscription which is the poem. "If they be two," they must rely upon such visible signs. For as several readers of the poem have noted, there is a movement in the opening stanzas from a soft, barely audible sound (the "whisper" of line 2) toward utter silence. The murmur around the death bed in lines 3–4 (in which the virtuous men's "sad friends doe say" a few words, guessing about the precise moment of death) subsides in line 4 with the speaker's insistence that there be "no noise" at all. To "tell" (8) of their love would, he says, be "prophanation" (7); the poem thus forbids not only mourning, but speech, audible language itself. As Baumlin argues, the work calls the lady "and the reader alike to meditative silence" (202).

It does not follow, however, that "the poem is itself an effacement of poetry" (Baumlin, 202). On the contrary, "A Valediction" moves toward a definition of lyric as a poem written rather than sung or spoken, and of a poem as sacrament, as visible rather than audible sign. The persona becomes an inscriber—the drawing leg of the compass—rather than a "speaker," and though the soul of the reader/addressee "hearkens" after him, he implies that she will receive, once he is gone, no audible word from him. Nor does the poet/persona promise to send her letters, written texts through which "friends absent speake" (*HWKiss*, 2) silently yet visibly. Instead, he offers only the text of the "Valediction" itself and, through it, an image of their paradoxically divided union: the compass.

The male leg of the compass is the one that writes, that makes a mark; he draws the circle, as the persona "far doth rome" (30) and as the poet writes the poem. The female "foot," in contrast, "makes no show / To move" (27–28); she produces no visible signs, no written text designed to move and direct a reader's emotions (as this text is attempting to move and direct its reader's). But her foot of the compass "doth" move, he goes on to say, "if the'other doe" (28). She is thus, in essence, an ideal reader, a stable perceiver content to "sit," moved only by the writer who addresses her, "in the center" (29) of his conceit as its subject and intended receiver.

It is only insofar as this reader does not confine herself to the visual imagination, however, that she will receive the fullness of what he offers. For, as Graham Roebuck argues, the inscription made by the compass in lines 25–36 of the poem is not so much a concrete visual image as a conceptual challenge to which the reader must rise. Indeed, as a number of critics have argued, the effectiveness of "A Valediction forbidding mourning" as a visible artifact and the reliability of the visual imagination itself are both called into question when a reader attempts simply to visualize the compass conceit. The poem, these scholars propose, engages the reader's sense of sight only to force a movement beyond or away from the visual. Gilman, for example, points out that "the compasses cannot really be visualized at all: if the moving foot 'comes home' it must rejoin the 'fixt foot' at the center of the circle and cannot at the same time inscribe a 'circle just' by completing the circumference" (136). As Gilman explains it, then, the conceit

> first tempt[s] us to visualize the love praised in the poem by an appeal to "sense," offering the kind of pictorial representation that even "Dull sublunary lovers" can perceive. The "failure" of that image suggests the mystery of a love "so much refin'd" that the appeal to sensual analogues . . . cannot encompass it. (136)

As Gilman's quotation marks suggest, however, it is too simple to say that the compass image is a "failure"; though understanding it requires more than a simple act of the visual imagination, the conceit does work, as Freccero demonstrates in his learned explication of the compass's motion as a *spiral*. The spiral, which—in Renaissance astronomy—is the geometrical pattern traced by planetary motion, combines the divine (which is circular) and the human (which is linear) (Freccero, "Donne's 'Valediction'").[39] A "determined reader" like Freccero may thus, as Roebuck observes, "push on from desire for a resolved image into the realm of thought as mathematics, whence visual furniture dissolves into the geometry of the mind" (40). Indeed the reader is called upon to do so by the poem itself, which urges an ascent above the realm of the physical senses and scorns those "Dull sublunary lovers" (13) who, not having studied the higher mathematics of love's astronomy, remain earthbound, in a realm delimited by sensory experience.

The point is, however, at least as much theological as it is mathematical. Like *La Corona*, the "Valediction" depends upon a distinction between true communicants and those carnal persons who rely upon the presence of the flesh. In his sermons, Donne objects to the doctrine of transubstantiation because he believes that it misleads the ignorant laity and allows them to confuse sacramental Presence with mere physical presence, to worship the visible bread as God. But in "A Valediction forbidding mourning," the speaker's attitude is less sympathetic toward ignorant folk; he has no Protestant interest in disabusing the common man of his misconceptions. On the contrary, he would keep the sacred rites of love's priesthood, the spiritual alchemy by which all things are transmuted, definitively secret: "T'were prophanation of our joyes / To tell the layetie our love" (7–8).[40] The unenlightened "layetie" (not comprehending the mystery of absent presence that informs the speaker's attitude and the poet's inscription) are excluded from the priesthood of true belief. They, like the "Dull sublunary lovers" of the poem's fourth stanza are mired in mere

carnal perception; like those who cling to Christ's fleshly presence in the Eucharist, relying too much "upon . . . corporall,
and personall presence" (*Sermons* 7:267), such lesser lovers
and readers "cannot admit / Absence" (14–15). But with a sacramental inscription as their seal of assurance, the lover and
his lady can. And thus, like Jesus forbidding Mary Magdalen
to touch him after his resurrection, the speaker can insist
upon controlled emotions, telling his lady (as Jesus tells the
Magdalen) that she should "Dwell not upon this passionate
consideration of my bodily, and personall presence" (Donne,
Sermons 7:267, paraphrasing John 20:16 in a sermon on the
Eucharist).

Similarly, the inscriber of the circle (who is also the writer
of the poem) calls the reader/communicant to a leap of faith.
Because the love of the speaker and his lady is itself a mystery
that cannot be seen or touched—it is so "refin'd" that they
themselves "know not what it is" (17, 18)—he offers her a
tangible sign that figures forth their inward assurance of
mind, a visible work with the power to seal that assurance
sacramentally if only she will not limit her response to the
merely visual and carnal. In offering the poem to his beloved,
the poet/speaker imitates God, who institutes the sacraments
as "external and visible means and seals of grace" so that
Christians can "assure [themselves] of the mercies of God"
despite the fact that grace "it self cannot be discerned by the
eye, nor distinguished by the touch" (Donne, *Sermons* 2:254).[41]
Like a believing Christian, then, the lady is to receive the
sign with faith—with a "firmnes" that validates the poem's
circular structure and makes it a "just" representation of their
union.

If it is thus received, the sacramental text will act upon the
receiver as Baptism did upon Augustine; he was relieved of "a
trembling, a jealousie, a suspition" and "imprint[ed]" with
"security" and "assurance" in "the outward seales and marks,
and testimonies of [God's] inseparable presence with [him]"

(Donne, *Sermons* 5:73–74). As Donne explains in his 1619 sermon to the Prince and Princess Palatine, "[T]he outward seals of the Church upon the person [are] . . . visible sacraments, . . . the outward seal of the person, to the Church, visible works, . . . [and] the inward seal of the Spirit, assurance"—that is, assurance of the final "fruition" that the soul will experience in its union with God (*Sermons* 2:266). In the poem, the outward seal of the written text is the visible sacrament that ensures the two lovers' inward faithfulness and trust in one another.

The speaker's sacramental relation to his female reader does not, however, simply cast him in the divine role. He is at once both the institutor of love's seal and, as in *La Corona*, the human priest whose sacramental offerings or "visible works," as Donne puts it in the sermon, depend upon the action of another Spirit. The circle of the poem will be "just," its utterance an effectual seal of absent presence and unbroken union, only if its inspiration is true. The lady's "firmnes" is what "makes" the speaker's circle complete (35); that is, her faithfulness to him is the real maker of the poem, the poetic agency that underlies the written seal. Just as *La Corona* will be a worthy eucharistic offering only if the Holy Spirit has raised the poet's muse, so the "Valediction" will be a truly effectual sign only if the woman's/reader's "firmnes" or constancy holds the compass steady; and the poet/speaker is, as the poem demonstrates, willing to take the risk of relying on her. Through "A Valediction forbidding mourning," then, Donne faces the lurking fear of female infidelity not—as does the speaker of "Twicknam garden"—by seeking magical assurances that must ultimately prove poisonous; rather, he offers his reader a poetic inscription that is itself a sacramental assurance, a support to the weakness of faith in both man and woman.

EIGHT

⊰⊱

Equivocal Devotion

The poet/speaker of "A Valediction forbidding mourning" presents his work as a sacramental seal that confirms and strengthens the faith of its receiver. But when Donne addresses poems to his social superiors, and to aristocratic women in particular, decorum dictates that he must take a humbler position, not claiming any quasi-divine power for himself or for his poetry, but assuming instead the role of human priest or penitent in relation to his patroness's "divinity" (*BedfReas*, 2). In verse epistles to noblewomen, Donne does not always abandon the idea of poem as sacrament; but he presents that idea ironically, and in contexts that suggest his ambivalence toward the poetry of praise.

Two Churches and Two Countesses: The Presentation of "Man to Gods image"

In May or June of 1609, Donne wrote a letter to his friend Henry Goodyer in which he responded to two subjects of an earlier letter from Goodyer. The first topic was the news

223

that, in some quarters, Goodyer was suspected of irresolute commitment to reformed religion. The second subject was Goodyer's praise of Elizabeth Stanley Hastings, Countess of Huntingdon, and his suggestion that Donne write complimentary verses to that lady.

In the first two thirds of his letter, Donne discusses religion, warning Goodyer against the dangers of appearing too ecumenical while at the same time approving "that sound true opinion, that in all Christian professions there is way to salvation" (*Letters*, 100). In the last third of the letter, Donne abruptly switches subjects to discuss "the other part of [Goodyer's] Letter" (103). He says he has "two reasons to decline" his friend's request that he write verses for the Countess: he does not want to appear undignified in her eyes and in the eyes of her family; and he fears that writing such a poem would compromise his "integrity to" the Countess of Bedford, for whom he has "reserved" his services as a poet (103, 104). Donne has no sooner expressed these reasons for refusal, however, than he consents to write the poem anyway, revealing that it is not only already written, but enclosed in the letter.

On both subjects—the competing claims of two religions and the competing claims of two countesses—Donne maintains a cautious neutrality even as he seeks to cloak that neutrality in the guise of preference and commitment. He affirms the good of both churches and both patronesses, using language that demonstrates his loyalty to one, yet not refusing to render a somewhat backhanded and negative-sounding tribute to the other. Together, the prose letter and the verse letter illustrate Donne's sense of the reader's role in creating meaning; and both texts play upon commonplaces of sacramental theology in order to manipulate reader response.

The prose letter to Goodyer is a complex artifact, constructed as a Chinese box of analogies within analogies. An implied parallel between religion and patronage links the first part of the letter to the second, and each part is in its turn filled with analogies. In the first part of the letter, Donne compares the "formes, and dressings of Religion" (*Letters*, 101) with bodily diet and dress, Catholicism with Copernican astronomy, and individual Christian souls with coins. In the second part, he uses the language of spiritual autobiography to describe the history of his relationship with the Countess of Bedford. Even more interesting than the analogies within and between the letter's two parts, however, are the connections between the prose of Donne's letter as a whole and the poetry of the enclosed verse epistle to the Countesses of Huntingdon, "Man to Gods image."[1] The prose letter to Goodyer provides a context for the reception and interpretation of the poem, and a close reading of the two texts in relation to each other helps to explain the theological images and rhetorical strategies of the verse epistle. An analysis of the connections between the prose letter and the verse epistle also underscores the crucial role that Goodyer—the first reader of both texts—played in determining the poem's meaning and function; studying those connections reveals the prose letter's mediating function as an envelope or conveyance that affects the meaning of the sacramental language in the enclosed verse letter.[2]

In order to appreciate the complex structure of Donne's prose letter to Goodyer, one must begin by considering the analogies in its first part, the part dealing with religion, which takes up three and one-half of its five and one-half pages. Donne opens by responding to Goodyer's account "of the book, and the nameless Letters" (*Letters*, 100). The book is apparently a Roman Catholic apologetic work, while the letters seem to be anonymous attacks on Goodyer written by persons who "think . . . [Goodyer has] in [his] Religion peccant humours, defective, or abundant," or that the book in question has "work[ed] upon" him; that he is, in short, "irresolved or various" in his religion (*Letters*, 100).[3]

Donne says that he harbors no "jealousie or suspicion of

a flexibility in" his friend and declares himself "angry, that any should think" such things of Goodyer (100). He stresses the need for discretion, however, explaining his fear that Goodyer has invited the advances of proselytizers (both Roman Catholic and nonconformist) through his rash candor in airing ecumenical opinions and through his "having friends equally near [him] of all the impressions of Religion"; both of these things, Donne says, "may have testified such an indifferency, as hath occasioned some to further such inclinations, as they have mistaken to be in you" (100–01). Donne is writing here as a fellow Protestant; two years earlier, in a 1607 letter to Goodyer, he had spoken of the English Church as "ours" (*Letters*, 87). Here, too, he speaks in the first person plural, confirming his own faith—both in that Church and in his friend—by speaking as a circumspect advisor who does not wish to see Goodyer depart from the *via media*:

> As some bodies are as wholesomly nourished as ours, with Akornes, and endure nakednesse, both which would be dangerous to us, if we for them should leave our former habits, though theirs were the Primitive diet and custome: so are many souls well fed with such formes, and dressings of Religion, as would distemper and misbecome us . . . (*Letters*, 101)

By comparing the "nakednesse" of "Primitive" people with the religious practices inappropriate for "us," Donne warns Goodyer against Genevan Calvinism, a religion stripped bare by its objection to vestments and its insistence on a return to the "Primitive" Christianity of the Early Church. But in warning also against a diet of acorns, Donne alludes to English Protestants' rejection of the Catholic Eucharist, the staple diet of their ancestors which they can no longer digest.

Throughout this part of the letter, Donne maintains a stance of detached objectivity even as he writes of matters that bear directly on his own case as a recusant-turned-Protestant. "You shall seldome see a Coyne," he tells Goodyer, "upon which the stamp were removed, though to imprint it better, but it looks awry and squint. And so, for the most part, do mindes which have received divers impressions" (*Letters*, 101–02). Given Donne's Catholic background, the "lack of self-consciousness" in passages like this is, as Richard Strier has observed, distinctly "odd" (357). But Donne's language is remarkably free of any reminder that he is, himself, a re-stamped coin. He no doubt speaks from experience when he says that one will suffer "in the opinion of men" if one changes one's religion (*Letters*, 101); but he eschews the opportunity to personalize such observations by citing his own history.

Instead, he preaches to his friend. First he insists that "I will not, nor need to you, compare the Religions"; they are so much alike, he urges, that it is pointless to incur the dangers of leaving one for the other: "they are sister teats of [God's] graces, yet both diseased and infected, but not both alike" (*Letters*, 102). Having said this much, however, Donne cannot resist continuing the comparison he said he would not make; he exercises his wit, constructing an amusing analogy between Roman Catholicism and Copernican astronomy:

> . . . as *Copernicisme* in the Mathematiques hath carried earth farther up, from the stupid Center; and yet not honoured it, nor advantaged it, because for the necessity of appearances, it hath carried heaven so much higher from it: so the *Roman* profession seems to exhale, and refine our wills from earthly Drugs, and Lees, more then the Reformed, and so seems to bring us nearer heaven; but then that carries heaven farther from us, by making us pass so many Courts, and Offices of Saints . . . in all our petitions . . . (*Letters*, 102)

This witty critique of Catholicism is also, by implication, a critique of Protestantism: Copernicanism carries earth up from its inert place at "the stupid Center," putting it in motion around the sun; similarly, Catholicism puts human beings into the celestial motion of otherworldly holiness; Protestantism is, by implied contrast, Ptolemaic—that is to say, an earth-centered, worldly system.

The analogy is a deliberately ingenious display of wit, clearly meant to divert and cheer Goodyer more than to enlighten him; for Donne follows his astronomical conceit with the advice that Goodyer must at all costs avoid melancholy: "Sir, . . . labour to keep your alacrity and dignity, in an even temper: for in a dark sadnesse, indifferent things seem abominable, or necessary, being neither; as trees, and sheep to melancholique night-walkers have unproper shapes" (*Letters*, 103). Religious melancholy here takes on the contours of imagination, that force that Shakespeare's Theseus finds in lunatics, lovers, and poets, as well as in nocturnal wanderers: "in the night imagining some fear, / How easy is a bush suppos'd a bear!" (*A Midsummer Night's Dream* 5.1.21–22). In Donne's letter, the things transformed by the imagination are "indifferent things," matters not essential to the faith. If Goodyer's melancholy imagination becomes overactive, Donne concludes, if he begins to see these "indifferent things" as either "abominable, or necessary," he will cheapen himself in demeaning attempts at self-explanation. Indeed, he will sell himself as cheaply as any whore: "[W]hen you descend to satisfie all men in your own religion, or to excuse others to al; you prostitute your self and your understanding, though not a prey, yet a mark, and a hope, and a subject, for every sophister in Religion to work on" (*Letters*, 103).

This warning provides Donne with a transition to his second topic, Goodyer's praise of the Countess of Huntingdon and his suggestion that Donne write verses in her praise. As becomes clear immediately, Donne feels that he has himself been made, "though not a prey, yet a mark, and a hope, and a subject" for a proselytizing friend "to work on." He responds delicately to Goodyer's dearly held belief: "For the other part of your Letter, spent in the praise of the Countesse, I am always very apt to beleeve it of her," Donne says, "and can never beleeve it so well, and so reasonably, as now, when it is averred by you." He responds negatively, however, to Goodyer's request that he become an active practitioner of this faith: "but for the expressing it to her, in that sort as you seem to counsaile, I have these two reasons to decline it . . ." (*Letters*, 103). The irony is immediately apparent: Donne will "descend to satisfie" his friend, to explain and defend himself in precisely the way that his just-penned advice warns Goodyer not to do.

First, Donne explains, he does not want to appear light or frivolous in the Countess of Huntingdon's eyes: "that knowledge which she hath of me, was in the beginning of a graver course, then of a Poet, into which (that I may also keep my dignity) I would not seem to relapse" (*Letters*, 103). The parenthetical phrase here—"that I may *also* keep *my* dignity"—clearly refers back to his earlier words of advice, "labour to keep your alacrity and dignity"; Donne is paralleling his own case with that of Goodyer. Just as "it hath hurt very many . . . in their reputation . . . that others have thought them fit to be wrought upon" in matters of religion (*Letters*, 101), so it may compromise Donne's reputation if he allows Goodyer to manipulate him in matters of literary devotion. Indeed, the phrase, "I would not seem to relapse," when read in the context of the letter's first topic, casts light on Donne's sense of his reputation not only as a former poet, but also as a former Catholic.

Donne had explicitly paralleled the two practices—that of the poet and that of the Catholic—in "Satyre II," in which the speaker calls the state of poets "poore, disarm'd, like Papists, not worth hate" (10). In the letter, too, Donne dismisses poetry with an attitude of condescending superiority. Invoking the Spanish proverb "that he is a fool which cannot make one Sonnet, and he is mad which makes two" (*Letters*, 104), Donne assumes the aristocrat's blandly dismissive attitude toward writing: every accomplished gentleman has the skill, but to be an inspired practitioner of the art is to be a lunatic. Thus, with his allusion to the proverbial observation that poets are madmen, Donne completes the subtle parallel between Goodyer and himself, between the perils of religious melancholy and the perils of poetic practice. As he counsels Goodyer against the night-walking lunacy of religious melancholy, so he declares his own resolution to avoid the madness of those other melancholy insomniacs, the sonneteers.[4] The parallel between the two kinds of "madness" allows Donne to sidestep any direct confrontation with the subject of his own spiritual biography. Instead of alluding to that personal religious history or explicitly confirming his loyalty to the English Church, he introduces a parallel discussion in which he alludes to the history of his relations with two noble ladies and asserts the firmness of his loyalty to one of them.

Indeed, though Donne is concerned about what Lady Huntingdon will think of him if he "relapse[s]" into poetry, he worries even more about what the Countess of Bedford will think if he writes poems for anyone but her. His "other stronger reason" to reject Goodyer's suggestion is, he says, "my integrity to the other Countesse[;] . . . for her delight (since she descends to them) I had reserved not only all the verses, which I should make, but all the thoughts of womens worthinesse" (*Letters*, 104).[5] As these lines reveal, Donne has not really abandoned the practice of poetry; he has merely restricted himself to writing verses for and about a lady who "descends" to them, not moving heaven out of reach, like a Catholic or a Copernican, but making it more accessible to a staunch believer. It would be going too far to say that Lucy thus symbolizes the more accommodating English Church; but it is clear that, in scrupulously maintaining his "integrity" to her, Donne can avoid being accused, as Goodyer has been, of "flexibility" (*Letters*, 100). Thus, within the parameters of Donne's letter, loyalty to Lucy will stand as the secular and literary equivalent of loyalty to the established religion.

As he insists upon his faithfulness to Lucy, moreover, Donne acknowledges that he originally became that lady's devotee through Goodyer's influence. She is "the other Countesse, of whose worthinesse though I swallowed your opinion at first upon your words, yet I have had since an explicit faith, and now a knowledge" (*Letters*, 104). Donne here traces his relationship with Lucy through stages corresponding roughly to a Protestant-eye-view of a converted recusant's spiritual development. He begins as a credulous communicant; lacking any real faith, he relies on the "words" with which Goodyer consecrates the Countess, the declaration that *hoc est* "worthinesse"; he "swallow[s]" whole the "opinion" thus conveyed. Subsequently, he becomes a more mature believer, achieving "an explicit faith" in his deity's goodness; and now, having entered Lucy's service, he resembles the saints in heaven, no longer seeing through a glass darkly, but possessing direct "knowledge" of the deity.

No sooner has Donne declared his reasons for holding firm in his service to Lucy, however, than he reveals his acquiescence to Goodyer's suggestion. He has written verses for Elizabeth Stanley Hastings, and he has enclosed them in the letter. He hopes, he says, that the Countess of Bedford "will not disdain, that I should write well of her Picture" (*Letters*, 104). If Lucy Harrington is willing to think of the younger Countess of Huntingdon as her "Picture," and if she is not an iconoclast who condemns the veneration of images, all will be well.

Donne thus cements the analogy between the letter's first and second topics. He has concurred with Goodyer's religious ecumenism, declaring that the two religions are "sister teats of [God's] graces" (*Letters*, 102); now, he concludes that he can suckle nourishment from more than one pap of female patronage. But the risks are as considerable in the second case as in the first. Goodyer, who first converted Donne to the service of Lady Bedford, has now persuaded the poet to pay literary homage to a lady firmly associated with the sphere of his earlier social and religious loyalties. Donne begs his friend to ensure that "by this occasion of versifying, I be not traduced, nor esteemed light in that Tribe, and that house where I have lived" (*Letters*, 104). Flynn explains this remark by noting that Donne would originally have made Elizabeth Stanley's acquaintance during his youthful service in the stubbornly (though equivocally) recusant household of her grandfather, Henry Stanley, Fourth Earl of Derby.[6]

Not surprisingly, Donne remains uneasy with his decision to "relapse" into poetry by writing verses for a daughter of this ancient Catholic house. His concern to avoid praising any woman but Lucy Harrington and to reserve for her all his "thoughts of womens worthinesse" (*Letters*, 104) helps to account for the language of the enclosed poem, which attempts to harmonize sexist remarks about women in general with compliment to the female addressee, and solves the problem by denying that Elizabeth Stanley Hastings *is* a woman at all. Unlike Lucy, who "descends" to her devotee's level, Elizabeth is one of those "heavenly things" (22) to which virtue—having "fled" like Astraea from the human realm (22)—has been "rais'd" (21). Given her sex, Lady Huntingdon's "active good" (10) is not "rare" (6) like a "comet" (10), but a "miracle" (8, 11) like a "new starre" (6).

In these lines, the poet resorts to the language of Catholicism, with its emphasis on miracles, and of Copernican astronomy, which made possible Kepler's discovery of new stars. In the prose letter, Donne points out Catholicism's similarity to the new science, declaring that both exalt the earthly without really honoring or advancing it; here he applies the terminology of both systems to the praise of the Countess of Huntingdon in order to declare her "heavenly" while, at the same time, refusing to honor any woman but the Countess of Bedford. Elizabeth Stanley Hastings is, he argues, no woman, but virtue herself. While virtue "guilded" others, the Countess is "gold" (25); while virtue "inform'd" others, she "transubstantiates" the Countess (26). In short, Donne praises Elizabeth by invoking the miracle of the Catholic sacrament; to avoid praising any woman but the Countess of Bedford, Donne celebrates a Catholic Mass and elevates not the Countess of Huntingdon, but her transubstantiated elements. He praises, he says in the poem's closing couplet, not her, but God *in* her: "I was your Prophet in your younger dayes, /And now your Chaplaine, God in you to praise" (69–70). Clearly, the mysteries Donne associates with a member of the Stanley family are Catholic mysteries; the reverence he gives her is reverence for the "miracle" of transubstantiation.

Having composed and resolved to send this Catholic-flavored sacramental tribute, Donne remains understandably ill at ease. He thus builds into the conclusion of the accompanying prose letter several defense mechanisms. These help to complete the analogy between the letter's two topics while at the same time shielding him from blame. First, he attempts to plant in Goodyer's mind any number of reasons to retain the poem for his own reading pleasure rather than give it to Lady Huntingdon:

> If those reasons which moved you to bid me write be not constant in you still, or if you meant not that I should write verses; or if these verses be too bad, or too good, over or under her understanding, and not fit; I pray receive them, as a companion and supplement of this Letter to you; and as such a token as I use to send, which use, because I wish rather they should serve (except you wish otherwise) I send no other. (*Letters*, 104–05)

Donne here resigns to Goodyer the office of "Chaplaine" claimed in the poem; it is Goodyer who will be the priest and mediator, deciding whether or not to offer up to the deity/ addressee the sacrifice of Donne's Mass-like poem. If Goodyer decides not to present it, the poem will be a gift to him, not to the Countess, a "token" of the sort Donne says he encloses quite often in his letters to his friend. But if Goodyer does

decide to give the poem to the lady, he will be taking respon-
sibility for it, vouching that it is a "fit" offering.

The result Donne hopes for, so he says, is that Goodyer
will decide to use the verse letter as a poem for his own diver-
sion rather than as a gift for the Countess. Though Donne
expresses anger in the first part of the letter "that any should
think" Goodyer "had in [his] Religion peccant humours, defective, or abundant," he relies on a version of that possibility in his own case, hoping that Goodyer will find his verse
either "defective"—beneath the lady's intellectual capacities—
or "abundant"—over her head. Indeed, Donne expresses a hope
that Goodyer himself will after all—in this matter if not in
religion—prove "irresolved or various," that he will waver in
his conviction that Donne ought to write verses. Or perhaps,
he says, edging toward another possible escape route, Goodyer did not mean that he should write verses; perhaps he has
misunderstood Goodyer's request, just as the judgment of
Goodyer's attackers "mistakes" him, misinterpreting things
that "have been ... incommodiously or intempestively ...
uttered by" him (*Letters*, 100). Donne explains that he has
not enclosed any other verses because he hopes that his friend
will indeed decide against giving the enclosed piece to the
lady and will instead keep "Man to Gods image" for himself. This gesture undercuts the acquiescence he displayed
in agreeing to write the poem.

So, too, do the letter's closing remarks undercut the quasi-
Catholic eucharist of the verse letter. For in ending, Donne
calls attention to his participation in the celebration of another sacrament in another Church: "here at a Christning at
Peckam, you are remembered by divers of ours," he says, in
what is probably a reference to the baptism of his nephew
Arthur Grymes, the child of Anne More's sister, Margaret
Grymes (Bald, 180, n.1.) The christening, recorded in the
records of the Parish of Camberwell, would have been performed according to the rubric of the *Book of Common Prayer*,

and the "divers of ours" who send their regards to Goodyer
are not just members of John's and Anne's family, but a community of faith, conforming members of the English Church.
As Donne had included himself in that community earlier
in the letter by using the first person plural "ours" and "us"
(*Letters*, 101), he now closes with a glance at his and Goodyer's
shared place in that community of belief.

Finally, however, he narrows his focus to a more intimate
community, the relation of friend to friend that he has already
invoked in begging Goodyer to shield him from any disgrace
in the eyes of the Stanleys: "I . . . intreat you by your friendship" (*Letters*, 104). Elsewhere, Donne calls letters "friendships sacraments" (unpublished letter, quoted in Simpson,
311); here, that sacred function is marked by Donne's use of
the word "seal"—a Protestant synonym for sacrament—as
he concludes the letter that will soon be held by Goodyer: "I
kisse your hands, and so seal to you my pure love, which I
would not refuse to do by any labour or danger" (*Letters*, 105).
Donne's language reminds Goodyer of the danger Donne in-
curs by his ongoing closeness to a man others think "various"; but it also declares that they remain coreligionists, men
in communion with one another. In the first part of the letter,
Donne is the soul of caution, expressing his agreement with
Goodyer's ecumenical tolerance from the safe and solid ground
of their shared English Protestantism, preaching wittily to his
friend from an essentially *via media* pulpit. He becomes more
daring in the second part of the letter, in which Goodyer is
cast as the priest of patronage, the mediator who may or may
not present the offering of Donne's quasi-Eucharistic poem to
the Countess of Huntingdon. But the poem's conclusion is,
one might say, the boldest stroke of all: it privileges the religion of friendship, making it the only reliable locus of "pure
love." And the letter, the sacrament of that religion, is signed
neither by Donne the English Protestant, nor by Donne the
former Catholic, nor by Donne the servant of this or that

Countess, but by Goodyer's *"very true friend and servant,* J. Donne" (*Letters*, 105). It is within the protected space that friendship provides—within the letter that is the sacrament of his "second religion, friendship" (*Letters*, 85)—that Donne has the freedom to survey and appraise the relations between things similar yet dissimilar, things "both diseased and infected, but not both alike": Catholicism and Protestantism, religion and patronage, poetry and prose.[7]

From the vantage point of this 1609 correspondence with Goodyer, moreover, the status of "Goodfriday, 1613," sent to the same friend a scant four years later, seems all the more bound to the question of human versus divine audience. In the case of his verse epistle to the Countess of Huntingdon, Donne tells his friend that, if the verses are "too bad, or too good, . . . and not fit," Goodyer should "receive them, as a companion and supplement of [Donne's] Letter to" him, withholding the work from the Countess and keeping it for his own delectation. Does this precedent bear upon the reception of "Goodfriday, 1613," helping to define its artistic or spiritual function? For Donne, perhaps, only his "true friend" Henry Goodyer was authorized to judge.

Bad Confession and Good Art: Desunt Cætera

If "Man to Gods image" and the letter in which it was enclosed were written in the early summer of 1609, as Hester estimates (*Letters*, xix), then it would seem that Donne avoided alienating the Countess of Bedford on that occasion. For most editors and biographers of Donne estimate that the Countess's patronage of Donne lasted until 1615. In that year, as he prepared to enter the ministry, Donne complained in a letter to Goodyer that the Countess entertained some "suspicion of [his] calling" and that his request for her aid in paying his debts had yielded a mere £30 (*Letters*, 218, 219). Donne's relations with Lady Bedford up to this point must have remained cordial, for in the 1615 letter he expresses surprise at this "diminution in her" and tells Goodyer that "her former fashion towards" him "had given a better confidence" (*Letters*, 219). Even in his disappointment, moreover, he credits the truth of her excuses: "that her present debts were burdensome, and that I could not doubt of her inclination, upon all future emergent occasions, to assist me" (*Letters*, 219). It is clear, then, that Lady Bedford did not cut off her patronage of Donne in a fit of pique over a poem in praise of another lady.

Nevertheless, Donne's own concern about questions of loyalty and sincerity surfaces frequently in Donne's writings to and about the Countess. Indeed, throughout the verses Donne wrote for Lucy Harrington and other noble ladies, Donne confronts his own uneasiness with being one of those poets "who write to Lords, rewards to get"—as he puts it in "Satyre II" (21). He frequently addresses the problem of self-contradiction involved in bestowing superlatives upon more than one patroness, as well as the problem of credibility and decorum involved in bestowing superlatives upon any mortal being. As Margaret Maurer points out, "The speaker of these poems repeatedly confronts the possibility that his praise may be construed as flattery" and the disconcerting sense that he must "reconcile other praises with those to the Countess of Bedford" ("John Donne's Verse Letters," 256, 257). Indeed, as Maurer argues, Donne's "verse letters to the Countess of Bedford are remarkable for the way they transform the difficulties prescribed by the circumstances of their inspiration into poetry that very often achieves its praise through scrupulous attention to the integrity of its author" (252).

For Donne, I would argue, the problem with writing complimentary poems about the virtues of his patrons is not just that it involves flattery, but that it seems to undermine the ambiguous and fictional status of poetry itself.[8] "The poet," Sidney insists in his *Defense of Poesy*, "nothing affirms, and therefore never lieth" (235); but in writing poems of praise,

Donne feels called upon to eschew the ambiguity and un-
certainty that give life to so much of his poetry. In "Satyre
III," the speaker urges "Seeke true religion," only to ask "Oh
where?" (43). And the answer remains as indirect as the route
up Truth's "huge hill" (79). In "Show me deare Christ," the
speaker seeks but is never able to affirm the identity of Christ's
Bride. And in "I am a little world," both the conceit and the
speaker's salvation depend upon verbal ambiguity. But in poems of praise such as "Madame, You have refin'd mee," it
would seem that Donne must affirm something; he must
assert his unwavering ability to recognize virtue and to "say,
This is shee" (*BedfRef*, 12).

Because he is *un*certain that such certainties can be the
stuff of poetry, Donne's complimentary verse letters often challenge the mode's reliance upon affirmation; and one of his most
interesting strategies for doing so is to inject his poems of praise
with a secularized version of the unresolved theological questioning that suffuses "Satyre III" and "Show me dear Christ."
In "Man to Gods image," he tempers his praise of the Countess of Huntingdon by tapping the language of the Catholic
Eucharist. Likewise, in his hymns of praise to the Countess of
Bedford, Donne inquires into the relative importance of Faith
and Reason in the poetic pursuit of "divinity" (*BedfReas*, 2);
weighs how much "care" should be lavished on "Temples
frames, and beauty," how much on "Rites within" (*BedfRef*,
35–36); and generally seeks to question and explore the practice of complimentary poesy as though it were a religion and
he a theologian engaged in doctrinal controversy.[9]

In "To the Countess of Bedford. Begun in France but never
perfected," this process of inquiry pushes the poetry of praise
to, or perhaps past its breaking point. The poem is Donne's
confession to his patroness, in which he asks her forgiveness
for having gone a-whoring after strange gods: that is, for the
very sin he begins to commit when he writes "Man to Gods

image" for the Countess of Huntingdon in 1609. Given the controversial status of confession as a sacrament of the Roman Church rejected by Protestants, Donne's attempt to make his poem a confession and to address that confession to a Protestant lady, is fraught with ambiguity. He not only takes his usual liberties in applying the language of theology to secular praise, but risks presenting the Calvinistically inclined Lucy with a Romanistically inclined conceit.[10] But the real essence of the poem's wit is its self-declared imperfection; for the piece is left, as I will argue, deliberately unfinished. It is through the poem's intentionally unfinished status, its witty failure to affirm either the poet's repentance or his patroness's divinity, that Donne strikes at the very core of complimentary poetry.

The "incomplete" verse epistle to Lady Bedford has received scant critical attention, most scholars noting only that it must be the poet's apology to the Countess for having written or published the *Anniversaries*. But Donne's "A Letter to the Lady Carey, and Mrs. Essex Riche, from Amyens," which was also written during the poet's 1611–1612 sojourn in France, could just as easily have provided the occasion for Donne's incomplete apology to Lucy.[11] The Countess might well have seen or heard about Donne's verse compliment to the daughters of the notorious Penelope Rich; and as Bald observes, "If some of Donne's contemporaries felt that he had overstepped the bounds of propriety in the *Anniversaries*, they must have felt that he had done so even more recklessly in his praise of these two living ladies" (249). In short, the Amyens "Letter" could also have occasioned the Countess of Bedford's irritation (or the poet's nervous anticipation thereof) and Donne's apology.

Whether or not the two poems are so directly linked, they both rely upon denominationally charged religious language to engage in and at the same time question the poetry of praise; a brief glance at the religious conceits of the Carey/ Rich poem can thus provide a helpful context for the interpretation of the apologetic verse epistle to the Countess. In the "Letter to the Lady Carey, and Mrs. Essex Riche," Donne remarks on the questionable principles that underlie poetic praise by drawing a parallel between French Catholicism and his own practice in composing the verse epistle:

> Here where by All All Saints invoked are,
> 'Twere too much schisme to be singular,
> And 'gainst a practice generall to warre.
>
> Yet turning to Saincts, should my'humility
> To other Sainct then you directed bee,
> That were to make my schisme, heresie.
>
> (1–6)

When in Amyens, he shrugs, he'll do as the Frenchmen do. And what they do is address their prayers to the saints: both the holy ones of heaven and the fair ones of Petrarchan sonnets.

As is frequently the case in Donne's poetry, the conventional language of romantic compliment is here associated with specifically those Catholic traditions of worship rejected by Protestants. By underscoring his playful conformity to Continental forms of worship and/or poetic modes, the poet can pay his respects to the ladies while stressing that he does not fully endorse the mode of discourse he is employing. And as he goes on to joke, any excesses that he may commit in practicing this French form of devotion will be answered for by the system he has temporarily adopted: "If this be too bold, / Pardons are in this market cheaply sold" (8–9).

In the poem "Begun in France but never perfected," however, Donne seeks full absolution from his patroness rather than the weaker consolation of a purchased indulgence. Fearing that he has incurred her wrath by writing poetry in praise of other ladies besides herself, he is determined to convince

her that he is sorry for his transgression; thus, he characterizes his poem as a confession. The poet is to Lucy as a sinful human being is to God. The religious overtones of his
language are, moreover, distinctly Catholic. As he explains
in lines 7–10, Lucy is the sun who nourishes his newly-
sprouting poesy and the deity whose grace works powerfully
in the holy springtime seasons of Lent and Easter:

> This season as 'tis Easter, as 'tis spring,
>> Must both to growth and to confession bring
> My thoughts dispos'd unto your influence, so,
>> These verses bud, so these confessions grow . . .
>
>> (7–10)

The lines allude to the Catholic practice of going to confession at least once a year, in preparation for Easter. Rome had
decreed this annual confession mandatory for all Catholics in
the year 1215, and as Thomas Tentler explains in his book *Sin
and Confession on the Eve of the Reformation*, the practice
was, by the late Middle Ages, deeply embedded in folk tradition: "If there was a time to venerate your patron saint, pray
for your dead relatives, get your throat blessed, invoke a variety of protectors, . . ., so there was also a time, most clearly
and emphatically defined, to confess your sins" (81). In the
poem, Donne characterizes his Eastertide confession to the
Countess as this kind of instinctual or liturgically determined
response to the season. In doing so, he casts the entire proceeding in a gently ironic light, suggesting that he will offer
the Protestant Lucy only the sort of "vegetable piety"—to
adapt Marvell's famous phrase—that could be expected from
a lowly papist carrying out his Lenten obligation.

Any such irony has, however, been overlooked by twentieth century readers. Maurer, one of the few critics who
discusses the poem at all, approvingly quotes R. C. Bald's comment: "It is more ingenious than convincing, and Donne
was probably wise to leave the poem unfinished." She adds

that "It is, of course, most illustrative of his capacities that he dared write it at all" ("Real Presence," 213). But what makes Donne's poem truly provocative and witty, given its ruling metaphor of confession, is its conspicious incompleteness. For the phrase *Desunt cætera* has a particular import and urgency when attached to a confession.

Any work may be left unfinished, but the particular significance of an incomplete *confession* will be clear to any reader familiar with the Catholic sacrament of penance. Medieval and Renaissance penitential manuals stress vehemently that each confession must be complete. One such manual is *A Short Treatise of the Sacrament of Penance* by Fr. Vincent Bruno, S.J. Bruno's treatise—published in 1597—explains that for a confession to be valid, "it must be entire" (18); that is, the penitent must "manifest" all his sins, "expressing every one in particuler, in the kind and number," including "not only that which he hath committed, by outwarde action, but also by thought, and by wordes" (19, 22).

Donne clearly has such a paradigm of thoroughness in mind when he begins the substance of his confession to the Countess in line 11 of the verse epistle:

> First I confesse I have to others lent
>   Your stock, and *over prodigally spent*
> *Your* treasure, for since I had never knowne
>   Vertue or beautie, but as they are growne
> In you, I should not *thinke or say* they shine,
>   (So as I have) in any other Mine; . . .
>
>   (11–16; emphasis added)

These lines conform to the model confession outlined by Bruno. Donne is careful to confess sins of thought and word as well as of deed, words and works being distressingly inseparable for a poet. His financial imagery serves, moreover, to reveal that the situation calls for reparations: he owes the Countess because he has misspent *her* "treasure." In Bruno's terms, Donne's sin involves a "circumstance . . . necessarily to be expressed, in respecte of some satisfaction which the Penitent is to make" (Bruno, 26–27).

Donne's scrupulous observation of rules such as those outlined by Bruno sets up several currents of wit. For Luther, the Catholic's obligation to confess comprehensively, rehearsing every sin without omission of a single particular, was an onerous burden inconsistent with Christian liberty. It was one of the most important issues leading to his reevaluation of faith versus works, and his eventual break with Rome. On one level, then, Donne's incomplete confession is a playfully Protestant-minded compliment to Lucy's "divinity." Demonstrating that it would be impossible to make account of all his transgressions against her, the poet surrenders himself utterly and submits an imperfect confession as evidence that he has abandoned any reliance upon his own works and will trust to the mercy of her quasi-divine grace. In short, Donne implies that his inability to complete his request for forgiveness is the surest testimony to his faith in her.

Donne's wit extends, however, beyond and below such association of devotion with failed self-expression. For, despite their conviction that one has no obligation to reveal one's sins to a *priest*, English Protestants stressed that a Christian must confess sincerely and comprehensively to *God*. Thus, the confessional idiom of Donne's verse epistle allows for the possibility that its Protestant addressee will take Donne's metaphor seriously and forgive him—as God would a sinner— only if he confesses as he ought. And how *ought* an Englishman to confess? The answer, it would seem, is a paradox: artfully, yet candidly. In a 1610 collection of sermons on repentance, the English preacher Richard Stock emphasizes the need for a complete and guileless confession of one's sins to the Lord. The language he uses, however, ironically underscores the inherent tension in any confession between artful role-playing and perfect openness or sincerity. The sinner must "*play the part* of an informer by . . . accusing himselfe before God" (emphasis added); yet he must do so "by making a simple, plaine, and full confession, al excuses, pretences, and shifts being laid aside" (Stock, 81).[12] Clearly, the process of total self revelation remains a challenge for the Protestant mind. Stock's idea of a good penitent, like Hamlet's idea of a good actor, involves a convincing fiction, not elaborate or overdone; the penitent must hold, as 'twere, a mirror up to his own sinful nature.

For Donne, too, confession is an art. One of his sermons on the penitential psalms begins by declaring the text of Psalm 32:5, on which the whole sermon is a commentary: "I acknowledged my sin unto thee, and mine iniquity have I not hid. I said, I will confesse my transgressions unto the Lord, and thou forgavest the iniquity of my sin." "This," Donne explains, "is the Sacrament of Confession; So we may call it in a safe meaning; That is, The mystery of Confession: for true Confession is a mysterious Art" (*Sermons* 9:296). And like any poetic art, confession is on one level the spontaneous—and therefore sincere—overflow of powerful feeling, and on another level an artfully crafted performance, a fiction. Donne explains the paradox in a Lincoln's Inn sermon: The only action that can make our sins "none of ours," Donne tells the congregation, is "the avowing of them, the confessing of them to be ours":

> Onely in this way, I am a holy lier, and in this the God of truth will reward my lie; for, if I say my sins are mine own, they are none of mine, but, by that confessing and appropriating of those sins to my selfe, they are made the sins of him, who hath suffered enough for all. . . . (*Sermons* 2:102)

The Christian poet who confesses himself to God in writing is thus becoming "a holy lier," or—to put it another way—a divine poet.

Similarly, when addressing his *human* "divinity," Lucy, Donne tends to shift the burden of verity onto her, to make her nature as his subject and her responses as his reader the only loci for truth. As he puts it in "Honour is so sublime perfection": "Should I say I liv'd darker then were true, / Your radiation can all clouds subdue" (19–20). Similarly, Lucy alone can "perfect" Donne's confessional poem "Begun in France." It can "never" be "perfected" by its author, for as the opening lines stress, he is totally dependent upon his reader:

> Though I be *dead*, and buried, yet I have
>   (Living in you,) Court enough in my grave,
> As oft as there I thinke my selfe to bee,
>   So many resurrections waken mee.
> That thankfullnesse your favours have begot
>   In mee, embalmes mee, that I doe not rot; . . .
>
>   (1–6)

Unpolished and inconsistent, these lines immediately confirm the headnote's promise that the poem will be imperfect. The images of resurrection mingle uncomfortably with those of embalming; and the explicit reference to "Court" mars the effect of the religious analogy between Lucy's favors and divine grace. The imagery is, moreover, radically incompatible with the ruling conceit of all that follows, for the dead are beyond both repentance and confession. As Stock explains, "In this life and upon the earth there is only place for repentance, men onely heere can repent and turne to God. . . . because the ministry of the word is onely of use in this life" (262). Similarly, if Lucy demands Donne's repentance, if she insists that he confess to her as only a living man can, she must also vouchsafe him the preventing grace that will resurrect him from the death of her disfavor and make his confession possible.

As Donne explains in his sermon on Confession as Art, the verb tenses in Psalm 32:5 say it all; David's act of confession is in the future, but God's act of forgiveness is in the past: "I said, I will confesse my transgressions unto the Lord, and thou forgavest the iniquity of my sin." As Donne explains, "David's is but *Actus inchoatus*, He sayes *he will confesse*,

And Gods is *Actus consummatus, Thou forgavest,* Thou hadst already forgiven . . . my sin." Thus, Donne concludes, the "*And,* in [the] Text, is as a ligament, as a sinew, to connect and knit together that glorious body of Gods preventing grace, and his subsequent grace; if our Confession come between and tie the knot, God, that moved us to that act, will perfect all" (*Sermons* 9:312). But if the goddess Donne addresses in his verse confession has not already granted him the grace that would make his confession both possible and perfect, then she has confirmed his status as a dead man and must accept the fact that he is beyond repentance or confession. She must leave his corpus to rest in peace, embalmed with the "thankfullnesse" he feels for her past favors and sprouting no new verses in her praise.

The poem's confessional idiom is built on shifting ground, then, from the very start; and as Donne's catalogue of his sins proceeds, the confession begins to implode and collapse upon itself. The first offence he confesses is that of lending Lucy's "stock" to other women by writing poems to them instead of her, but the second sin he lists is the one he is in the process of committing by writing this poem:

> Next I confesse this my confession,
>> For, 'tis some fault thus much to touch upon
> Your praise to you, where half rights seeme too much,
>> And make your minds sincere complexion blush.
>
>   (17–20)

These lines remind the addressee of the protestations she ought to make at being divinized by a poet. They undermine the legitimacy of the indignation that ostensibly occasioned the current poem and suggest that as a woman of devout sincerity, Lucy ought to demur at the thought of being put in God's place. She should view the slackening of his former idolatrous behavior as a virtue, rather than a vice.

And indeed, the final sin Donne confesses proceeds logically from just such thinking: he is not truly sorry, after all, as he has been behaving charitably, not sinfully, in writing the praises of humbler ladies:

> Next I confesse my'impentitence, for I
>   Can scarce repent my first fault, since thereby
> Remote low Spirits, which shall ne'r read you,
>   May in lesse lessons finde enough to doe,
> By studying copies, not Originals,
>   *Desunt cætera.*   (21–26)

Donne's wit comes full circle here, playing upon the traditional doctrine that true repentance has three essential components: Contrition (which is a movement of the heart), Confession (declared with the lips), and Satisfaction (the work of the hands that confirms one's rejection of sin and makes restitution for any ill-gotten gain).[13] The *desunt cætera*, the something missing from Donne's poem, is thus contrition itself.

If a sinner is not truly contrite to begin with, he cannot proceed either to confession or to absolution, and his acts of satisfaction—in the form of prayers, charitable acts, or reparations—will be worthless. On this, despite the radical disagreement of Catholics and Protestant about whether or not human works can be said to "merit" anything, Father Bruno and the Reverend Stock reach essentially the same conclusion. Bruno explains that "he which is in mortall sinne, looseth all the good works which he doth: because they availe not to obtaine any meritt of everlasting life" (9). And Stock puts it even more vividly: "[A]ll their good workes be they never so glorious and many, comming from a corrupt fountaine, of an unrepentant and unbeleeving heart, are accounted sins before God" (46). Thus, in the ingeniously inconclusive conclusion of his poem to the countess, Donne admits that "something is missing" from this poetic work of confession and satisfaction, both because he is not sincerely sorry and because he continues to view what "are accounted sins" in Lucy's eyes as good works, which is to say, valid poems.

From beginning to end, Donne invests his poem with witty commentary on its own nonfeasiblity. As a dead man, cut off from Lucy's life-giving favor, he cannot confess at all; as a Catholic, rattling off his sins in rote succession, he cannot confess deeply; and as a Protestant, convinced that no man can give a satisfactory account of himself, he cannot confess comprehensively. Finally, as an unrepentant practitioner of the sin called poetry, he cannot write a poetic confession unless he insures that it will cancel and undercut itself. The truest poetry is the most feigning, and in this case, the worst confession is the best art.

In his sermon on Confession as Art, Donne says that "As liquors poured out leave a taste and a smell behinde them, unperfected Confessions (And who perfects his Confession?) . . . leave a taste, and a delight to thinke, and speake of former sins, sticking upon thy selfe" (*Sermons* 9:314–15). Donne's unperfected confession to the Countess of Bedford leaves Donne, and us, savoring the sweet residue of poetry— unaffirming, uncomplimentary, ambiguous—that always clings to his work.

AFTERWORD

Conveying Donne

Throughout his career as a poet, a correspondent, and a priest, Donne is concerned with the ways in which one person—human or Divine—conveys himself or herself to another.[1] Tracing the frequent images of self-conveyance and delivery in his writing, one detects a common thread linking texts (written or spoken) to bodies as conduits for souls, and in turn linking both bodies and texts to Sacraments, God's visible means of conveying grace incarnate.

"Loves mysteries in soules doe grow," says the speaker of "The Extasie," "But yet the body is his booke" (71-72); for bodies "us, to us, at first convay" (54). But the body's function of conveying the self may be performed by a letter as well. In a 1613 letter to Martha Garrard, Donne explains that in visiting him, her brother George has brought her along "as well by letting me see how you do, as by giving me occasions, and leave to talk with you by this Letter" (*Letters*, 40). He thinks often of her, he says, but his thoughts "have seldome the help of this conveyance to [her] knowledge" and thus he is "loth to leave" off writing:

> [F]or as long as in any fashion, I can have your brother and
> you here, you make my house a kinde of Dorney [the Garrard
> estate]; but since I cannot stay you here, I will come thither
> to you; which I do, by wrapping up in this paper, the heart of
>
> Your most affectionate servant
> J. Donne.   (*Letters*, 41)[2]

So complete is the illusion of presence evoked by this letter
that Bald believes it was written "acknowledging a visit which
[Martha Garrard] made to Donne with her brother" (278); but
in commenting on the letter as one of the means by which
George has given him access to Martha, Donne stresses that
she is present to him and he to her, not in the flesh, but through
George's oral communication, which lets Donne "see how"
Martha is doing, and through the "conveyance" of the written text, which allows Donne to send his heart to her. Indeed,
as Donne says in another letter (printed in Simpson, 311) "letters are friendships sacraments. & wee should be in charyty
to receaue at all tymes." The Eucharistic conceit is telling;
friend is in full communion with friend, and Real Presence is
possible through the text as sacramental medium.

Between human beings and God, too, there are means of
conveyance; and one of the most powerful of these, as Donne
explains in an oft-quoted passage from a 1617 sermon, is a
kind of love poetry:

> *Salomon*, whose disposition was amorous, and excessive in
> the love of women, when he turn'd to God, he departed not
> utterly from his old phrase and language, but . . . conveyes all
> his loving approaches and applications to God, and all Gods
> gracious answers to his amorous soul, into songs, and Epitha-
> lamions . . . (*Sermons* 1:237)

Finally, the deity's "gracious answers" to man are transmit-
ted to man through God's own conveyances: "[T]hen does God
truely shine to us," Donne explains in a 1622 sermon, "when
he appears to our eyes and to our ears, when by visible and

audible means, by Sacraments which we see, and by the Word which we heare, he conveys himself unto us" (*Sermons* 4:105).

Body, letter, sermon, poem, sacrament: all are means by which the self may convey itself to another self who is "in charyty to receave." Embracing a hermeneutics of suspicion, late twentieth century readers may avoid being ravished by Donne's God, seduced by his lyrics, or impregnated by what Donne himself calls his "words masculine perswasive force" (*ElFatal*, 4); but it is a dear-bought chastity. The alternative is a dangerous, a pleasurable, a wise "charyty to receaue" the poetry by which—like Sir Henry Wotton in "Sir more then kisses" we still "have DONNE."

APPENDIX

૨☙

The Doctrine of Eucharistic Sacrifice

On the subject of Christ's presence in the Eucharist, Roman Catholics of the Reformation era did not disagree; but on the question of how and in what sense the Mass might be called the sacrifice of Christ's Body and Blood, they differed widely. Ambrose Catharinus (1487–1553), whom Donne cites occasionally in his sermons, argued that while the death of Jesus on the cross was a sacrifice for the remission of original sin, Christ—in instituting the Eucharist and commanding his disciples to celebrate it—instituted a new priesthood "for doing away with the faults which are continually repeated under the new covenant." In the Eucharist, Catharinus explained,

> We have blood, and real blood, which we offer to appease God for the new faults, because without blood there is no remission; and the outpouring of this blood, which took place once, ought always to be of profit, provided it is continually offered. (*Commentary on the Epistle to the Hebrews*, quoted and translated in Stone 2:71)

Catharinus's explanation seemed quite erroneous to some Catholics, however. Melchior Cano (1520–1560)—one of the Dominican theologians present at the Council of Trent and a man whom Donne refers to as "a great man in the *Roman Church*" (*Sermons* 4:217), "a wise Author of theirs" (*Sermons* 7:123), and "a good Author in the Roman Church" (*Sermons* 8:135)—condemned

> the madness of the idea of Ambrose Catharinus that sins com-
> mitted before Baptism are remitted by means of the sacrifice of
> the cross, but all sins committed after Baptism by means of
> the sacrifice of the altar. For the sacrifice of the cross is the
> universal cause of the forgiveness of sins, whether committed
> before or after Baptism. (*De locis theologicis*, quoted and trans-
> lated in Stone 2:359)

Cano nevertheless asserted that the Mass was a propitiatory sacrifice; and, indeed, the doctrine of propitiatory sacrifice was promulgated in 1562 by the Council of Trent:

> [Christ], at the Last Supper, on the night He was betrayed, that
> He might leave to His beloved spouse the Church a visible
> sacrifice, such as the nature of man requires, whereby that
> bloody sacrifice once to be accomplished on the cross might be
> represented, the memory thereof remain even to the end of the
> world, and its salutary effects applied to the remission of those
> sins which we daily commit, . . . offered up to God the Father
> His own body and blood under the form of bread and wine, and
> under the forms of those same things gave to the Apostles,
> whom He then made priests of the New Testament, that they
> might partake, commanding them and their successors in the
> priesthood by these words to do likewise: *Do this in commemo-*
> *ration of me* [Luke 22:19; 1 Corinthians 11:24f.]. ("Doctrine
> Concerning the Sacrifice of the Mass," Chapter 1)[1]

The distinction between the bloody sacrifice on the cross and the
unbloody sacrifice of the Mass is central to the Roman Catholic teaching. It had been very clearly defined in 1531 by Cardinal Cajetan
(whom Donne cites approvingly on several occasions in his *Sermons*):

> The blood of Christ on our altar is none other than the blood
> of Christ shed on the cross. But the way in which this identi-
> cal victim is offered is different. The unique, original, and basic

way of offering was in a bloody manner, when in its own proper form the body was broken on the cross and the blood shed.
But the daily, representative, and derived manner is unbloody,
under the form of bread and wine, as Christ once offered on the
cross is present again in the mode of an offering. (Cajetan, 197)[2]

For theologians such as the Jesuit Robert Bellarmine, however,
the word "sacrifice" could have no meaning unless it referred the
destruction of the thing sacrificed: "it is required for a sacrifice that
what is offered to God as a sacrifice be wholly destroyed, that is, that
it be so changed as to cease to be that which it was before" (*De
Missa*, quoted and translated in Stone 2:366). Hence, Bellarmine
asserts that

> In the consecration of the Eucharist, three things take place
> in which the method of a real and actual sacrifice consists.
> First, a profane thing becomes sacred; for the bread otherwise
> earthly and common is turned by consecration into the body
> of Christ. . . . Secondly, in the consecration that thing which
> has been made sacred from being profane is offered to God. . . .
> Thirdly, by means of the consecration the thing which is of-
> fered is destined to a real, actual, and outward change and de-
> struction, which has been declared necessary to the method of
> a sacrifice. For by means of consecration the body of Christ
> receives the form of food; and food is destined to be eaten, and
> in this way to change and destruction. (*De Missa*, quoted and
> translated in Stone 2:366)

Bellarmine's emphasis on the Eucharistic sacrifice as involving the
immolation of the transubstantiated Host was particularly obnox-
ious to Protestants, for it implied (as Donne puts it) that men could
both "*make* a Christ" and then "*kill*" him (*Sermons* 7:429).

But Reformers found the Catholic doctrine of Eucharistic sacrifice objectionable at a more fundamental level as well. For Luther,
the doctrine obscured both the true nature of the Eucharist and the
priesthood of all believers. In his 1520 "Treatise on the New Testament, that is, the Holy Mass," Luther stresses that Christ's words of
institution ("This is my body. . . . This is my blood which is poured
out for you, a new eternal testament") bestow a "testament" or legacy

to "heirs" ("Treatise," 86). The practice of the priest's pronouncing the consecration in a low voice inaudible to the laity[3] hides "these words of the testament" ("Treatise," 90) and suppresses the truth that "we do not offer Christ as a sacrifice, but that Christ offers us" ("Treatise," 99). Indeed, Luther argues,

> all those who have the faith that Christ is a priest for them in heaven before God, and who lay on him their prayers and praise, their need and their whole selves, presenting them through him, . . . are true priests. . . . Faith alone is the true priestly office. . . . On the other hand all who do not have such faith but who presume to make much of the mass as a sacrifice, and perform this office before God, are anointed idols. ("Treatise," 101)

In the *Institutes*, John Calvin expresses a similar belief, emphasizing that the Eucharist is "the sacrifice of prayse" made by all Christian people, who are for that reason called "a kingly Presthode" (4.18.17). But he rejects Catholic doctrine even more violently than Luther does, expressing revulsion at the very idea of propitiatory sacrifice. The Roman Mass is, he insists, an abomination, a "pestilent error"; the belief that it "is a sacrifice and oblation to obtein the forgevenesse of sinnes . . . whereby the sacrificyng Prest . . . offereth up Christ . . . dishonoreth Christ, burieth and oppresseth his crosse, putteth his death in forgetfulnesse, taketh away the frute that cometh thereof unto us, [and] doth weaken and destroy the Sacrament wherein was left the memorie of his death" (*Inst.* 4.18.1). Calvin's influence shows clearly in the 31st of the *Thirty-nine Articles*, which declares that "The offeryng of Christ once made, is the perfect redemption, propiciation, and satisfaction for all the sinnes of the whole worlde, . . . and there is none other satisfaction for sinne, but that alone. Wherefore the sacrifices of Masses, in the whiche it was commonly sayde that the priestes did offer Christ for the quicke and the dead, to have remission of paine or gilt, were blasphemous fables and dangerous deceiptes."

But English theologians of Donne's day were not always so vehemently negative on the subject of Eucharistic sacrifice. As one would expect, Archbishop Laud insisted that the priesthood of all believers did not exclude a particular function for the ordained priest, and this insistence led him to a very different definition of the Eucharistic sacrifice:

> [A]t and in the Eucharist we offer up to God three sacrifices: One by the priest only, that is, the commemorative sacrifice of Christ's death, represented in bread broken and wine poured out. Another by the priest and the people jointly, and that is the sacrifice of praise and thanksgiving for all the benefits and graces we receive by the precious death of Christ. The third, by every particular man for himself only, and that is the sacrifice of every man's body and soul, to serve Him in both all the rest of his life. (*Works* 2:339–40; quoted in Stone 2:269)

Nor was Laud the only English Protestant to entertain the notion of sacrifice. Richard Field (1561–1616) argued that

> a man may be said to offer a thing unto God in that he bringeth it to His presence, setteth it before His eyes, and offereth it to His view, to incline Him to do something by the sight of it, and respect had to it. In this sort Christ offereth Himself and His body once crucified daily in heaven, and so intercedeth for us. . . . And in this sort we also offer Him daily on the altar in that, commemorating His death and lively representing his bitter passions endured in His body upon the cross, we offer Him that was once crucified and sacrificed for us on the cross, and all His sufferings, to the view and gracious consideration of the Almighty . . . (*Of the Church*; quoted in Stone 2:303)

Lancelot Andrewes (1555–1626) went even farther. In an effort to find common ground with Cardinal Bellarmine, Andrewes wrote that the doctrine of sacrifice would not be objectionable to Protestants if Catholics did not insist on transubstantiation as the means by which Christ is present in the Eucharist. English Protestants feel, Andrewes explained, that the doctrine of transubstantiation may be placed "among the theories of the school," but that it should not be made an article of faith:

> We believe no less than you that the presence is real. Concerning the method of the presence, we define nothing rashly, and, I add, we do not anxiously inquire. . . . Our men believe that

the Eucharist was instituted by the Lord for a memorial of Himself, even of His sacrifice, and, if it be lawful so to speak, to be a commemorative sacrifice. . . . Do you take away from the Mass your Transubstantiation; and there will not long be any strife with us about the sacrifice. (Quoted and translated in Stone 2:264, 265, 266).[4]

Some devout Protestants were scandalized by such conciliatory gestures. Donne's friend and mentor Thomas Morton (1564–1659), who (according to Izaak Walton) was instrumental in convincing Donne to enter the priesthood, wrote in his treatise *Of the Institution of the Sacrament of the Blessed Body and Blood of Christ, (by some called) the Masse of Christ*:

It would be a wonder to us to hear any of our own profession to be so extremely indifferent concerning the different opinions of the manner of the presence of Christ's body in the Sacrament as to think the Romish sect therefore either tolerable or reconciliable upon pretence that the question is only *de modo*, that is, of the manner of being, and that consequently all controversy about this is but vain jangling. (Quoted in Stone 2:289).[5]

On the contrary, Morton insisted, all heresies "albeit their difference from the orthodox were only *de modo*," must be abandoned. As for the Catholic doctrine of Eucharist sacrifice, Morton declared it "sacrilegious," asserting that "the body of Christ in this Sacrament is not a proper sacrifice nor properly sacrificed" and that "This (except men have lost their brains) must needs be every man's conclusion" (quoted in Stone 2:287).

But of course, it was by no means every man's conclusion. Nor was it Donne's. The poet's position on this question—which plays an important part in determining the function of his Eucharistic sonnet cycle, *La Corona*—cannot be easily pigeon-holed. In the preface to *Pseudo-Martyr*, he is—as always in that work—equivocal and evasive. Constructing an analogy to defend his position as a layman writing on the Oath of Allegiance issue and addressing his Jesuit opponents, he insists that it is

meerly of temporall matters, that I write. And you may as justly accuse Vitruvius, who writ of the fashion of building Churches, or those Authors which have written of the nature of Bees and use of Waxe, or of Painting, or of Musique, to have usurped upon the office of Divines, and to have written of Divinity, because all these are ingredients into your propitiatory medicine, the Masse, and conduce to spirituall and divine worship: as you may impute to any, which writes of civil obedience to the Prince, that he meddles with Divinity. (B3v)

The reference to the Sacrifice of the Mass as "your propitiatory medicine" is sarcastic, but it is placed within a sentence that categorizes that sacrifice not as a sacrilegious heresy but as "spirituall and divine worship." Years later, in his *Sermons*, Donne defines the English Church's notion of Eucharistic sacrifice very carefully in terms that evoke the Tridentine notion of "applying" Christ's sacrifice even as they reject Bellarmine's insistence that sacrifice necessarily involves the destruction of that which is sacrificed. Donne's phrasing recalls Field's emphasis on the presentation of Christ's merits to the father; but the Dean makes the idea sound closer to Catholic doctrine by referring repeatedly to the *"body"* of Jesus's merits:

> The *Communion Table* is an *Altar*; and in the *Sacrament* there is a *Sacrifice*. Not onely a Sacrifice of *Thanksgiving*, common to all the Congregation, but a *Sacrifice peculiar to the Priest, though for the People*. There he *offers up* to God the Father, (that is, to the *remembrance*, to the contemplation of God the Father) the *whole body* of the *merits of Christ Jesus*, and begges of him, that in contemplation of that *Sacrifice* so offered, of that Body of his merits, he would vouchsafe to return, and to apply those merits to that Congregation. A Sacrifice, as farre from their blasphemous over-boldnesse, who constitute a *propitiatory Sacrifice*, in the *Church of Rome*, as from their over-tendernesse, who startle at the name of *Sacrifice*. We doe not, (as at *Rome*) first invest the power of God, and make ourselves able to *make* a Christ, and then invest the malice of the Jews, and *kill that Christ*, whom we have made; for *Sacrifice*, Immolation, (taken so properly, and literally as they take it) is a *killing*; But the *whole body* of *Christs actions* and *passions*, we sacrifice, wee represent, wee offer to God. (*Sermons* 7:429)

In this passage, taken from a sermon preached at Paul's Cross on May 6, 1627, Donne's language draws upon many different Catholic and Protestant formulations; it is equivocal, much more open to interpretation and misinterpretation than are the statements of Laud and Andrewes. He defines the nature of Eucharistic sacrifice specifically over against the most extreme Roman Catholic formulations of the doctrine, yet his repeated references to "the *whole body*" sacrificed, represented, and offered in the Eucharist emphasize his refusal to separate the idea of sacrifice from a less than figurative interpretation of the words "Hoc est corpus meum."

Donne edges even closer to the Roman Catholic doctrine of Eucharistic sacrifice in a sermon delivered in Calvinist Heidelberg before the Prince and Princess Palatine; he says that the priest offers up "Christ Jesus crucified . . . *for the sins of the people*, so, as that that very body of Christ, which *offered himself for a propitiatory sacrifice upon the cross, once for all*, that body, and all that that body suffered, *is offered again*" (*Sermons* 2:256; emphasis added). The language of this passage makes the priest's sacrifice sound propitiatory even though the "which" clause that follows restricts the act of propitiation to Christ's offering of himself "once for all."

NOTES

Notes to Introduction

1. This image originated with Donne's seventeenth century biographer, Izaak Walton, and was endorsed by R. C. Bald, who took Walton as his guide in writing what has until recently been accepted as the "definitive" twentieth century biography, *John Donne: A Life*. The view of Donne as a conservative "Anglican" preacher is exemplified in the commentary of Potter and Simpson's edition of Donne's *Sermons* and in Davies. Critics portraying Donne's politics as essentially absolutist include Goldberg and Shuger.

2. Shami cites Sharpe, Cogswell, and Cust.

3. See Chanoff, who, though he retains the anachronistic term "Anglican," presents a nuanced account of how Donne came to find "his spiritual home in the English Church" (154) and of how "sacramental" poems like *La Corona* reflect that process. Helpful in accounting for the inadequacy of traditional categories are Patterson ("All Donne") and Norbrook, who stresses Donne's ties to English divines such us Thomas Morton and Joseph Hall and notes that Morton and Hall "have been labeled without too much of a sense of oxymoron as 'Puritan bishops'" (20). Shami calls these bishops and Donne "participants in a theological 'middle group'" ("Donne's Sermons," 381). For a stronger emphasis on Donne's affinity for "Puritan" views, see Doerksen (356, 361). Other reassessments of Donne's religious and political alignments include Patterson, "John Donne, Kingsman?"; Guibbory, "'Oh, Let Mee Not Serve So'"; and Scodel. Major historical studies providing a context for the reevaluation of theological and ecclesiological factions in the English Church include those of Fincham and Lake.

4. Shami cites Davies, *Like Angels* (195–203), and Lewalski (17) Donne himself was suspicious of the tendency to quote selectively for polemical purposes; see "Satyre II," in which the speaker says that a lawyer deliberately leaves key phrases out of documents "As slily'as any Commenter goes by / Hard words, or sense; or in Divinity / As controverters, in vouch'd Texts, leave out / Shrewd words, which might against them cleare the doubt" (99–102).

5. Chamberlain argues that Donne "shared in the High Church reaction against the Puritan methods of developing Scripture by reductive topical logic and preferred to follow the patristic and medieval example of reading the text with attention to the rich and interrelated significations of the words" (108). Despite his rhetorical techniques, however, Donne's position on the power and necessity of preaching resembles that of Hooker's opponents more closely than that of Hooker. See my discussion in the fourth section of chapter 1, below.

6. See Hester, Young, and Flynn. See also Eleanor J. McNees's insightful chapter on Donne in her book *Eucharistic Poetry: The Search for Presence in the Writings of John Donne, Gerard Manley Hopkins, Dylan Thomas, and Geoffrey Hill.* McNees's analysis of Donne's poetry in light of English Protestant theology of the Eucharist does much to explain how sacramental theology shapes Donne's use of figurative language. Also sensitive to the poet's synthesis of disparate theologies is Gilman.

7. Flynn points out that there was "a fertile dialectic of continuity and discontinuity" between pre-Reformation and post-Tridentine English Catholicism; many Catholics clung to what they called "the Old Religion" and found little in common with those—especially "the new breed of post-Tridentine Jesuits"—committed to the dogmatic and political militancy of ultra-montane Catholicism ("'*Annales* School,'" 3–4, 8). Flynn argues that "Donne's Catholicism, like that of the Heywoods and More, was of a sort that could survive the Council of Trent only through fierce resistance on its own terms. . . . Their isolation became increasingly painful and confounding, and became also the source of their increasingly ineffectual ironies about religion: the ironies of *Utopia,* of John Heywood's plays and poems, of Jasper Heywood's antic disposition, and ultimately of John Donne's love poems, satires, and other writings" ("'*Annales* School,'" 8). Donne's grandmother, Joan Rastell, was the niece of St. Thomas More; she married John Heywood, a protégé of More, and their sons, Jasper and Ellis Heywood, were both Jesuits. Flynn's work is informed in part by the historical scholarship of Bossy, who explains the tensions dividing the secular clergy, the Jesuits, and the Catholic gentry, and Haigh, who stresses the concept of English Catholic

"resistance" both to English Protestantism and to post-Tridentine Catholicism.

8. The Elizabethan Homily on the Sacrament urges that "truely as the bodily meat cannot feede the outward man, unlesse it be let into a stomacke to bee digested, which is healthsome and sound: No more can the inward man be fed, except his meate be received into his soule and heart, sound and whole in faith" (*Homilies*, 200). See also John Bale, who uses the word "digested" to describe devout reception of the Eucharist in his anti-Catholic treatise, *A mysterye of inyquyte* (1545): "Whereae his [Christ's] fleshe is eaten and surelye dygested / there is seane nomore whoremongynge / theft / fornicacyon . . ." (37v). And as is clear from Calvin's objections to Catholic ceremonies in which the consecrated Host was merely surveyed—"shew[n] foorth in a common gazing to be loked upon" (*Inst.* 4.17.37)—Protestants felt that mere surveying was not enough. The *Book of Common Prayer* recalls Calvin's objections when it urges members of the congregation to participate in the Communion, not to "stand by as gazers and lookers on them that do communicate, and be no partakers of the same yourselves" (256). By contrast, the Jesuit writer Thomas Wright says, "he that seeth this sacrament, seeth God, as those that saw Christs sacred humanity, the vaile of his person, were said to see his diuinitie" (*A Treatise . . . of the Reall Presence*, fol. 74v).

9. See the discussion of the phrase "ex opere operato" in note 11 below.

10. In order to demonstrate the high degree of nuance involved in Eucharistic controversy over the centuries, and to sketch the nature of Donne's response to its complexities, I have included an appendix tracing one subject of debate—the doctrine of Eucharistic sacrifice—through a number of the writers Donne might have encountered in his broad program of controversial reading and showing how he himself eventually addressed the doctrine. I have included works written later than *Pseudo-Martyr* as well as before it in order to demonstrate the range of different opinions Donne had to "digest"—before and after he entered the English Church—in formulating his own positions.

11. See Donne, *Sermons* 2:258 (quoted below, page 13). For a detailed explanation of the Latin expression "ex opere operato" (which means, literally, "by the work worked" or "by force of the action itself"), see Leeming 5ff. The Council of Florence (*Decree for the Armenians*, 1439) defined the difference between the sacraments of the Old Law, which "only prefigured" the grace "to be given through the Passion of Christ" and the Sacraments of the Church, which "both contain grace and confer it upon those who receive them worthily" (Leeming, 28). The doctrine that sacraments convey grace

specifically *ex opere operato* "in the case of those who place no impediment" ("*non ponentibus obicem*") was promulgated by the Council of Trent in 1547. The teaching was originally meant to stress that the effects of a sacrament are the *result* neither on the goodness of the priest nor that of the recipient, but that—as Leeming sums it up—"the will to receive God's gift is . . . a *conditio sine qua non*, a prerequisite, like dryness in wood before it can be burnt" (Leeming, 6). Leeming explains: "In so far as the expression *ex opere operato* excludes such efficacy from the minister, all Protestants who reject Donatism accept an *ex opere operato* doctrine," as is evident, for example, in Article 26 of the Thirty-nine Articles. He notes, however, that the expression "since the controversy of the sixteenth century, is more generally taken as excluding Luther's teaching that the sacraments are effectual exclusively through the faith of the recipient" (10). "Trent did not define that the sacraments *cause* grace, but only that they *confer* it," Leeming continues, noting that in so doing, the council was able to accommodate the Scotist view "that the sacraments were not causes of grace in any exact sense of the word 'cause,' but were, as one may say, infallible occasions, God having settled that he himself would produce grace in the souls of those who received the sacraments" (10, 12).

12. McNees is here commenting specifically on a passage from Donne's *Devotions* (Expostulation 14); she acknowledges that Donne's poetry "defies . . labeling" that would classify it as specifically Roman Catholic or Calvinist, but she emphasizes that the poet "advances toward Anglicanism as the most catholic of all religions" (37). While I find it more useful to dispense with labels altogether rather than to try to define what McNees calls "Donne's particular breed of Anglicanism," I am nevertheless indebted to her chapter on Donne's poetry, which very clearly and accurately outlines Donne's response (in sermons and poetry) to the most commonly emphasized features of the English Church's Eucharistic theology.

13. In this passage, quoted from a sermon preached at St. Paul's, 21 June 1626, Donne digresses from an argument against the doctrine of Purgatory, in which he has cited Cardinal Bellarmine's use of 1 Corinthians 15:29; Donne wishes to insist on a literal reading of that verse, and so he recalls Bellarmine's own insistence on the literal interpretation of Matthew 26:26 ("Hoc est corpus meum"), arguing that English Protestants have no objection to that interpretation. See Cardinal Cajetan's discussion of the same verse, in which he asserts that "These words, 'This is my body,' in their most literal sense signify that the substance indicated beneath the accidents of bread is the body of Christ. If these words, spoken literally, do not suffice, then no words would suffice" (Cajetan 165).

14. Calvin bases his teaching on Augustine's distinction "betwene

a Sacrament [*sacramentum*] and the thyng of the Sacrament [*res sacramenti*]" (*Institutes* 4.14.15). The Latin text of the *Institutes* is quoted from *Ioannis Calvini Opera Quae Supersunt Omnia,* vol. 2.

15. Compare the Council of Trent's insistence on the "wonderful and singular change of the whole substance of the bread into the body and the whole substance of the wine into the blood, the appearance only of bread and wine remaining, which change the Catholic Church most aptly calls transubstantiation" (Thirteenth Session, "Canons on the Most Holy Sacrament of the Eucharist," Canon 2). The Tridentine catechism further stresses that "the accidents which present themselves to the eyes or other senses exist in a wonderful and ineffable manner without a subject. All the accidents of bread and wine we can see, but they inhere in no substance, and exist independently of any; for the substance of the bread and wine is so changed into the body and blood of our Lord that they altogether cease to be the substance of bread and wine" (*Catechism,* 229).

16. Hooker also defends kneeling against Cartwright's objections that "sitting agreeth better with the action of the Supper" and that "Christ and his Apostles kneeled not" (Cartwright 165; quoted in the notes to Keble's edition of Hooker's *Works,* 2:365, n. 1). The rubric in *The Book of Common Prayer* instructs the minister to distribute "the communion in both kinds . . . to the people in their hands kneeling" (*BCP,* 263–64). Calvin does not object to the kneeling posture for prayer (*Inst.* 4.10.30), but on the question of whether or not the sacrament should be received kneeling, he says only that the communicants should "in becoming order . . . partake of the most holy banquet" (*Inst.* 4.17.43).

17. See, for example, Lancelot Andrewes's *Responsio ad Apologiam Cardinalis Bellarmini:* "'Christ said 'This is My body' He did not say, 'This is My body in this way.' We are in agreement with you as to the end; the whole controversy is as to the method . . . We believe no less than you that the presence is real" (quoted in Stone, 2:264). See also the conclusion of Hooker's analogy between art appreciation and devout reception of the sacrament: "Let it therefore be sufficient for me presenting myself at the Lord's table to know what there I receive from him, without searching or inquiring of the manner how Christ performeth his promise" (*Laws* 5.67.12).

18. See also Spenser's letter to Ralegh explaining the "darke conceit" of *The Faerie Queene.* The Calvinist Spenser is, of course, self-conscious about the idolatrous potential of art; and he knows that his "Methode will seeme displeasuant" to some who "had rather have good discipline deliuered plainly . . ., or sermoned at large, . . . then thus clowdily enwrapped in Allegoricall deuises" (737).

19. See Sidney's *Defense of Poesy:* "[T]he poet, disdaining to be

tied to any .. subjection, lifted up with the vigour of his own invention, doth grow in effect another nature. . . . [T]he skill of the arti-
ficer standeth in [the] idea or foreconceit of the work. . . . And that
the poet hath that idea is manifest, by delivering them forth in
such excellency as he had imagined them" (216).

20. This passage conveys a view not unlike that of the Scotist
school of Roman Catholic theologians (see note 11 above); but it is
clear from Donne's wording that he, like other Protestants, interpreted the Tridentine formula *ex opere operato* as positing a causal
relation between the performance of sacramental actions and the
transmission of grace. See also *Sermons* 2:217: "God is not tyed to
any *place*; not by essence; . . . but he is tyed *by his promise* to a
manifestation of himselfe, by working in some certain places."

21. See also Calvin's more extended discussion of the Holy Spirit's
role in the sacraments (*Inst.* 4.14.8–10).

22. The sixth book of Hooker's *Laws* was not published during
Donne's lifetime, but the principles underlying this passage clearly
derive from a conservative Protestant reading of Calvin and are similar to those underlying the passage from Donne's *Sermons* 2:258,
quoted above.

23. For Calvin, the function of the Eucharist does not essentially
differ from that of a sermon: "[T]he offering up of Christ is there [in
the Lord's Supper] so shewed in us, that the spectacle of the crosse is
in a maner set before our eyes: as the Apostle sayth that Christ was
crucified in the eyes of the Galathians, when the preaching of the
crosse was set before them [Galatians 3:1]" (*Inst.* 4.18.11). Comparing
preaching to sacraments in a more general sense, Calvin asserts that
justification is "communicated unto us no lesse by the preachyng of
the Gospell, than by the sealyng of the Sacramente" (*Inst.* 4.14.14).
Both are instituted in order "to offer and set foorth Christ unto us,
and in hym the treasures of heavenly grace" (*Inst.* 4.14.17).

24. This doctrine is based on Romans 10:13–15. See also Donne's
sermon for Easter, 1628 (*Sermons* 8:220, 228).

25. See *Paradise Lost* 1, lines 6–16; Milton aspires to emulate the
"shepherd, who first taught the chosen seed" (8) or the singers of
"Sion Hill" (10) and "Siloa's Brook" (11).

26. In the *Institutes*, Calvin rejects the *ex opere operato* formula
specifically because it underlies the idea that the act of receiving a
sacrament is a meritorious work: "whatsoever the Sophisters have
triflingly taught concerning the worke wrought, is not only false,
but disagreeth with the nature of the Sacramentes, which God hath
ordeined, that the faithful being voide and nedy of al good things
should bring nothing thether but beggerie Whereupon foloweth that
in receiving them, these men do nothing wherby they may deserve

praise: or that in this doing (whiche in theyr respecte is merely passive) no worke can be ascribed unto them" (*Inst.* 4.14.26).

27. See the "Pangc lingua," the Eucharistic hymn by St. Thomas Aquinas that is sung after Communion on Holy Thursday: "Pange lingua . . . / Corporis mysterium / Sanguinisque pretiosi" ["Sing my tongue . . . / The mystery of the Flesh / And precious Blood"] (*Missal*, 336–37).

28. See Cardinal Cajetan's explanation that in the Eucharist, Christ's body "is present in a spiritual manner that the human mind cannot grasp. In the same way we cannot grasp how the Word is united with the assumed humanity, nor how the one God is three persons. But we believe these, in spite of our lack of understanding" (161). McNees believes that the elements of Catholic imagery in "The Canonization" are parodic, that the poem mocks "Roman Catholic reverence for miracles by exaggerating the lovers' transformation" and that line 19 ("Call us what you will, wee'are made such by love") "pokes fun at the ease with which the Roman Catholics perform transubstantiation." She concludes that the poem succeeds in wielding Roman Catholic imagery to criticize earthly or visible love" (*Eucharistic Poetry*, 46).

29. The reservation and veneration of the host were, of course, particularly offensive to Protestants. Article 28 of *The Thirty-Nine Articles* specifies that "The Sacrament of the Lordes Supper, was not by Christes ordinaunce reserved, caryed about, lyfted up, or worshypped." The Council of Trent, however, anathematized anyone claiming that the Sacrament is "neither to be venerated with a special festive solemnity, nor to be solemnly borne about in procession according to the laudable and universal rite and custom of holy Church, or is not to be set publicly before the people to be adored" ("Canons on the Most Holy Sacrament of the Eucharist," Canon 6); also declared anathema was anyone claiming "that it is not lawful that the Holy Eucharist be reserved in a sacred place" (Canon 7).

30. I read the opening of stanza 5—"And thus invoke us"—as a declarative (the second verb and direct object in the clause that begins with "all shall approve / Us"), not an imperative.

31. In "Resurrection, imperfect" (17), the phrase "credulous pietie" is used to describe a pious superstition that, at the moment of death, "a Soule one might discerne and see / Goe from a body" (18–19). Ferry links the future projected in "The Canonization" to the "age" of "mis-devotion" in "The Relique" (*All in War with Time*, 120).

32. Herz argues that there is often no identifiable persona at all in a Donne poem; "rather, marvelously crafted, self-propelling, self-generating poems speak out of their own rhetorical systems, the

putative speaker of each disappearing into his own rhetorical excesses" ("'An Excellent Exercise,'" 5).

33. See Guibbory, "A Sense of the Future" and Wollman.

34. Donne speaks of having "descended to print any thing in verse" in 1612 letters to George Garrard and Henry Goodyer responding to criticism of his *Anniversaries*. The letters are quoted in their entirety in Stringer et al., eds. 6:239–40.

35. See the discussion of this remark in Marotti, Introduction, *Critical Essays*, 4.

36. For discussions of Donne's conscious cultivation of difficulty (as opposed to the Sidneyan poet's attempt to teach by delighting), see the first chapter of Alvarez ("Donne and the Understander"), especially 25–28, and Hester, "'Let me love.'" Both Alvarez (27–28) and Marotti (Introduction, *Critical Essays*, 5) note the 1633 elegists' emphasis on the difficulty of Donne's verse.

37. See also Donne, *Sermons* 2:362. The communicant's preparation to receive the Eucharist is also a matter of great concern to Roman Catholics; but whereas the English Church stresses readiness of soul and *intellect*, the Roman Catholic emphasis falls upon the preparation of soul and *body*. The council of Trent's canon dealing with the question of what constitutes "sufficient preparation for receiving the sacrament" declares that "sacramental Confession, when a confessor can be had, must necessarily be made beforehand by those whose conscience is burdened with mortal sin" (Canon 11). The Trent Catechism extends the preparation of the soul to include as well the need to "discern the body of the Lord," but it defines such discernment as an act of faith: "This we do when we firmly believe that there is truly present the body and blood of the Lord. . . . We should venerate the greatness of the mystery rather than too curiously investigate its truth by idle inquiry" (247). The Catechism also urges preparation of the body through fasting and abstention "from the marriage debt for some days previous to Communion" (248). As for intellectual preparation, the Catechism does stress that "the faithful are on no account to be left in ignorance" regarding the doctrine of the Eucharist (228); but it does not make understanding of transubstantiation a prerequisite for the reception of communion: "To explain this mystery is extremely difficult. The pastor, however, should endeavor to instruct those who are more advanced in the knowledge of divine things on the manner of this admirable change. As for those who are yet weak in faith, they might possibly be overwhelmed by its greatness" (238). Thus, at the beginning of his 1596 devotional handbook *The Disposition or Garnishmente of the Soule To receive worthily the blessed Sacrament*, Fr. Thomas Wright contrasts the handbook's function with

that of his earlier *Treatise, Shewing the Possibilitie, and Conveniencie of the Reall Presence*: "it concerneth us with no lesse industrie to preparc ourselves to receive it [the sacrament], then profoundly to understande it. Therefore having declared the speculative parte in the precedent booke, the practicall we reserved for this present: not that those Meditations weare not ordeyned, or not most apt meanes to induce oure hartes to receive this foode of life with all respecte, love, & affection (for all knowledg of God distillethe into the harte a certaine sweete motion or impulsion to love him) but because they weare somthing remote from practise, they taught not fully the way & particuler meanes how oure soules ought to be disposed, to participate this holy Sacrifice" (1–2). Wright then proceeds to outline the usefulness of physical mortifications in preparing oneself for the Eucharist (26–28) and to "reduce" spiritual preparation for the Sacrament "to sixe actes of fyve vertues. And the verie same which the Councell of Trente reckeneth, as dispositions to justification: those I Judge most fitt preparations for the sacred communion: Feare, Faith, Hope Charitie, Repentance, which I devyde into two operations, detestation of oure passed lyfe, and a firme resolution, not to falle again . . ." (28–29).

38. See also McNees's reading of "The Extasie" (*Eucharistic Poetry*, 40–43) and Hester, "'this cannot be said'" (374).

39. In the sermon, preached in the public setting of Paul's Cross on the Anniversary of King James's succession, 24 March 1616/17, Donne speaks in the first person plural of "*purifying Puritans*" as what "we shall become" if we are always "quarreling with men, with States, with Churches, and attempting a purifying of Sacraments, and Ceremonies, Doctrine and Discipline, according to our own fancy" (*Sermons* 1:189). He warns also against "*purified puritans*, that think they . . . need ask no forgiveness" (189). Donne is careful to insist, however, that "if we shall imagine a third sort of Puritans, and make men afraid of the zeal of the glory of God," we are contemptuous of Christian piety itself: "So I say, let me live the life of a *Puritan*, let the zeal of the house of God consume me, let a holy life, and an humble obedience to the Law, testifie my reverence to God in his Church, and in his Magistrate: For, this is Saint *Pauls Puritan*" (188). See also Doerksen, "'Saint Paul's Puritan.'"

Notes to Chapter One

1. Sherwood discusses Donne's emphasis on the connection between salvation and the believer's imitation of Christ crucified (*Fulfilling the Circle*, 116–30); and McNees, examining the importance

of that connection in what would come to be the Anglican position on the Eucharist, applies *via media* English Protestant doctrines to her readings of Donne's divine poems, including "The Crosse" (*Eucharistic Poetry*, 33–40, 51–54).

2. The sermon in which Donne uses this phrase to refer to the sacraments was preached 16 June 1619 to the Prince and Princess Palatine during Donne's visit to Heidelberg as part of the entourage of King James's ambassador, the Viscount Doncaster. The definition of a sacrament as a visible sign of invisible grace is traditional, carrying over from Augustine to the medieval theologians, and from them to the Reformers, including Calvin, whom Donne specifically cites in the Heidelberg sermon. For Calvin, Augustine's phrase "visible forme of invisible grace" is not entirely satisfactory, since in its "brefenesse there is some darknesse, wherein many of the unskillfuller sort are deceived" (*Inst.* 4.14.1). But for Donne, the "darknesse" of the Augustinian definition is a fruitful ambiguity.

3. See also Donne, *Sermons* 4:288–89 and 5:136; Herbert's "The Sacrifice," lines 245–47 (*The English Poems*, 55); and Tuve's discussion of Herbert's stanza in typological and iconographic terms (54–55 and Plates 2, 3 a,b). For a medieval example, see Chrysostom's sermon on Matthew 27:45–48 (*PG* 58:573) and *The Golden Legend*: "[W]hen the soldier opened his side with a spear, . . . this was the sacrament of our redemption" (Voraigne, 1:74). Also of interest is the title page of the Jesuit Thomas Wright's 1596 *Treatise, Shewing the Possibilitie, and Conveniencie of the Reall Presence of Our Saviour in the Blessed Sacrament*, which features the seal of the Society of Jesus (the letters IHS ["In Hoc Signo"] surmounted by a cross resting on the horizontal bar of the H with the three nails of the crucifixion beneath them and a border of flames enclosing the whole). The cross as it is rendered in the detail-rich version of the seal on Fr. Wright's title page is a crucifix with large drops of blood springing from the hands and side of the corpus. Around the flames which form the border of the seal is inscribed a motto (taken from Psalm 78:25): "MAN HATH EATEN THE BREAD OF ANGELS." The motto directly links the crucifixion as depicted in the engraving with the Eucharistic subject of Wright's treatise.

4. In this passage from his *Tractates on the Gospel of John*, Augustine is contrasting the use of sacramental signs by the virtuous, for whom they are effectual means of contact with Christ, with their empty use by the wicked: "If thou art good, thou belongest to the body of Christ now and hereafter: now by faith, by sign, by the sacrament of Baptism, by the bread and wine of the altar . . . But if thou livest wickedly, thou mayest seem to have Christ now, because thou enterest the Church, signest thyself with the sign of Christ, art

baptized with the blood of Christ, minglest thyself with the members of Christ, and approachest his altar, but [thou art no true member of the mystical body]." Calvin cites this passage in an argument against the local presence of Christ's body in the Eucharist: "How rightly he reckeneth a superstitious usage among the Signes of the presence of Christ, I doe not now dispute: but he that compareth the presence of the fleshe to the signe of the crosse, sufficiently sheweth that he fayneth not a twoo bodyed Christ, that the same he maye lurke hidden under the bred, which sitteth visible in heaven" (Inst. 4.17.28).

5. See Augustine, *Tractates on the Gospel of John*: "The word is added to the element, and it becomes a sacrament, tantamount to a visible word" (quoted and trans Pelikan 4:54). The "element" that makes the word visible in a poem is, of course, ink on paper. In a sermon, Donne compares the sacraments to the seal that is inscribed upon the foreheads of the just by an angel with a "writer's inkhorn by his side" (Ezekiel 9:3); the angel, Donne explains, "had a visible thing, *Inke*, to marke them withall" (*Sermons* 10:53); similarly, "Church-Angels, the Ministers of the Gospell" apply God's visible seals to men "in all emergent necessities" (*Sermons* 10:54). Donne probably had not yet taken orders when he wrote "The Crosse," but the poem certainly anticipates the role of priest and preacher he was to assume. On the cross in relation to the seal in Ezekiel, see Danielou, *Primitive Christian Symbols* (140–42) and *The Theology of Jewish Christianity* (154).

6. Donne owned an annotated a copy of Barlow's *Summe and Substance*; Keynes notes that Donne's copy was "Bound for him with five other tracts" and that it contains "many of Donne's pencil markings in the margins" (210).

7. Shawcross's note to line 2 of the poem acknowledges the baptismal sign of the cross as the poem's subject: "Christ's death absolved of original sin those who had died before; baptism is a sacrament continuing such absolution for the living. Puritans were, however, averse to using the sign of the cross in baptism" (*Complete Poetry*, 409). The practice of crossing the forehead of the baptized person is very ancient; on the history of the ritual, see Danielou, *Primitive Christian Symbols*: "The first appearance of the sign of the cross is in baptismal rites" and "ancient writers often use[d] the sign of the cross to indicate baptism itself. For example, at the end of the second century the Abercius inscription speaks of the people 'who bear the glorious seal': the word 'seal' (σφραγίς) means the sign of the cross traced on the forehead" (136). See also Danielou, *The Theology of Jewish Christianity* (329–31).

8. Elsewhere, Donne stresses that the crossing of the child's forehead during the baptismal rite is "not . . a part of the Sacrament, or

any piece of that armour, which we put on of spirituall strength" (*Sermons* 8:198). Yet he does recognize it as a valid testimony of "whose Souldiers wee [become]" in putting on that armor (198); in another sermon, he calls it one of the "sacramental and ceremonial things, which God (as he speaks by his Church) hath ordained" (2:258). See the discussion of "sacramentals" in chapter 7 below.

9. Article 27 of the Thirty-nine Articles explains that, in baptism, the believer is "as by an instrument, . . grafted into the Church." Hooker calls sacraments in general "the powerful instruments of God to eternal life" (*Laws* 5.50.3), being careful to specify that "they are not physical but *moral instruments* of salvation" (5.57.4). Donne says that the apostles Jesus chose for his ministry were but instruments of "the Workman" himself (*Sermons* 2:274). "[T]he Sacrament" is ambiguous, and may refer to either the Eucharist or baptism, evoking Donne's sense that both sacraments are a partaking in Christ's cross. The verb "dew'd" suggests both the waters of life that descend upon the believer in Baptism and manna, a type of the Eucharistic bread, which fell upon the camp of the Israelites with the morning dew (Exodus 16:13–14). McNees reads the passage as referring to the Eucharist. She says that "The tight compression of 'dew'd on me in the Sacrament' slices through time to capture the actual moment of Christ's blood falling from the cross. . . . The sacrament leads inward until the speaker becomes his own cross or part of Christ" (*Eucharistic Poetry*, 52). On the typological significance of dew see Nohrnberg (167 n. 178); see also the discussion of Marvell's "On a Drop of Dew" in Dickson (2–10).

10. This is the poem's title in all printed editions and in the Group I manuscript *C57*; however, it is entitled "On the Crosse" in *TCD* and "Of the Crosse" in *TCC, DC, Dob*, and *O'F* (*Complete Poetry*, 486). The two-word title most directly supports the reading of Donne's poem *as* a cross, a poetic crucifix. However, the variants by no means rule out such an interpretation. The ambiguity of the word "On" in the title "On the Crosse" suggests that the poem is not only a literary work *about* the cross but an utterance from or inscription upon Christ's cross. And the word "Of" in the title "Of the Crosse" may go beyond the designation of subject matter to define the work as a product or offspring of Christ's cross, one of "That Crosses children," as the last line of the poem puts it.

11. See Danielou, *Primitive Christian Symbols* (138–39) on the possibility that some early Christians may actually have borne tattoos of the cross on their foreheads.

12. Asals cites this passage as an expression of "a *via media* Anglican position" (*Equivocal Predication*, 23). She notes that, like Donne, Herbert connects "the *act or ceremony* of writing a poem . . . with the *event* on the Cross" (18) and conceives of poetry as "an

efficacious sign of Christ's *victory* on the Cross. . . . a rewriting of the former handwriting 'which is against us'" (22).

13. As Donne sees it, they engage in this practice, this imitative handwriting, when they "admit patiently [God's] Fatherly chastisements in the afflictions and tribulations in this life" (*Sermons* 10:196). See Harland, who stresses that both the sermon and the poem call the believer "to reincarnate the real presence of Christ in the world" (170).

14. See Luke 19:23: "Take up your cross and follow me." For a similar emphasis on the believer's eye, see Lancelot Andrewes's Good Friday 1597 sermon on Zechariah 12:10 ("and they shall look upon me whom they have pierced"). Andrewes discusses John 19: 37, where the verse from Zechariah is quoted as a prophecy of the crucifixion: "it is we that have 'pierced Him' that are willed to 'look upon Him.' Which bringeth home to us . . . and *applieth it most effectually to every one of us*, who seeing that we were the cause of this His piercing, if our hearts be not too hard, ought to have remorse to be pierced with it" (*Works* 2:125).

15. See Gilman, chapter 2.

16. When Christians consume the body and blood of the "crucified Serpent," Donne concludes, they are "mystically, and mysteriously, and spiritually, and Sacramentally united to him in this life" (*Sermons* 10:190). See Luther's comment on how the crucified Christ "even appears like the snake . . ., the Devil" (*Werke* 47:67f.; quoted and trans. Nohrnberg, 172). See also Donne's Latin poem to George Herbert (*Complete Poetry*, 368).

17. See Gilman (37–38).

18. Baker-Smith ("John Donne and the Mysterium Crucis") argues that Donne's images in "The Crosse" and "Good Friday 1613" are reminiscent of the *mysterium crucis* tradition, especially as it is expressed in the works of the humanist writers Lipsius and Gretser. Reproduced in Baker-Smith's article is a plate that was used to illustrate Lipsius 1593 work, *De Cruce*; the plate depicts many cross-shaped things also mentioned in Donne's poem: a swimmer, a praying man, a bird in flight, and several other items. The first scholar to discuss the relation between "The Crosse" and Lipsius's work was Bennett. See also Baker-Smith, "John Donne as Medievalist."

19. See Labriola on Donne's "Hymn to God my God, in my sicknesse" (18–20); when reading these lines, "the reader who makes the connections or draws the lines from Anyan to Sem, Magellan to Cham, and Gibralter to Japhet will inscribe the *iota chi*, the sacred hieroglyph" representing the name of Jesus Christ. This hieroglyph "engirds the land and sea traveled by the descendants of Sem to Asia, of Cham to Africa, and of Japhet to Europe. The Christogram thus

encloses the world within the name of Jesus" ("Donne's 'Hymn,'" 3–4). Labriola reads "The Crosse" as a related commentary on the "countless and reenacted inscriptions of the Christogram" in the physical universe and in human experience (5).

20. On the Greek "tau," which is T-shaped and the Hebrew "taw," which is shaped as + or × in the Hebrew alphabet of the first century AD., see Danielou, *Primitive Christian Symbols* (139–42). Both letters are hieroglyphs for the Name of God. The form of the letter "t" varies in Donne's handwriting; the character is distinctly cruciform, for example, throughout much of a receipt Donne wrote for Egerton in 1602 (reproduced in Bald, plate 8); in some words, however, it resembles the number 4. One may observe a similar mixture in the holograph epitaph Donne wrote on his wife Anne in 1617 (reproduced in Stringer et al., 8:186). Of course, there is no extant holograph manuscript of "The Crosse."

21. See Calvin, *Inst.* 4.14.17, 26.

22. As a noun, *physic* can mean "Natural science, the knowledge of the phenomenal world = PHYSICS" (*OED* 1) or "MEDICINE" (4), especially (4b) "a cathartic or purge" See also the word's adjectival meanings: "physical, natural" (1) or "medical, medicinal" (2). The phrase "good physicke" in Donne's poem thus contributes to an argument that assumes an anti-Manichaean stance in defense of ritual and ceremony; compare Hooker, who cites Augustine's response to the Manichaeans in his response to Cartwright (*Laws* 4.7.2). See also Donne, *Sermons* 6:237–38.

23. See Calvin, *Inst.* 4.14.18.

24. In another sermon, Donne refers to the miracle at Cana, insisting that if God "doe fill all your vessels with water, with water of bitternesse, that is, fill and exercise all your patience, and all your faculties with his corrections, yet he shall doe that, but to *change your water into wine*, as he did there, he shall make his very Judgements, Sacraments, conveyances and seals of his mercy to you . . ." (*Sermons* 2:114).

25. Fabricius discusses a direct connection between alchemy and the Eucharist and reproduces an engraving (fig. 258) of the alchemist as a priest celebrating Mass; his "secret identification with the Christ figure is spelled out by the image of the Saviour embroidered on the back of his chasuble and also by the gesture of surrender, which imitates the crucified arms of the suffering Christ" (138). The engraving is taken from Michael Maier, *Symbola aureae mensae duodecim nationum* (Frankfort, 1617); it was used to illustrate a treatise by Melchior Cibenensis in which, as Fabricius explains, "the alchemical process of transformation is expounded in the form of the Catholic Mass" (138). Notably, one of the prayers from

Cibenensis's alchemical Mass specifically asks that the practitioners of spiritual alchemy may "Gaze on the brazen crucified serpent" (quoted in Fabricius, 138). See also Frost on "The alchemical context" (239–43) of Donne's "Resurrection, imperfect."

26. See the Decree on the Eucharist in *Trent* (77–79); the Trent *Catechism* (245–48); Wright's *Disposition or Garnishmente of the Soule* (especially the first part, "Preparation"); the *BCP* (256–59); and the two-part Elizabethan "Homilie of the worthy receiving and reverend esteeming of the Sacrament of the body and blood of Christ" (*Homilies*, 197–205).

27. See Donne, *Sermons* 7:321; quoted above, page 16. See also Harland (166).

28. McNees explicates lines 33–36 as an illustration of the transformation that Eucharistic participation effects in the communicant's soul; Christians "must duplicate Christ's sacrifice to stand in sacramental relation to him . . . These lines mark Donne's middle stance between Roman Catholicism and Protestantism. The cross is not mere icon to be adored for itself nor accidental symbol to be discarded when one reaches colloquy with God; internalized in a person, it demonstrates Real Presence, the intersection of divine and human natures" (*Eucharistic Poetry*, 52–53).

29. As sculptors, crosses act upon human beings as Christ did upon the Apostles: "A cunning Statuary discerns in a Marble-stone under his feet, where there will arise an Eye, and an Eare, and a Hand, and other lineaments to make it a perfect Statue. Much more did our Saviour . . . foresee in these fishermen, an inclinablenesse to become usefull in that great service of his Church. . . . Hee tooke them weatherbeaten with North and South winds, and rough-cast with foame, and mud; but he sent them back soupled, and smoothed, and levigated, quickned, and inanimated with that Spirit, which he had breathed into them" (Donne, *Sermons* 2:276).

30. See Sherwood, *Fulfilling the Circle* (122).

31. Donne does not directly evoke the image of the reader picking up the material text of the poem and thus taking up "The Crosse." But he does include the general directive "Be covetous of Crosses, let none fall" (59), which reminds the reader that he or she holds at least one "Crosse" in his or her hands. See also Donne's anticipation of the moment when Lady Herbert's hand will touch the paper on which his verse epistle, "To Mrs. M. H.," is written. In the verse epistle, it is the reader's "warme redeeming hand" (17) that will bestow grace on the poem, rather than vice versa. The self-conscious evocation of a poem's text in a reader's hand is a Renaissance commonplace. See, for example, the opening distich of Ben Jonson's *Epigrams*: "Pray thee, take care, that tak'st my book in hand, / To read

it well: that is, to understand." For an example from a religious poem, see Crashaw's "On Mr. G. Herberts booke intituled the Temple of Sacred Poems, sent to a Gentlewoman": "When your hands unty these strings, / Thinke you have an Angell by th' wings. /. . . / These white plumes of his heele lend you, / Which every day to heaven will send you:/ . . . / And though Herberts name doe owe / These devotions, fairest; know / That while I lay them on the shrine / Of your white hand, they are mine" (5–6, 11–12, 15–18).

32. See Donne's assertion that "Absolution is conferred, or withheld in Preaching . . the proposing of the promises of the Gospel in preaching, is that binding and loosing on earth, which bindes and looses in heaven" (*Sermons* 7:320). On Reformation views of the sermon as an "apocalyptic event" in which the listener's response determines whether he is saved or damned, see Oberman, who argues that, in the Reformation-era sermon, "man's real existence is revealed in confrontation with Jesus Christ, and so even his religious and pious questions are unmasked as expressions of self-love" (18).

33. On Donne's objections to such mockery and labeling, see a particularly powerful passage preached to King Charles in 1630: "This man is affected when he heares a blasphemous oath, and when he lookes upon the generall liberty of sinning; therefore he is a Puritan; That man loves the ancient formes, and Doctrines, and Disciplines of the Church, and retaines, and delights in the reverend names of Priest, and Altar, and Sacrifice, therefore he is a Papist" (*Sermons* 9:216); see also *Sermons* 1:188 and 2:58, 117; Clancy; and Doerksen (353–56).

34. See Harland on these lines: "The secret exaltation in personal adversity is not really a participation in Christ's suffering, but a pseudo-martyrdom, a heightening of the unhealthy experience of self-sufficiency" (164). By contrast, Harland notes, Donne's sermons stress that a true "imitation of Christ is not merely the creation in private devotion of an inner memorial, but an engagement in the issues and problems that are current in one's time and place" (172).

35. See Donne's use of the alchemist trope to attack the "Pharisaicall Superstition" and "carnall" Eucharistic doctrines of the Roman Church (*Sermons* 7:289). Just as alchemists claim to transmute lead into gold, Donne says in an early sermon, so the *"Romane Chymists"* believe that they "can *transubstantiate bread into God"* (*Sermons* 1:203). Like the alchemist-"coyners" of the poem, who devalue gold itself by turning out vast numbers of worthless coins, the Roman clergy as Donne defines them in the sermon are counterfeiters. Positing the daily miracle of Transubstantiation, accomplished every time a priest pronounces the words of consecration,

they "dishonour miracles, by the assiduity and frequency, and multiplicity of them" (7:294). By claiming too much for the sacrament, Donne suggests in his sermons, priestly charlatans invalidate the terms of their own arguments. Their lavish excess is both their sin and their folly.

36. See the Trent *Catechism*, which, in explaining the importance of spiritual preparation for the reception of communion, notes that, "It is characteristic of the best and most salutary things that, if seasonably made use of, they are productive of the greatest benefit, but if employed out of time, they prove most pernicious and destructive" (246). See also the exhortation against "unworthy receiving" of the Eucharist included in the communion liturgy of the *BCP*, which McNees cites in explicating these lines of "The Crosse" (*Eucharistic Poetry*, 53).

37. See *Sermons* 4:105, quoted above, p. 15.

38. See also *Sermons* 2:276–77 and 5:146, where Donne stresses that the minister's function is "the breaking of the bread, the applying of the Gospell according to [the congregation's] particular indigences, in the preaching thereof." These passages draw on a traditional analogy between preaching and Eucharist, between Christ as Word of God and Christ as Bread of Heaven. The analogy originates in the language of the Gospel of John: "the Word was made flesh" (John 1:14) and declared himself to be "the living bread which came down from heaven" (6:51). See Merrill, especially chapter 9, "The Sermon as Sacrament." As Merrill notes, Donne did not wish "to downgrade the sacraments" in comparing their effect to that of preaching, but rather to exalt "the sacramental quality of the sermon" (166).

39. Christian doctrine generally affirms that there is no sacrament, no communion between the individual soul and Christ, outside of the community of faith, the Church. But for Calvin, this doctrine implied that "private" Masses celebrations of the Eucharist in which only the priest partook of the consecrated bread and wine were not truly Eucharistic. See the discussion of this issue in chapter 2, page 92 below.

40. Lucius Cary, Second Viscount Falkland (1610–1643) is best known as the addressee of Ben Jonson's ode on the death of Cary's friend, Henry Morison ("To the Immortall Memorie, and Friendship of That Noble Paire, Sir Lucius Cary, and Sir H Morison"). He was the son of Elizabeth Cary, author of *The Tragedy of Mariam, The Fair Queen of Jewry*, who became a convert to Catholicism in 1625. As Weller and Ferguson note in their introduction to the play, Lucius inherited his mother's "deep interest in theological questions. His two houses near Oxford, stocked with books, became centers for

relatively liberal discussions of religion. . . . An eloquent defender of religious toleration, Lucius leaned toward conversion [to Catholicism] for some time but eventually resisted his mother's pressure" (8). Lucius's biography casts an interesting light on lines 51–54 of his elegy on Donne: "Experience makes us see, that many a one / Owes to his Countrey his Religion; / And in another, would as strongly grow, / Had but his Nurse and Mother taught him so" (*Poems*, 390).

41. The *OED* explains that the word "anthem" derives from the Greek αντίφωνα via the Latin *antiphona* and is a synonym of the English "antiphon" (a "composition in prose or verse, consisting of verses or passages sung alternately by two choirs in worship" ["antiphon," def 2]). " The note on "anthem" further explains that "some English spellings indicate an attempt to explain the word as *anti-hymn, ant'hymn.*"

42. The lines stress the power of an "an-theme" to convey a "theme": a "theme" can be a "subject of discourse" (*OED* 1), but also "the text of a sermon" (2), the principal melody in a contrapuntal piece" of music (4), or a "subject treated by action; hence . . the cause *of* or *for* specified action" (1b); compare Shakespeare's *Hamlet* 5.1.266.

Notes to Chapter 2

1. See McNees, who finds that Donne's divine poems are "preoccupied with the repentance and confession of sins *before* participation in the act of Holy Communion" (*Eucharistic Poetry*, 36). Asserting that the divine poems "are only by analogy eucharistic sacraments themselves," McNees nevertheless argues that "Donne's divine poems attempt to emulate the language and ritual of the sacraments, specifically of the Passion and its extension in the Eucharist. The poem's language offers the sacramental link between divine action and personal internalization of that action. One must devour the words . . . to realize presence. This presence fuses the poet with Christ and, by extension, the reader with the Christ-poet persona" (*Eucharistic Poetry*, 34, 38). McNees's discussion of Donne's divine poems includes *Cross, Annun, Sickness*, and several of the Holy Sonnets; she does not discuss *La Corona*. See also Martz on "brief acts of mental communion" frequent in seventeenth century religious poetry, especially that of George Herbert (90–91, 288–95) and Lewalski on the preparatory Eucharistic meditations of Henry Vaughan and Edward Taylor (157–58).

2. Martz compares the meditational structure of *La Corona* to

that of the seven-part *"corona* of our Lady" (also known as the "Bridgettine rosary"); he finds many parallels between Donne's work and a 1619 devotional tract by the Jesuit Sabin Chambers, *The Garden of Our B Lady.* Fr. Chambers's work instructs readers in various meditations (upon such subjects as the Five Wounds of Christ) and in saying the rosary two different ways: the Dominican rosary with its 15 decades and the shorter Bridgettine "corona."

3. See O'Connell, "'La Corona.'" For a critique of criticism that oversimplifies seventeenth century theology, see Young, "Donne's Holy Sonnets" (20–23).

4. The "Suscipiat" is the response to the priest's prayer "Orate fratres" (*Roman Liturgy,* 99).

5. The Latin text reads, "Suscipe, sancte Pater, . . hanc immaculatam hostiam, quam ego indignus famulus tuus offero tibi . . . pro innumerabilibus peccatis, et offensionibus, et negligentiis meis, et pro omnibus circumstantibus, . . . ut mihi, et illis proficiat ad salutem in vitam aeternam" (*Roman Liturgy,* 83).

6. For a discussion of this passage and others on the same topic in Donne's sermons, as well as an overview of theological debate on "The Doctrine of Eucharistic Sacrifice," see appendix below.

7. The concept of commemorative sacrifice does not in itself contradict the Roman doctrine of propitiatory sacrifice. Thus, both Donne's sermon and *La Corona* can recall the language of another prayer in the Tridentine Mass: "Receive, O holy Trinity, this oblation which we make to Thee, in memory of the Passion, Resurrection and Ascension of our Lord Jesus Christ [ob memoriam passionis, resurrectionis, et ascensionis Jesu Christi Domini nostri]" (*Missal,* 635; *Roman Liturgy,* 95). See also the Trent *Catechism* (218, 258); the Council of Trent's "Decree Concerning the . . . Eucharist," chapter 2; and its "Decree Concerning the Sacrifice of the Mass," chapter 1.

8. Citing the Vulgate translation of Isaiah 28 (which is the Matins reading for the third week of Advent in the Roman Breviary), Gardner notes that the opening sonnet's "ideas and much of its phrasing are derived from the Advent Offices in the . . Breviary" (57). The chapter from Isaiah is also, however, assigned as a First Lesson for Morning Prayer during Advent in the almanac of the 1559 *Book of Common Prayer.* See also Petrarch's *Rime sparse* 23, line 31: "La vita el fin, e'l dì loda la sera"; "The end crowns the life, the evening the day." The literal meaning of "loda"—which Durling renders as "crowns"—is "praises." Petrarch laments, "I . . . saw my hairs turning into those leaves which I had formerly hoped would be my crown" (41–44); and he stresses that his poetry has never succeeded in winning Laura's pity, though he has tried "to make myself in her eyes from unworthy, worthy of mercy" (101–02).

9. In the Tridentine Mass, the priest prays these psalm verses just before consuming the Precious Blood.

10. See additional quotations from this sermon above, page 16 and below, pages 72, 73, 77, 80, 81, 85, 86 and 275 (n. 35). McNees discusses it as a particularly helpful guide to Donne's Eucharistic theology (*Eucharistic Poetry*, 38–40).

11. In the Roman liturgy, too, communion is preceded by a penitential rite; but in the Tridentine Mass, the "Confiteor" is said near the beginning of the liturgy, not—as in the *Book of Common Prayer*—just preceding the Canon.

12. The *sursum corda* is also the opening exchange of the preface to the Canon in the Tridentine Mass.

13. Luke 21 (the Gospel for the First Sunday of Advent in the Roman Missal and the Second Sunday in the *BCP*) stresses that "your redemption draweth nigh" (verse 28). See also Psalm 144:18, 21 ("The Lord is nigh unto all them that call upon Him: to all that call upon Him in truth. My mouth shall speak the praise of the Lord . . ."), which serves as the Gradual in the Tridentine liturgy for the Fourth Sunday of Advent.

14. Both the *BCP* and the Tridentine liturgy designate Romans 13 as the Epistle for the first Sunday of Advent.

15. Chambers, noting that *Cor1* announces both the first Advent and the second, explains that line 4 alludes to "that time forecast by St. Paul, in a lesson for Christmas Day, when all 'shall be changed' and only God remain 'the same' (Heb. 1:12)" ("Uses of Time," 165). See also 1 Corinthians 15:51.

16. See Asals on a similar word-play in George Herbert's "The Call" (*Equivocal Predication*, 56).

17. On the Virgin's role in these lines, see Asals, "*Davids* Successors" (34–35). The images Donne uses are commonplaces; Gardner notes that the second and third sonnets of *La Corona* recall "the *Horae B.V.M.*, which made part of the *Prymer*, the prayer book of the laity in the Middle Ages" (59). Within the Eucharistic liturgy, however, the Preface for Christmas in the English Protestant liturgy is the clearest analogue for the opening of *Cor3*. The Christmas Preface in the Tridentine Mass has different emphases.

18. See the discussion of this poem in Young, "Herbert and the Real Presence" (181). For a Roman Catholic paean to priests' "dignitie of consecrating the bodye of Christ," see Wright, *A Treatise* 32r (quoted below, n. 53). For an English Protestant mockery of such belief, see Tuke's 1625 poem *Concerning the Holy Eucharist and the Popish Breaden-God*.

19. See my discussion of sacramental covenant above, page 13.

20. These phrases are taken from Donne's Christmas sermon

for 1621, in which he objects to the devaluation of either sacraments or sermons: "He that undervalues *outward things*, in the religious service of God, though he begin at *ceremoniall* and *rituall* things, will come quickly to call *Sacraments* but outward things, and *Sermons*, and *publique prayers*, but outward things, in contempt. . . . [However,] outward things apparell God; and since God was content to take *a body*, let not us leave him naked, nor ragged; . . . [rather], execute cheerfully in outward declarations, that which becomes the dignity of him, who evacuated himselfe for you" (*Sermons* 3:368); see also Asals, "*Davids* Successors" (33).

21. Martz notes a similar compression in the Jesuit Sabin Chambers's guide to the seven-part rosary called the "*corona* of our Lady": "Part 3 of Chambers's sequence covers exactly the same compass of events [from Nativity to the flight into Egypt], though more events are included" (Martz 108–09). See also A. B. Chambers, "Uses of Time" (162).

22. See also Chambers ("Christmas," 120) on the Nativity sonnet in relation to Psalm 2:12.

23. See also McNees on Donne's effort "to transform mundane words into revelatory instruments of grace" (*Eucharistic Poetry*, 35).

24. This is line 24 of St. Thomas Aquinas's Eucharistic hymn, "Pange lingua gloriosi," which is sung during the solemn procession at the conclusion of Mass on Holy Thursday (*Missal*, 336–38). See also Young, "Herbert and the Real Presence" (185–86).

25. See Chambers on the relation between *Cor4* and biblical commentaries that stress the Finding in the Temple as affirming Christ's dual nature as God and man ("The Meaning of the 'Temple'" and "Uses of Time," 161). Gardner (xxii) points out the correspondence between *Cor4* and the fifth Joyful Mystery of the Dominican Rosary.

26. Nania and Klemp stress the sonnet's central position as the fourth of seven sonnets in *La Corona*.

27. See also Gilman (*Iconoclasm and Poetry*, 122) on how the compression of temporal and spatial imagery in the Annunciation sonnet anticipates the related compression in "Crucifying."

28. See Tuke: "Is't not ynough for Him, and for us all / That He was once borne, and once vnder thrall, / But that He must yet also, day by day, / By you be made, and offred, as ye say?" (page 25, lines 224–27).

29. The analogy between the Pharisees and the Roman clergy was a common one among Protestant writers; see Booty (*BCP*, 363) for a long quotation from Thomas Cranmer drawing such an analogy.

30. The word "span" may suggest temporal as well as spatial measurement, for a "span" can be a measure of either time or length.

Gardner interprets it in terms of time: "the infinity of life itself was reduced to the length of a human life—indeed to less, for Christ did not live out the alloted span" (61); this reading is consistent with Donne's use of the terms "span" and "inch" in *HSScene* 4.

31. Communion wafers were used by the English Church as well as by Roman Catholics; the 1559 *BCP* rubric indicates that "to take away the superstition, which any person hath or might have in the bread and wine, it shall suffice that the bread be such as is usual to be eaten at the table . ." (*BCP*, 267). But as Booty explains in a note, the English Church continued to use small, round wafers: "This rubric was continued from the 1552 Book, but it was ignored when in the Royal Injunctions (1559) order was given 'that the same sacramental bread be made and formed plain, without any figure thereupon of the same fineness and fashion round, though somewhat bigger in compass and thickness, as the usual bread and wafer heretofore named singing cakes'" (*BCP*, 402, quoting *Visitation Articles and Injunctions* 3:28). For an English Protestant objection to the idea that Christ's body is contained in the host, see the remarks of Sir Thomas Smith, principal secretary under Edward VI, in a speech made at the December, 1548 debate on the Mass: "Christ must have a small body, or else his length and thickness cannot be there, which things declare that it cannot be no true body, or else he must want his head or his legs or some part of him" (quoted in Booty, 363–64).

32. See McNees, *Eucharistic Poetry* (33–68) for a discussion of Donne's belief in relation to *Cross, Goodf*, and several of the Holy Sonnets; see also Harland, "'A true Transubstantiation.'"

33. See Chambers, "Uses of Time" (157, 164).

34. Hooker's text contains a Protestant qualifying phrase ("by them we draw out, *as touching efficacy, force and virtue,* even the blood of his gored side") that is not included or implied in Donne's poetic evocation of the Eucharist. Keble notes (Hooker, *Works* 2:361, n. 1) that Hooker's passage adapts Arnold of Chartres, *De Coena Domini* (part 6 of his *Liber De Cardinalibus Operibus Christi, PL* 189:1646). See also a passage from St. Chrysostom's Homily 84 on the Gospel of John, cited in the Jesuit Sabin Chambers's devotional manual, *The Garden of our B. Lady*: "Thinke when thou commest to drinke of the holy Chalice, thou doest put thy mouth unto christ his side, and sucke thence his sacred bloud" (201–02).

35. Donne also says that Jesus' words, "Touch mee not, for I am not ascended to my Father," are a command applicable to Eucharistic piety: "Dwell not upon this passionate consideration of my bodily, and personall presence, but send thy thoughts, and thy reverence, and thy devotion, and thy holy amorousnesse up, wither I am going,

to the right hand of my Father" (*Sermons* 7:267). On this interpretation of John 20:17 in the works of Donne and Herbert, see also Asals, *Equivocal Predication* (96).

36. See the description of Fr. Edmund Campion's 1581 execution in Flynn, *John Donne and the Ancient Catholic Nobility* (105); Campion and eight other priests executed in 1582 were "drawn" (i.e., disembowelled) after being hanged until dead, though the penalty for treason technically specified that the torture be performed while the prisoner was still living. Flynn notes, "How many, if any, of these executions young Donne witnessed is not known; but, given the near presence of his Jesuit uncle, the terror of a family's vulnerability was surely impressed on his developing mind." See also Flynn, "Donne the Survivor."

37. For a Catholic reader, moreover, the phrase "Now thou art lifted up" might evoke the climax of the Mass: the elevation of the consecrated Host. A practice dating from the twelfth century, the Elevation was condemned by Reformers because it confirmed the Catholic conception of the Mass as a propitiatory Sacrifice in which the Body of Christ is offered up to the Father by the priest. Article 28 of the Thirty Nine Articles specifically insists that "The Sacrament . . . was not by Christes ordinaunce . . . lyfted vp" and elevation was also forbidden by the 1549 *BCP*. The rubric which indicated that the consecration be said "without any eleuation, or shewing the Sacrament to the people" was, however, omitted—along with all other directions for manual acts—in the 1552 and 1559 versions of the book, and liturgical conservatives advocated the restoration of gestures modeled on those of Christ at the Last Supper (when he took the bread, blessed it, and gave it to his disciples). The continued omission of any instructions about manual gestures in the 1559 version of the prayerbook gave "great offence to the conservatives" and Andrewes was probably a leader in the move to restore the dominical action: "At any rate the practice spread quickly among his followers and disciples, such as Wren and Laud, until it came to be described as 'the custom of the Church of England' when the question arose in connexion with the Scottish Liturgy of 1637"; Presbyterian protesters at that time were outraged by "the gestures used . . . by the clergy whom they attacked. They even charged them with elevating the Host" (Frere, 224). Frere doubts the validity of the accusation, but admits "that there was a great deal of prostration and a multitude of reverences customary at the consecration" (224).

38. The doctrine of a change in use has its roots in the teachings of the more radical reformers; see a 1528 sermon by Zwingli (quoted in Stone 2:41). Davies calls the stress upon the change in use one of

three "clear landmarks in the cloudiness of the Anglican doctrine of the Eucharist" (*Worship* 2:297). According to Davies, the other two Eucharistic doctrines widely embraced by English Protestants are that of the Church's self- oblation and that of the sacrament as a seal of grace; McNees (*Eucharistic Poetry*, 33) cites these "three elemental points" as her framework for interpreting Donne's Eucharistic poetics; but see also note 39 below.

39. McNees (*Eucharistic Poetry*, 38–40) cites these passages from Donne's 1626 Christmas sermon on Simeon to demonstrate that Donne's views on the Lord's Supper reflect the most important emphases of English Protestant Eucharistic theology. But by equating a "new use" with a "new essence," I would note, Donne subtly conflates the Protestant doctrine of a change in use with the Catholic doctrine of transubstantiation. Compare the Trent *Catechism*'s comment on the particular fitness of bread and wine to be transubstantiated into Christ's body and blood: "As, then, the body of Christ the Lord furnishes nourishment unto eternal life to those who receive this Sacrament with purity and holiness, rightly is the matter composed chiefly of those elements by which our present life is sustained. . . . Although no change of the bread and wine appears externally, yet their substance is truly changed into the flesh and blood of Christ. . . . What bread and wine are to the body, the Eucharist is to the health and delight of the soul . . ." (222, 223, 242).

40. See Simon, 34: "It is as though the appeal at the end of sonnet 5 had been heard, for in the next, *Resurrection*, the verb *moist* (prayer in 5, l[ine] 14) becomes an adjective: the poet's soul is, or will be, moist, that is, has received (or at least, is confident that she will receive) the drop of blood for which he begs. Through his trust in the Grace of God, Donne will now be able to conquer the dryness of his heart and thereby conquer death." The shift in meaning is also noted by Fuller: "[T]he metamorphosis of the link-line's verb from an imperative into a participle silently anticipates the desired redemption, brings it (though still in the imagination) one stage nearer" (42). A. B. Chambers, though he does not discuss the change in the verb, points out the reason for the change in the speaker: "Donne's soul, '*moyst with one drop*' of Christ's blood, is freed from being '*starv'd*' [*Cor6*, 4], presumably because it now has been nourished by the Eucharistic elements" ("Uses of Time," 163).

41. See the quotation from Donne's *Sermons* 7:321, page 16 above; my discussion of spiritual transformation in "The Crosse," pages 42–43 above; and the quotation from Hooker, *Laws* 5.67.11, page 82 below. The Trent *Catechism* also discusses the change which the Eucharist brings about in the soul of the communicant: "This admirable change of the elements [transubstantiation] also helps to shadow

forth what takes place in the soul. Although no change of the bread and wine appears externally, yet their substance is truly changed into the flesh and blood of Christ; so, in like manner, although in us nothing appears changed, yet we are renewed inwardly unto life, when we receive the Sacrament of the Eucharist the true life. . . . This Sacrament is not, like bread and wine, changed into our substance; but we are, in some wise, changed into its nature, so that we may well apply here the words of St. Augustine: '*I am the food of the grown. Grow and thou shalt eat Me; nor shalt thou change Me into thee, as thy bodily food, but thou shalt be changed into Me*' [*Confessions*, book 7]" (*Catechism*, 223, 242).

42. Simon notes that "Whereas Sonnet 5 dealt with Christ, then with 'mee,' here Christ and 'mee' are really inseparable" (38).

43. See *Devotions*, Expostulation 14, where Donne draws an analogy between preparation for death and preparation to receive the Eucharist. McNees discusses the Eucharistic theology underlying the passage from *Devotions* and cites Donne's last sermon, "Deaths Duell," as an example of how Donne compared "preparing . . . for the sacrament of Holy Communion" to the penitential acts of a man preparing for death (*Eucharistic Poetry*, 66–67, 60). On the Eucharist as *Viaticum*, see the Trent *Catechism* (215). Also see the *Catechism* on the effects or "fruits" (241) afforded to communicants by the Eucharist: "Finally, . . . by the grace of this Sacrament men enjoy the greatest peace and tranquillity of conscience during the present life; and, when the hour of departing from this world shall have arrived, they, . . . invigorated by the strengthening influence of this (heavenly food), will ascend to unfading glory and bliss" (244).

44. See also the Trent *Catechism*, which asserts the Roman Catholic doctrine that "by the Eucharist are remitted and pardoned lighter sins, commonly called venial" (243).

45. Compare the Council of Trent's portrayal of those who communicate both sacramentally and spiritually as wearers of the "wedding garment" (quoted below, page 92). The "Yee" of *Cor7* may also be read as addressing the saints, members of the Church Triumphant; see the invocation of the saints in the Tridentine liturgy (*Roman Liturgy*, 151; *Missal*, 651, 652).

46. Compare also the invocation of the Holy Spirit during the Offertory in the Tridentine Mass, as well as the prayer before Mass: "Asperges me, Domine, hyssopo, et mundabor: lavabis me, et super nivem dealbabor"; "Thou shalt sprinkle me, O Lord, with hyssop, and I shall be cleansed; Thou shalt wash me, and I shall become whiter than snow" (*Missal*, 610, 611). The *BCP*'s emphasis on "the thoughts of our hearts" is, however, particularly relevant to the poet's struggle for sincerity.

47. See also Chambers, "Uses of Time" (165): "Advent, from the office for which Donne takes his materials . . is threefold: the first coming which enables a rebirth in the heart and prepares for the *Parousia*."

48. Ferry contrasts the prayer of *La Corona* with common prayer as Donne describes it in *Sermons* 7:233 ("And though thou know thine own prayers unworthy to come up to God, . . though this make thee thinke thine own prayers uneffectuall, yet beleeve that some honester man then thy selfe stands by thee, and that when he prayes with thee, he prayes for thee; and that, if there be one righteous man in the Congregation, thou art made the more acceptable to God by his prayers"). By contrast, Ferry argues, the speaker of *La Corona* "ceases to pray with or for other petitioners at the moment he sets himself apart in the knowledge that his own Muse's language is pure by virtue of its truth to what is in his heart" (225).

49. See also the *Catechism* (223).

50. See also "The Prayer Book and the Idea of Communion," pages 368–72 of Booty's appendix on the history of the *BCP*.

51. See the discussion of "Communion of the Sick" below, page 114. In addition, see the *BCP* exhortation of those disinclined to take Communion, which does not consider the possibility that they may communicate spiritually rather than sacramentally: "if ye stand by as gazers and lookers on them that do communicate, and be no partakers of the same yourselves . . . what can this be else, but even to have the mysteries of Christ in derision?" (*BCP*, 256).

52. The prayer of Oblation follows the distribution of communion; but see Booty (*BCP*, 380–81) on the conservative movement to make it precede the Communion and thus to underscore the sacrificial nature of the oblation.

53. See the Jesuit Thomas Wright, who argues that the Protestant ministry has less dignity than the Roman Catholic priesthood because it lacks "the dignitie of consecrating the bodye of Christ," while the Roman clergy has "power over his reall body by consecration" no less than "over his mystical bodye [the congregation] by remission of sinnes"—that is, by the power of the keys in confession (*A Treatise*, 32r). Wright goes on to ask, "What greater authoritie can wee imagine God could give to man, than to put in his hand the use of his infinite power, to worke so many myracles, to effect such a worke as surpasseth the creating both of heaven and earth, when, where, and as often as hee woulde?" (*A Treatise*, 32r). Donne responds to such charges and questions by insisting that the English clergy lack nothing but presumptuous pride: "They may be pleased to pardon, this, rather *Modesty*, then *Defect*, in us, who, so we may work fruitfully, and effectually upon the *mysticall* body of Christ,

can be content that his reall, and true body work upon us. Not that
we have no interest to work upon the reall body of Christ, since he
hath made us Dispensers even of that, to the faithfull, in the Sacrament; but for such a power, as exceeds the *Holy Ghost*, who in the
incarnation of Christ . . . did but make man of the woman, who was
one part disposed by nature thereunto, whereas these men make
man, and God too of bread, naturally wholly indisposed to any such
change, this power we confesse it is not in our Commission; and
their Commission, and ours was all one . . ." (*Sermons* 10:129).

54. See Donne's claims for "A Litanie," "That neither the Roman Church need call it defective, . . nor the Reformed can dis-
creetly accuse it . . ." (*Letters*, 34).

55. See Nania and Klemp, who note that *corona* may mean "an
assembly or crowd of men." They suggest that, in "Temple," "Donne
may be punning on this second meaning by referring to Christ sitting in the centre of an assembly of doctors" (52). On the corona of
sonnets as a genre, see Martz (107–08). See also Baumgartner.

56. Though Donne probably wrote *La Corona* some years before
1615, when he was ordained as a priest of the English Church, he
was almost certainly an active communicant in that Church by the
time he composed it. Based on sketchy evidence from Walton's *Life
of Herbert*, Grierson argues that the poem was written in July of
1607; and Shawcross retains this date in his "Chronological Schedule of the Poems" (*Complete Poetry*, 413). However, Novarr argues
for a date as late as 1609; and Gardner, taking Novarr's argument
into account, conjectures that the work may have been written circa
1608, in the same year as the liturgically inspired "Upon the Annunciation and Passion falling upon one day. 1608" and "A Litanie"
(xxi, xxiv, 151–52). Thus, though the work cannot be dated with
absolute certainty, it was probably written no earlier than 1607; and
in a 1607 letter to Henry Goodyer, Donne refers to the English Church
as "ours" (*Letters*, 87).

57. Asals quotes Odo of Cluny from Garth (78); Smeaton (137–
38); and Herbert (*Latin Poetry*, 153).

58. In his "Elegie upon Dr Donne," Izaak Walton asks rhetorically, "Did his full soule conceive, / And in harmonious holy numbers weave / A *Crowne of sacred sonets*, fit to adorne / A dying
Martyrs brow: or, to be worne / On that blest head of Mary Magdalen:
/ After she wip'd Christs feet, but not till then?" (*Poems*, 383). A
marginal gloss in the 1633 *Poems* confirms that Walton is here referring to *La Corona*; but the lines also seem to allude to the Donne
sonnet asking Magdalen Herbert to take Donne's poems into her
care. Gardner notes that there is no proof that Grierson was right in
linking the Magdalen sonnet to *La Corona*; though they are "the

only extant poems which fit the descriptions" in Donne's letter and the introductory sonnet, "we cannot assume as certain that the poems which Donne sent to Mrs. Herbert have survived: indeed Walton follows the sonnet with the comment that 'These *Hymns* are now lost to us'" (Gardner, 56). Nevertheless, Donne's letter to Mrs. Herbert does mention sonnets as well as hymns, and the Magdalen-oriented language of Walton's "Elegy" seems to encourage the idea that the Magadalen-sonnet and *La Corona* are linked.

59. See Asals, "*Davids* Successors" (35).

Notes to Chapter 3

1. Even in Petrarch's *Rime sparse*, as Freccero has shown, the poet's idolatrous love for Laura is elided with his equally idolatrous desire for the laurel crown. The solipsistic self-referentiality of his poetics, the detachment of his art from any end or purpose outside itself, makes Petrarch's verse "a poetry whose real subject matter is its own act" ("The Fig Tree," 34).

2. Compare the prominence of the word "I" in Marvell's "The Coronet," which may be read as a more strictly Calvinist counterargument to the sacramental poetics of Donne's *La Corona*; and see Walker's discussion ("The Religious Lyric as a Genre") of *La Corona*, "The Coronet," and Herbert's "A Wreath."

3. This is the translation of the phrase *ex opere operato* in Norton's English translation of Calvin's *Institutes* 4.14.26; see above, introduction, (n. 11).

4. See also Young, "Donne's Holy Sonnets" (35–36).

5. On the title "Divine Meditations," which is found in Group III manuscripts, see Gardner (65); see also McNees, *Eucharistic Poetry* (56): "The language of 'Goodfriday,' 'Hymne to God my God, in my Sicknesse,' and the Holy Sonnets internalizes the public eucharist . . of the previous poems to depict the persona's own private spiritual struggle."

6. See also McNees, *Eucharistic Poetry* (61–65), on those Holy Sonnets in which penitence and communion "seem to offer separate routes toward redemption" (63).

7. See also the Trent *Catechism* (189–90), Article 16 of the *Thirty-Nine Articles*, and *Homilies* (261).

8. For the English Church's assertion that there are only "two Sacramentes ordeyned of Christe," see Article 25 of the *Thirty-Nine Articles*; against the Catholic requirement of "auricular confession," see *Homilies* (266–67). For Calvin on the idea that the penitent need only devoutly recall the forgiveness of his sins in baptism, see *Inst.*

4.15.3–4. The Council of Trent specifically anathematizes anyone promulgating this doctrine; see the Seventh Session, "Canons on Baptism," Canon 10.

9. Line 4 thus contrasts sharply with *Cor6*, where the speaker feels himself released from "Feare of first or last death" (7).

10. The delayed turn is noted by Martz (53) and Empson (75). McNees also notes that this sonnet "deviates from the octet-sestet" structure (*Eucharistic Poetry*, 65).

11. See *Sermons* 8:280–81: "When I have had ... true *Absolution* . . . still to suspect my state in Gods favour, . . . still to call my repentance imperfect, and the *Sacramentall seales ineffectual*, still to accuse myselfe of sinnes, thus devested, thus repented, . . . this is *to blaspheme mine owne soule.*" See also *Sermons* 5:85–86, 102–03; 7:110–17, 9:329, and 10:118.

12. See the vivid evocations of a despairing sinner's state of mind in Donne's *Sermons* 7:413 and 2:84.

13. This is the Geneva Bible translation. The King James renders the phrase "fiery indignation, which shall devour the adversaries." See also 2 Peter 2:20–21.

14. The sermon, which was preached at Whitehall, is undated; but Potter and Simpson (*Sermons* 10:15) conjecture that it was delivered during the reign of King Charles. The thrust of the sermon is to defend the godliness of those who remained within a largely corrupt Roman Catholic Church prior to the Reformation and, as Potter and Simpson explain, to defend "the English Church against those Puritans who wished to secede from it, or to despoil it of all the ceremonies derived from the primitive and the medieval Church" (*Sermons* 10:19).

15. See also *Sermons* 1:189 for Donne's account of "*purified puritans*" as those that "think they . . need ask no forgiveness."

16. See also Clark (77) and McNees, *Eucharistic Poetry* (66).

17. From the third *Devotion*, "The Patient takes his bed." Interestingly, Donne mentions recusancy here only to deny any inclination toward it and to confirm his desire to be restored to communal worship in the Church of England.

18. In one sermon, Donne associates "zeale / Of . . [God's] house" with accusations of crypto-Catholicism: "Let a man be zealous, and fervent in reprehension of sin, and there flies out an arrow, that gives him the wound of a *Puritan*. Let a man be zealous of the house of God, and say any thing by way of moderation, for the *repairing* of *the ruines* of that house, and *making up the differences* of the Church of God, and there flies out an arrow, that gives him the wound of a *Papist*" (*Sermons* 2:58). But as this passage itself suggests, the word "zeal" was more commonly associated with Christians of a Puritan

bent, as is the case with the character of Zeal-of-the-land Busy in Ben Jonson's *Bartholomew Fayre*. See also Donne, *Sermons* 1:188: "let me live the life of a *Puritan*, let the zeal of the house of God consume me."

19. Of course, the Roman Catholic Church also provides both for Communion of the Sick (the reservation of the consecrated Host making a separate Communion liturgy in the sick person's room unnecessary) and for the act of mental communion (see the quotations from Ignatius Loyola and Francis de Sales in Martz [90, 288]). See also page 92 above for a quotation from the Trent *Catechism* on the distinction between spiritual and sacramental reception of the Eucharist.

20. See Belette, who notes that the sonnet's "resolution, the harmonizing, of its separate parts lies not in argument and debate but in recognition and acceptance: specifically recognition and acceptance of Christ's sacrifice. When this occurs, the sonnet form regularizes itself and is seen once again to embody within itself an orderly movement towards a reconciling conclusion" (334).

21. Gardner's gloss identifies them as "discoverers generally: astronomers who find new spheres and explorers who find new lands" (76). Smith's note on the lines includes not only those mentioned by Gardner, but also "the blessed who have ascended to a heaven beyond our comprehension" (627). He does not, however, link the lines to 2 Peter 3:13. Shawcross glosses the "you" as "Christ" himself (*Complete Poetry*, 347).

22. This passage is quoted from Donne's memorial sermon on Magdalen Herbert Danvers, preached about one month after her death.

23. For a different emphasis, see McNees, *Eucharistic Poetry* (65–66): "Here Donne transfigures the word 'burne' from its secular to sacred use by imploring God's intervention as opposed to that of secular explorers. With this transformation he surrenders his temporal control over language to God's sacred control."

24. "God was . . zeale in *Paul*" (*Sermons* 8:233).

25. See *Sermons* 3:214, where Donne recalls the coming of the Holy Ghost at Pentecost "in Tongues, and fiery Tongues. Christ was not, a Christian is not justified in silence, but in declarations and open professions; . . . and not in dark and ambiguous speeches, nor in faint and retractable speeches, but in fiery tongues; fiery, that is, fervent; fiery, that is, clear." See also the discussion of human speech in relation to the divine Word in Asals, "John Donne and the Grammar of Redemption."

26. Belette notes that the "sonnet, too, is 'a little world made cunningly'" (334).

290 Notes to Pages 117–19

27. Galenist physiology defines digestion as a process in which the body's heat breaks down and transmutes food. See Milton, who describes digestion as "concoctive heat / To transubstantiate" (*Paradise Lost* 5:437–38).

28. On the issues at work in the conclusions of Donne's devotional lyrics, see Linville.

29. The adverb "cunningly" evokes a connection between the poetic activity of the poet's "Angelike" spirit and the divinely inspired and commissioned work of the craftsmen chosen to make the cloth of the tabernacle, which is to be adorned with "broidered" cherubim (Exodus 26:1), "That is," as the 1560 Geneva Bible's marginal gloss indicates, "of moste conning or fine worke." In the King James translation, the language is even closer to that of the sonnet: "with cherubim of cunning work shalt thou make them." On the speakers of some of Donne's Holy Sonnets as self-conscious poets exploring the nature of poetic sincerity, see Ferry, *The 'Inward' Language* (226–46).

30. See O'Connell, who argues that "Goodfriday, 1613" "could almost be subtitled 'I am a little world (expanded)': structural, verbal and thematic parallels would seem to indicate that Donne had this sonnet in mind, if not in hand, as he composed the later couplet poem. Both begin with a microcosm-macrocosm analogy, proceed to the speaker's recognition of his own sinfulness, and conclude by addressing the Lord directly, in each case to ask for the purifying action of fire" ("'Restore Thine Image,'" 13).

31. The structure of "Goodfriday, 1613" has frequently been discussed; Martz divides the poem into a three-part mediation in which the first 10 lines are the "composition" (the part of meditation in which the faculty of memory is engaged), lines 11–32 are the "analysis" (the part of the meditation in which the faculty of the reason or understanding is engaged), and the final 10 lines—perfectly symmetrical to the first 10—are the "colloquy," in which the faculty of the will is engaged (54–56). This schema is disrupted somewhat by the fact that the composition of place is completed only in lines 11–32 and by Donne's reference to the faculty of memory in lines 33–35 rather than in lines 1–10. For alternative accounts of the structure of Donne's work, see Bellette and Severance, who builds on the analysis of the poem proposed by Bellette and sees "Goodfriday, 1613" as dividing into sections of symmetrically proportioned groups of lines— 8,2,4,6,2,6,4,2,8—where lines 1–8 correspond to lines 35–42, lines 9–10 to lines 33–34, etc., with the couplet describing Christ's "hands which span the Poles, / And turne all spheres at once" (21–22) at the poem's center. Severance's argument that this symmetrical pattern indicates the work's status as a "circle" (24) seems to me to be undercut by Bellette's accurate observation that, "The poem is not

totally symmetrical. The last eight lines are in many ways greatly opposed to the first eight. They are full of anguish, far from the intellectually controlled sureties of the opening. We have not returned to the same emotional and spiritual place" (345).

32. Subsequent quotations from Sidney's sonnet sequence are cited parenthetically as *A&S* by sonnet and line number.

33. The work is, of course, composed of rhyming couplets rather than quatrains, but the poem's grammatical and semantic dividing lines repeatedly echo the 8/6 proportions of the Italian sonnet so important in Sidney's *Astrophil and Stella*.

34. See McNees on Donne's presentation of the speaker's "outdated Ptolemaic analogy as a superficial (and incorrect) rationalization" (*Eucharistic Poetry*, 56–57).

35. See Steinberg's landmark study, which explores the "sexual Christology" articulated through the representation of Christ's genitalia in Renaissance painting and sculpture. Steinberg stresses that the works he analyzes "set forth what perhaps had never been uttered" and "are themselves primary texts" rather than illustrations of a "preformed" doctrine. For Steinberg, the paintings and sculptures of Jesus' circumcision imply a contrast between Christ and the phallic fertility gods of the Greeks ("The sexual member exhibited by the Christ child . . . concedes . . . God's assumption of human weakness; it is an affirmation not of superior prowess but of condescension to kinship. . . And instead of symbolizing, like the phallus of Dionysus, the generative powers of nature, Christ's sexual organ—pruned by circumcision in sign of corrupted nature's correction—is offered to immolation. The erstwhile symbol of the life force yields not seed, but redeeming blood" [47–48]). Donne, I am arguing, takes a step beyond these circumcision images in portraying the erection of the crucified Christ as supernaturally and spiritually procreative. Though Steinberg—taking great care to refute the "fallacy of naturalism"—finds "the folklore of hanged men's erections . . . irrelevant" to his inquiry (82, n. 82), Donne seems to be contrasting that supposed natural tumescence with the supernatural phallic potency that, in the paintings Steinberg discusses, is figured by billowing loincloths that "convert the *ostentatio genitalium* decently into a fanfare of cosmic triumph" (93). See especially figure 101, a *Crucifixion* (1503) by Lucas Cranach in which the loincloth of Christ contrasts with that of the hanged thief facing the viewer.

36. See O'Connell, who also links line 27 to the creation of Adam ("'Restore Thine Image,'" 23).

37. The question of whether the verb in line 22 is "tune" (as in the seventeenth century print editions of the poem and many manuscripts) or "turne" (as in the Group II manuscripts and the Dobell manuscript) is decided in favor of "turne" by Shawcross (see his

explanation in the "Index of Textual Differences," *Complete Poetry*, 497–98). The appropriateness of "turne" seems all the clearer in light of a reading that underscores the contrast between the poet/speaker's artful sonnet-turns and Christ's super-Natural actions as *primum mobile* and begetter of redemption. On lines 21–22 as "the exact mid-point of the poem," see Bellette (344); Severance (37–38); Stanwood (114–15); and Brooks (295).

38. See O'Connell: "the logic of the question points to the impossibility of not seeing" ("'Restore Thine Image,'" 22). I would stress that the ambiguity of the rhetorical questions in "Goodfriday, 1613" contrasts markedly with the ringing imperatives and less equivocal rhetorical questions in "The Crosse," in which the poet/speaker and the reader must not refuse to see the cross of Christ in all its myriad manifestations.

39. Compare the conclusion of Marvell's "Coronet." Unlike the author of Genesis, who excludes any mention of Sarah from his account of the Sacrifice of Isaac, Donne identifies with the mother whose husband—Abraham obeying God in Genesis, and God the Father himself in the Gospels—is willing to sacrifice their only Son. This sympathy is not subversive, for it presupposes the rightness of the mother's submission to the Father's will; but it points up the analogy paralleling the bond of flesh and blood between the female parent and her child with the bond of ink and inspiration between the poet and his work. See also *Astrophil and Stella* 1, where Sidney's speaker goes through labor pains in an effort to give birth to his poetry.

40. Petrarch's phrase is "micidiali specchi" (*Rime sparse* 46:7). See also Petrarch on "that lovely clear gaze where the rays of love are so hot that they kill me before my time" (*Rime sparse* 37:83–85) and on the "assault" of Laura's eyes (*Rime sparse* 39:1).

41. See Brooks's discussion of the word "turne" (297); she argues that the "residual tension within the poem's future-oriented closing lines attests to . . the recognition of the [human soul's] lifelong dependency on Christ's saving Grace, a dependency that Protestant thinking had greatly intensified" (298). I would argue that the conclusion does precisely what Brooks contends that it does *up until* the concluding half-line, which breaks away from reception of grace to assert the independent action of the "I."

42. The refrain is repeated with a slight variation in the mode of address in verse 7 ("Turn us again, O God of hosts . .") and in verse 19 ("Turn us again, O Lord God of hosts, cause thy face to shine; and we shall be saved"), which concludes the psalm.

43. Donne follows a similar sequence in his "Hymn to God the Father," where he begs that "at my death thy Sunne / Shall shine"

(15–16), concluding by surrendering all to God: "And, having done that, Thou hast done, / I have no more" (17–18).

44. "Zenith to us and to'our Antipodes" (24), "The seat of all our Soules" (26), and "that Sacrifice, which ransom'd us" (32).

45. See also Stanwood's reading of "Goodfriday, 1613" as "an implicitly liturgical poem that makes individual prayer possible within a carefully wrought form suitable for all times and individuals" (115).

46. See Marotti's reading of Donne's divine poems as "witty performances designed for an appreciative readership" and of "Goodfriday, 1613" as "particularly adjusted to the receptivities of a primary audience" (*John Donne, Coterie Poet*, 245, 266). Marotti takes issue with Friedman's conclusion that the poem is meant as a vehicle for the reader's conversion, arguing that, "[I]n the context of [Donne's] actual behavior, the religious thematics of 'Goodfriday, 1613' and of the other preordination religious and philosophical poetry were rendered deeply problematic, and would have been perceived as such by a knowing coterie readership" (268).

47. See Walker, "The Religious Lyric as a Genre" and Friedman.

48. See Flynn, "'Awry'" for a discussion of the possibility that the "E. of D." is William Stanley, sixth Earl of Derby rather than Richard Sackville, third Earl of Dorset, as Gardner (64, citing Grierson) conjectures. Flynn argues that, since the dating of the Holy Sonnets between 1609 and 1611 is based partly upon the assumption that Sackville is the addressee of the poem to "E. of D.," that dating may in fact be erroneous; he notes that the sonnets may have been written as early as the 1590s, when the vogue for writing sonnet-sequences was at its height in England. Flynn points out, moreover, that the heading associating the "E. of D." poem with the Holy Sonnets exists in only two manuscripts; it is possible, then, that the piece addressed to "E. of D." may have accompanied secular poems rather than holy sonnets.

49. The letter to Goodyer, dated "Jan 19" was clearly written in 1614, a little less than a month after Somerset's wedding, which took place on 26 December 1613. The letter suggests that Donne might write in defense of the "Nullity" or annulment that had been granted to the bride shortly before the wedding, noting that "it may prove possible, that my weak assistance may be of use in this matter, in a more serious fashion, then an Epithalamion" (*Letters*, 180). Donne thus excuses the fact that he has not yet written a wedding poem, that he has—as he puts it—been "abstinent in that kinde"; but he goes on to say that "by my troth, I think I shall not scape" writing and presenting an epithalamion. *Eclog* must therefore date from early 1614 rather from December of the previous year when the wedding itself took place.

50. For a reading of "Thou hast made me" and "As due by many titles" as applying to God the strategies used in the letter to Carr, see Schoenfeldt, "Poetry of Supplication."

Notes to Chapter 4

1. The danger, Herbert implies in a number of poems, lies not so much in the use of Petrarchan conventions, but in the idolatrous tendencies of the poetic imagination itself. In "Jordan (II)," for example, he uses the language of horticulture to capture the luxurious excesses of that faculty: "My thoughts began to burnish, sprout, and swell, / Curling with metaphors a plain intention" (4–5). See also Marvell's "The Coronet," which draws on the language of pastoral rather than Petrarchism (the speaker "Dismantl[es] all the fragrant towers / That once adorned my shepherdess's head" (7–8) in order to make a new crown for Christ), but nevertheless finds his sacred "chaplet" (11) inextricably entwined with sinful "wreaths of fame and interest" (16).

2. See Low on the Petrarchan emphasis in this poem, in which the "absent God . . seems as distant and unobtainable as any Petrarchan mistress" ("John Donne," 216–17).

3. See Mueller, who stresses that the opening lines describe "a categorically higher order of experience, an exaltation of emotion that voids the ordinary operation of [the speaker's] mind and senses" (86). Mueller observes that she departs from most critics' interpretation of the poem's opening lines as "an allusion to previous amours," noting that "the utter stupefaction that attended Dante's early sight of Beatrice and Petrarch's of Laura will suggest the gratuitousness of the inference, as an importation of the reader and not of the poet" (93, n. 7). Critics who infer a libertine past include De Sa Wiggins (88–90) and Young ("Angels," 3–4). See also Spinrad, who links the Petrarchan angelolatry of the poem with the alleged practice of Roman Catholics.

4. Docherty alludes briefly to Theseus's theory of the imagination in discussing "Aire and Angels," but only to comment on the word "pinnace": "a ship of fools may be one thing, but a ship of love or of lovers is another, even if Shakespeare may have aligned 'the lunatic, the lover and the poet' in terms of imagination in *A Midsummer Night's Dream*" (196).

5. See Mueller, who argues "that 'Aire and Angels' is a Renaissance sonnet sequence . . containing just two sonnets" and that the lover of this "cameo sonnet sequence . . . finally offers testimony much like that of Sidney's Astrophil, who more lengthily but no

more conclusively suffers depletion of a personal and social erotic economy by seeking to operate within a Petrarchan construction of gender roles and sexual difference" (89, 92).

6. Calvin is describing the Catholic laity's visual adoration of the consecrated Host. See also Gilman (38).

7. See also Wyatt's translation of this sonnet as "My galley chargèd with forgetfulness" and Spenser's less despairing adaptation, "Lyke as a ship. . ." (*Amoretti* 34).

8. See Labriola: "First as a Platonist, then as an Ovidian he fails; for his changed outlook on the woman does not empower him to act sexually, merely to fantasize" ("'This Dialogue,'" 81).

9. See Donne's *ElVar*, 25–26: "The last I saw in all extreames is faire, / And holds me in the Sun-beames of her haire." Shawcross glosses "in all extreames" as "in all extremities of the body" (*Complete Poetry*, 73).

10. The poem's conclusion is a much-debated crux; for an overview of the controversy about these lines, see Roberts, "'Just such disparitie.'"

11. See De Sa Wiggins (94) and Schoenfeldt, "Patriarchal Assumptions" (23).

12. On relation to and communication with "Thou" versus perception or experience of "He," "She," or "It," see Buber. See also Guibbory: "The poem . . . makes clear how difficult it is to love someone else for her(him)self, as (s)he is, rather than as a reflection or mirror of the lover's needs and desires" ("Donne, the Idea of Woman," 111).

Notes to Chapter 5

1. Phrygius (62–64), who is portrayed as avoiding women altogether, is—as Hester explains—"some sort of purist . . who believes that all current forms of the Church fail to fulfill Christian principles. He does not believe in the possibility of a pure Church any more than some of Donne's lyrical personae believe in 'a woman [both] true and faire'" (*'Kinde Pitty'*, 121). Hester discusses various purist sects, including the Seekers and the Barrowists, that might be Donne's target in the portrayal of Phrygius.

2. See *Rime sparse* 16, where Petrarch compares himself to an old man who wanders away "to Rome, following his desire" (9) to gaze on a true icon of Christ; similarly, Petrarch seeks Laura's "longed-for true form" (14). The speaker's comparison of Mirreus's reverence to that which "wee here" give to the monarch's "statecloth" points up the ironic parallel Donne perceives between the alleged Mariolatry of

Roman Catholics and the cult of the Virgin Queen; see Hester, who comments on how English "Establishment poets . . . had reformed Roman Mariologies to support an imperial Protestant Petrarchism" ("'this cannot be said,'" 382). Hester reads Donne's love poetry as "a witty critique of the poetry, the poetics, and the Protestant polemic best represented by Sidney's works, as a sort of witty 'counter-reformation' endorsement of the recusant Donne's early motto— *Better dead than changed*" and as an "attempt to distance himself from the views of love, religion, and poetry represented by the example of Sidney" ("'Let me love,'" 131). My only quarrel with Hester's reading is that he does not sufficiently underscore the irony implicit in Donne's strategy: the poet may well be engaged in a "counter-reformation" reply to Sidneyan Protestant poetics, but he does not always portray the "Catholic" alternative as an anti-Petrarchan "apology for sexual desire" ("'Let me love,'" 132). On the contrary, Donne's Petrarchan speakers often use Catholic-sounding language (as in poems like "Loves Deitie" and "The Funerall") in ways that represent their religion of unrequited love as a specifically papistical species of folly. What Donne most objects to in Protestant Petrarchism, I would argue, is its essential, ironic likeness to the equally unsatisfactory "Catholic" love-religion embraced by such speakers.

3. See Donne's *EpEliz*, the first two stanzas of which are addressed to "Bishop Valentine" (1).

4. I use the term in its anthropological sense See Freccero, "Fig Tree." Freccero draws on the work of Kaufmann, who identifies "the Jews' conception of idolatry as a kind of fetishism" (Freccero, "Fig Tree," 37).

5. See Donne, *Sermons* 5:135 and 7:267; the appendix on Eucharistic sacrifice below; and the discussion of *Cor5* above, pages 76–77.

6. See Estrin (180–91), who stresses that the speaker of "The Funerall" "deprives [the Petrarchan mistress] of a duly reverential Petrarchan following: she has no audience left to confirm her laurelization" (187).

7. "To safeguard in every possible way the dignity of so august a Sacrament, not only is the power of its administration entrusted exclusively to priests, but the Church has also prohibited by law any but consecrated persons . . to dare handle or touch the sacred vessels" (*Catechism*, 254).

8. This is the heading for chapter 2 in the "Table of the Chapters handled in this Booke." See Flynn, "Irony" (57–59) on Donne's circulation of the table of contents for his book, which "included more than one covert joke," in advance of *Pseudo-Martyr*'s publication.

9. From the headings from Chapters 3 and 4 in Donne's "Table of the Chapters."

10. Donne's uncles Jasper and Ellis Heywood were both Jesuits, and his response to the order reflects the range of different attitudes toward the order among various sectors of the English recusant community; see Bossy, particularly the chapter on "The Archpriest Controversy" (33–48), which explains the secular clergy's hostility towards the Jesuits and the varied perspectives of the clergy and the lay gentry on how best to approach the issue of allegiance to a Protestant monarch. On conflicts among the Jesuits themselves, see Flynn's discussion of the disagreement between Donne's uncle Jasper Heywood and his more powerful colleague, Robert Persons, over the conduct of the Jesuit mission in England (*John Donne and the Ancient Catholic Nobility*, 101–02, 108). Flynn reads both of Donne's overtly anti-Jesuit prose works, *Ignatius His Conclave* and *Pseudo-Martyr*, as deeply ironic and ambivalent. *Ignatius*, though it sets up the founder of the Jesuits as the supreme rival to Lucifer himself, is also (Flynn convincingly argues) a covert attack on Robert Cecil, the most assiduous anti-Catholic persecutor in the English government. And as Flynn also demonstrates, *Pseudo-Martyr*'s overt function (to repudiate the Jesuits' claim to martyrdom and to argue in favor of Catholics' taking the Oath of Allegiance) masks its broader purpose, which is to satirize the whole pack of religious controversialists, Protestant and Catholic alike, as men who—as Donne put it in a letter—"write for Religion, without it" (*Letters*, 160).

11. Though the close reading of the sentence from *Biathanatos* is my own, I am indebted to Flynn's account of Donne's controversial prose as essentially ironic; see notes 8 and 10 above.

12. See Andreasen, *Conservative Revolutionary* (133), Parish, and Richards.

13. "Always the Same" was the motto of the Virgin Queen, Elizabeth I. On the Jesuit claim to be in search of their own martyrdoms rather than in any way guilty of plotting the Queen's demise, see the passages quoted from Southwell's *An Humble Supplication to her Maiestie* in Hester, "'this cannot be said'" (373). To the speaker's portrayal of "this place" as a doomed "Paradise," compare the famous speech by Shakespeare's Gaunt in praise of "This other Eden, demi-paradise, / . . . / This blessed plot, this earth, this realm, this England" (*Richard II* 2.1.42).

14. See the section on "Metamorphosis" in the introduction to Durling's edition of Petrarch (26–33).

15. Shelburne has argued for the validity of the variant "growe" in place of "groane" in line 17; as Shawcross's textual notes indicate (*Complete Poetry*, 451), "growe" occurs in all print editions of Donne's poems 1633–69, as well as in C57, TCC, Dob, and O'F. Noting that "n" and "w" are often nearly indiscernible in seventeenth

century handwriting, Shelburne argues that "'groue' violates the sense because the speaker doesn't want to be part of the process: when the mandrake groans it dies, but also stimulates reproduction. Our speaker wants to feel nothing at all[;] . . . he'd prefer to keep 'growing' and avoid the participation in the death/birth cycle" (Shelburne, Personal e-mail [20 June 1997]). I am less sure, however, that the speaker "wants to feel nothing at all."

16. See discussions of the sacramental imagery in Stampfer (173–74), Andreasen (146–48), Richards (182), Sherwood, *Fulfilling the Circle* (111, 213, n 7), McNees, *Eucharistic Poetry* (47–48), Sheppeard (70), and Baumlin (174).

17. The imagery calls to mind abuses of the Eucharist that Protestants saw as an ongoing threat. The first Edwardian Prayer Book proscribes communicants' taking communion in the hand lest they take the bread and convey it "secretelye awaye" to use as a magic charm (*First and Second Prayer-Books*, 230). See also Thomas (34–35) and Scot's 1584 treatise *The Discoverie of Witchcraft*, which catalogues "Popish" superstitions and abuses, including the use of consecrated wine to cure a cough (148).

18. The sermon is undated by Potter and Simpson, but I would conjecture that it was preached some time in 1622, in the same spirit as the Lincoln's Inn sermon for Ascension Day 1622 (quoted below, p. 171) that portrays Jesuits as spiritual seducers of men's wives. As Potter and Simpson note in introducing the Lincoln's Inn sermon, "There was some cause for alarm at this time, because James, in his anxiety to please the Spanish ambassador [Diego Samiento De Acuña Gondomar], had relaxed many of the restrictions imposed on the entry of foreign priests. Arthur Wilson (*History of Great Britain*, 195) wrote of this period: 'At home the *Prisons* are set open, *Priests* and *Jesuits* walk about at noon day to deceive'" (Potter and Simpson, *Sermons* 4:31). And James was quick to punish anyone criticizing or interfering with his policies; as Norbrook notes, Thomas Winiffe "was sent to the Tower in 1622 for a sermon in which he attacked Gondomar" (34, n. 81). In the undated sermon preached at St. Paul's, Donne comments on 2 Corinthians 5:20 ("We pray ye in Christs stead . . ."), contrasting agents of the Roman Church, whom he represents as self-serving ambassadors of the Pope, devoted to "their owne businesse" with priests of the English Church, whom he represents as God's true ambassadors (*Sermons* 10:125–27). Donne's extended discussion of the proper function of ambassadors seems like a discreet way of alluding to Ambassador Gondomar's role in reopening England to Jesuit influence; by commenting in general terms on what ambassadors ought and ought not to do, Donne could implicitly criticize James's accommodation of Gondomar without

explicitly denouncing the Spanish ambassador and thus offending the king. Donne carefully distances himself from those preachers who were more directly criticizing James's policies; he distinguishes between the priest, who is sent to "intreat" the people of God, and the prophet, who is given an "extraordinary Commission" to criticize monarchs. But even as he condemns the usurpation of the prophets' "Commission," Donne uses equivocal language that suggests that such a commission may currently be in effect; he says that "over-zealous" Protestants who criticize monarchs are "assuming to themselves . . . whatsoever God, upon extraordinary occasions, was pleased to give *for the present*, to his extraordinary Instruments the Prophets" (*Sermons* 10:121; emphasis added). While the primary meaning of "for the present" is clearly, "for the duration of a specific occasion in the past," the phrase might also be taken to mean "for now."

19. See Calvin, *Inst* 4.17.37 and 18.7–8, as well as Article 25 of the *Thirty-Nine Articles*: "The Sacramentes were not ordeyned of Christ to be ga[z]ed upon, or to be caryed about: but that we shoulde duely use them."

20. The tale of the jealous husband spans chapters 33–35 in part 1 of *Don Quijote.*

21. See Ariosto, *Orlando Furioso* 42.98–104.

22. The Wine of Truth will poison him See a story of priests killing a king with a poisoned host (Donne, *Sermons* 7:295, 9:302); as Thomas Browne tells it, the chalice is tainted, so the victim "receive[s] his bane in a draught of his salvation" (1:607).

23. See the introductory paragraph of Trent's "Decree Concerning the Most Holy Sacrament of the Eucharist," which "forbids all the faithful of Christ to presume henceforth to believe, teach or preach with regard to the Holy Eucharist otherwise than is explained and defined in this present decree." Chapter 1 of the "Decree" declares that, since Christ's words in instituting the Eucharist ("Hoc est corpus meum"; "This is my body") "embody that proper and clearest meaning in which they were understood by the Fathers, it is a most contemptible action on the part of some contentious and wicked men to twist them into fictitious and imaginary tropes by which the truth of the flesh and blood of Christ is denied, contrary to the universal sense of the Church, . . . *the pillar and ground of truth* [1 Timothy 3:15]."

24. See Flynn ("Irony") and Marotti (*John Donne, Coterie Poet*, 214–18), who discusses "Twicknam garden" as an expression of Donne's ambivalence towards literary patronage.

25. On recusant wives' preservation of Roman Catholic practice even in families where the male head of household was a conforming Protestant or a "Church-Papist," see Bossy (152–61).

26. Donne would not, of course, have known anything about the religion more properly referred to as vodoun; his term in the poem is "witchcraft." But the practice he fears is the making of an effigy for purposes of working harm, a practice associated in Donne's time with witches and the Old Religion (see 159 above on "witchcrafts charms") and in the popular imagination of our time with the much-maligned religion of Haiti, which is practiced by many men and women who also practice Catholicism.

Notes to Chapter 6

1. Mayne's elegy includes a number of verbal echoes of Donne's work and begins by asking, "Who shall presume to mourn thee, Donne, unlesse / He could his teares *in thy expressions* dresse" (1–2; emphasis added). It seems likely, then, that the cloister image is a conscious allusion.

2. For a Roman Catholic commentary on the words of institution, see the Trent Catechism, which specifies that "The word *this* expresses the entire substance of the thing present; and therefore if the substance of the bread remained, our Lord could not have truly said: *This is my body"* (236); see also Cajetan (162–67). For a Protestant counterargument, see Calvin (*Inst.* 4.17.20–23).

3. See Calvin's acknowledgment that "before that we goe any further, we must entreate of the selfe institution of Christe: specially because this is the most glorious obiection that our adversaries have, that we departe from the woordes of Christe. Therefore that we may be discharged . . . our fittest beginnyng shall be at the exposition of the woordes" (*Inst.* 4.17.20).

4. A lyric, as Shawcross explains, is "a briefer poem in which the author intends to produce a successful literary creation by specific chosen techniques, devices, form, language, strategy, and the like in an ultimately competitive spirit for evaluation by the readers. It implies a fictive voice that may appear to be an authorial one, and that may owe its substance to an authorial voice; it is a fictive voice speaking to an auditor, implied or also fictive, who always also is the reader" (*Intentionality*, 86). In the white spaces between its stanzas, "The Flea" provides ample opportunity for the reader to identify with the lady who is the fictive auditor; and the battle-ready speaker of the poem bears a strong resemblance to Donne himself as he enters the flea-poem arena in a "competitive" attempt (Shawcross, *Intentionality*, 86) to rework and outdo previous lyrics of that type. In order to judge the poet's attempt "successful" while insisting that the seduction attempt fails, a reader will find it necessary to cling very closely to a condemnation of the intentional fallacy. For

an insistence on precisely this sort of distinction, see Rudnytsky (187–89).

5. See David B. Wilson and Brumble.

6. The sighing note of the interpolated "alas," somewhat out of keeping with the matter-of-fact tone he has maintained up until this point, anticipates the more emotional argument of the second stanza. In implying, subtly, that he would actually prefer it if they *could* have a child together, he cunningly evokes an attitude of commitment without avowing it. Only a Donnean speaker could manage to say, "Don't worry, you won't get pregnant" and sound, at the same time, as if he were singing, "Would you marry me anyway? Would you have my baby?"

7. See Brumble (150) on Donne's adaptation of Petrarchan convention in stanza two.

8. Brumble (150) notes the movement from mere analogy in stanza one to more literal claims in the second stanza.

9. See Gilman (chapter 5) on Donne's ambivalence toward images and the frequent recurrence in his poetry of what the speaker of "Witchcraft by a picture" calls "pictures made and mard." Gilman does not discuss "The Flea."

10. Augustine makes this assertion—"[A]liud est Sacramentum, aliud virtus Sacramentum"—in his *Tractates on the Gospel of John* (*PL* 35:1611).

11. Winny is one of seven twentieth century critics noted by Perrine in an "annotated list of critics who believe that the seduction attempt in 'The Flea' is successful" (16). The list also includes Helen Gardner (introduction, xx) and Patricia Meyer Spacks. Perrine blasts their readings as unfounded, insisting that the evidence provided "in the poem . . . favors the inference that this attempt on the young lady's virginity is as unsuccessful as those that have preceded it" (6). For Perrine, the poem dramatizes a witty game—as sexually fruitless as any Petrarchan ritual—played "for the 'fun' of the thing" by a perennially unrequited lover and his definitively coy mistress (7). But recent criticism of the poem—Perrine's list extends only through 1970—has persisted in taking the speaker's rhetoric considerably more seriously. See, for example, Baumlin's argument, discussed below, 186; Rudnytsky's assertion that "Donne secures [the lady's] assent to the irrational assumptions that support his . . . aim" (188); and Docherty's observation that "Prediction is tantamount to the generation of factuality in this poem" (59).

12. See the appendix on *The Doctrine of Eucharistic Sacrifice* below.

13. See Calvin: "They consecrate an host, as they call it, which they may carie about in pompe, which they may shew foorth in a common gazing to be loked upon, worshipped, and called upon"

(*Inst* 4.17.37). For a concise explanation of medieval Catholic "communion through the eyes," see the section entitled "The Gaze that Saves" in Emminghaus (80–83).

14. See Donne's insistence that we must "apply [Christ's] bloud . . shed for us, by those meanes which God in his Church presents to us," since not to do so would be a "wastfull wantonnesse" (*Sermons* 3:163, 162).

15. See Rajan's argument that the *Songs and Sonets* invite resistance, that they evoke a response much like the one Donne solicited for the *Paradoxes and Problems* when he described them as "swaggerers" and "alarums to truth" (809).

16. Marotti concludes that the poem pits "a shame morality that views loss of virginity before marriage as a woman's greatest dishonor . . against a personalist morality that regards the intention of commitment (and marriage) as largely legitimizing the premarital intercourse of mutual lovers" (94).

17. As LeComte notes, the exact dates of Constance's birth and baptism are unknown.

18. Because Donne's *Songs and Sonets* cannot be dated with any certainty, the parallels between the poem and the letter cannot reliably be applied to a biographical account of the poet, either; but as Shawcross stresses, such applications tend at any rate to limit rather than enrich our understanding of Donne's lyrics ("Poetry, Personal and Impersonal"). What I am exploring in this reading is not "The Flea" as biographical document, but rather the parallel between the rhetorical project Donne undertook in the letter and the lyric project he undertook in "The Flea."

19. The letter to George More, for its part, did not persuade its addressee; far from convincing Anne's father to bless the match, Donne's rhetoric seems, understandably, to have incensed him further—just as the speaker's argument provokes the lady to extreme measures in the first two stanzas of "The Flea." When Donne wrote to Sir George again on 11 February, it was from the Fleet Prison, where he was held for a brief period after having been dismissed from Egerton's service.

Notes to Chapter 7

1. See the Renaissance humanist Lipsius, who cites St. Jerome's quotation (epistle 42) of Turpilius, a Roman comic writer: "This is the one thing which makes the absent present" (9). See also Young and Hester in their introduction to Lipsius' treatise: "The letter is the most 'logocentric' of genres, and this, to a large extent, accounts

for its importance among the humanists" (xxiii); indeed, "the rendering of the full presence of the absent subject in writing . . . is the goal of Lipsius' epistolography" (xxiv).

2. The first of the four poems is a longer piece (comprised of four 8-line stanzas) in which Donne addresses Woodward as "sweet Poët." The most detailed discussion of the "T. W." poems is Klawitter's.

3. See Baumlin's discussion of the poem, which stresses the tension between the poem as a Catholic sacrament that "might claim, if even blasphemously, the capacity to substantiate the poet through his own words of (self)-invocation" and the poem as a "more radically Protestant" Eucharist "restricting the words of Eucharistic celebration to a figural representation rather than a re-presenting or presencing of its transcendental subject" (167–68).

4. For an alternative reading, which takes the poem as a genuine expression of melancholy born of frustrated homosexual desire, see Klawitter (98–99).

5. In his note on *HWKiss* 1, Milgate (226) also cites Ambrose: "in quibus etiam cum amico miscemus animum, et mentem ei nostram infundimus" (*PL* 16:1151).

6. "[I]f yᵒ coole not in friendship be not loath to write for letters are frendships sacraments & wee should be in charyty to receaue at all tymes" (from a letter printed in Simpson, *A Study of the Prose Works*, 292). Marotti quotes this letter in his discussion of *HWKiss*, noting that it dates from the same period as the poem, and that it was "probably also to Wotton" (*John Donne, Coterie Poet*, 121).

7. On the date of the poem, see Pebworth and Summers, "'Thus.'"

8. Milgate notes that the idea of the soul-mingling kiss descends from an epigram ascribed to Plato in the *Greek Anthology* (226); see note 11 below. See also Perella (4–9, 26–27, 130–32), who notes that in the erotic poetry of the Renaissance the kiss becomes a "Neoplatonic sacrament" (169).

9. Shawcross (*Complete Poetry*, 195) cites the psalm verse. For a similar emphasis on a letter as necessary nourishment, see Donne's verse epistle *TWPreg* (quoted above, page 320). See also the Eucharistic transition from *Cor5* to *Cor6*, which pivots around the word *"moyst"* (*Cor5*, 14, *Cor6*, 1) and Donne's insistence that Christ's blood must moisten his *"dry soule"* (*Cor5*, 14, *Cor6*, 1) if it is to be saved "from being starv'd, hard, or foule" (*Cor6*, 4).

10. Donne cites Augustine as his source. See also Articles 12 and 13 of the Thirty-Nine Articles: "[G]ood workes, which are the fuites of fayth, and folowe after justification, are . . . pleasing and acceptable to God in Christe and do spring out necessarily of a true and

lively faith"; but ""Workes done before the grace of Christe, and the inspiration of his spirite, are not pleasaunt to God . . .: yea rather for that they are not done as God hath wylled and commaunded them to be done, we doubt not but they have the nature of sinne." See also the Council of Trent's "Decree Concerning Justification," chapter 16: ". . . Christ Jesus Himself . . . continually infuses strength into the justified, which strength always precedes, accompanies, and follows their good works, and without which they could not in any manner be pleasing and meritorious before God . . ." Trent anathematizes, however, the idea that "all works done before justification . . . are truly sins, or merit the hatred of God" ("Canons Concerning Justification," Canon 7).

11. Grierson believed that both "Sir, more then kisses" and "'Tis not a coat of grey" were entries in a literary debate then current among the members of Essex's coterie over the relative merits of country, town, and court; at the heart of this supposed debate was Francis Bacon's poem "The World." Donne's language does seem to allude to the "The World" at several points; but Pebworth and Summers argue convincingly that the similarities among the various poems cited by Grierson are best explained by the fact that they all "reflect their authors' current study of the Planudean Anthology" which contains a number of epigrams that may be sources for various conceits in Bacon's work as well as Donne's ("'Thus,'" 363).

12. See *Sermons* 1:246, where Donne stresses that God is to be found "at home" within the believer's heart and within his native Church rather than "beyond the Sea . . in a forrein Church." For a discussion of the distinctions Donne saw between the English Catholic tradition in which he was raised and the ultra-montane "Papism" of post-Tridentine Europe, see Flynn, "'*Annales* School.'"

13. Flynn builds upon Haigh's accounts of Catholic "resistance."

14. See also Chanoff (155–63).

15. Though Wotton wrote and circulated *The State of Christendom* in 1594, the work was not published until 1657, after his death. Flynn discusses Wotton's work, the ambivalent Protestantism of his family, and his friendship with Donne ("Donne, Henry Wotton, and the Earl of Essex").

16. As Pebworth and Summers observe, "[T]hrough the pun on his own name at the poem's conclusion, he identifies completely with his friend" ("Donne's Correspondence," 8).

17. As Walker points out in a review of *John Donne, Undone*, Docherty employs the term "Other" in a vaguely Lacanian sense without specifying Lacan as his source ("Left/Write/Right," 137). It is the "Other" in Lacan's sense of the word that the self recognizes and identifies with in "Sir, more then kisses." However, Docherty's

sense of the relation between Self and Other also seems strongly influenced by Hartman's conception of author and reader in *The Fate of Reading*. "Sir, more then kisses" demonstrates the inaccuracy of Docherty's conclusion—derived from his reading of Hartman—that "In the ideal, dialogical or poetic reading of poetry, namable personal identity is lost" (197). Such loss of identity is the case neither in the creation of the Church as corporate body (see 1 Corinthians 12, which stresses that the one body has many members, each unique), nor in the creation of the corporate identity in which Donne and Wotton are joined.

18. See Walker, "'Here,'" and "Anne More." Walker demonstrates that, according to the system of gematria developed by John Skelton in his *Garland of Laurel*, in which each letter has a numerical value, the names JOHN DONNE and ANNE MORE, as well as the phrase MY NAME, are all numerically equivalent, being composed of letters whose values add up to 64. See also Shawcross's note (*Complete Poetry*, 401).

19. Walker qualifies this point, noting that "the male in question is absent, and we have instead the NAME as object of the female gaze"; she also observes that "it is only a partial statement of dual identity, for the female subject is allowed to see the male as object, but the male subject identifies himself with the female object" (101).

20. See also Hester's more extended reading of "Valediction of my name, in the window" ("'Let me love,'" 136–41).

21. The phrase "hallmark of Popery" is Dugmore's (82).

22. Donne owned a copy of Rogers's commentary on the Thirty-nine Articles, which discusses in great detail the doctrines repudiated by them. Cardinal Cajetan, it should be noted, denies that Catholics believe any such thing: "when one refers the sacrifice of the altar to the death of Christ, a sign is involved and not the reality, since neither the death of Christ nor Christ in death is present in itself. Since Christ lives and reigns in heaven, his death is consequently not contained in this sacrifice but is rather signified. . . . Christ himself is both signified and contained, while his death is indeed signified but not contained. There is no need therefore that Christ die each time this sacrifice is offered . . ." (169).

23. See the discussion of Spenser's Protestant objections to "the worship of Corpus Christi . . and the veneration of relics" in Nohrnberg, who notes (175) that John Bale's *A mysterye of inyquyte* (Geneva, 1545) sums up the Protestant attitude toward Roman Catholic ceremonial when it calls Catholicism "ydolatrie and necrolatrie" (fol. 54v). Bale's treatise responds to a doggerel verse-polemic by one P. Pantolabus that defends transubstantiation and condemns the Protestant martyr Johan Frith because "he did denye. / That Christ

unfayned / Was there contayned. / Both ryallye / And substancyallye" (quoted in Bale, *A mysterye,* fol. 46r). Coincidentally, Bale anticipates Donne's reference to the mock-Eucharistic inscription of his "ragged bony name" ("Valediction," 23) when he belittles Pantolabus's lame verse as "ragged rymes of rustycall rudeness" (fol. 38v) and dismisses the Catholic writer's scholastic terminology as "youre ragged realyte / borrowed of the paganes lernynge" (fol. 47r).

24. In another reading of the poem, Hester argues that "the final claim of the speaker returns to the Catholic insistence on Real Presence: in the sacrament of love the glass and lines of the speaker's worship of his divine mistress—like the cup and words of the priest in the rite—are merely the accidentals of the Feast; but they are not the *firma,* the physical signature or Real Presence that makes the ceremony substantial . . . The point . . . is that the presence of the body alone makes this *sermo* substantial . . . Presence alone can overcome the speaker's murmuring doubts" ("'Let me love,'" 140).

25. See also Estrin (202–12), who reads the "Valediction" as "a deconstruction of the Petrarchan mentality" (204).

26. See also my "Ambivalent Mourning."

27. Hooker's nineteenth century editor, John Keble, goes so far as to use the traditional Roman Catholic term to refer to "things, which (to use Hooker's own expression) though not sacraments, are *as* sacraments, and which perhaps it might not be amiss to denominate *sacramentals*" (*Works* 1:xcvii).

28. Compare Whitgift's remarks on the roundness of the ring to Donne's "Sonnet. The Token," in which the speaker tells his beloved not to send him any token of affection save to "Swear thou think'st I love thee." Among the rejected tokens is a "Ring to shew the stands / Of our affection, that as that's round and plaine, / So should our loves meet in simplicity" (7–9).

29. See also the mixture of serious and bawdy meanings in Shakespeare's *Merchant.* In act 3 scene 2, Portia gives her ring to Bassanio and tells him that she gives herself and all of her possessions to him "with this ring, / Which when you part from, lose, or give away, / Let it presage the ruin of your love" (171–73). The ring is thus clearly defined (as is the insect in the first stanza of "The Flea") as a sign that participates in what it signifies. Whereas the lady in "The Flea" resists such a definition, however, Bassanio endorses it, pledging that "when this ring / Parts from this finger, then parts life from hence!" (183–84). Later, when Portia is disguised as the young doctor of law, Balthasar, "he" asks Bassanio for the ring in terms that correspond to those of the seducer in "The Flea": "you in love shall not deny me this" (4.1.429). Bassanio responds by insisting that he cannot give the wise young judge such a "trifle"

(430); and the double-entendre of the following line further extends the analogy between female honor and the ring: "I will not shame myself to give you this." "Balthasar" responds with a punning line that clinches the joke: "I will have *nothing* else but only this" (emphasis added).

30. In "Sonnet. The Token," Donne's speaker implies a parallel between rings and poesy when he rejects both, telling her to send him neither a ring nor any of the "witty Lines" that abound in her "Writings" (15).

31. See Estrin on "A Jeat Ring" as a poem in which Donne offers "in exchange for [the woman's] gift, . . an 'I' to match her 'you'"; Estrin stresses "the ring as a *shifting* signifier" that is "initially the woman's way of getting the man off her back" but that "emerges in the end [as] the vehicle that frees him from the obligation she initially felt" (183). Both "A Jeat Ring sent" and "The Funerall," Estrin argues, feature speakers who subvert Petrarchan tribute: "He writes out its Petrarch in 'Jeat Ring' and its Laura in 'The Funerall'" (191).

32. See the discussion of the poem in an *Explicator* query signed L.P. and in the replies by Armstrong and Daniels, Pope, and Wertenbaker.

33. As Shawcross's note points out (*Complete Poetry*, 145), there is a possible pun on "jet" and the French "jet"—throwing.

34. For an excerpt from Cartwright, see pages 208–09 above.

35. The addressee of "Valediction forbidding mourning" is, of course, unidentified within the poem; this fact is often obscured by readers' reliance upon Izaak Walton's account of the lyric as having been written for Anne More Donne on the occasion of Donne's voyage to France with Sir Robert Drury in 1611. As Herz points out, however, "we know nothing of the poem's circumstances." And thus, she asks, "Why not imagine Donne exercising the valedictory mode as virtuoso piece?" ("Reading," 141). The poem certainly functioned as virtuoso performance in the seventeenth century, no matter what its original occasion, insofar as it was widely circulated in manuscript and made available for the admiration of readers other than the woman who is the implied reader/addressee. Janice Whittington notes that, "Although not the most copied Donne poem (Peter Beal lists 54 manuscript transcriptions—'The Anagram' has 69), 'A Valediction forbidding mourning' exists in more copies than most other Donne poems" (125). Though the poet/speaker disdains "To tell the layetie our love" (8), the trope with which he begins the piece—that of the dying men whose "sad friends" watch and comment upon their breathing—suggests that the lovers' parting and the poem that describes it are to be observed by a sensitive audience capable of appreciating the quiet spectacle.

36. In combining the analogy between the poem and the wedding ring with that between poem and Eucharist, Donne's wit again plays upon a context of controversy; for the reception of the Sacrament by the newly married couple was, like the use of the wedding ring, a practice much debated among English Protestants. For Cartwright and others who wished to see more stringent reforms in the English Church, it was an abuse of the Eucharist to offer communion to the bride and groom alone: "As for the receiving of the Communion when they be married, that it is not to be suffered, unless there be a general receiving, I have before at large declared; and as for the [idea] . . . that those that be Christians may not be joined in marriage but in Christ, . . . it is very slender and cold: as if the Sacrament of the Supper were instituted to declare any such thing; or they could not declare their joining together in Christ by no means but by receiving the Supper of the Lord" (quoted in Hooker, *Works* 2:433, n. 1). In Hooker's *Laws*, the discussion of nuptial communion immediately follows the section on wedding rings; he quotes Tertullian's opinion that "the Sacrament . . . confirm[s]" the bond of wedlock" (5.73.8).

37. Redpath eliminates the confusion and the ambiguity by silently emending the punctuation of line 17; he puts a comma after "we" and removes the commas after "love" and "refin'd." For a discussion of the textual ambiguities in the "Valediction," see Whittington.

38. See also Cunnar and the discussion of alchemical transmutation as Eucharist above, chapter 1, n. 25.

39. The speaker says that his foot of the compass "far doth rome" (30), and that it must "obliquely runne" (34). See Freccero on the astronomical implications of the terms "rome" and "oblique," as suggesting planetary wandering along an ecliptic ("Donne's 'Valediction,'" 284–87). Freccero draws upon theological, philosophical, astronomical, and astrological sources to explain the compass image: "The 'circle' which ends the poem is no circle in the ordinary sense, but is rather a circle joined to the rectilinear. . . . This explains the apparent inconsistency in Donne's image. . . . Two different movements are executed by the compass: . . . a movement along a radius, from a center to a circumference and back to the center again . . . [and a] circular motion" ("Donne's 'Valediction,'" 281–82). Freccero cites the explanation of a compass' spiraling movement in Chalcidius's commentary on the *Timaeus* and concludes: "The spiral is . . . a kind of circle whose outline is unfixed until outward motion ceases and inward motion begins, retracing the same gyre in the opposite direction toward the central point of origin" (283).

40. See Freccero, "Donne's 'Valediction,'" 300.

41. In making this point, Donne is quoting directly from the Latin text of Calvin's *Institutes* (4.14.3).

Notes to Chapter 8

1. See Bald (111, n. 1; 179–80) on the poem ("Donne's other epistle to the Countess") and the letter in which it was enclosed.

2. See Maurer, who observes that "We must regard a letter to Goodyer, especially one written to him when he seems to have been an agent for two countesses, as more a public statement than a private confidence. That is, it is probably as artful as the poems it is often invoked to explain" ("John Donne's Verse Letters," 252).

3. The book may well have been one of the pamphlets written by Robert Persons, S.J. during the controversy over the Oath of Allegiance; in 1608, in response to King James's defense of the Oath, Persons wrote and published *Judgment of a Catholicke English-man living in banishment for his religion . . . concerning a late booke set forth, and entituled, Triplici nodo, triplex cuneus.* Donne himself made a contribution to the controversial literature on this subject with *Pseudo-Martyr* in 1611.

4. At one point in his poetic career, Donne *is* a sonneteer writing for and to a beloved object more exalted than either the Countess of Huntingdon or the Countess of Bedford. We cannot be certain about whether his "Holy Sonnets" date from the same period as the letter to Goodyer (as Shawcross conjectures in his "Chronological Schedule of the Poems" [*Complete Poetry*, 414]) or were written as early as the 1590s (as Flynn argues to be a possibility; see above, chapter 3, n. 48). But whenever they were written, the sonnets unite in their form and subject matter the two halves of the submerged analogy structuring the letter to Goodyer. In the "Holy Sonnets," Donne's choice of the sonnet form and application of Petrarchan conventions invite the reader to think the sonnets' poet/speaker "mad" enough— that is, in the Spanish proverb's terms, poet enough—to make more than one such lyric precisely because he is spiritually "melancholique." In the letter, however, Donne keeps the two issues carefully separated; he counsels Goodyer against the night-walking lunacy of religious melancholy while declaring his own resolution to avoid the madness of sonnet-spewing poet/lovers.

5. Gosse has the two countesses confused; he takes the Countess of Bedford to be the lady for whom Goodyer wishes Donne to write, and assumes that the "other Countess" is Lady Huntingdon (2:76–77).

6. Flynn discusses the household of Henry Stanley in chapter 10 of *John Donne and the Ancient Catholic Nobility*; see particularly pages 172 and 226, n. 46.

7. The letter in which Donne refers to friendship as his second religion was also addressed to Goodyer; Hester (*Letters*, xviii) estimates that it was written in the summer of 1607.

8. See Donne's famous assertion—in a 1624/25 letter to Sir Robert Carr—that he "did best" as a poet "when [he] had least truth for [his] subjects" (*Complete Poetry*, 267). Donne contrasts "this present case," in which he seeks to write true praise of Carr's deceased friend, James Hamilton: "In this . . . there is so much truth as it defeats all Poetry" (*Complete Poetry*, 267). As Maurer explains, "He argues that there is too much truth in Hamilton to admit poetry, an artful use of the old idea that truth and poetry are incompatible. Thus a complimentary motive is behind Donne's celebrated comment on his earlier work. The poetry of 'least truth' which Donne recalls . . . probably refers to his various defenses of his poetry of compliment in the years just prior to his taking orders, when he justified his praises of noblewomen, conspicuously Elizabeth Drury, on the grounds that he hardly knew them and so presumed the best he could imagine about them. In Hamilton's case, however, Donne argues that there is no need to poetize to produce a poetic compliment: 'Call therefore this paper by what name you will,' truth or poetry" ("John Donne's Verse Letters," 240).

9. See also Maurer ("John Donne's Verse Letters," 251–53) on Donne's use of theological language in these poems.

10. In his 1615 letter to Goodyer complaining about the "diminution" in the Countess's generosity, Donne speculates that the Countess's "suspicion of [his] calling" may have something to do with the influence of her spiritual mentor, the Calvinist physician and clergyman John Burges. As Thomson explains in a brief sketch of his career, Burges strongly influenced the Countess with his strict Calvinist teachings; Thomson concludes that "There were grounds for a disagreement in religious outlook between Donne and the Countess, a disagreement which may well have become more evident about 1613, when Burges appeared, and which was probably most marked in 1614 and 1615, when Donne was busy trying to rid himself of debt and preparing to enter the Church" (334–35). Lucy's association with strict Calvinism would perhaps not have been as strong in 1612, when Donne wrote the epistle "Begun in France but never perfected"; but as I have argued in my analysis of Donne's May/June 1609 prose letter to Goodyer, the poet saw fit to draw an implied analogy between Lucy and Protestantism even before she became involved with Burges.

11. Shawcross dates *BedfDead* around Easter 1612, *Carey* having been written in late 1611 (*Complete Poetry*, 415).

12. See also the emphasis on artless candor in Bruno's treatise: confession must be "plaine and simple, not arteficially composed" (20).

13. The three parts of repentance are outlined in Bruno's treatise; Stock, like Hooker (*Laws* 6.3.5), retains the idea of a three-part repentance, though the official Elizabethan *Homilies* take a polemical stand against this scholastic formulation. The "Homilie of Repentance, and of true reconciliation unto God" insists that there are "foure parts of repentance": contrition, confession, faith, and amendment of life. "[T]hey that teach repentance without a lively faith in our Saviour Jesus Christ," the homilist urges, "doe teach none other but Iudas repentance as all the Schoole-men doe, which only doe allow these three parts of repentance: the contrition of the heart, the confession of the mouth, and the satisfaction of the worke" (*Homilies*, 268). I am indebted to Hugh Wilson for drawing my attention to the Homily's insistence upon a four-part repentance.

Notes to Afterword

1. See also Marotti: "In his letters, Donne set forth a model of communication with his coterie reader that . . he sought in most of his poetry and much of his prose. In one missive, he told his close friend Henry Goodyer that he conceived of letters as 'conveyances and deliverers of me to you': the interpersonal relationship, then, not the circumstantial content, is what mattered" (Introduction, *Critical Essays*, 4; quoting *Letters*, 109).

2. As Gosse notes, Dorney is misprinted as "Dorvey" in the 1651 *Letters* (2:18).

Notes to Appendix

1. See also the Tridentine *Catechism*: "[T]he Sacrifice of the Mass is and ought to be considered one and the same Sacrifice as that of the cross, for the victim is one and the same, namely, Christ our Lord, who offered Himself, once only, a bloody Sacrifice on the altar of the cross. The bloody and unbloody victim are not two, but one victim only, whose Sacrifice is daily renewed in the Eucharist, in obedience to the command of our Lord. . . . This being the case, it must be taught . . . that . . . the sacred and holy Sacrifice of the Mass is not a Sacrifice of Praise and Thanksgiving only, or a mere commemoration of the Sacrifice performed on the cross, but also truly a propitiatory Sacrifice, by which God is appeased and rendered

propitious to us. If, therefore, with a pure heart, a lively faith, and affected with inward sorrow for our transgressions, we immolate and offer this most holy victim, we shall, without doubt, obtain mercy from the Lord . . ." (258–59).

2. From the 1531 treatise "The Sacrifice of the Mass and Its Rite— Against the Lutherans." Cajetan was one of the greatest defenders of scholastic doctrine, and his commentary on Matthew 26:26 ("this is my body"; "hoc est corpus meum") exemplifies the Roman Catholic insistence that the substance of bread is, through the consecration, transformed into the substance of Christ's body. For Donne's approving citations of Cajetan, see *Sermons* 7:385, where (in a discussion of the disputed canon of scripture) he quotes Cajetan as an example "even in the later Roman Church" of "a good Author that gives us a good rule" for approaching the question of canonicity. In another place, Donne quotes the same passage from Cajetan's discussion of canonicity, calling him a "great Author of theirs" (*Sermons* 4:218). But he disapproves of Cajetan's teachings on attrition as sufficient for salvation (*Sermons* 1:204), and he makes a punning (and probably sarcastic) allusion to Cajetan's emphasis on the substantial presence of Christ in the Eucharist when, in a discussion of Holy Orders, he calls him "a man great in matter of substance" (*Sermons* 8:183; preached at Whitehall in 1627).

3. See the rubric preceding the consecration of the host in the Tridentine Liturgy, which indicates that the priest is to speak the words "secrete, distincte, et attente" (*Roman Liturgy*, 135). Likewise, the consecration of the wine is to be spoken "secrete super calicem" (143). The Council of Trent defended these rubrics, saying that "since the nature of man is such that he cannot without external means be raised easily to meditation on divine things, holy mother Church has instituted certain rites, namely, that some things in the mass be pronounced in a low tone and others in a louder tone." Through such practices, "the majesty of so great a sacrifice" is "emphasized and the minds of the faithful excited . . . to the contemplation of those most sublime things which are hidden in this sacrifice" ("Doctrine Concerning the Sacrifice of the Mass," chapter 5).

4. Stone translates Andrewes's *Responsio ad Apolgiam Cardinalis Bellarmini* (London, 1610) as reprinted in his *Works* 8:13, 250, 251.

5. The treatise was published 1631, the year Donne died. Morton was a major contributor to the early seventeenth century outpouring of controversial writings on the question of Jesuit influence in England and Catholic loyalty to the English Crown, and Donne was on familiar terms with him during the time that he wrote his own contributions to that controversy, *Pseudo-Martyr* and *Ignatius His Conclave*. See Bald (202–28). Bald notes that there is no concrete

evidence to support Jessop's claim that Donne assisted Morton in writing controversial treatises from 1606–1610, but he notes circumstantial evidence that Donne read one of Morton's works (*A Catholike Appeale*; 1609) in manuscript "a full eighteen months before that work was published" and that Donne showed Morton the manuscript of *Conclave Ignati* (the Latin version of *Ignatius His Conclave*) before its publication.

BIBLIOGRAPHY

Alvarez, A. *The School of Donne*. New York and Toronto: New American Library, 1967.

Andreasen, N. J. C. *John Donne, Conservative Revolutionary*. Princeton: Princeton University Press, 1967.

Andrewes, Lancelot. *Works*. 11 vols. Ed. J. P. Wilson and J. Bliss. Oxford: Oxford University Press, 1841–1845. Rpt. New York: AMS Press, 1967.

Ariosto, Lodovico. *Orlando Furioso*. Trans. John Harington. N.p.: Centaur Press, 1962.

Armstrong, Ray L. and Edgar F. Daniels. "Donne's 'A Jeat Ring Sent.'" *Explicator* 30 (1972): Item 77.

Asals, Heather Ross. "*Davids* Successors: Forms of Joy and Art." *Proceedings of the PMR Conference: Annual Publication of the Patristic, Medieval, and Renaissance Conference* 2 (1977): 31–37.

———. "John Donne and the Grammar of Redemption." *English Studies in Canada* 5 (1979): 125–39.

———. *Equivocal Predication: George Herbert's Way to God*. Toronto: University of Toronto Press, 1981.

Augustine, Saint, Bishop of Hippo. *Expositions on the Book of Psalms*. 6 vols. Oxford: J. H. Parker, 1847–57.

Baker-Smith, Dominic. "John Donne and the Mysterium Crucis." *English Miscellany* 19 (1968): 65–82.

———. "John Donne as Medievalist." *Sacred and Profane: Secular and Devotional Interplay in Early Modern British Literature.* Ed. Helen Wilcox, Richard Todd, and Alasdair MacDonald. 185–93. Amsterdam: Vrije Universiteit Press, 1996.

Bald, R. C. *John Donne: A Life.* 2nd ed. Oxford: Clarendon, 1986.

Bale, John. *A mysterye of inyquyte contained within the heretycall genealogye of P. Pantolabus.* Geneva: M. Woode,1545.

Barlow, William. *The Summe and Substance of the Conference . . .* London: John Windet for Mathew Law, 1604.

Baumgartner, Jill. "'Harmony' in Donne's 'La Corona' and 'Upon the Translation of the Psalms.'" *John Donne Journal* 3 (1984): 141–56.

Baumlin, James S. *John Donne and the Rhetorics of Renaissance Discourse.* Columbia and London: University of Missouri Press, 1991.

Belette, Anthony F. "'Little Worlds Made Cunningly': Significant Form in Donne's *Holy Sonnets* and '*Goodfriday, 1613.*'" *Studies in Philology* 72 (1975): 322–47.

Bennett, J. A. W. "A Note on Donne's *Crosse.*" *Review of English Studies* ns 5 (1954): 168–69.

Booty, John E. "History of the 1559 Book of Common Prayer." Appendix to *The Book of Common Prayer 1559. The Elizabethan Prayer Book.* Ed. John E. Booty. 327–82. Charlottesville: University Press of Virginia, 1976.

Bossy, John. *The English Catholic Community 1570–1850.* London: Darton, Longman & Todd, 1975.

Brooks, Helen B. "Donne's 'Goodfriday, 1613. Riding Westward' and Augustine's Psychology of Time." *John Donne's Religious Imagination: Essays in Honor of John T. Shawcross.* Ed. Raymond-Jean Frontain and Frances M. Malpezzi. 284–305. Conway, AR: University of Central Arkansas Press, 1995.

Browne, Thomas. *Pseudodoxia Epidemica.* 2 vols. Ed. Robin Robbins. Oxford: Clarendon, 1981.

Brumble, H. David, III. "John Donne's 'The Flea': Some Implications of the Encyclopedic and Poetic Flea Traditions." *Critical Quarterly* 15 (1973): 147–54.

Bruno, Vincent. *A Short Treatise of the Sacrament of Penance.* [Douay?], 1597.

Buber, Martin. *I and Thou.* Tr. Ronald Gregor Smith. 2nd edition. New York: Charles Scribners Sons, 1958.

Cajetan [Thomas de Vio, Cardinal Gaetano]. *Cajetan Responds: A Reader in Reformation Controversy.* Ed. and trans. Jared Wicks. Washington, D.C.: The Catholic University of America Press, 1978.

Calvin, John. *The Institution of the Christian Religion.* Trans. Thomas Norton. London: Thomas Vautrollier for Humfrey Toy, 1578.

———. *Ioannis Calvini Opera Quae Supersunt Omnia.* Eds. Guilielmus Baum, Eduardus Cunitz, and Eduardus Reuss. Vol. 2. Corpus Reformatorum 30. Brunsvigae: C. A. Schwetschke et Filium, 1864.

Cameron, Allen Barry. "Donne's Deliberative Verse Epistles." *ELR* 6 (1976): 369–403.

Carey, John. *John Donne: Life, Mind, and Art.* Oxford: Oxford University Press, 1980.

Cartwright, Thomas. *A Reply to an answere made of M. Doctor Whitegift.* London: J. S. Wandsworth, [1574?].

Cervantes Saavedra, Miguel de. *Don Quijote de la Mancha.* 2 vols. Ed. Florencio Sevilla Arroyo and Antonio Rey Hazas. Madrid: Centro de Estudio Cervantinos, 1996.

Chamberlain, John S. *Increase and Multiply: Arts-of-Discourse Procedure in the Preaching of John Donne.* Chapel Hill: University of North Carolina Press, 1976.

Chambers, A. B. "The Meaning of the 'Temple' in Donne's *La Corona.*" *Journal of English and Germanic Philology* 59 (1960): 212–17.

———. "Christmas: The Liturgy of the Church and English Verse of the Renaissance." *Literary Monographs* 6 (1975): 111–51.

———. "*La Corona*: Philosophic, Sacred, and Poetic Uses of Time." *New Essays on Donne.* Ed. Gary A. Stringer. 140–72. Salzburg: Institut für Englische Sprache und Literatur, 1977. Rpt. in *Essential Articles for the Study of John Donne's Poetry.* Ed. John R. Roberts. 349–52. Hamden, CT: Archon Books, 1975.

———. *Transfigured Rites in Seventeenth-Century English Poetry.* Columbia, MO and London: University of Missouri Press, 1992.

Chambers, Sabin. *The Garden of Our B. Lady.* [St. Omer], 1619. Facsimile rpt. Ilkley, Yorkshire: The Scholar Press, 1978.

Chanoff, David. "Donne's Anglicanism." *Recusant History* 15 (1980): 154–67.

Church of England. *Articles whereupon it was agreed by the Archbishoppes and Bishoppes . . . 1562.* London: Richarde Jugge and John Cawood, 1571.

———. *The First and Second Prayer-Books of King Edward the Sixth.* New York: E. P. Dutton, 1910.

———. *Visitation Articles and Injunctions of the Period of the Reformation.* Ed. W. H. Frere. 3 vols. London: Longmans, Green, 1910.

———. *Certaine Sermons or Homilies Appointed to be Read in Churches In the Time of Queen Elizabeth I (1547–1571). A Facsimile Reproduction of the Edition of 1623.* Intr. Mary Ellen Rickey and Thomas B. Stroup. Gainseville, FL: Scholars' Facsimiles and Reprints, 1968.

———. *The Book of Common Prayer 1559. The Elizabethan Prayer Book.* Ed. John E. Booty. Charlottesville: University Press of Virginia, 1976.

Clancy, Thomas H. "Papist-Protestant-Puritan: English Religious Taxonomy 1565–1665." *Recusant History* 13 (1976): 227–53.

Clark, Ira. *Christ Revealed: The History of the Neotypological Lyric in the English Renaissance.* Gainesville: University Press of Florida, 1982.

Cogswell, Thomas. *The Blessed Revolution: English Politics and the Coming of War, 1621–1624.* Cambridge: Cambridge University Press, 1989.

Corbett, Richard. *The Poems of Richard Corbett.* Ed. J. A. W. Bennett and H. R. Trevor-Roper. Oxford: Clarendon, 1955.

Cranmer, Thomas. *The Remains of Thomas Cranmer.* 4 vols. Ed. Henry Jenkyns. Oxford: Oxford University Press, 1833.

Crashaw, Richard. *The Poems . . . of Richard Crashaw.* 2nd ed. Ed. L. C. Martin. Oxford: Clarendon, 1957.

Cunnar, Eugene. "Donne's 'Valediction: Forbidding Mourning' and the Golden Compasses of Alchemical Creation." *Literature and the Occult: Essays in Comparative Literature.* Ed. Luanne Frank. 72–110. Arlington: The University of Texas at Arlington, 1977.

Cust, Richard. *The Forced Loan and English Politics, 1626–1628.* Oxford: Clarendon, 1987.

Daniélou, Jean. *Primitive Christian Symbols.* Trans. Donald Attwater. Baltimore: Helicon Press, 1964.

———. *The Theology of Jewish Christianity.* Trans. and ed. John A. Baker. London: Darton, Longman, & Todd, 1964.

Davies, Horton. *Worship and Theology in England.* 5 vols. Princeton: Princeton University Press, 1970–1975.

———. *Like Angels From a Cloud: The English Metaphysical Preachers 1588–1645.* San Marino: Huntington Library, 1986.

De Sa Wiggins, Peter. "'Aire and Angels': Incarnations of Love." *English Literary Renaissance* 12.1 (1982): 87–101.

Dickson, Donald R. *The Fountain of Living Waters: The Typology of the Waters of Life in Herbert, Vaughan and Traherne.* Columbia: University of Missouri Press, 1987.

DiPasquale, Theresa M. "Ambivalent Mourning: Sacramentality, Idolatry, and Gender in 'Since she whome I lovd hath payd her last debt.'" *John Donne Journal* 10.1–2 (1991): 45–56. Rpt. as "Ambivalent Mourning in 'Since she whome I lovd.'" *John Donne's 'desire of more': The Subject of Anne More Donne in His Poetry.* Ed. M. Thomas Hester. 183–95. Newark: University of Delaware Press, 1996.

Docherty, Thomas. *John Donne, Undone.* London and New York: Methuen, 1986.

Doerksen, Daniel. "'Saint Paul's Puritan': John Donne's 'Puritan' Imagination in the *Sermons.*" *John Donne's Religious Imagination: Essays in Honor of John T. Shawcross.* Ed. Raymond-Jean Frontain and Frances M. Malpezzi. 350–65. Conway, AR: University of Central Arkansas Press, 1995.

Donne, John. *The Sermons of John Donne.* 10 vols. Ed. George R. Potter and Evelyn M. Simpson. Berkeley: University of California Press, 1953–1962.

———. *The Complete Poetry of John Donne.* Ed. John T. Shawcross. Garden City, NY: Doubleday, 1967.

———. *Selected Prose.* Chosen by Evelyn Simpson. Ed. Helen Gardner and Timothy Healy. Oxford: Clarendon, 1967.

———. *Poems, By J. D. with Elegies on the Authors Death.* London: Printed by M. F. for John Marriot, 1633. Facs. rpt. Menston, England: Scholar Press, 1970.

————. *Pseudo-Martyr*. London: W. Stansby for Walter Burre, 1610. Facsimile rpt. introd. Francis Jacques Sypher. Delmar, NY: Scholars' Facsimiles and Reprints, 1974.

————. *Devotions Upon Emergent Occasions*. Ed. Anthony Raspa. Montreal and London: McGill-Queen's University Press, 1975.

————. *Letters to Severall Persons of Honour*. London: J. Flesher for Richard Marriot, 1651. Facsimile rpt. introd. M. Thomas Hester. Delmar, NY: Scholars' Facsimiles and Reprints, 1977.

————. *Biathanatos*. New York and London: Garland, 1982.

Dugmore, Clifford W. *Eucharistic Doctrine in England from Hooker to Waterland*. New York: Macmillan, 1942.

Emminghaus, Johannes H. *The Eucharist: Essence, Form, Celebration*. Trans. Matthew J. O'Connell. Collegeville, MN: The Liturgical Press, 1978.

Empson, William. *English Pastoral Poetry*. Freeport, NY: Books for Libraries Press, 1972.

Estrin, Barbara L. *Laura: Uncovering Gender and Genre in Wyatt, Donne, and Marvell*. Durham, NC: Duke University Press, 1994.

Fabricius, Johannes. *Alchemy: The Medieval Alchemists and their Royal Art*. London: Diamond Books, 1994.

Ferry, Anne. *All in War with Time: Love Poetry of Shakespeare, Donne, Jonson, Marvell*. Cambridge, MA: Harvard University Press, 1975.

————. *The "Inward" Language: Sonnets of Wyatt, Sidney, Shakespeare, Donne*. Chicago: University of Chicago Press, 1983.

Fincham, Kenneth. *Prelate as Pastor: The Episcopate of James I*. Oxford: Clarendon, 1990.

Fish, Stanley. "Authors-Readers: Jonson's Community of the Same." *Representations* 7 (1984): 26–58.

Flynn, Dennis. "Irony in Donne's *Biathanatos* and *Pseudo-Martyr*." *Recusant History* 12 (1973): 49–69.

————. "Donne's Catholicism: I." *Recusant History* 13 (1975): 1–17.

————. "Donne's Catholicism: II." *Recusant History* 13 (1975): 178–95.

————. "The 'Annales School' and the Catholicism of Donne's Family." *John Donne Journal* 2 (1983): 1–9.

————. "Donne the Survivor." Summers and Pebworth 15–24.

———. "Donne's *Ignatius His Conclave* and Other Libels on Sir Robert Cecil." *John Donne Journal* 6 (1987): 163–83.

———. "'Awry and Squint': The Dating of Donne's Holy Sonnets." *John Donne Journal* 7 (1988): 35–46.

———. "A Biographical Prolusion to Study of Donne's Religious Imagination." *John Donne's Religious Imagination: Essays in Honor of John T. Shawcross.* Ed. Raymond-Jean Frontain and Frances M. Malpezzi. 28–44. Conway, AR: University of Central Arkansas Press, 1995.

———. "Donne, Henry Wotton, and the Earl of Essex." *John Donne Journal* 14 (1995): 185–218.

———. *John Donne and the Ancient Catholic Nobility.* Bloomington, IN: Indiana University Press, 1995.

Freccero, John. "Donne's 'Valediction: Forbidding Mourning.'" *ELH* 30 (1963): 335–76. Rpt. in *Essential Articles for the Study of John Donne's Poetry.* Ed. John R. Roberts. 279–304. Hamden, CT: Archon Books, 1975.

———. "The Fig Tree and the Laurel: Petrarch's Poetics." *Diacritics* 5.1 (1975): 34–40.

Frere, W. H. *The Principles of Religious Ceremonial.* London: Longmans, Green, and Co., 1912.

Friedman, Donald M. "Memory and the Art of Salvation in Donne's Good Friday Poem." *English Literary Renaissance* 3 (1973): 418–42.

Frontain, Raymond-Jean and Frances M. Malpezzi, eds. *John Donne's Religious Imagination: Essays in Honor of John T. Shawcross.* Conway, AR: University of Central Arkansas Press, 1995.

Frost, Kate Gartner. "*Magnus Pan Mortuus Est*: A Subtextual and Contextual Reading of Donne's 'Resurrection, imperfect.'" *John Donne's Religious Imagination: Essays in Honor of John T. Shawcross.* Ed. Raymond-Jean Frontain and Frances M. Malpezzi. 231–61. Conway, AR: University of Central Arkansas Press, 1995.

Fuller, John. *The Sonnet.* London: Methuen, 1972.

Gardiner, Anne Barbeau. "Donne and the Real Presence of the Absent Lover." *John Donne Journal* 9 (1990): 113–24.

Gardner, Helen, ed. General Introduction. *John Donne: The Elegies and The Songs and Sonnets.* Ed. Helen Gardner. Oxford: Clarendon, 1965.

———. *The Divine Poems of John Donne.* 2nd ed. Oxford: Clarendon, 1982.

Garth, Helen Meredith. *Saint Mary Magdalene in Medieval Literature.* Baltimore: Johns Hopkins University Press, 1950.

The Geneva Bible: A Facsimile of the 1560 Edition. Madison, WI: University of Wisconsin Press, 1969.

The Geneva Bible: A facsimile of the 1599 edition with undated Sternhold & Hopkins Psalms. Ozark, MO: L. L. Brown, 1995.

Gibb, John, and James Innes, trans. *Tractates on the Gospel of John.* By Saint Augustine, Bishop of Hippo. Select Library of the Nicene and Post-Nicene Fathers 7. New York: Christian Literature Co., 1888.

Gilman, Ernest. *Iconoclasm and Poetry in the English Reformation: Down Went Dagon.* Chicago: University of Chicago Press, 1986.

Goldberg, Jonathan. *James I and the Politics of Literature: Jonson, Shakespeare, Donne and their Contemporaries.* Baltimore: Johns Hopkins University Press, 1983.

Gosse, Edmund. *The Life and Letters of John Donne.* 2 vols. Gloucester, MA: Peter Smith, 1959.

Grierson, Herbert J. C. "Bacon's Poem, 'The World': Its Date and Relation to Certain Other Poems." *Modern Language Review* 6.2 (1911): 145–56.

Guibbory, Achsah. "A Sense of the Future: Projected Audiences of Donne and Jonson," *John Donne Journal* 2 (1983): 11–21.

———. "Donne, the Idea of Woman, and the Experience of Love." *John Donne Journal* 9 (1990): 105–12.

———. "'Oh, Let Mee Not Serve So': The Politics of Love in Donne's Elegies." *ELH* 57 (1990): 811–33.

———. "Fear of 'loving more': Death and the Loss of Sacramental Love." *John Donne's 'desire of more': The Subject of Anne More Donne in His Poetry.* Ed. M. Thomas Hester. 204–27. Newark: University of Delaware Press, 1996.

Haigh, Christopher. *Reformation and Resistance in Tudor Lancashire.* Cambridge: Cambridge University Press, 1975.

———. "The Fall of a Church or the Rise of a Sect? Post-Reformation Catholicism in England." *Historical Journal* 21 (1978): 181–86.

———. "The Continuity of Catholicism in the English Reformation." *Past and Present* 93 (1981): 37–69.

———. "From Monopoly to Minority: Catholicism in Early Modern England." *Transactions of the Royal Historical Society* 5th ser. 31 (1981): 129–47.

———. *English Reformations*. Oxford: Clarendon, 1993.

Halley, Janet E. "Textual Intercourse: Anne Donne, John Donne, and the Sexual Poetics of Textual Exchange." *Seeking the Woman in Late Medieval and Renaissance Writings: Essays in Feminist Contextual Criticism*. Ed. Sheila Fisher and Janet E. Halley. 187–206. Knoxville: University of Tennessee Press, 1989.

Harland, Paul W. "'A true transubstantiation': Donne, Self-love, and the Passion." *John Donne's Religious Imagination: Essays in Honor of John T. Shawcross*. 162–80. Conway, AR: University of Central Arkansas Press, 1995.

Hartman, Geoffrey. *The Fate of Reading*. Chicago: University of Chicago Press, 1975.

Harvey, Elizabeth D. and Katharine Eisaman Maus, eds. *Soliciting Interpretation: Literary Theory and Seventeenth-Century English Poetry*. Chicago: University of Chicago Press, 1990.

Herbert, George. *The Latin Poetry of George Herbert*. Trans. Mark McCloskey and Paul R. Murphy. Athens: Ohio University Press, 1965.

———. *The English Poems of George Herbert*. Ed. C. A. Patrides. London: Dent, 1974.

Herz, Judith Scherer. "'An Excellent Exercise of Wit That Speaks So Well of Ill': Donne and the Poetics of Concealment." *The Eagle and the Dove: Reassessing John Donne*. Ed. Claude J. Summers and Ted-Larry Pebworth. 3–14. Columbia, MO: University of Missouri Press, 1986.

———. "Resisting Mutuality." *John Donne Journal* 9 (1990): 27–31.

———. "Reading [out] Biography in 'A Valediction forbidding Mourning." *John Donne Journal* 13 (1994): 137–42.

Hester, M. Thomas. *'Kinde Pitty and Brave Scorne': John Donne's 'Satyres'*. Durham, NC: Duke University Press, 1982.

———. "Donne's (Re)Annunciation of the Virgin(ia Colony) in Elegy XIX." *South Central Review* 4 (1987): 49–64.

———. "'this cannot be said': A Preface to the Reader of Donne's Lyrics." *Christianity and Literature* 39 (1990): 365–85.

———. "'let them sleepe': Donne's Personal Allusion in Holy Sonnet IV." *Papers on Language and Literature* 29 (1993): 346–50.

———. "'Let me love': Reading the Sacred 'Currant' of Donne's Profane Lyrics." *Sacred and Profane: Secular and Devotional Interplay in Early Modern British Literature.* Ed. Helen Wilcox, Richard Todd, and Alasdair MacDonald. 129–50. Amsterdam: Vrije Universiteit Press, 1996.

———, ed. *John Donne's 'desire of more': The Subject of Anne More Donne in His Poetry.* Newark: University of Delaware Press, 1996.

The Holy Bible . . . Set Forth in 1611 and Commonly Known as the King James Version. New York: American Bible Society, n.d.

Hooker, Richard. *The Works of that Learned and Judicious Divine Mr. Richard Hooker.* Ed. John Keble. 7th ed. Rev. R. W. Church and F. Paget. Oxford: Clarendon, 1888. Facsimile rpt. Ellicott City, MD: Via Media, Inc., 1994.

Jonson, Ben. *Bartholomew Fair.* Ed. E. A. Horsman. Cambridge, MA: Harvard University Press, 1962.

———. *The Complete Poems.* Ed. George Parfitt. London: Penguin, 1975.

Juergens, Sylvester P. *The New Marian Missal for Daily Mass.* New York: Regina Press, 1950.

Kaufmann, Yehezkel. *The Religion of Israel.* Trans. Moshe Greenberg. Chicago: University of Chicago Press, 1960.

Keynes, Geoffrey. *A Bibliography of Dr. John Donne, Dean of St. Paul's.* Cambridge: Cambridge University Press, 1958.

Klawitter, George. "Verse Letters to T. W. from John Donne: 'By You My Love Is Sent.'" *Homosexuality in Renaissance and Enlightenment England: Literary Representations in Historical Context.* Ed. Claude J. Summers. 85–102. New York: Harrington Park Press, 1992.

Labriola, Albert C. "'This Dialogue of One': Rational Argument and Affective Discourse in Donne's 'Aire and Angels.'" *John Donne Journal* 9 (1990): 77–83.

———. "Donne's 'Hymn to God my God, in my sicknesse': Hieroglyphic Mystery and Magic in Poetry." *Ben Jonson Journal* 2 (1995): 1–7.

Lake, Peter. *Moderate Puritans and the Elizabethan Church.* Cambridge: Cambridge University Press, 1982.

———. *Anglicans and Puritans?: Presbyterianism and English*

Conformist Thought from Whitgift to Hooker. London: Unwin Hyman, 1988.

Laud, William. *Works*. Ed. W. Scott and J. Bliss. 7 vols. Oxford: J. H. Parker, 1847–1860.

LeComte, Edward. "Jack Donne: From Rake to Husband." *Just So Much Honor: Essays Commemorating the Four-Hundredth Anniversary of the Birth of John Donne*. Ed. Peter Amadeus Fiore. 9–32. University Park: Pennsylvania State University Press, 1972.

Leeming, Bernard. *Principles of Sacramental Theology*. 2nd ed. Westminster, MD: Newman Press, 1960.

Lewalski, Barbara K. *Protestant Poetics and the Seventeenth-Century Religious Lyric*. Princeton, NJ: Princeton University Press, 1979.

Linville, Susan E. "Contrary Faith: Poetic Closure and the Devotional Lyric." *Papers on Language and Literature* 20 (1984): 141–53.

Lipsius, Justus. *Principles of Letter Writing: A Bilingual Text of Justi Lipsi Epistolica Institutio*. Ed. and trans. R. V. Young and M. Thomas Hester. Carbondale and Edwardsville, IL: Southern Illinois University Press, 1996.

Low, Anthony. *Love's Architecture: Devotional Modes in Seventeenth-Century English Poetry*. New York: New York University Press, 1978.

———. "John Donne: 'The Holy Ghost is Amorous in His Metaphors.'" *New Perspectives on the Seventeenth-Century English Religious Lyric*. Ed. John R. Roberts. 201–21. Columbia and London: University of Missouri Press, 1994.

Luther, Martin. *Werke*. 6 vols. Weimar: H. Böhlau, 1912–21.

———. "A Treatise on the New Testament, that is, the Holy Mass." Trans. Jeremiah J. Shindel. Revised by E. Theodore Bachmann. *Luther's Works*. Vol. 35. Ed. E. Theodore Bachmann. Philadelphia: Muhlenberg Press, 1960.

Maier, Michael. *Symbola aureae mensae duodecim nationum*. Frankfort, 1617.

Marotti, Arthur F. *John Donne, Coterie Poet*. Madison: University of Wisconsin Press, 1986.

———. Introduction. *Critical Essays on John Donne*. Ed. Arthur F. Marotti. 1–16. New York: G. K. Hall, 1994.

Martz, Louis L. *The Poetry of Meditation: A Study in English Religious Literature of the Seventeenth Century.* New Haven, CT: Yale University Press, 1954.

Marvell, Andrew. *The Complete Poems.* Ed. Elizabeth Story Donno. London: Penguin, 1985.

Maskell, William. *The Ancient Liturgy of the Church of England According to the Uses of Sarum, York, Hereford, and Bangor and the Roman Liturgy Arranged in Parallel Columns.* 3rd ed. Oxford: Clarendon, 1882. Facsimile rpt. New York: AMS Press, 1973.

Maurer, Margaret. "John Donne's Verse Letters." *Modern Language Quarterly* 37 (1976): 234–59.

———. "The Real Presence of Lucy Russell, Countess of Bedford, and the terms of John Donne's 'Honor is so sublime perfection.'" *ELH* 47 (1980): 205–34.

McNees, Eleanor J. "John Donne and the Anglican Doctrine of the Eucharist." *Texas Studies in Literature and Language* 29 (1987): 94–114.

———. *Eucharistic Poetry: The Search for Presence in the Writings of John Donne, Gerard Manley Hopkins, Dylan Thomas, and Geoffrey Hill.* Lewisburg: Bucknell University Press, 1992.

Merrill, Thomas F. *Christian Criticism: A Study of Literary God-Talk.* Amsterdam: Rodopi, 1976.

Milgate, W., ed. *The Satires, Epigrams and Verse Letters.* By John Donne. Oxford: Clarendon, 1967.

Milton, John. *Paradise Lost.* Ed. Alastair Fowler. London: Longman, 1971.

Mueller, Janel. "The Play of Difference in Donne's 'Aire and Angels.'" *John Donne Journal* 9 (1990): 85–94.

Nania, John and P. J. Klemp. "John Donne's *La Corona*: A Second Structure." *Renaissance and Reformation* ns 2 (1978): 49–54.

Nohrnberg, James C. *The Analogy of "The Faerie Queene."* Princeton, NJ: Princeton University Press, 1976.

Norbrook, David. "The Monarchy of Wit and the Republic of Letters: Donne's Politics." *Soliciting Interpretation: Literary Theory and Seventeenth-Century English Poetry.* Ed. Elizabeth D. Harvey and Katharine Eisaman Maus. 3–36. Chicago: University of Chicago Press, 1990.

Novarr, David. "The Dating of Donne's *La Corona.*" *Philological Quarterly* 36 (1957): 259–65. Rpt. in *The Disinterred Muse*. Ithaca, NY: Cornell University Press, 1980.

O'Connell, Patrick F. "'Restore Thine Image': Structure and Theme in Donne's 'Goodfriday.'" *John Donne Journal* 4 (1985): 13–28.

———. "'La Corona': Donne's *Ars Poetica Sacra.*" *The Eagle and the Dove: Reassessing John Donne*. Ed. Claude J. Summers and Ted-Larry Pebworth. 119–30. Columbia, MO: University of Missouri Press, 1986.

Oberman, Heiko A. "Preaching and the Word in the Reformation." *Theology Today* 18 (1961): 16–29.

P., L. [Query on "A Jeat Ring Sent"]. *Explicator* 29.3 (1971): Query 2.

Parish, Jon E. "Donne as a Petrarchan." *Notes & Queries* ns 4 (1957): 377–78.

Patrides, C. A. "'Above Atlas His Shoulders': An Introduction to Sir Thomas Browne." *Sir Thomas Browne: The Major Works*. Ed. Patrides. 21–52. New York: Penguin Books, 1977.

Patrologiae Cursus Completus. Series Graeca. 161 vols. Ed. J. P. Migne. Paris: Migne, 1857–1866.

Patrologiae Cursus Completus. Series Latina. 221 vols. Ed. J. P. Migne. Paris: Migne, 1844–1903.

Patterson, Annabel. "All Donne." *Soliciting Interpretation: Literary Theory and Seventeenth-Century English Poetry*. Ed. Elizabeth D. Harvey and Katharine Eisaman Maus. 37–67. Chicago: University of Chicago Press, 1990.

———. "John Donne, Kingsman?" *The Mental World of the Jacobean Court*. Ed. Linda Levy Peck. 251–72. Cambridge: Cambridge University Press, 1991.

Pebworth, Ted-Larry, "Sir Henry Wotton." *Seventeenth-Century British Nondramatic Poets: First Series*. Ed. M. Thomas Hester. 286–95. Vol. 121 of *Dictionary of Literary Biography*. Detroit, London: Gale Research, 1992.

Pebworth, Ted-Larry and Claude J. Summers. "'Thus Friends Absent Speake': The Exchange of Verse Letters between John Donne and Henry Wotton." *Modern Philology* 81.3 (1984): 361–77.

———. "Donne's Correspondence with Wotton." *John Donne Journal* 10 (1991): 1–36.

Pelikan, Jaroslav. *The Christian Tradition: A History of the Development of Doctrine.* 5 vols. Chicago and London: University of Chicago Press, 1971–91.

Perella, Nicolas James. *The Kiss Sacred and Profane.* Berkeley: University of California Press, 1969.

Perrine, Laurence. "Explicating Donne: 'The Apparition' and 'The Flea.'" *College Literature* 17.1 (1990): 1–20.

Petrarch, Francesco. *Petrarch's Lyric Poems.* Trans. and ed. Robert M. Durling. Cambridge, MA: Harvard University Press, 1976.

Pope, Myrtle Pihlman. "Donne's 'A Jeat Ring Sent.'" *Explicator* 34 (1976): Item 44.

Quinn, Dennis. "Donne's Christian Eloquence." *ELH* 27 (1960): 276–97.

Rajan, Tilottama. "'Nothing Sooner Broke': Donne's *Songs and Sonets* as Self-Consuming Artifact." *ELH* 49 (1982): 805–28.

Redpath, Theodore, ed. *The Songs and Sonets of John Donne.* 2nd ed. New York: St. Martin's, 1983.

Richards, Bernard. "Donne's 'Twickenham Garden' and the *Fons Amatoria.*" *Review of English Studies* ns 33 (1982): 181–83.

Roberts, John R., ed. *Essential Articles for the Study of John Donne's Poetry.* Hamden, CT: Archon Books, 1975.

———. "'Just such disparitie': The Critical Debate about 'Aire and Angels.'" *John Donne Journal* 9 (1990): 43–64.

———, ed. *New Perspectives on the Seventeenth-Century English Religious Lyric.* Columbia and London: University of Missouri Press, 1994.

Roebuck, Graham. "Donne's Visual Imagination and Compasses." *John Donne Journal* 8 (1989): 37–56.

Rogers, Thomas. *The Faith, Doctrine, and religion professed & protected in the Realme of England: Expressed in 39 Articles* Cambridge: J. Legatt, 1607. Rpt. as *The Catholic Doctrine of the Church of England: An Exposition of the Thirty-Nine Articles, by Thomas Rogers, A.M., Chaplain to Archbishop Bancroft.* Ed. J. J. S. Perowne. Cambridge: Cambridge University Press, 1854.

Roman Catholic Church. *Catechism of the Council of Trent for Parish Priests.* Trans. John A. McHugh and Charles J. Callan. London: B. Herder; New York: Joseph F. Wagner, 1923.

———. *Canons and Decrees of the Council of Trent.* Trans. J. J. Schroeder. London: B. Herder, 1941; Rockford, IL: Tan Books and Publishers, Inc., 1978.

Rudnytsky, Peter L. "'The Sight of God': Donne's Poetics of Transcendence." *Texas Studies in Literature and Language* 24 (1982): 185–207.

Schoenfeldt, Michael C. "Patriarchal Assumptions and Egalitarian Designs." *John Donne Journal* 9 (1990): 23–26.

———. "The Poetry of Supplication: Toward a Cultural Poetics of the Religious Lyric." *New Perspectives on the Seventeenth-Century English Religious Lyric.* Ed. John R. Roberts. 83– 86. Columbia and London: University of Missouri Press, 1994.

Scodel, Joshua. "John Donne and the Religious Politics of the Mean." *John Donne's Religious Imagination: Essays in Honor of John T. Shawcross.* Ed. Raymond-Jean Frontain and Frances M. Malpezzi. 45–80. Conway, AR: University of Central Arkansas Press, 1995.

Scot, Reginald. *The Discoverie of Witchcraft.* London: W. Brome, 1584; New York: Dover Publications, 1972.

Sellin, Paul. *"So Doth, So Is Religion": John Donne and Diplomatic Contexts in the Reformed Netherlands, 1619–20.* Columbia: University of Missouri Press, 1989.

Severance, Sibyl Lutz. "Soul, Sphere, and Structure in 'Goodfriday, 1613. Riding Westward.'" *Studies in Philology* 84 (1987): 24–41.

Shakespeare, William. *The Riverside Shakespeare.* Ed. G. Blakemore Evans. Boston: Houghton Mifflin, 1974.

Shami, Jeanne. "Donne's *Sermons* and the Absolutist Politics of Quotation." *John Donne's Religious Imagination: Essays in Honor of John T. Shawcross.* Ed. Raymond-Jean Frontain and Frances M. Malpezzi. 380–412. Conway, AR: University of Central Arkansas Press, 1995.

———. "'The Stars in their Order Fought Against Sisera': John Donne and the Pulpit Crisis of 1622." *John Donne Journal* 14 (1995): 1–58.

Sharpe, Kevin. "Introduction: Parliamentary History 1603–1629: In or Out of Perspective?" *Faction and Parliament: Essays on Early Stuart History.* Ed. Kevin Sharpe. 1–42. London: Methuen, 1978.

Shawcross, John T. "Poetry, Personal and Impersonal: The Case of Donne." *The Eagle and the Dove: Reassessing John Donne.* Ed.

Claude J. Summers and Ted-Larry Pebworth. 53–56. Columbia, MO: University of Missouri Press, 1986.

———. *Intentionality and the New Traditionalism: Some Liminal Means to Literary Revisionism.* University Park: The Pennsylvania State University Press, 1991.

Shelburne, D. Audell. "John Donne's 'Twicknam Garden': The Problem of Line 15." Twelfth Annual Conference of the John Donne Society. Gulfport, MS, 22 Feb. 1997.

Sheppeard, Sallye. "Eden and Agony in 'Twicknam Garden.'" *John Donne Journal* 7 (1988): 65–72.

Sherwood, Terry G. "Conversion Psychology in John Donne's Good Friday Poem." *Harvard Theological Review* 72.1–2 (1979): 101–22.

———. *Fulfilling the Circle: A Study of John Donne's Thought.* Toronto: University of Toronto Press, 1984.

Shuger, Deborah K. *Habits of Thought in the English Renaissance: Religion, Politics, and the Dominant Culture.* Berkeley: University of California Press, 1990.

Sidney, Philip. *Sir Philip Sidney: A Critical Edition of the Major Works.* Ed. Katherine Duncan-Jones. Oxford: Oxford University Press, 1989.

Simon, Irène. "Some Problems of Donne Criticism." *Revue des Langues Vivantes* 18 (1952): 317–24, 393–414; 19 (1953): 14–39, 114–32, 201–02.

Simpson, Evelyn M. *A Study of the Prose Works of John Donne.* Oxford: Clarendon, 1924.

Slights, Camille Wells. "Air, Angels, and the Progress of Love." *John Donne Journal* 9 (1990): 95–104.

Smeaton, Johannes. *S. Mary Magdalens Pilgrimage to Paradise.* London 1617.

Smith, A. J., ed. *John Donne: The Complete English Poems.* London: Penguin, 1986.

Southwell, Robert. *An Humble Supplication to Her Maiestie.* Ed. R. C. Bald. Cambridge: Cambridge University Press, 1953.

———. *The Complete Poems of Robert Southwell, S.J.* Ed. Alexander B. Grosart. London, 1872. Facsismile rpt. New York: AMS Press, 1971.

Spacks, Patricia Meyer. "In Search of Sincerity." *College English* 29 (1968): 591–602.

Spenser, Edmund. *The Poetical Works of Edmund Spenser.* Ed. J. C. Smith and E. De Selincourt. London: Oxford University Press, 1912.

Spinrad, Phoebe S. "'Aire and Angels' and Questionable Shapes." *John Donne Journal* 9 (1990): 19–22.

Stampfer, Judah. *John Donne and the Metaphysical Gesture.* New York: Funk and Wagnalls, 1970.

Stanwood, P. G. "Liturgy, Worship, and the Sons of Light." *New Perspectives on the Seventeenth-Century English Religious Lyric.* Ed. John R. Roberts. 105–23. Columbia and London: University of Missouri Press, 1994.

Steinberg, Leo. *The Sexuality of Christ in Renaissance Art and in Modern Oblivion.* New York: Pantheon/October, 1983.

Stock, Richard. *The Doctrine and Use of Repentance.* London: F. Kyngston for E. Weaver, 1610.

Stone, Darwell. *A History of the Doctrine of the Holy Eucharist.* 2 vols. London: Longmans, Green, 1909.

Strier, Richard. "John Donne Awry and Squint: The 'Holy Sonnets,' 1608–1610." *Modern Philology* 86 (1989): 357–84.

Stringer, Gary, et al., eds. *The Variorum Edition of the Poetry of John Donne.* 8 vols. Bloomington, IN: Indiana University Press, 1995–.

Summers, Claude J. and Ted-Larry Pebworth, eds. *The Eagle and the Dove: Reassessing John Donne.* Columbia, MO: University of Missouri Press, 1986.

Tentler, Thomas. *Sin and Confession on the Eve of the Reformation.* Princeton: Princeton University Press, 1977.

Thomas, Keith. *Religion and the Decline of Magic.* New York: Scribner, 1971.

Thomson, Patricia. "John Donne and the Countess of Bedford." *Modern Language Review* 44 (1949): 329–40.

Toal, M. F., ed. and trans. *The Sunday Sermons of the Great Fathers.* 4 vols. Chicago: Henry Regnery Co., 1958.

Tuke, Thomas. *Concerning the Holy Eucharist and the Popish Breaden-God.* London, 1625. In *Miscellanies of the Fuller*

Worthies' Library. Vol. 3. Ed. Alexander B. Grosart. Blackburn: St. Georges, 1872. 9–44. Facsimile rpt. New York: AMS Press, 1970.

Tuve, Rosemund. *A Reading of George Herbert.* London: Faber and Faber, 1952.

Voraigne, Jacobus de. *The Golden Legend: Readings on the Saints.* Trans. William Granger Ryan. 2 Vols. Princeton, NJ: Princeton University Press, 1993.

Walker, Julia. "'Here you see me': Donne's Autographed Valediction." *John Donne Journal* 4 (1985): 28–33.

———. "The Religious Lyric as a Genre." *English Language Notes* 25.1 (1987): 39–45.

———. "Left/Write/Right: Of Lock-Jaw and Literary Criticism." *John Donne Journal* 7 (1988): 133–39.

———. "Anne More: A Name Not Written." *John Donne's "desire of more": The Subject of Anne More Donne in His Poetry.* Ed. M. Thomas Hester. 89–105. Newark: University of Delaware Press, 1996.

Weller, Barry and Margaret W. Ferguson. Introduction. *The Tragedy of Mariam, The Fair Queen of Jewry.* By Elizabeth Cary, The Lady Falkland. Ed. Weller and Ferguson. 1–59. Berkeley: University of California Press, 1994.

Wertenbaker, Thomas J., Jr. "Donne's 'A Jeat Ring Sent.'" *Explicator* 35.4 (1977): 27–28.

Whittington, Janice. "The Text of Donne's 'Valediction forbidding mourning.'" *John Donne Journal* 13 (1994): 127–36.

Wilcox, Helen, Richard Todd, and Alasdair MacDonald, eds. *Sacred and Profane: Secular and Devotional Interplay in Early Modern British Literature.* Amsterdam: Vrije Universiteit Press, 1996.

Wilson, Arthur. *History of Great Britain, being the Life and Reign of King James the First.* London: Printed for Richard Lownds, 1653.

Wilson, David B. "*La Puce de Madame Desroches* and John Donne's 'The Flea.'" *Neuphilologische Mitteilungen* 72 (1971): 297–301.

Winny, James. *A Preface to Donne.* New York: Scribners, 1970.

Wollman, Richard. "The 'Press and the Fire': Print and Manuscript Culture in Donne's Circle." *SEL* 33 (1993): 85–97.

[Woodward, Thomas?], "To Mr. J. D." In *The Satires, Epigrams and Verse Letters.* Ed. W. Milgate. 212. Oxford: Clarendon, 1967.

Wright, Thomas. *The Disposition or Garnishmente of the Soule To receive worthily the blessed Sacrament.* Antwerp: Joachim Trognesius [false imprint, actually printed in London by a press associated with James Druckett? and Henry Owen], 1596.

————. *A Treatise, Shewing the Possibilitie, and Convenience of the Reall Presence of our Saviour in the Blessed Sacrament.* Antwerp: Ioachim Trognesius [false imprint, actually printed in London by a press associated with James Druckett? and Henry Owen], 1596.

Young, Robert V. "Donne's Holy Sonnets and the Theology of Grace." *"Bright Shootes of Everlastingnesse": The Seventeenth-Century Religious Lyric.* Ed. Claude J. Summers and Ted-Larry Pebworth. 20–39. Columbia: University of Missouri Press, 1987.

————. "'O My America, My New-Found Land': Pornography and Imperial Politics in Donne's Elegies." *South Central Review* 4 (1987): 35–48.

————. "Angels in 'Aire and Angels.'" *John Donne Journal* 9 (1990): 1–14.

————. "Herbert and the Real Presence." *Renascence* 45 (1993): 179–96.

————. "Donne, Herbert, and the Postmodern Muse." *New Perspectives on the Seventeenth-Century English Religious Lyric.* Ed. John R. Roberts. 168–87. Columbia and London: University of Missouri Press, 1994.

INDEX